WAR
AND THE
20TH CENTURY

A STUDY OF WAR AND MODERN CONSCIOUSNESS

Christopher Coker

BRASSEY'S
London • Washington

First English edition 1994

UK editorial offices: Brassey's, 33 John Street, London WC1N 2AT
UK orders: Marston Book Services, PO Box 87, Oxford OX2 0DT

North American orders: Macmillan Publishing Company,
201 West 103rd Street, Indianapolis, IN46290

Christopher Coker has asserted his moral right to be identified as
author of this work.

Library of Congress Cataloging in Publication Data
available

British Library Cataloguing in Publication Data
A catalogue record for this book is available
from the British Library

ISBN 1-85753-055-1 Hardcover

Typeset by Solidus (Bristol) Limited
Printed in Great Britain by Bookcraft (Bath) Limited

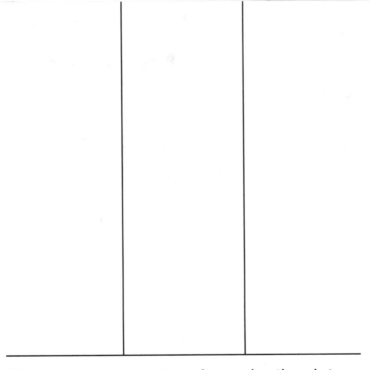

Please renew or return items by the date shown on your receipt

www.hertsdirect.org/libraries

Renewals and enquiries: 0300 123 4049

Textphone for hearing or speech impaired users: 0300 123 4041

L32

Hertfordshire

WAR

AND THE
20TH CENTURY

A STUDY OF WAR AND MODERN CONSCIOUSNESS

Also available from Brassey's

CLARKE/SABIN
British Defence Choices for the Twenty-First Century

CLARKE
New Perspectives on Security

SIMPKIN
Race to the Swift

Contents

The present day European requires not merely war but the greatest and most terrible wars – thus a temporary relapse into barbarism – if the means to culture are not to deprive him of his culture and of his existence itself.

Nietzsche, *Human All Too Human (1878)*

... war educates for freedom. For what is freedom? That one has the will to assume responsibility for one's self ... that one is prepared to sacrifice human beings for one's own cause not excluding one's self ... the free man is a warrior.

Nietzsche, *The Twilight of the Idols (1888)*

Prologue

I began writing this book three years ago, although I had thought about it for much longer. Books have many different births. Delivering this into the world required an exhaustive reading of European literature. It demanded as well a knowledge of the most recent historical accounts of two world wars and the Cold War that followed – a Promethean labour indeed.

Inevitably this study is impressionistic. Is this necessarily a bad thing? My readers will have to arrive at their own conclusions. What I have tried to offer is an *interpretation* of the phenomenon of 20th century warfare, an inductive rather than deductive look at a century of Western history, a discussion of the ideas and beliefs which encouraged men to go to war and which sustained them so long at the Front. Trying to unlock that meaning through literature and philosophy I am aware of making demands of my English-speaking readers whose pragmatic approach to history and social science distinguishes them from their colleagues in most other countries.

I offer this interpretation, nevertheless, in the hope that it will be seen as an interpretation and nothing more. It is not the only interpretation, of course. The 20th century can be understood in altogether different terms, in terms of economic forces and sociological perspectives. There are many other historical explanations whose interpreters might find my comprehensive approach unfamiliar or questionable.

In writing this book I have received much help from friends and associates, too numerous to name. I am particularly grateful, however, to Mark Almond, Michael Bloch, Inga Haag, William Pearsall and James Sherr for putting me on the track of some of the more obscure analyses of war. I am obliged, too, to Mats Berdal for reading the manuscript in its various forms and to Elaine Childs and Susan Hunt for putting together the manuscript in its final form. I owe a particular debt of gratitude, of course, to Jenny Shaw and Tony Trythall who encouraged me throughout a long and frequently difficult delivery. Any mistakes of fact or interpretations of dubious value, are, of course, entirely my own.

Christopher Coker
February 1994

1

War and the 20th Century

'Out there I used to think how each army was like a sprawling, living creature, a powerful but rudimentary creature ... bursting and dying incessantly.... Two vast stagnant armies, oozing and jellying backwards and forwards like immense protozoa trying to feed off each other.'

(Philip George Chadwick, *The Death Guard (1939)*)

PROLOGUE

Cocteau recounts meeting an elderly newspaper vendor in 1919 selling copies of *Le Figaro* at double the standard price. His curiosity piqued, he purchased a copy only to discover that it was two years out of date. When he protested that he had been cheated, the vendor replied: 'But, *cher monsieur*, that is precisely why it is more expensive because there is still a war in it'. Even now the two world wars still exercise an extraordinary hold over our imagination. For some they are a metaphor, for others they are still a memory.

Sixty years later the American writer Norman Podhoredz recalled a conversation with the poet Robert Lowell who had said to him in answer to certain criticisms he had made of the poetry of W.H. Auden, 'after all, if not for Auden we wouldn't have known about the Second World War'. Podhoredz, at first, was puzzled by the remark and then it struck him that Lowell meant it literally. If he had never read about the outbreak of war in Auden's poem 'September 1, 1939', if he had only read about it in the newspapers, for example, 'he would never have believed its reality'. War in terms of our consciousness takes many forms – poems, or collective memories, or stories we have heard from those who have actually fought it.

In fact, I would argue that it has been so central to our experience of the 20th century that even in the word 'peace' there is a paradox. Whenever we see it in print we think immediately of war. Such a diametric transference of meaning might be interpreted as a symptom of the

1

abnormality of the modern age. In reality, I believe what it implies is the exact reverse. War has been the accredited theme of modern life.

I have written this book in an attempt to describe the imaginative life of Western culture in the 20th century. I am concerned primarily with the high culture, rather than the popular culture of the day, and within that primarily with its intellectual and imaginative literature. If I am granted that point of view I hope to show how many of the writers whose works I shall be analysing became in their own minds the voice of the 20th century. Through their writings they provided a definitive interpretation of what it meant to be modern, as well as what the 20th century meant to those who lived through it.

One of the most important developments after 1914, however, was the creation of a mass market for new ideas in the form of concepts that had seeped into the newspapers, much of the popular literature and even films of the time. The 20th century was one in which the ideas of the 'salon' escaped into the streets. In the wake of that catastrophe even members of the avant-garde were forced to keep in step with political life, to make comments, to join parties, to align with popular movements, to be *used* as politicians saw fit. Julien Benda was one of the first to recognise and denounce this development in a book he wrote in 1927, *The Treason of the Intellectuals*.

The 20th century, in short, was also one in which undigested concepts and ideas entered popular currency, Freud's death-wish and Jung's Collective Unconscious being two cases in point. In other words, even if most people did not read Heidegger, or Freud, or Nietzsche, many of their ideas were conveyed in popular phrases and political clichés, the small change of modern political discourse. In Orwell's vision of the future, of course, the people are prisoners of slogans that are largely empty of content, but the masses believe them nonetheless. Ultimate reality in *1984* has no existence outside the mind that observes it. Big Brother's mind contains all others. The mind is not an individual one, but a collective consciousness.

Perhaps, a better example of this phenomenon is the last of the century's great novels about totalitarianism, Ismael Kadare's *Palace of Dreams*. An Albanian novelist writing towards the end of the Cold War in the last Stalinist state in Europe, Kadare produced the most complete totalitarian vision yet, that of a country with an omnipotent Department of Dreams. The task of its members is to scour every town and village to collect the citizens' dreams, then to sift and classify them and ultimately interpret them in order to identify the 'master dream' that will provide a clue to the state's destiny. An entire nation's unconscious is tapped into and meticulously laid bare in the form of the images and symbols of the dreaming mind.

In my defence let me add that I am not claiming that the explanations and writings I have chosen to discuss are the only important contribution to understanding 20th century warfare – if only because my focus of attention is the West and – towards the end of the book, the impact on the West itself of its contact with the outside world. Of course, wars were fought and experienced by other societies – over a hundred million people, after all, died in the course of the century. But I think it is fair to say that the Western experience was by far the most important because it encompassed the whole world. For much of the modern era war and the West were synonymous, if only because war was a medium of modernisation.

In short, I intend to discuss what Kant would have called the *Ideologiekritik* – that is, the discourse within Western culture about war, its meaning, its significance, its impact, even its nature. This study not only encompasses the two world wars, but the Cold War as well, which, of course, forced itself into the consciousness of everyone in the most inescapable form of all: the fear of a nuclear holocaust.

In pursuit of this quest I have chosen to look at a wide-ranging discussion about the human condition, the meaning or futility of history, the unconscious forces at work in the human mind as well as the aesthetic response to war – in a word, the unique colloquy conducted between the Western nations. Let me start, however, by explaining what the 20th century – as a phase of history – meant to the Western world, a world that had been prepared for some time for its coming.

WHAT WAS THE 20TH CENTURY?

Before the late 18th century the major transformations of human life never corresponded to the consciously held objectives of the historical participants. Consciousness had little role in the processes by which war became a fact of human discourse. Of course, men were conscious of the world about them and learned what they thought to be the lessons of history, but they did not try to self-consciously revise or rewrite it.

The change, symbolically at least, came with the French Revolution, and more to the point the 25 years of war into which it plunged western Europe. The young Goethe saw the World Spirit at the battle of Valmy (1792) when the finest army in Europe was defeated by a rabble infused with a revolutionary ambition to make the world anew. Hegel saw a somewhat different World Spirit at work at the battle of Jena in 1806, this time in the person of Napoleon, carrying forward the revolutionary principles of a new age.

Hegel's formative years were those of the French Revolution. Writing in 1817 he called the last 25 years 'the richest that world history has had and for us the most destructive because it is to them that our world and our ideas belong'. Hegel viewed Napoleonic France as the spearhead of liberalism, and the Napoleonic age as one which had opened up new avenues for rational progress, even though the forces of conservatism, nationalism and catholicism had succeeded in 'halting the march of the Spirit' for a time.

For Hegel and Clausewitz war was the main instrument of political change, the chief mechanism by which man could become no longer the object, but the subject of history. As Marx wrote in *German Ideology* 'up to now history has made man; from now on man can make history'.

The French Revolution, however, had a historical significance that was even more profound. As Alfred de Musset wrote in 1834,

'All the sickness of the present century stems from two causes: the nation which has experienced 1793 and 1814 carries two wounds to its heart. All that was is no more; all that will be is not yet. Do not seek elsewhere the secret of our ills.'[1]

Musset may have been writing specifically of his own age but his complaints struck a convincing enough note 100 years later in a world in which men, believing they had been dispossessed of their past, had a particularly urgent need to repossess the future.

For much of this period Western man, conscious of the economic and social influences at work in the world, tended to see war as the chief medium of change. At no time was this more true than in 1914 when European society seemed to be waiting for a change in the World Spirit, or plotting like Lenin in Zürich to bring it about. It was almost an accepted fact that by mere force of will an inspired individual or people could change history or revise it, that history could be made most effectively by those who acted in conformity with the *Zeitgeist* of the age.

In that sense the 20th century meant different things to different people. Many hoped that it would be continuous with the past, that it would complete what the previous century had left unfinished, or unattempted – in short, that it would represent a further advance on the road to progress. The 20th century impressed those who were enthused by the speed of development, especially of scientific invention, even when the scientists turned their energies to fighting wars.

Others drew comfort from the hope that the century would represent a break with the past, a conscious effort to make man for the first time autonomous of history. For them the future promised a new world, that would emerge from the ruins of the old. Where the 19th century had had its great engineers, its road builders and shipwrights, the 20th century saw the birth of something quite new, engineers of human souls.

There was also, however, another 20th century, one which threatened to make the age discontinuous with the past and the future, that threatened to end in an apocalyptic struggle. Instead of expressing optimism, many Europeans were profoundly anxious that the whole human project would never be finished, that the advanced nations of the world would disinherit themselves as well as everyone else. It was a mood expressed tellingly by H G Wells in his novel *War in the Air* (1908): 'This was no slow decadence that came to the Europeanised world – other civilisations rolled and crumbled down, the Europeanised civilisation was, as it were, blown up.'[2]

The vision of a world blown up compounded the view that modern life was fragile, that human progress was by no means assured. For much of the 20th century many people had no belief in the future, in part because they had so little faith in themselves.

The First 20th Century

If the 20th century was continuous with the past, it was continuous with one version of it – a post-Enlightenment belief in human progress. In the wake of the Industrial Revolution the mechanical sciences progressed faster than ever before. Intellectual enquiry was no longer held back by religious or ethical constraints. The age was expressed eloquently by Henry Adams who noticed on the eve of the new century '1830:1860:1890 – X and X always comes out not 1920 but infinity'.[3] Adams was proposing one of the laws of proliferating modern energy, but he might also have been writing of the sense of change which Americans, in particular, found so exhilarating.

In that sense there was little reason to think in 1900 that an era was drawing to an end. The general shape of the late 19th century was easily recognized in the 20th. The continuities between the two periods are as visible even today as the discontinuities between them. It was, of course, not a necessarily comforting fact for those who, like Theodor Adorno, suspected that the future might not be a continuation, but an intensification of the present – a present that they had hoped to escape.

As many Europeans discovered to their dismay, 20th century warfare had much in common with its practice in the 19th century. Many of its features would not have been unfamiliar to the generals who had fought the Franco–Prussian War (1870). Indeed, most of the great technological developments of war before 1945 came about at the very end of the 19th century – the invention of the internal combustion engine, the use of electricity and oil as new sources of power, the revolution in communications produced by the telephone and the tape machine (the foundations of modern bureaucratic organisation), even the production by the chemical industry of the first synthetic materials which enabled societies like Nazi Germany to fight on long after they had been denied access to the natural resources of the world.

Even the weapons used in the First World War were not so different from those that had been employed by the Europeans against the relatively unarmed societies of Africa or Asia. The machine guns used so effectively at the Front after 1914 were merely a technological extension of the Maxim gun 40 years earlier. Closely formed groups of men walking in tight formation across barbed wire defences were slaughtered just as effectively as had been massed hordes of natives in Africa. The only difference between the battle of the Somme (1916) and that of Omdurman (1898), the last of the great colonial battles, was that both sides in the European war had the same technology.

Nor were high casualty lists unique to the 20th century. High rates of attrition had been seen in the Wilderness campaign in the closing months of the American Civil War, as well as during the siege of Paris in 1871. The actual proportion of casualties to the total number of combatants was not significantly higher in the First World War than in any other major conflict the previous century. Long before the Great War, in fact, soldiers had already begun to see themselves no longer as professionals but 'assets' to be used as their commanders saw fit, workers with a job to be done. War had become a form of life not so entirely different from an industrial process. As an American general wrote in 1917, the principal task of a state was to produce a fighting unit, a machine that would work independently 'of the quality of the men who turned the crank'.[4]

Nor must it be imagined that even in the age of the blitzkrieg the mechanisation of warfare was taken to its ultimate conclusion. The Wehrmacht in Russia won the great battles of 1941 principally with infantry. The battle of Stalingrad, like Verdun before it, was fought not by tanks but by men – with the same intention on both occasions, not out-manoeuvring the enemy, but, bleeding it white.

Later in the war the Germans went even further by *demodernising* the battlefield, re-establishing in the process an even more direct link with the past. As Omer Bartov writes, by the end of 1942 the Germans recognised that the striking imbalance between their own forces and those of the Red Army had made technology an enemy, not an ally. In France the Wehrmacht may have fought a modern style war based on the decisive battle achieved in a short, sharp, relatively bloodless campaign. In Russia it found in its last offensive at Kursk in 1943 that it could only advance for ten days, despite throwing a million men and nearly 3,000 tanks into the battle.

The Wehrmacht only managed to hold on for so long by fighting a quite different style of campaign, based on endless battles, a refusal to concede ground or to surrender, a glorification of death in which soldiers were proud, even anxious to die for the Fatherland. War became a condition of existence, the will to win everything. The Russians, of course, had an equal will to win, plus the manpower reserves to prevail. There is some truth in arguing, nevertheless, that the war on the Eastern Front was the last of the great 19th century campaigns, one whose ultimate reality, of course, would have outstripped even Clausewitz's powers of imagination.[5]

Technological similarities between the two centuries did not stop at weaponry. The armies which were despatched into the field in 1914 were assembled, fitted out and transported to the battlefield by a state bureaucracy that was able to master logistic problems with the same efficiency Prussia had shown in 1870. In all three of the wars fought by the French between 1870 and 1945 the means of getting their men to the Front was the railway.

'The railway makes man a chattel, transports him by the box and ton, he waits on it', wrote Emerson in the late 19th century.[6] He was not the first American writer to see the railway as more threatening than promising. In the 1890s Henry Adams wrote that the railway network that spanned the American continent had absorbed the energy of an entire generation. The generation of the 1860s, he added, had been 'mortgaged to the railways.... No-one knew it better than the generation itself'.[7]

To judge from the faces peering out at us from fading sepia photographs of the first volunteers of the Great War en route to the Front, it looks as though they had booked their passage years in advance. In Paris, the Gare d'Est – 'this man-eater' as one Frenchman called it – witnessed another set of scenes 20 years later, another series of leavetakings and emotional farewells, the vivid expression of a nation on the move, this time leaving for the Maginot Line in 1939.[8] Only towards the end did the mood change. In April 1945 the Parisians turned out to welcome home the first contingent of women prisoners from Ravensbrück. Their arrival was an altogether more sombre affair, marked by little shouting, and few expressions of joy. The silence that greeted them was an expression, one observer wrote at the time, 'of the emotion of an hour that penetrated beyond that to something nearer pain'.[9] Too much human suffering lay behind their homecoming.

Even the shape of 20th century warfare had been glimpsed during the American Civil War. By then it had become clear that the country that could mobilise its population and industry more effectively than its adversary would almost certainly prevail, as proved to be the case in the North's victory over the Confederacy. In the 20th century, thundered Thomas Edison in 1915, the nation that could out-produce rather than out-fight its competitors would always win. With its huge industrial plants, naval stockyards and assembly lines he predicted that the United States could out-produce any country or combination of countries in the world.[10]

It was a persuasive argument, if a deeply worrying one. For once warfare became a contest of industrial might, cities became a legitimate object of attack. During the First World War Edison's grandchildren collected scrap metal from their neighbours to feed the machines of war. They lived to see a world in which they themselves became the targets. Some years before the first atomic attack on Japan painted an apocalyptic picture of the future role of airpower, the expatriate Russian pilot Alexandre de Seversky had argued that the era of war fronts and struggles for a few miles of disputed territory had ended for ever: 'The key now is no longer occupation but destruction ... and the destruction is now systematic, scientific – the planned wrecking of a great nation.'[11]

In the first novel of his *Alexandria Quartet*, Lawrence Durrell painted a vivid scene of an air raid during the Second World War:

> 'To our surprise we found ourselves shouting at each other. We were staring at the burning embers of Augustus's Carthage. I thought to myself, we are observing the fall of city man'.[12]

By the 1940s the old urban geometry had come to conform to the new geometry of industrial warfare. The very vulnerability of the highest state of life – the city, the modern world in its most perfect form, the *civitas*, the place where people communicated – was ultimate confirmation that mankind could not be protected from its own powers of invention.

City man did not disappear during the course of the 20th century, but the process of bombing came to its logical conclusion in the Pacific War in which more Japanese civilians died than soldiers. By the 1950s political scientists in the West were turning their attention from the means of production to the means of destruction as the guiding motor of the modern age. The nuclear era, wrote the sociologist Wright Mills, had legitimised 'the principle of obliteration as the defining principle of modern life'.[13]

Even in the nuclear age, however, Clausewitz's *central* proposition about war was still deemed to be valid – that victory in modern conflicts tended to go to the side that prevailed upon its enemy to surrender. The country that lost was the one that was persuaded to concede defeat.

The methods by which an army could break through a well defended trench line were partly tactical and partly technological, but in the end, in a century in which infantrymen still counted for more than tank crews, victory or defeat was a matter of will. As Hegel had concluded, wars were the ultimate test of the 'ethical life', or political health, of a nation. The willingness of its citizens, soldiers and civilians alike to fulfil their patriotic obligation depended, in Hegel's view, on their ability to rise above self-interest. And that in turn required them to put the survival of their ethical community above their own material interest, even personal survival.

In war, wrote Hegel, 'the power of the association of all with the whole is in evidence'. The secret of success in modern warfare lay not so much in the display of personal bravery or individual heroism, but in organised, disciplined, collective action. Courage, he wrote in *The Philosophy of Right* had become 'mechanical'. Victory and defeat were no longer technical matters to be decided by opposing armies in the field, but final conclusions to be drawn about the viability of an entire society and its way of life.[14]

If this were true in the 1830s how much more so was it the case in the 20th century when simply to have a nationality was to be part of a military process. Not only were men conscripted to fight, both women and children as well endured passive recruitment. There were no non-combatants, no real conscientious objectors. By the beginning of the Second World War even military historians had begun to recognise that it was their task not to describe armies at war so much as societies in conflict. While the socialisation of war, as much as the industrialisation of warfare, was one of the features of the 20th century, it was also one of the elements of continuity with the era in which Clausewitz and Hegel had lived.[15]

As Clausewitz's English translator Colonel Maude wrote before the First World War:

> The chances of victory turn entirely on the spirit of self-sacrifice of those who have to be offered up to gain an opportunity for the remainder.... The true strength of an army lies essentially in the power of each or any of its constituent factions to stand up to punishment, even to the verge of annihilation if necessary.[16]

In one of his essays in 1919 Hermann Hesse observed that the Allied armies had won the Great War not because they had superior resources, but because they had 'better nerves'.[17] A society with better nerves could take greater losses. A country with a more assertive will to power could still assert itself over an adversary which on paper was superior but lacked the will to win. As John Keegan writes, the outcome of battles in the 20th century was no different from that in the 19th – it was determined in the end by the human factor, the behaviour of men struggling to reconcile their instinct for survival with their sense of honour. The factors which turned victory into defeat or vice versa were as operative in 1940 as in 1814. The vices that accounted for the disintegration of armies in the field – anxiety, uncertainty and misapprehension, in a word loss of morale – were the same.[18]

What was different was that men were prepared to die for their beliefs in greater numbers than ever before. As Susan Sontag remarks, they so loved the ideas that impelled them to fight that they wanted to die *of* them (as though they were a disease). In an age which craved ideological certainty, armies seemed to be willing enough to lock themselves in almost endless engagements so that they could redeem the past or repossess the future. In the 20th century, wrote Elias Canetti, people did indeed seem 'most alive while dying'.[19] Why men were prepared to die so readily for their beliefs is the subject, of course, of this book. The paradoxes elaborated by Sontag and Canetti lie at the heart of our question – what was the 20th century about? It brings us also to what was significantly different about the 20th century compared with the classic Clausewitzian age.

The Second 20th Century

Historical continuity is a concept which people find less or more comforting at different times in history. As the German writer Eric Tuchkolovsky wrote in the aftermath of the Great War, having lived through one historical era he and his generation had no wish to live through a second.[20]

In the 20th century, however, many men did believe that they could break with the past altogether, that they could aim for an objective which had always remained out of reach, to make man autonomous of history. Marx had predicted that the victory of communism would bring history to an end. The United States, although far less millenarian in its expectations, believed that the spread of free trade would create a different kind of man, an economic being dedicated to the pursuit of peace.

In this respect, two of the ideologies that competed for dominance in the century promised discontinuity with what had gone before. Indeed, in making this claim both the United States and the Soviet Union, in the eyes of observers such as Oswald Spengler, seemed to be remarkably similar. In one sense neither were countries at all but promises to the world, or contracts with history. Both saw themselves not as actors, but historical agents with the power as well as the will to give history a push. Both saw themselves as revolutionary powers implacably opposed to the weight of tradition. Both entered the 20th century within months of each other, when Woodrow Wilson took the United States into the First World War, and Lenin arrived from Zürich intent on sweeping away Russia's Tsarist past.[21]

It was in the Soviet Union that men first tried to make a future more promising than the past. The Soviet Union was born in a world war. Indeed, but for the experience of the civil war that followed, the form that Soviet communism took in the 1930s might have been very different.

'Revolution is nothing more than war' wrote Hermann Hesse, 'like war it is a continuation of politics by other means'.[22] In Russia it was a tragedy that the 1917 Revolution produced a civil war in which up to nine million people died in the greatest social catastrophe which had ever afflicted Europe. It was a tragedy because Lenin deliberately plunged the country into war to consolidate his own position. The methods he used in the name of a national emergency would probably not have been acceptable, even to many of his fellow communists, in any other circumstances.

By late 1918 it had become a common practice for the government to call up workers for state service exactly as they drafted recruits into the Red Army. The compulsory labour scheme was identical in many respects to the mediaeval *tiaglo* system in Muscovy, only this time it was seen as a permanent obligation, not an ad hoc response to a particular crisis or threat. In the countryside the first task of the Red Army was to fight the peasant producers. Despite the fact that no campaign medals were issued, the war against the peasants, the *muzhik*, provided the Red Army with its first combat experience.[23]

The civil war also provided the imagery of the first Five Year Plan with its persistent references to political struggle. War socialism, if not the model, became the reference point for many of the policies associated with rapid industrialisation, the collectivisation of farms, the state distribution of supplies, the compulsory requisition of food, even the introduction of state planning. The Red Army became the model for the control of transport and industry.[24]

It was natural that after the civil war Trotsky, the architect of victory, should have transferred his attention from the army to the economy. 'It is obvious', he wrote in 1918, 'that Soviet power is organised civil war against the landlords, the bourgeoisie and the kulaks'. Two years later, he admitted, 'if we are serious about a planned economy then labour must be distributed, shifted and ordered in the same way as soldiers are'.[25]

As usual Trotsky's arguments required rather than compelled agreement. Bukharin, the party's chief ideologue, nevertheless produced a theoretical justification for the shift of emphasis from the spontaneous activity of the masses to what he called 'the organised coercion of a proletarian state'. Labour conscription was one of the first reform measures. Proletarian coercion in all its forms, Bukharin added, 'beginning with shooting and ending with labour conscription is ... a method of creating communist mankind out of the material of the capitalist epoch'.[26]

As for the forcible movement of people in the 1930s, their fate too can be traced to the experience of war. In 1916 Stalin passed through the POW camp at Krasnoyarsk, one of the larger camps for German prisoners. Most of them were transported in appalling conditions, packed into modified boxcars, often 40 men to a carriage. The journey to the White Sea could take days. The journey to Siberia or Turkestan could last for weeks. POWs in transit frequently spent days at a time waiting on railway sidings, often without food. A great many died en route.

Did the widespread system of POW camps that existed in the last days of Tsarist Russia suggest the *gulag*, the vast network of prison camps in which over 13 million citizens of the Soviet Union were condemned by Stalin? All we know is that 20 years on the trains were at work again. At the height of the purges special *zak* trains left Moscow Northern Station at 17.00 hours on odd numbered days and 06.00 hours on even numbered ones.

One of the more distinguished of these reluctant travellers, the novelist Solzhenitsyn, writing of his journey by train to a labour camp in 1950, argued that the experience of the political prisoner and the soldier were much the same. The transport, he observed in *The First Circle*:

> has the life/death experience for a prisoner as being wounded for a soldier. And just as a wound can be light or serious, curable or fatal, so a transport can be long or short, a momentary distraction or a short cut to death.

It was a journey that over a million Poles were forced to take when evicted from their homes after the Soviet invasion in September 1939. All the politically suspect elements of Polish society, whether ex-soldiers, state officials, forestry workers, or even small farmers, were deported east in green painted cattle cars with the members of their family, the sick, the elderly, even the very young. It was only when they passed through the Ukraine that they recognised that, for the Ukrainians at least, their plight was not at all extraordinary:

> From Kiev onwards scarcely one of the people hurrying to and fro on the crowded platforms so much as glanced twice in the direction of the cars or their freight.... It was still very difficult for people coming from outside [Russia] to take in that such things could be everyday sights; that members of these people's own families, their fellow workers or neighbours might as easily have been transported in similar trains to similar destinations.... The citizens of Kiev and Kharkov could not be expected to turn their heads because this time the trains came from Lvov or Tarnopol or Stanislavov or Pinsk or any other town to them equally remote and unknown.[27]

Few citizens of Kiev would have seen the Poles as POWs. They would probably have seen them as victims of a political age in which war and peace could no longer be distinguished, for they themselves had become prisoners of peace, victims of the purges, the show trials, of forced collectivisation – a programme which had amounted to a declaration of war by the state against its own citizens.

Outside the Finland Station in St Petersburg stands a statue of Lenin in place of the traditional man on horseback as civic hero. Finland Station is one of the five railway terminals through which a visitor may enter or leave the city. There he will see Lenin's finger pointing at an imaginary crowd, making a point, striking a political gesture. There he will glimpse another image of the 20th century, Lenin standing on an armoured car, the symbol of a society continually mobilised for war.

The Finland Station is still symbolic of an age. The trains, in fact, began leaving for the *gulag* soon after Lenin's arrival. The station still stands as a permanent reproach to the name that St Petersburg was forced to bear after Lenin's death. It stands, notes the poet Joseph Brodsky, 'as a terminus for a rail journey into the future with the *gulag* and the gas chamber as waystations along the route'.[28]

It was not only totalitarian regimes which wanted to remake history on the understanding that all things were possible, a proposition alas that often ended not with the impossible but the unthinkable: the Final Solution. The United States too was a society which came into existence through revolution, that wished to create a new order, to rewrite history in its own idiom. The United States entered the First World War not to defeat Germany, but to create a new world order based on a form of democratic internationalism. Its wish to break with the past came out even more clearly during the Second World War. When Churchill and Roosevelt published the Atlantic Charter in August 1941, Roosevelt insisted that Britain endorse his four freedoms: freedom of speech, freedom of worship, freedom from fear and freedom from want.

In the course of the Cold War no-one took America's role more seriously than John Foster Dulles. In a book written before he became Secretary of State he had argued that the severest test for America was to redeem the world. The United States had been created as 'an experiment in human liberty'; its institutions reflected the Founding Fathers' belief that the country's destiny was to free mankind, and that it could not survive unless it showed mankind the way to a better life.[29]

Dulles was the most fundamentalist of all America's Secretaries of State, the most consistent believer in redemptionism. His contempt for the non-aligned nations of the Third World who wished to distance themselves from both superpowers was typical of a man who believed that the lowest circles of hell were reserved for those who refused to stand with God or against him, those who refused to make a choice, those who refused to make the future something better than the past. One of his favourite quotations was Woodrow Wilson's 'our civilisation cannot survive materially unless it is redeemed spiritually'.[30] Ultimately, he believed that the United States had the moral authority to lead because it had chosen the path of virtue before seeking power. If political balance requires a politician with a fine eye for the shade of grey, Dulles saw politics in terms of sharply defined antipathies and antagonisms.

So too did William Fulbright, who as Chairman of the Senate Foreign Relations Committee was to be one of the greatest critics of America's role in Vietnam. In his early years, however, far from condemning the 'arrogance of American power', Fulbright believed the world could be redeemed by the United States provided it used its power boldly, not timidly.[31] He supported the Marshall Plan, the Truman Doctrine and the Atlantic Alliance as organisations or projects that offered America scope to pursue its ends. By the 1960s, of course, many Americans had begun to doubt whether the United States could actually rewrite history anew.

As the Mexican poet Octavio Paz argued, the United States wanted to be outside the world but was in the world. This was the contradiction of contemporary American society 'having been founded against history yet being itself history'. Just as the Soviet Union was forced to come to terms with its inability to play the role of a historical agent, so the United States began to question the role conferred on it by its founding fathers: that of an actor outside history, an example to some, a crusader to others, a country which would ultimately redeem the human race.[32] It is, perhaps, significant that even so pragmatic a politician, and so inveterate a Cold War warrior as Zbigniew Brzezinski, a man who had once written that being 'historically relevant and militarily powerful' were both mutually reinforcing, should have concluded his memoirs many years later with an observation by the Russian philosopher, Pytor Chaadaev:

> We are one of those nations which do not appear to be an integral part of the human race, but exist only in order to teach some great lesson to the world. Surely the lesson we are destined to teach will not be wasted; but who knows when we shall rejoin the rest of mankind and how much misery we must suffer before accomplishing our destiny.[33]

For most of the 20th century the United States saw itself as a country once removed from the historical constraints within which others had to manoeuvre for advantage, or to survive by cunning. For most of the Cold War the United States tried to make history or seek various ways of escaping from it. None succeeded. Neither containment in the 1950s nor detente in the 1970s secured its future. Of course, it eventually prevailed – it won the Cold War. One of the ironies of contemporary politics, however, was that only after achieving so complete and comprehensive a victory did the Americans discover that they could no longer create a new world order – that they no longer had either the resources or the amibition.

The Third 20th Century

Of the three interpretations of the century that I have chosen to discuss, the third was by far the most significant, in the world that really mattered, the imagination of men. All periods are prey to their own versions of the future. After 1945 the world was reduced to a level of consciousness which threatened to deny man a future altogether. Many were haunted by the fear of genocide, whether of a particular people or of the entire human race – the fear of what Christa Wolf called 'a bomb induced futurelessness'.[34] Haunted by such dreams men were concerned that the 20th century might bear no relation to either the past or the future, that it might be discontinuous with itself.

In 1945 the soldiers of the advancing US First Army uncovered the worst possible confirmation of human perversity, the most eloquent challenge to man's belief in progress and the power of human reason. It stumbled upon Hitler's death camps, the first intimation of the apocalypse. A few months later, the United States dropped the first atomic bomb on Hiroshima.

Two quite different but telling episodes illustrate the quiet despair that the returning American veterans felt in witnessing the world's disgrace.

In some American cinemas members of the audience tried to flee the first films to show the familiar concentration camp victims, the survivors caught by the camera, those gaunt, almost inhuman figures, a people dejected and defeated before its time. In some cinemas the returning soldiers barred the doors and forced the civilians to look upon scenes they themselves had witnessed.[35] In Hiroshima and Nagasaki, however, the Americans averted their gaze. Rather than garrison the two cities they preferred their allies to do so. They wished to spare their own soldiers scenes of what they had accomplished.

The Holocaust and the atomic attack on Japan are the two events that have remained most vividly in the consciousness of the Western World. 'After the Second World War', writes Robert Von Hallberg, the problem the world confronted was less how to evade history than to survive 'history's evasion of humanity'.[36]

The United States had known other crimes that had challenged man's faith in reason. It was implicated in two of them – in the genocide of American Indians, three million of whom died in forced marches, random massacres and the forcible resettlement of the population. In the Middle Passage, the euphemism for the transatlantic slave trade, as many as 15 million Africans were transported from their homes to work the cotton and sugar plantations of the New World.

In these two cases, however, there had been a reason for what had transpired, whether the 'necessity of history' (the exploitation and development of the wilderness), or the commercial development of the young republic. Neither were inexplicable. The murder of the Jews, by comparison, was terrifying because it had no economic or political rationale. It marked 'the abrogation of causation', an ultimately 'unhistorical' act, one dictated by human perversity, not historical necessity.

Fear of the irrational in human affairs was compounded by the recognition that genocide had become the currency of military power. The two superpowers did not necessarily wish to eliminate each other, but war was now played out at the level of life itself. The most important date in the 20th century, wrote Arthur Koestler, was 6 August 1945, the day the atom bomb was first dropped on Hiroshima. Before that date man had to contend with his own mortality, with the terror of his own death. After the explosion, men had to confront the death of the entire species.

Twenty-five years earlier Salvador de Madariaga had claimed that America's entry into the First World War had been the first 'world event' – that it had seen the birth of a world community, one in which America had become the common reference point, at least in mankind's imagination.[37] In 1940 the American sociologist Robert Park had predicted that

America's impending entry into the Second World War would move the world towards 'a common historical life'.[38] After Hiroshima the world tended to ask whether it could survive America. If only two atomic bombs were dropped it counted for much that the world's only real superpower exploded them. History, wrote the psychologist Erik Eriksson, had begun to presume 'a coercive universality' – one country could now bring the curtain down on the whole human race.

The experience of Hiroshima led the French novelist Michel Tournier to make the subsidiary hero of his novel *Gemini* the owner of a rubbish dump. He is depicted in the late 1930s presiding over a vast empire of vegetable peelings and cheap household goods. His livelihood is threatened only by what he sees as a peculiar modern vice: an obsession with keeping everything, however valueless, with creating goods that will last forever, a society in which the two great processes of production and consumption are carried out with no waste at all – the dream of a completely constipated city. Tournier conjures up an entirely disposable world in which a whole city could be thrown on the scrapheap. 'But isn't that just what we are promised in the next war', he asks, 'with the aerial bombing that we shall have?'[39]

As Tournier recalls in his memoirs the rubbish dumps of his novel are modelled on those that were inherited from her father by Louise Falque, a gnome of a woman with close-cropped grey hair whom the novelist encountered during her retirement in Barbizon when she was more than 80 years old. Falque had been raised by her father, a garbage scavenger who had lived off the rubbish dumps that served Marseilles. Forty years earlier she had received the first load of rubbish from Paris after the human exodus of June 1940. In Tournier's novel a rubbish dump is a society in microcosm, a society of form without substance, made up of newspapers, advertising leaflets, poison-pen letters and empty declarations of love. In Tournier's vision the 20th century is the ultimate disposable age.[40]

During the Cold War the concept of disposable cities reached its final realisation. Nuclear war promised what conventional bombing never could, not even the bombing of Tokyo or Dresden, that the world might well go in for designer-made disposable cities or spares. In the early 1960s the nuclear strategist Hermann Kahn imagined a dialogue in which the President of the United States might say to his advisers: 'How can I go to war – almost all America's cities will be destroyed?' And they in turn would answer: 'That's not entirely fatal – we have built some spares.' It was a chilling vision, one no less real for being imaginary. The fact that Kahn endorsed it made it all the more chilling.[41]

How do we judge in retrospect such an age? Were the men of the 20th century morally defective, or only more brutalised by war? Or does the real answer lie in the way they fought it? We must remember Clausewitz's dictum that victory in modern warfare went to the side that persuaded its adversary to surrender – the side whose nerve held longer, who 'willed' itself to survive.

Hitler always warned the German people that they would be destroyed if the war was lost. He did his best to deny the Allies victory by taking his threat to its logical conclusion – by destroying Germany himself, and thus at the eleventh hour robbing his enemies of their prize. His scorched-earth policy in November 1944 was far more ruthless than the Soviet Union's own policy had been in 1941 – for Hitler was determined to destroy no less than the *collective memory* of the German nation. He gave orders for the destruction of every ration card and historical record, every birth certificate and bank account number, every church and museum, everything that made up the German identity in the imagination not only of the Germans but the world as well. Historians have tended to interpret his programme (which was obstructed successfully, though secretly, by Albert Speer) as final confirmation of his nihilism – his will to destruction. But it was perfectly in keeping with a certain strain of military thinking unique to the century in which he lived.[42]

Long before Hitler's rise to power the *Reichswehr* had drawn up its own plans in the 1920s for the defence of Germany against a French invasion. In such an eventuality it concluded Germany would have to be treated like an African colony, and the Germans themselves as a subject people. The only defence, the generals concluded, was to destroy every road, bridge and telephone line, to drop mustard gas bombs on German citizens to delay the French advance, and to engage in semi-permanent guerrilla operations in which no distinction could be made between civilians and soldiers. It might be necessary, the generals insisted, to destroy Germany in order to save it.[43]

After the mid-1950s the same philosophy was applied to the defence of a democratic Germany against Soviet attack. Estimates of the true extent of civilian casualties in a nuclear war vary, but in the course of the 1983 Wintex exercise, a 'nuclear release' ordered on 9 March (six days into the war) – a limited release involving only a few 25 megaton weapons – resulted in the death of 400,000 soldiers and seven million civilians.[44] It was ironic that at the end of the Cold War the Germans were prepared to do to themselves what they had done to the Jews – to play the role of both persecutor and persecuted, to send their enemies to the gas chambers and then go to them uncomplainingly themselves. In that sense Arnold Lustig was quite right to call Auschwitz 'the visiting card of the 20th century'.

Eli Wiesel has long argued that the events that led logically to the Holocaust, the other to the bombing of Hiroshima, can only be understood together. 'The only way for the world to save itself', he once wrote, 'is by remembering ... the Holocaust. There could have been no Hiroshima, symbolically without Auschwitz'.[45] In the early 1980s, during the renewed fear of the outbreak of nuclear war, Wiesel added:

> 'only Auschwitz can save the planet from a new Hiroshima.... We recall the ultimate violence in order to prevent its recurrence. Ours then is a twofold commitment: to life and death.'[46]

As Elias Canetti expressed it in a journal entry in 1945, by the end of the war the whole world had become Jewish,[47] just as vulnerable to the suicidal instincts of the superpowers.

The survivors of the Holocaust like Samuel Pisar talked of an 'Auschwitz fever' taking hold of mankind, leading it to absolute perdition. Pisar believed that nuclear deterrence not only devalued human life, it suggested something far worse, that Auschwitz itself had been merely 'a pilot scheme for the apocalypse'.[48] As for some of the Jewish scientists who worked on the Manhattan Project, many later in life drew an analogy with the Nazi death camps they themselves had been spared. Forty years later one of the most prominent was to insist that the only difference between America's nuclear strategy and the Final Solution was one of comparative advantage. Instead of marching into the ovens like the prisoners of Auschwitz, man had decided to wait for more efficient ovens to be built.[49]

Even at the Nuremberg trials some among the Allies were aware of the irony of parading before the court of world opinion criminals who were held responsible for brutally prosecuting a war, when the ruins of the city above attested to a brutality of a different kind. 'Sixty thousand bodies under the ruins', wrote Albert Camus in his notebooks, 'it is prohibited to drink the water – one doesn't feel like washing in it either. It is water from the morgue. Above the decomposition, the trial'.[50]

THE TOTALITARIAN STYLE OF WARFARE

What is become of the Princes of Germany? Blown up. Where are the Estates or the power of the people of France? Blown up. Where is that of the people of Aragon and the rest of the Spanish Kingdoms? Blown up ... Nor shall any man show reason that will be holding in providence why the people of Oceana have blown up their king but that the king did not first blow up them.

(John Harrington, *Oceana (1656)*)

The 20th century, in a word, was conceptually imagined at the same time as it was experienced and lived. It existed in the consciousness of those who made it. It represented different things to different people – its historical significance or meaning was a question of which interpretation one preferred to follow – as well as whether one preferred to look to the past or the future. Ordinary people may not have consciously looked for meaning or tried to understand the times through which they lived, but they did, on the whole, understand that war had become a condition of life and thus implicitly accepted the meaning given to it by others.

By 1945, from the dizzying height of B-29s flying at 20,000 feet, the world did indeed look like a potential bombsite. It was a world that intruded into the modern consciousness, not immediately but at intervals. It was discovered or occasionally rediscovered, in the course of the next 20 years – in 1949 when the Russians exploded their first atomic bomb, in 1953 when they narrowed the gap with the United States and constructed their first hydrogen weapon; in 1956 when the Americans deployed an intercontinental bomber (the B-52) that could fly to Moscow and back. Was this not AD1, asked one observer, the first year of the atomic era?[51]

Nuclear war became part of everyone's private consciousness as the two superpowers, once uncertain allies in the war against Hitler, now implacable foes, found themselves locked in a posture of readiness, committed to each other's destruction. War had finally become definitively totalitarian for democrats and dictators alike – as Khrushchev later reminded his own people: the 'bomb' did not recognise the 'class principle'.

If the threat of nuclear war was part of man's interior life it was a private nightmare that belittled, indeed diminished, the dreamer. As Robert Oppenheimer, the man responsible for building the first atomic bomb later admitted, the nuclear age would be seen by historians as a transitory, dangerous and degrading phase in human history.[52] Degrading perhaps, but not, alas, transitory. For 45 years the super-powers terrorised themselves into silence, falling back on blackmail when argument failed. In the 1950s, when men were more honest, both sides referred to nuclear deterrence as 'the balance of terror' and it is as a form of terror, both degrading and dangerous, that nuclear deterrence should be understood.

It was a form of terror that would not have been unfamiliar to the early 20th century anarchists who had longed not only to throw bombs into parliaments or to assassinate heads of state, but to blow up entire societies. In *The Secret Agent* (1907), Joseph Conrad created Mr Vladimir, a shadowy figure running an anarchist cell from the Russian Embassy in London. In keeping with the temper of the time, Vladimir aspires to commit the ultimate blasphemy in the post-Enlightenment age, a crime not against God but against Reason. Blowing up a restaurant or a church or a factory would not terrorise anyone, he contends, not even the liberal bourgeoisie who would ascribe such an attack to a personal, even justifiable discontent. Blowing up an idea like pure mathematics, however, would have all the 'shocking senselessness of gratuitous blasphemy'. Such an outrage would combine 'the greatest possible regard for humanity with an alarming display of ferocious imbecility'. Such an act would make it clear to the bourgeoisie that its enemies were perfectly determined 'to make a clean sweep of the whole social creation'.[53]

In the Cold War the West threatened to blow up not only the Soviet Union but the *idea* of Soviet man. In turn, the Soviet Union posed a threat to the continued existence not of individual Americans so much as the entire capitalist system. Deterrence was in essence a crude expression of self-alienation, a naked form of terrorism based on the willingness of both systems to destroy each other. As a rational threat it represented an ultimate challenge to reason.

Like modern terrorists today both superpowers also held the enemy population responsible for the actions of its own government. 'The communalisation of guilt', writes Octavio Paz, 'included the communalisation of punishment.'[54] In its extreme consequence it executed the proposition of Christian humanism – that we are all bound together, all responsible for whatever actions are performed in our name. The late 20th century made the whole world collectively responsible for the political order which governed it. It was a proposition of universal responsibility which was, in itself, terroristic in essence. For in its essentials the nuclear state was really no different from the Palestinian terrorist movement holding Western citizens to account, not for their actions, but for those of their governments, for the plight of the politically dispossessed or disadvantaged in the squalid refugee camps of the Gaza Strip.

The nuclear state and today's terrorists were similar in one other respect. Just as Islamic Fundamentalists in Beirut kept their hostages in suspense about their fate in the late 1980s, so the people of the industrialised world were suspended in an eternal stay of execution. For 45 years they had to confront the threat of not being reprieved or ransomed when the hour finally came. By the early 1960s the first intercontinental ballistic missiles could reach their targets in 30 minutes. This was a world in which once done, nothing could be undone. Bombers might be ordered back, missiles could not. No-one would survive even through ingenuity;

no-one would be reprieved by luck. Even if the missiles overshot their targets people were as much threatened by what they would find if they did survive a nuclear attack, a radioactive wasteland in which even the initial survivors would probably envy the dead.

By the 1960s mankind found itself living in a totalitarian world similar in many respects to the world of Kafka's *Trial*. Does not Josef K learn at the end that in an age in which men may stand accused of unnamed or unlisted crimes, in which merely to survive is to plead guilty, that all that can be hoped for is a deferral of sentence, for the trial to never end so that the inevitable sentence can never be pronounced.

We are all hostages and we are all terrorists, concluded the philosopher Jean Baudrillard at the height of the second Cold War:

'This circuit has replaced that other one of masters and slaves, the dominating and the dominated, the exploiters and the exploited. Gone is the constellation of the slave and the proletarian, from now on it is the hostage and the terrorist. Gone is the constellation of alienation; from now on it is that of terror.'[55]

But perhaps the conventions of the nuclear age were determined less by the example set by the anarchists in the 1900s than by governments in the 1930s who turned to terror as the very basis of organised life. As Walter Benjamin once wrote, life in the 20th century was indeed like living in a 'permanent state of emergency'. And so it was, not only in Stalin's Russia or Hitler's Germany but also for Russia and Germany in the nuclear era.

In Stalin's Russia everyone was on trial, everyone was guilty until judged otherwise by the state, even the police whose leaders were shot from time to time for showing insufficient zeal in rooting out dissidents. At the height of the purges the Soviet people were literally terrorised into submission. In this respect, the interrogator in Sinyavsky's *Daniel* is almost as frightening a figure as Dostoevsky's Grand Inquisitor, more so, perhaps, because he is the instrument of a totalitarian rather than an authoritarian order:

Please remember (cries Seryozha) I have not been so far condemned. I am only on trial.
The interrogator looked amused and threw back the window curtain ...
That's where they are, the people who are on trial. See how many of them.
The interrogator pointed at the crowd milling below ...
You are different now, my boy. You are not on trial, you are condemned.[56]

Clearly a state that spent 30 years terrorising its own citizens had few moral qualms about building the bomb. Consistent to the end with its own past, it used the slave labourers in the *gulag* to build the *Tupamarov,* the Soviet Union's first intercontinental bomber. In a world in which the enslaved became party to the principle of terror by constructing instruments which could terrorise people beyond the state's reach, war became the agency as well as the instrument of the totalitarian state. Was not the apotheosis of 20th century warfare the state's ability to invade the *consciousness* of its enemies as well as its own citizens, to encroach upon their sense of self, to deny them *peace of mind* in the pursuit of 'peace'?

ON MODERNITY AND MODERN WARFARE

Modern (modern art; modern world). There is the modern art that, in lyrical ecstasy, identifies with the modern world. Apollinaire. Glorification of the technical fascination with the future.... But opposite Apollinaire is Kafka: the modern world seen as a labyrinth where man loses his way.

(Milan Kundera, *The Art of the Novel (1987)*)

Beset by fear of nuclear annihilation Arnold Toynbee was the first major writer to use the term 'post-modern', not in its present connotation as a critique of modernity but as a term which best summed up the final institutionalisation of warfare. For Toynbee the First World War was the first post-modern war, which together with the Second challenged the foundations of post-Enlightenment thought. One foundation was the belief in eternal progress, based largely but not entirely on technological invention. The onset of the nuclear era suggested that technological progress could itself be at fault. Before the First World War, H G Wells had talked of the end of the modern age, one which offered man a 'safe, satisfying modern life' based on a 'timeless present'. In taking exception to this view Toynbee predicted the onset of a post-modern future in which war would be the natural condition of life.[57]

Both Wells and Toynbee were wrong. The 20th century was not the post-modern age, it was the apotheosis of the modern era. And if that era was indeed beset by war it was largely because modernity and war were synonymous.

(1) They were synonymous to begin with because of the aggressive nature of modernisation. If modernisation was the end of progress it was inevitable that an unmodern people, or an unenlightened political class would be swept aside, or condemned to oblivion because of the failure to come to terms with its own historical obsolescence. Karl Kraus once described the modern age as a dumb puppet show in which only modern

men could perform. The unmodern were condemned to watch from the stalls. 'The feeling of man's superiority', he wrote in 1914 'triumphed in the expectation of a spectacle to which only modern men had access'.[58] One lesson to draw from this view was that the unmodern were historically irrelevant, perhaps not really true men at all.

The brutality of the 20th century, which has taken many forms, including that of the mass displacement, even deportation, of people, is easier to understand if we see the totalitarian features of warfare as a reflection of modernity itself. A people who could not be improved or reformed, whether Stalin's *kulaks* or the Christian Armenians of Turkey, were ruthlessly excluded. Those who, in Lenin's description of the bourgeoisie, were 'objectively hostile' to modernity were considered expendable and were frequently expended.[59]

The French anthropologist Claude Levi-Strauss once defined modern civilisation as 'anthropoemic' – modern cultures did not devour their adversaries as did anthropaphagic or primitive ones, they vomited them out, separating, segregating, excluding them from the realm of human obligation. Communists excluded not only the bourgeoisie, but also the *lumpenproletariat*, religions of all denominations, as well as most Asiatic and African races. All, at one time or another in the history of the Soviet Union, were considered to be irredeemably reactionary, an obstacle to be swept aside on the road to the creation of a truly modern state. Many were killed indiscriminately, others more methodically, while many more were sent to be re-educated at the 'preparatory school' of the penal colony.

The modernising imperative had been seen at its most ruthless in the colonisation of Africa after 1870. What was the use, asks Kurtz in Conrad's *Heart of Darkness*, of sympathising with a people 'on the verge of extinction'. In such cases, argued the late 19th century scholar of the unconscious Eduard von Hartmann, there was little humanity in prolonging a people's death agony – 'the true philanthropist should accelerate the process and labour to that end'.[60] Such sentiments were soon to be echoed by Europeans of their fellow Europeans, particularly the Jews.

There were many explanations, of course, for the Holocaust, but surely one that has been paid insufficient attention by historians is the fateful encounter of Germans and Jews on the Eastern Front after 1915 that helped to prepare the way psychologically for the catastrophe that was about to befall Europe. It was an encounter with a society whose very existence had not even been suspected. While serving in Russia the artist Oskar Kokoschka discovered 'a strange people from the ghetto who regarded war as a typical Christian amusement from which they chose to remain detached'.[61] The squalor of the Jewish ghettoes in the towns and villages through which the Austrian and German armies passed had no equivalent, not even in Eastern Europe.

For the extent of the horror they inspired in those who saw them we might quote a 'neutral' observer, the American reporter John Reed, who crossed into Russia with the German army in 1915. In the streets of the Jewish quarter of Rovno he discovered a multitude of little shops, a veritable warren of houses in which far too many people were huddled together. He discovered 'a pale, stooping, inbred race', a race of faintly bearded boys with unhealthy faces, girls prematurely aged with ceaseless labour, a people who smiled deprecatingly and hatefully as they stepped aside to let the Gentiles pass. For a thousand years, Reed observed, the Russians had tried to exterminate the Jews with little success. Instead, thousands had shored themselves up in the impregnable world of the ghetto, scrupulously observing their own religion, practising their own customs, speaking their own language, and above all hating the outside world and being hated by it.[62]

It was, of course, one of the ironies of the Holocaust that this medieval structure that had survived a thousand years was swept away almost overnight by the Second World War. In mass shootings such as those at Rovno in 1941 and the deportation of Russian Jews to the death camps, the Nazis ironically emancipated the survivors from the claustrophobia of their medieval tradition, the *shetl*, a narrow-bounded world in which ritual practice had separated Jews from Gentiles far more effectively than the walls of the ghetto. It was a terrible salvation, nevertheless.[63]

Even in the democracies, wrote Engels in a letter to Marx, history 'leads a triumphal car over heaps of corpses, not only in war but in peaceful economic development'. 'Progressive' and 'reactionary' were terms frequently used by non-Marxists as well to define their own society in relation to history. A progressive state was one that kept in step with history, a non-progressive people one that fell behind. The idea of history as constant movement was an integral part of the modern consciousness. It was progress of a kind. If people got in the way they tended to get knocked down. In a sense, they invited their fate.

In that respect, the resignation of men and women to the awful circumstances that attended them in the 20th century is one of the most depressing, if characteristic, features of the modern age. Once the forces of history had been unleashed nothing could be done to reverse or arrest them. History pronounced its judgement without benefit of a court of appeal. As one of the survivors of the death camps later remarked, 'Of course, we wanted to survive but we were not at all sure we had the right to'.[64]

(2) The modern age was inherently aggressive in another respect. It was

predicted on the principle of constant struggle. The present was seen as
a period of transition to a predetermined end. Young artists such as André
Breton who were influenced by the Surrealist movement of the 1920s saw
all art as traditional and all creativity as conflictual. 'To live our life in
beauty', he wrote in the journal *L'Action d'Art*, 'we know we must struggle.
Revolt for us is the action of art.'[65]

What was so remarkable about the generation of 1914 was the extent to
which they implicitly recognised that they were on the threshold of a
world that was about to change forever. And it was indeed the awareness
of this change that encouraged them to believe that their generation was
special, that it had a unique mission – that in the words of Ortega y Gasset,
history was trembling to its very roots because a new reality was about to
be born.[66]

If the journey into the future was transitional, transitional periods
provided fertile ground indeed for men peddling grand designs, final
struggles, or even 'final solutions'. Every modern ideology of the 20th
century promised the end of history. Every one anticipated a long and
bitter period of conflict before the journey could be completed. History, in
a word, offered a vista of unending conflict with no certainty of what to
expect at the end of the journey. History was inherently pernicious. While
serving in the trenches Henri Barbusse was puzzled to find his fellow
soldiers so fearful of the future since there was nothing to be said for the
present which threatened their lives. 'The contract signed by God'
nevertheless 'affirms without question that man must stay in the past ...'
an odd doctrine where making progress lies in marking time.[67]

With the rise of the totalitarian regimes of the 1930s the future seemed
more threatening still. The concept of progress, wrote Walter Benjamin,
had become associated with the notion of catastrophe. 'The fact that
"things move on" was the catastrophe'.[68] In moving one step forward men
seemed always to take two steps back. Was this not the dynamic of
progress? As Robert Musil wrote in the opening chapter of *The Man
Without Qualities*, his magnificent enquiry into the catastrophe of 1914:

> People who were not born then will find it difficult to believe but the fact is that
> even then time was moving as fast as the cavalry camel; but ... no-one knew what
> it was moving towards. Nor could anyone quite distinguish ... between what was
> moving forwards and what backwards.[69]

Musil himself never completed his novel. At his death in 1942 it remained
unfinished. History, he once wrote, was a 'chaotic succession' of unsat-
isfactory and false attempts at a solution. In the end, he could not present
his readers with a general outline of events because he was unclear

whether history would end on a positive note or not.

Looking back 50 years later it is strange that so many intellectuals were taken in by the quest for Utopia. What did Shaw or André Gide see in Moscow in the mid-1930s? Did they find a Utopia they wanted for themselves, one that they imagined the poor yearned for in the *banlieues rouges* of Paris, or the blackened terraced houses of Lancashire? Did the workers really dream of a promised land or of a society in which they would be free, in which they could live as self-determining individuals? Shaw saw in the white granite buildings, in the giant chunks of architecture that transformed the urban landscape of Moscow, the essence of modernity against which the West was in revolt.

In constructing his socialist Utopia, Stalin built an ersatz state, one of prestressed concrete, steel and plastic tiles. In taking possession of Russia he built over the Russian landscape, destroying the old populist institutions, including the village communes. For the peasants Utopia was withheld from them in the moment of its fulfilment. To Malcolm Muggeridge, the new paradise looked neither Russian nor socialist, or for that matter Utopian. More than anything else it looked frightening – the object of too much desire, of too much striving.

Twentieth century man, in fact, seemed to be condemned to live in a world in which movement was inherently dangerous, in which progress was often malign. It was a world discussed by the novelist Günter Grass in his semi-autobiographical novel *The Diary of a Snail*, a compelling defence of evolution against revolution, of the snail's pace against history's Great Leap Forwards, an apology for perseverance, not impatience, on the road to the future. Not for Grass Hegel's World Spirit mounted and galloping like Napoleon on the field of Jena (1806). Hegel had sentenced mankind to history. In his name every abuse of state power was explained as historically necessary, every war as historically inevitable. In his novel Grass recalls that his hero Hermann Ott had once written an article on totalitarianism, an essay that subsequently had been lost. Only the title had survived (perhaps a title for the times?): 'On the Consciousness of Snails – or Hegel will be overtaken'.[70]

(3) Finally, the modern age was intrinsically aggressive because it was self-referential and therefore self-validating. Without history there could be no self-conscious life. For Hegel, writes Hayo Krombach:

> being is meaningless without its relational becoming. There cannot be self-conscious life where there is no history, because it is only through its spiritualised manifestation that life recognises itself. The ultimate meaning of life itself is thus its historical self-recognition.[71]

Since 20th century man had no vantage point from which to look back on his life, success perforce became its own justification. A nation that won a long struggle or prevailed in battle surely validated its own ideas. 'You say it is the good cause that hallows every war', wrote Nietzsche, 'I tell you it is the good war that hallows every cause'. 'Of course our cause sanctifies battle', echoed Ernst Jünger, 'but how much more does battle itself sanctify the cause?'[72]

Nietzsche's archetypal hero was Napoleon on the field of Jena, the World Spirit on horseback, the man of battle. 'He lived the life of Europe' wrote Balzac, 'he inoculated himself with armies'.[73] As long as he was victorious, he was in the right. Nietzsche too saw himself as 'a man of catastrophe', a prophet who predicted that the 20th century would see upheavals never before witnessed. 'There will be wars', he warned, 'the likes of which have never yet been seen on earth'. He himself, however, was not an advocate of war as such. His wars of the spirits, the great ideological struggles of the century to come, were more rhetorical than real. He forecast not a war of guns but of words, 'a war without powder and smoke', a war not of soldiers but of thinkers. 'If you cannot be saints of knowledge', Zarathustra remarks, 'be at least for me her warriors'.[74]

Nietzsche may well have anticipated that the 20th century would be marked by conflicts unprecedented in their scope as well as the vigour with which they would be prosecuted, but he anticipated a struggle between warriors of knowledge, not warriors of war. He could hardly argue otherwise since he found war itself to be a ludicrous means of validating the truth of any idea. Does not Zarathustra say the 'blood is the worst witness of truth'? Did not Nietzsche also add that life should always prevail over knowledge, that 'if knowledge had destroyed life it had destroyed itself too'?[75]

Unfortunately, Nietzsche was to be confounded in his optimism. The battles of the 20th century may not have been his prophecy, but they were often fought in his name. Men did not debate big ideas, they preferred to die for them. They were prepared to kill for their truth, to annihilate spirits in opposition to their own. In the end, Nietzsche the prophet fell victim to his own belief in reason. As a phenomenon war rapidly outgrew the understanding of its phenomenologists.

2

On Consciousness and Modernity in Modern War

There are no more living mythologies you say? Religions are at their last gasp? Look at the religion of the power of history and the priests of the mythology of ideas with their scarred knees.

(Nietzsche, *The Use and Abuse of History (1874)*)

It is not at all unlikely that illnesses have their history, and every epoch has its own definite sickness which did not occur in such guise before.

(Troels-Lund)

France, wrote Martin Heidegger in 1940, had not been defeated by Germany; it had lost the will to survive.[1] War in the 20th century was a struggle of moral forces. By seizing the initiative one side could impose its will on the other while imbuing its own soldiers with the spirit needed to fight in conditions that probably were the worst that any soldiers in history had had to fight in. What this book sets out to discuss is the motivation that men had for fighting so fiercely, for going to war in the first place, for 'willing' their countries to survive. As the 20th century opened, the European generals knew well enough that the shape of the modern battlefield would require a degree of self-sacrifice that had rarely been asked of soldiers in the past. Would they in fact fight on the modern battlefield, could they be sent into 'a zone of death', into ground swept by the artillery and machine-gun fire of the enemy? Would their nerve crack on the "killing ground" of the future? The responses to these questions elicited two schools of thought. One, represented by the Polish writer Jean Bloch, was that firepower had made defence supreme, that war in effect had been abolished. The defenders would always win. An attack would result in little less than mass slaughter.

The second school of thought, associated in France with Foch, a director of the French War College, put its faith in the 'cult of the offensive'. Foch coined a series of epithets which were soon to enter general use: 'the will to conquer is the first condition of victory'; 'a battle won is a battle in which one will not confess oneself beaten'.[2] The cult of

29

the offensive swept through the military academies of Western Europe, including Britain. Writing in 1910 Ian Hamilton, an observer of the Russo-Japanese War a few years earlier, wrote:

> Blindness to moral forces and worship of material forces inevitably lead in war to destruction. All that exaggerated reliance placed upon *chassepots* and *mitrailleuses* by France before '70; all that trash written by M. Bloch before 1904 about zones of fire across which no living being could pass, heralded nothing but disaster.
>
> War is essentially the triumph ... of a line of men entrenched behind wire entanglements and fire swept zones over men exposing themselves in the open, *of one will over another weaker will*.[3]

In the course of the 20th century Hegel's belief in the 'ethical health' of nations – that strong nations produced strong armies, that the will to win was a reflection of a nation's will to survive – soon entered common discourse. Fascism and socialism, wrote Karl Polyani in *The Great Transformation*, were forces transforming international life, 'an *élan vital* which produced the inscrutable urge in the German and Russian people to claim a greater share in the record of the [Western] race'.[4]

It was also commonplace among writers of colonial Africa in the 1930s to stress the listlessness of native societies that had succumbed to colonialism in the last years of the previous century. In observations that could be taken to be commentaries on their own societies, anthropologists complained that war had given 'a keenness' to native life which was 'sadly lacking in times of peace'. The fate of the Africans, wrote one English anthropologist, was to become a 'cultural in-between'. The *Pax Britannica* denied them their old identity, as well as the chance to forge a new one through war. Africa, he added, had fallen from 'cultural maturity' into 'cultural infancy'. The most likely fate of a culturally destitute people was to 'literally die of boredom'.[5]

Even as they wrote, Hitler and Mussolini were parading similar ideas in public about the 'detribalised degraded natives of their time' – the cowardly proletariat living in barrack cities, drained of energy, needing war for their redemption. War had its appeal too in the democracies. 'I suppose that the desire to merge one's individual destiny in forces outside ourself', confided Evelyn Waugh in his diary in April 1926, 'is really only a consciousness that that is already the real mechanism of life'.[6] War was one way in which men chose to 'objectify' their lives, even if this meant – in Waugh's words – transforming themselves into 'subordinate forces'.

In this chapter I shall try to identify some of those forces which seemed to require war as a condition of life and self-sacrifice as proof of the 'ethical life' of a nation. In outlining those forces no-one wrote more compellingly than Nietzsche. Nietzsche was not alone in anticipating 'the will to power' that would lead men into war and sustain them on the battlefield. He was unique, nevertheless, in the intensity of his vision.

NIETZSCHE AND THE ABUSE OF HISTORY

They who manipulated and misused our youth
Smearing those centuries upon our hands
Trapping us in a welter of dead names
Snuffing and shaking hands at patent truth.
(Muriel Rukeyser, *Poem Out of Childhood (1935)*)

Nietzsche was the first modern philosopher to study the problem of excessive historical consciousness, a problem he believed prevented the Europeans from beginning history anew. He called it 'a historical sickness', and in a sense it was. It held men back. It prevented the early 20th century from developing a style uniquely its own. It forced men to borrow from what he called 'the vast warehouse of theatrical masks and costumes' that constituted the past. In preventing men from realising their true historical potential it denied them the chance of a profound transformation of the notion of humanity itself.

In *The Will to Power* Nietzsche argued that there was nothing wrong with a historical consciousness. Men must understand history if they were ever to become free agents, no longer answerable to the dead weight of tradition:

Man must first have learned to distinguish necessary events from chance ones, to think causally, to see and anticipate distant eventualities as if they belonged to the present ... Man must first of all become calculable, regular, necessary, even in his own image of himself, if he is to be able to stand security *for his own future*.[7]

The future was the key. The Europeans, he declared, were self-determining individuals, no longer governed by the laws of nature or by such abstract forces as hate or providence. Freedom had given the West a power denied Islam and China. It had made them uniquely, in Hegel's words, 'a people with history' because only they were aware of making history, of making a future different from everything that constituted the past. The Europeans were free not because they had invented democracy, but because they had freed themselves from superstition and tradition. They were able to make themselves autonomous of history. The problem was, he observed, that Europe seemed unwilling to realise its full possibilities. History was not so much made, but endured. Western man seemed to live in the shadow of an invented or useable past. The true historical consciousness, he argued, would be one which allowed history to serve man, not man history.[8]

Nietzsche correctly perceived that in the 20th century men, in serving history, would go to war. History had become dangerous, not least because towards the end of the 19th century certain nations began claiming that they *were* history, that they were able to speak in its name.

In his history of 19th century Europe the Italian philosopher, Croce, wrote at length about this unique phenomenon, the readiness of nations to see themselves as best able to liberate others:

> Even the hegemony or primacy claimed on behalf of such or such a nation by Fichte and others in favour of the German people, by Guizot and others in favour of the French people, by Mazzini and Giolerti in favour of the Italian people, by yet others in favour of the Polish people or the Slavs in general, that hegemony was the outcome of a theory that presented it as a right and a duty to be the leader of all peoples, an originator of civilisation, of human perfection and of spiritual grandeur.[9]

In the 20th century both the United States and the Soviet Union saw themselves as the agents of history, its custodians, its spokesmen. Of the two, the Americans probably took the claim more seriously. As Octavio Paz observes, the Americans were a people always rushing towards the future. The United States was a country made not of solid earth but that 'evanescent substance: time'.[10] The United States was a country without Romanesque or Gothic cathedrals, without a hereditary nobility, without a king. In that sense it was not a nation at all but 'a historical project', a contract with history entered into by the Founding Fathers in 1776.

The United States did not belong to the past: it was a programme whose field of realisation was the future. The space in which America itself had been created was not a land with a history but a virgin continent. 'The birth of the United States was the triumph of a voluntary contract over the fatality of history, of private ends over collective ends, and of the future over the past'.[11] It followed, of course, that as the future the United States could not take notice of the limits imposed on countries by fate or providence.

As such, of course, the Americans as a people came to be seen in the course of the 20th century as inherently dangerous. The problem with making the world 'safe for democracy' (democracy as history) was that little thought was given to making democracy itself safe for the world. Wilsonian internationalism was all very well, but America's claim to be the future established a cultural difference, even a temporal one, between itself and most other 'unmodern' people. In one of Saul Bellow's novels a Third World politician complains that the United States has robbed his country of its future by dispossessing it of its past. Recognising this threat, George Ball, one of the great American politicians of the 1960s, called Wilsonian interventionism 'Winthropism', or 'Williamsism,' after America's two great Calvinist preachers, John Winthrop and Roger Williams. Winthrop preached his sermon about establishing a 'city on the hill' not on American soil, but on board ship before the first colonists landed in Massachusetts Bay. One of the reasons why Roger Williams was driven from the Massachusetts Bay colony in 1637 was his insistence that the colonists were building their city on someone else's hill – in this case that of the American Indians.[12] Twain's hero in *A Connecticut Yankee at King Arthur's Court* destroys the pre-industrial society he is attempting to redeem by cutting it off from its past and its traditions. Herman Melville's Ahab tries to redeem himself but plunges into the infernal regions, taking his crew with him. These two heroes are pilgrims trying to redeem other people 'from time'. In the course of the 20th century the United States looked as though it was quite willing to obliterate time (or history) by cutting other people off from their roots. In his book *Of A Fire On The Moon*, Norman Mailer wrote that Americans were 'the most Faustian, barbaric, draconian, progress-oriented and root destroying people on earth'. Was it too fanciful, he asked, to suggest that the United States was unwilling to look history in the face? Redemptionism in the 20th century was not a creed for the faint-hearted.[13]

Nietzsche's challenge to the way that history was understood by his own age, his fear of how it would be used or interpreted for the next hundred years, went further than just an indictment of national destiny. He was equally appalled at the prospect of millions dying for the sake of national myths. Nietzsche was not alone in complaining about the way history was interpreted. Looking back upon the Great War, Hermann Hesse wrote in the weeks following the Kaiser's flight to Holland that history as taught in German schools had been a lie. It had not liberated Germany but belittled its children, crushing their spirit and keeping them in their place. It had denied them dignity by comparing their dull and uninspiring lives with a magnificent past that had been distinguished by bravery, self-sacrifice and redemption. It had been a profoundly theatrical view, of course, a caricature of history, a kind of pantomime offering a series of "scenes from grand opera".[14]

Hesse contended that the German people had discovered too late in 1914 that they were weighed down by their own historical consciousness. Young men were persuaded that their lives had no value unless tested in battle. Everyone who fought in the war was convinced that anything less than victory would constitute the most terrible defeat of the German spirit. What the politicians, in effect, offered the people was a sham greatness, a version of history that lured to their death those who 'thought historically', those who lived perpetually in the shadow of the past.

'For the rest of us, the poets and the religious minded', Hesse added, 'those who believed in God even on weekdays and [were] already familiar with the life of the soul', the war was a monstrous fraud. Only those who 'lived outside the time' managed to maintain their self-respect, even when being led to the slaughter.[15] As Nietzsche had predicted, the sickness of history had encouraged men to die for bogus causes and spurious historical roles. 'An excess of history', he had warned, had indeed exhausted 'the shaping power of life'.[16]

Both Nietzsche and Hesse, of course, wrote of a world that was in all essentials undemocratic. In a letter to a friend in May 1925 Thomas Mann hoped that the new Weimar Republic would repudiate an aristocratic version of German history, with its love of death (*Todesverbundenkeit*) and replace it with one more democratic in spirit, more friendly to life (*Lebensfreundlichkeit*). Perhaps the republic would turn its back on history once and for all.[17] Unfortunately, from his American exile in the 1940s, he learned too late that the masses could just as easily be conscripted to die for a populist version of the past.

It would be wrong, of course, to insist that all historical myths are life-denying. In 1940 the English people discovered that their myth was able to sustain them, a myth that went back to the Armada and to their resistance to Napoleon, a myth almost prophetic in its appeal to the logic of history – a logic that taught that the English always fought alone, but were rescued in the end by other countries coming into the war on their side, or by their enemies over-extending themselves, when they allowed their ambition to exceed their grasp.

In 1940 the past served Churchill particularly well in his dialogue with the nation. Of all leaders he could instil in those who listened to his radio broadcasts a sense of national purpose which he constantly evoked to fortify the present. It was a sense of destiny shared by historians such as Trevelyan, who accepted Churchill's rhetoric as a dogma of their faith and tried to convey it in their writings. It was the last time they were able to do so. As J H Plumb noted in his book *The Death of the Past*, there was something elegiac in the writings of Trevelyan and his colleagues in the years leading up to the war, a nostalgic respect for a past which was fast failing to catch up with the popular imagination, in part because it could no longer disguise Britain's decline.[18]

In an earlier essay Plumb had written that the past was not history, it was merely an interpretation of events which generations of scholars, poets and even novelists had shaped to give a sense of meaning and purpose to the events in which they found themselves involved. It was a highly useable commodity, since it helped a political élite to formulate its ideas and regulate its political discourse. In 1940 Britain was more deeply conscious of and committed to its national myth than at any other time in the 20th century, precisely because it forged a bond between the politicians and the public in their hour of maximum need. Churchill's speeches were effective because they 'rang true'. That is why Alan Taylor wrote that Churchill was the price the British people paid for reading history.[19] In the event Churchill proved to be the last great Englishman. Wells would have called him a historical effigy, a totem figure, a symbol, not a real person. Writing in 1943 the poet Julian Symons stated that all the great men of the time were the products of the peculiar historical consciousness, that they were 'monsters' that 'nature should have outgrown'.[20] And so it did. By the time Churchill was returned to power in 1951, he was already irrelevant, his message obsolete. In Plumb's words, Britain's myth had become 'a threadbare refuge for the ageing rulers of a society ... from which all strong emotion [was] rapidly draining away'.[21]

Another of Nietzsche's complaints was that the past served only the few, not the multitude. What he perhaps did not recognise was that the masses would come to reject history, that they would be reluctant to join up to fight future wars, not because of a more democratic spirit but because of a preoccupation with consumerism. Writing just before the outbreak of the Second World War, Thomas Mann complained:

> The German does not think in *economic* terms. And he doesn't think politically either: he thinks tragically, mythically, heroically – the dismemberment [of Germany] and its forced depoliticising would be a great psychic relief.[22]

The Germany to which Mann returned in 1947 from his self-imposed exile in America was very different from what it had been. The Germans were now divided politically; they had also begun to think in economic terms. As they became more prosperous they also became less and less the military power they once were. By the end of the Cold War they had become a post-military society, disinclined to see any political utility in the use of force, except in self-defence.

It was the coming of consumerism that explains why the Soviet system in Eastern Europe collapsed so quickly in 1989, why communist governments were swept out of power in Poland in ten months, in Hungary in ten weeks, in Czechoslovakia in only ten days. It also explains why rather than contest the issue at the very end of its life, the Soviet Union imploded without violence. Long before these events, however, history had given way to economics. Writing in the 1960s Raymond Aron observed:

> There [is] no point in trying to discover what the mental outlook of the manager of an Anglo-American company and the director of a Soviet trust have in common ... As economies become industrialised both must calculate expenses and income, make long-term plans – the production schedule – and translate all these data into comparable quantitative terms.[23]

In a word, qualitative estimates of social life lost their hold on the popular imagination. In the 1950s Khrushchev promised 'to bury' the United States, not by outfighting, but by outperforming it. Both systems offered the world a more effective way of enriching itself; both promised the Third World not so much a political Utopia as an opportunity for the first time to escape the poverty trap. That is why Ernest Gellner calls the last phase of the Cold War (1973–89) the Great Economic Competition – the country that won so decisively was the power that was able not only to promise but to provide its people with a higher standard of living.

If Nietzsche did not foresee this development, he also did not foresee another, that history would not so much end in war but that war itself would finally discredit history. After 1918, defeat in war meant far more than just signing an unfavourable peace treaty with the enemy or trading territory for peace, or conceding unfavourable terms of trade. In the modern age terms such as 'winning' and 'losing' referred to much more than just the specific outcome of a war. Writing of Germany's defeat in 1918 Walter Benjamin explained why the result had disinherited an entire people:

> Our linguistic usage is a marker of the depth to which the texture of our being is penetrated by winning or losing a war: it makes our whole lives richer or poorer in representation, images, treasures. We have lost one of the greatest wars in world history, a war intertwined with the whole material and spiritual substance of our people. The significance of that loss is immeasurable.[24]

Not only Hitler felt dispossessed of his past by the defeat of the Second Reich; millions more wished to repossess the war and determine its meaning. The signing of the peace treaty with France in the same carriage at Compiègne in which the Germans had surrendered in November 1918 was an attempt to put history in reverse, to remember the first rather than the last act, in a word to rewrite it.[25]

The Austrian novelist Joseph Roth put the case in similar terms. 'The Great War is now in my opinion rightly called the World War, not only because the whole world was involved in it but also because as a result of it we each lost a world, our own world.'[26] After every war in the 20th century its participants came to mourn an epoch that had passed on. 'Every epoch dreams about the next', wrote Benjamin, except the people who lose a war. They dreamed of a past that could never be recaptured. That, he added, was the nightmare of history in the 20th century.[27]

It was a nightmare that haunted the victors just as much as the vanquished, in the case of 1918 the principal victorious powers, England and France. Even the very word 'victory' became questionable. 'Even now', wrote Barbusse in 1920, 'we cannot hear [the word victory] without feeling nausea'.[28] The French, added Paul Valéry two years later, had been left by their victory in a terrible state of uncertainty. They had almost been destroyed by what they had destroyed. 'We do not know what is going to come into being and we have every reason to fear it.'[29] What they feared most, in the words of Gabriel Franconi, was that the ghosts of the fallen heroes might come back to rise against the civilian shirkers in the cities, against the old men who had remained behind the lines.[30]

In the event, of course, it was the living, not the dead, who felt disinherited. The English may have imagined that they lost a generation on the Somme, the French most certainly did. France lost a larger percentage of its active male population than any other participant in the fighting. So many young men perished at Verdun, writes Theodore Zeldin, that the young were quite unable to challenge the old politicians who continued to govern France by the old ideas.[31]

The English too may have won the war, but what had they won, asked many who returned from the Front? Did naval supremacy, or the acquisition of more colonies from Germany, or even maintaining the balance of power in Europe, really justify losing the sixty thousand or so officers who died on the killing ground of the Western Front? 'The Wasteland' of the 1920s was more than just T S Eliot's term for the nameless millions performing barren office routines, wearing out their souls in interminable labours which never seemed to bring much happiness. 'The Wasteland' had another definition. It was a place not merely of desolation but intellectual doubt. As Edmund Wilson wrote of Eliot's vision: 'In our post war world [1931] of shattered institutions, strained nerves and bankrupt ideals, life no longer seems serious or coherent – we have no belief in the things we do and consequently we have no heart for them.'[32]

In the 1920s many Englishmen believed that defeat would have been no worse than victory, indeed that their victory constituted a form of defeat, one which had dispossessed them not so much of the past, but of the future. It denied them a future in confirming that the years that lay ahead could never be more attractive or inspiring than those that had just passed. For the English, at least, the 1914 war still represents a watershed, a psychological *caesura* between a golden age and the less than golden years that followed.

This was all the more the case after the Second World War, a confrontation which many English came to suspect they had lost as decisively as if the German Army had marched up Whitehall. Many writers suspected this from the beginning. Asked in 1940 what he felt about the war E M Forster replied:

> 'I don't want to lose it. I don't expect Victory with a big V and I can't join in any bold-new-world. Once in a lifetime one can swallow that – but not twice.'

Fifteen years later the English had forfeited their empire and to some extent their own self-respect. Visiting England in 1947 Edmund Wilson found only a collection of ruins, a country whose gods were old and dishonoured.[33] The British people began to suspect that the Battle of Britain had not only been their finest hour but their last, in the words of Alan Taylor 'the last great moment in the English story'.[34]

Such views did not necessarily reflect the situation in which Britain found itself but they did have resonance for a society which unconsciously understood history in Hegelian terms. What was the decline in the English spirit, after all, but a decline in the ethical health of the nation? After 1945 the English were forever comparing themselves to what they had been in the past, drawing up an unfavourable balance sheet in the process. The English, wrote Emil Cioran, had become a nation of 'etiolated vikings'. Determined to be happy, they had sacrificed their role in history. 'Exempt from plenitude, from risk, from any *tragic* suggestion', the English had become a nation enveloped by mediocrity.[35] In choosing to become unhistorical, loved not feared, understood not detested, 'no longer a nightmare for anyone', they had disappeared from view:

> 'excess, delirium – he protects himself against these, sees them only as an aberration or impoliteness. What a contrast between his former excess and the prudence he invokes now. Only at the price of great abdication does a nation become *normal*'.[36]

NIETZSCHE AND THE 20TH CENTURY

Nietzsche discussed more than just the abuse of history, in particular the way in which it was (mis)used by governments to inspire their people to fight. He wrote also of the 20th century's uniquely catastrophic character, what would distinguish warfare in the new age from every other. Indeed, he saw three developments in the evolution of modern consciousness that would probably make war a condition of life.

(1) In an age of mass politics, he predicted, man would fight not over what to divide up, but over what was worth having. When he wrote that the conflicts of the future would be over 'the domination of the earth' he meant that nations would struggle over the right to impress their own beliefs and values on other people – the right, if you will, to speak for humanity in a world from which God had departed, much like Alexander the Great, leaving the field to the strongest of his generals.[37]

That is why Nietzsche criticised Bismarck's Germany for being a 'lie', not a universal truth – a conception of very limited appeal to Germans only. Anything that was not universal in the 20th century, that could not be sold as a universal truth, would probably deny a country victory. Writing in 1915 Max Weber complained that the Germans would probably lose the war to those other Anglo-Saxons, to the two countries, the United States and Britain, that lived in the imagination of other people in terms of the universal ideas in whose name they fought.[38]

Later in the Cold War the United States terrified people by the very comprehensiveness of its claims. As the Frenchman Raoul de Rusty wrote during the Second World War, when the Americans emerged victorious they would demand a unique tribute from their enemies and allies alike. They would demand not land, or strategic bases, but a moral tribute – they would require other countries to become more American.[39]

It was this prospect which frightened Stalin more than anything else, and which may or may not have precipitated the onset of the Cold War. Roosevelt, Stalin told the American Ambassador in 1941, was the first world figure to live in the imagination of the Russian people, just as Woodrow Wilson had been the first non-European to live in the imagination of the Germans and French. Stalin's true dilemma was that the influx of American ideas would destabilise the Communist Party in the Soviet Union, rendering it a more responsible power, or one more responsive to US wishes. Containment was not a US invention. Lenin invented the term in the 1920s. Stalin gave it wider currency still in his book *The Problems of Marxism-Leninism* (1947), in which he wrote that the Soviet Union would have to contain the United States by erecting a barrier against 'every manner of invasion'. In the event, for all its experiments with *détente*, arms control, and even partnership in the last days of the Soviet state, the United States never drew back from its demand for the latter's unconditional surrender. When 'truth' was at issue anything short of surrender would have been unthinkable.

(2) Nietzsche's second fear was that in a secular age men would replace God by their own man-made divinities. When he wrote in 1870 that God was dead he did not mean that men would live without religion. He argued, instead, that they would merely organise their lives without putting God at the centre. Humanity would live in a godless world even if it believed in the world hereafter. Shorn of the certainty of religious belief, it would crave the certainty of political truth.

It is important that we understand precisely what Nietzsche meant. In the lectures on the philosopher that Heidegger gave between 1936 and 1940 he spelt out his understanding of Nietzsche's meaning.

'The pronouncement "God is dead" means: the supra-sensory world is without effective power. It bestows no life. Metaphysics, i.e. for Nietzsche Western philosophy, understood as Platonism, is at an end.'

The passage that Heidegger singled out for particular analysis was from *The Gay Science* and it is worth quoting it at length here:

The madman. Have you not heard of that madman who lit a lantern in the bright morning hours, ran to the marketplace and cried incessantly, "I seek God, I seek God". As many of those who did not believe in God were standing around just then, he provoked much laughter.... "Whither is God", he cried. I shall tell you. *We have killed Him.* You and I. All of us are his murderers.... What was holiest and most powerful of all that the world has yet owned has bled to death under our knives.... Is not the greatness of this deed too great for us? Must we not ourselves become gods simply to be worthy of it? There has never been a greater deed; and whoever will be born after us – for the sake of this deed – he will be part of a higher history than all history hitherto.

Unfortunately, this was not how the 20th century turned out. Indeed, the madman in Nietzsche's fable goes on to remark that his 'time has not yet come', that the tremendous event he has described has not yet reached the ears of men.

As Nietzsche acknowledged, the need for God was so profound that such an 'abandonment would have consequences beyond the multitude's capacity for comprehension'. The death of religion would for many be the most 'terrible news'. Rather than accept the loneliness of man's new position, men would worship false gods – even human ones, 'even the very serpents that dwell among His [God's] ruins'. In time they would feel compelled to turn their own disbelief in a divinity into the worship of what Auden called 'a psychopathic God'. More than that, they would be prepared to martyr themselves as an earlier age had borne witness to Christ through martyrdom.[40]

(3) Finally, Nietzsche forecast that in the clash of wills wars would be fought on a scale never before seen. Long before the advent of the Cold War and the age of nuclear deterrence Nietzsche feared that domination of the world would be fought between the European powers who would use history as their tool and treat the world as a laboratory. 'Whole portions of the earth', he wrote, 'might be used for conscious experiments.'[41] 'This is the great spectacle in a hundred acts reserved for the next two centuries in Europe.'

Nietzsche was not alone in his presentiment that in the 20th century the Germans might even be prepared, if necessary, to sacrifice the subject of history: man. Where the great religions had once demanded the martyrdom of man, the new secular faiths might require the martyrdom of a species: 'The desire for knowledge has been transformed amongst us into a passion which fears no sacrifice, which fears nothing but its own extermination'.[42] As he speculated in *Beyond Good and Evil*, 'to perish through absolute knowledge may well form a part of the basis of being'.

By the end of the 19th century other writers too had noticed the disproportionate relationship between promise and reality, between the promise contained in the experiments of which Nietzsche wrote and the power required to achieve them. If the problem was to remake society or reinvent man, the means were destructive and omnipresent. Nietzsche feared that man's capabilities would outgrow his capacity to use them – that in the end men would lose control of their own inventions and of their politicians. Technologies would provide possibilities no-one could dream of; power would enable people to 'will' if not the impossible, the unthinkable – the Final Solution.

The question of man's *hubris* had already been posed much earlier in 1879 by the French chemist Berthelot, who had predicted that 'a hundred years from now, thanks to physical and chemical science, men would know of what the atom is constituted and would be able, at will, to moderate, extinguish and light up again the sun as if it were a gas lamp'. The brothers Jules and Edmond de Goncourt had raised no objection, but added in mitigation, 'we have the feeling that when this time comes in science, God with his white beard will come down to earth, swinging a bunch of keys and will say to humanity the way they say at five o'clock in the salon

"Closing time gentlemen".[43] After the atomic bomb was dropped on Hiroshima Elias Canetti was moved to speculate whether God had stolen away at the end of the 19th century and taken refuge in the atom, whether on that grim autumn day God had not 'revealed himself for the first time'.[44]

It is this particular catastrophic nature of history that has changed since the end of the Cold War in 1989. We know that there are limits to what can be found out about the world and ourselves – that there are ethical limits to our own experiments, as well as practical limits if the world is not to be destroyed. In particular there is a *historical* limit, a change of historical consciousness. We can never 'know' the truth by standing outside ourselves, observing the world by looking in. We can only discover truth by taking part in history, not as agents but as actors. It is a change of consciousness which began before the Cold War came to an end, that was inspired by the fear of nuclear destruction.

Even with that prospect before them, of course, there were many men who were still determined to keep in step with what Milan Kundera called 'the Great March of History', surprisingly, perhaps, when keeping in step had risks of its own:

> People never suspect that every step forward is also a step on the way to the end and that behind all the joyous "onward and upward" slogans lurks the lascivious voice of death urging us to make haste. If you question the need to keep in step it is only because the basis of modern consciousness was no longer God, or faith in mankind, or even progress but the Grand March, the splendid march on the way to brotherhood, equality, justice, even happiness, a march that went on and on "obstacles notwithstanding", for obstacles there must be if the march is to be the Grand March.[45]

By 1960, however, many people had begun to question the causes for which they marched, for which they had once been so ready to give their lives. As Kundera noted: 'When the crimes of the country called the Soviet Union became too scandalous, a leftist had two choices: either to spit on his former life and stop marching, or ... to reclassify the Soviet Union as an obstacle to the Grand March and march on'.

In exile from his native Czechoslovakia, Kundera drew hope from the fact that the march was coming to an end, that that space where it was occurring was now no more than a small platform in the middle of the planet, that the crowds that had once pressed eagerly up to the platform had long since departed. The Grand March was now taking place off stage, often outside Europe in the killing fields of the Third World, from Cambodia to Angola.[46]

After so much blood-letting the march had lost its hold over the imagination. By the mid-1980s its glory was equal to the 'comic vanity of its marchers'. And even its marchers now shambled rather than marched, having long since lost faith in their own marching songs. By 1989 there was little of the 'willed action in war' of which Robert Musil had despaired 60 years earlier, that war-like step that had always involved 'movements of the legs'.

Michelet had looked on history as epic poetry; Nietzsche as a theatrical performance, or more exactly that region where theatre ceases to be representation and becomes a living embodiment of the life and death of society. At the end of the Second World War the archetypes of conflict were no longer to be found in biology or theatre, but in communications theory. Nations were no longer interested in what the messages said or even who formulated them, but how they were expressed, for fear that the wrong transmission might lead to the wrong signal and the wrong signal to nuclear annihilation. What mattered were the means not the ends of each society. History as passion began to disappear.

No one any longer judged the world, they endured it – that is why the collapse of ideology in 1989 came so quickly – even if its end had been glimpsed by Herbert Marcuse and Daniel Bell 20 years earlier. The participants of the Great March stumbled along without music, displaying little of the brio of the past.

History has not ended, of course, even if the Great March has been abandoned. It has returned with a vengeance in countries previously under communist rule. A people disappointed in its past is unlikely to be reconciled or at ease with its present, still less hopeful of its future. 'We have turned the course of history' cried the guests of a May Day party in Warsaw encountered by the English writer Rory MacLean on a trip across Eastern Europe after the Berlin Wall had been breached:

> We have turned the course of history! all cried together. We started to feel quite mad, the poem and chants, the mantras of dogma were hypnotic. The words moved as though they were quite meaningless. Jacek and Anna, as the rest, felt torn between fear of the past and responsibility for the present. Where are we? What year is it? Has anything changed?

The 21st century, alas, is likely to be just as fraught with historical consequences as the last. The past has become an essential element, perhaps *the* essential element in the idea of nationalism. If there is no suitable past it can always be adapted or invented or 'remembered'. Such histories, writes Benedict Anderson, are limited imaginings. They are parochial and exclusive, not universal and inclusive. They sanction the exclusion of groups from the larger community; they discriminate against others; they reject the very idea of internationalism. In that respect, the end of the Cold War marks not the end of history, only the end of a historical era, that of the Great March. It is a momentous change nevertheless.

DOSTOEVSKY AND THE CULT OF SELF-SACRIFICE

... Dostoevsky and Tolstoy, as for Kierkegaard, human destiny was *either/or*. Thus their works cannot be truly understood in the same key as *Middlemarch* or *The Charterhouse of Palma*. We are dealing with different techniques and different metaphysics. *Anna Karenina* and *The Brothers Karamazov* are, if you will, fictions and poems of the mind, with central to their purpose is what Berdyaev has called "the question of the salvation of humanity".
(George Steiner, *Tolstoy or Dostoevsky: An Essay in Contrast*)[47]

If the writings of Nietzsche are useful in helping us to understand the importance that men attach to history, the works of Dostoevsky are helpful in understanding something else about the modern world, what the Italian novelist, Italo Calvino, once called the 'catastrophe complex' of the 20th century.[48]

As Octavio Paz argues, Dostoevsky is our great contemporary. Few writers of the past have his presence: to read his novels is to read a chronicle of the 20th century. He obliges us to go underground so that we can see what is really happening beneath the surface of modern life. He obliges us to see ourselves. 'Dostoevsky is our contemporary because he guessed what the dramas and conflicts of our age would be, and he guessed not because he had the gift of prophecy and was able to see future events, but because he had the ability to get inside souls.'

His world, of course, is not ours. In his tastes and aesthetic concerns he is a writer of another age, and that it why it is useful to approach his work, to understand its political import, through a 20th century commentator, perhaps the most important commentator of all, Mikhail Bakhtin.

Bakhtin was a Soviet critic who wrote several major studies, including one on one of Dostoevsky's novels, which was first published in 1929. It was a critical moment in Soviet politics. In the same year Bakhtin was arrested and sent into exile to Kazakhstan. There he spent a large part of his life, effectively silenced, immured from the world. He was not rediscovered until the late 1950s when his study of Dostoevsky's *Poetics* was republished, together with an appendix containing notes for a revised version of the work which was never produced.

Bakhtin was interested in Dostoevsky's view of heroic consciousness (rather than Nietzsche's view of man's historic consciousness). He was interested, in particular, in the way in which consciousness was formed in turning-points or crises in people's lives. Each crisis for Dostoevsky represented an existential conflict in which the value of life could be either affirmed or denied. Like Hegel, Dostoevsky accepted that value was a commodity that could not be realised except in an 'exchange', in a dialogue with another person, one which involved the process of reciprocal recognition. Indeed, the essence of Dostoevsky's heroes is that they have no personality unless they are heard, recognised or remembered. In what Bakhtin called in an infelicitous phrase 'the interdependence of consciousness', men have their true being in the 20th century: 'Justification cannot be self-justification, recognition cannot be self-recognition ... consciousness is in essence multiple ... the Underground man at the mirror'.[49]

Mutual recognition, Bakhtin maintained, was to be found particularly in crises or occasions in which man risked his life. Catastrophe, whether the death of an individual or death on a large scale in battle, represented the most critical dialogue of all.

This has been a perennial theme of 20th century fiction. In 1929 Georg Lukacs, one of the most perceptive literary interpreters of the century, argued that the psychological element of any character in a work of fiction 'not strictly requisite to the living dynamics of collision must be judged superfluous'.[50] Thirty years later Solzhenitsyn dismissed the greater part of Western literature on the telling, if specious grounds that it revealed little about human nature since the West had not known enough suffering.[51] The only effectual witness to the human condition in the modern age, both Lukacs and Solzhenitsyn argued, was that which described the cathartic clash of catastrophe leading to death or involving, at least, the prospect of it.

In the novels of Thomas Mann the idea of death as the realisation of life takes a related if somewhat different form, the end of the *will to live*. For in the 20th century, as Heidegger argued, catastrophe has taken not only the form of a nation willing another to death (Germany and the Soviet Union in 1941) but also of a nation like France in 1940 lacking the will to survive. The death of Thomas Buddenbrooks (1901) may be sudden but it is really the end of an unremitting, persistent disillusionment with the whole business of living. The sheer pointlessness of Thomas's life comes to him in his last summer. In *The Magic Mountain* (1924) the hero Hans Castorp is also given a unique insight into the pointlessness of his pending death. Released from his sanatorium, however, he dies the following year,

quite happily in the trenches, finally reconciled to death not in the
meaningless form of tuberculosis, of which he has been cured, but in a war
in which his death, at least, has meaning for others.[52]

Neither Buddenbrooks nor Castorp consciously will their death, but
they do not avoid it either. They die content in the knowledge that they
have understood life for the first time. In this respect, writes Jonathan
Stern, the modern consciousness is very much the enemy of life: 'as the
spirituality which exacts an understanding over and above the needs of
practical life, an understanding of the world and self at all costs – even at
the cost of life itself'.[53]

In the revised version of Dostoevsky's *Poetics*, Bakhtin noted Dostoevsky's influence on Thomas Mann, for Mann too was interested in
'those people ... with whom argument has not ended (for indeed, it has not
yet ended in the world)'. By argument Bakhtin meant an idea, a debate, an
intellectual dialogue. The death of a man does not mean that the idea for
which he died has necessarily been refuted, nor is a death wasted if the
argument is not won:

> In Dostoevsky's world ... a special place is occupied by the death departures of
> righteous men ... for the death of consciousness the person himself is always
> responsible.... Dostoevsky does not acknowledge death as an organic process, as
> something happening to a person without the participation of his responsive
> consciousness. Personality does not die. Death is a departure.... *The person
> departs having spoken his word but the word itself remains in the open ended
> dialogue.*

Was there not in this world a consciousness, an element of religious
excess? Faith in God may have died, but not faith in man. In allowing
themselves to be martyred did not 20th century man experience a
transcendent moment? And was it not one that they were unwilling to
surrender? The willingness of Stalin's victims in the 1930s to admit their
guilt rather than acknowledge their original error in joining the Party
(and thus denying the experience they had had) is not as astounding as it
often seems. A few centuries earlier the same was probably true of many
who were martyred for their faith. Their willingness to die, and to do so
uncomplainingly, was indeed a transcendent experience. Most martyrs of
the 20th century, perhaps, unlike their 17th century predecessors, may
have seen few visions, or heard fewer voices – but in the record of their
experiences at the Front we find episodes that, if they were not pathological in the exact sense of the word, were similar to pathological states
such as epilepsy. Let me quote from a passage in Dostoevsky's *The Idiot*

where the author describes Prince Myshkin's feeling just before the onset of an epileptic fit:

> Suddenly amid the sadness, spiritual darkness and depression, his brain seemed to catch fire, and with an extraordinary momentum his vital forces were strained to the utmost all at once. His sensation of being alive and his awareness increased tenfold ... his mind and heart were flooded by a dazzling light. All his agitation, all his doubts and worries, seemed composed in a twinkling, culminating in a great calm, full of serene and harmonious joy and hope, full of understanding in the knowledge of the final cause.[54]

Many who were conscripted in both world wars, but particularly the First, experienced a similar illumination, a similar presence of a truth greater and worthier than themselves at the moment of self-sacrifice. In that sense the 20th century can be seen as a period which encouraged, even exploited, a particular *political* sickness. Other visions of the world, of course, did not require war for their expression, or demand that those who espoused them should die for their beliefs. In our more materialistic world moments of transcendent understanding do not require violent action as a medium of communication either with God or with the 'world spirit'. In the first half of the 20th century this was not always the case.

Perhaps I should add that we do not devalue the experience of so many soldiers by labelling it 'hysterical' or neurotic in inspiration. For the people who had such experiences they were real enough. On this point Dostoevsky having had the first, may perhaps have the last word:

> He arrived at last at the paradoxical conclusion: What if it is a disease? ... What does it matter that it is an abnormal tension, if the result, if the moment of sensation, remembered and analysed in a state of health, ... gives a feeling, undivined and undreamt of till then, of completeness, proportion, reconciliation and an ecstatic and prayerful fusion in the highest synthesis of life? ... If in that second that is to say at the last conscious moment before the fit – he had time to say to himself, consciously and clearly 'yes, I could give my whole life for this moment', then this moment by itself was, of course, worth the whole of life.

Such was Dostoevsky's vision. It was in many respects a very Russian one (according to the age in which he lived). Balzac, and Flaubert in France, or Dickens in England, were not called upon to engage those forces that were to dissolve the fabric of society and with it the very nature of private life. Flaubert assured George Sand that the French Commune (1871) was merely a reversion to the factionalism of the Middle Ages, not the presage of a more nihilistic age. Only two writers, notes George Steiner, glimpsed the impulses towards the disintegration of private life:

Henry James and Joseph Conrad (and it is obviously significant that neither were West European).

Even in Russia, however, there were those who were inveterately opposed to Dostoevsky's insistence that life was nothing but a working out of the forces of history. What is the end of *Anna Karenina*, for example, but a refutation of this thesis? The book ends with Levin listening to Koznyshev's theory about a new world epoch inaugurated by the Slavic races, one which would require violent catharsis for its realisation. He is summoned to the nursery by his wife. On the way he thinks of the ideas that have been discussed, concerning providence, culture and history. He arrives to be told that his baby can now recognise him for the first time. It is a truth which means far more to him than the discovery of Russia's Slavonic future. It is a truth which alone gives his life meaning, a meaning he has the power to invest his life with. It is a human truth that can be grasped by everyone, not a private communication requiring a particular political consciousness. Perhaps, as Dostoevsky argued at the time, Levin will lose his faith again and 'tear himself on the same mental nail of his own making' – but that is Dostoevsky's prediction, not Tolstoy's end. We leave Levin (and his family) happy.[55]

We cannot leave the argument here, however. For the search for 'authentic death', for a death with meaning, was also a peculiarly 20th century quest, an attempt to escape the grand theories of the 19th century that had depersonalised death and thus rendered it more frightening. Ideas such as evolution, natural selection, the struggle for existence, the myth of race, all made death impersonal. Men were building blocks to a future they would never experience, or certainly never enjoy.

Heidegger argued in the wake of the First World War that the only thing that mattered was a personal death, to claim responsibility for one's death as much as one's life, to seize back the initiative from the impersonal forces of history moving inexorably to their end. When Heidegger talked of an authentic death he was talking of an existential one. In talking of 'conscious being unto death' he was offering men reassurance after the catastrophe that had befallen them. He was offering them a refuge from the industrialised, bureaucratised, totalitarian world of which I have written in the previous chapter.

In a world in which death was forever present, in which war seemed to be a condition of life, the best a man could do for himself was to prepare for death, so that he would know what he would be dying for when the moment arrived. 'As Anyone I always lived under the inconspicuous domination of the Other ... Everyone is the other and no-one is himself.' In Heidegger's view men live with the terrible realisation that 'Anyone ...

is Nobody', that 'Anyone' is 'the subjugated one', that the language of 'Anyone' is part of the universal 'talk'.[56] Only by grouping together with people of like mind could men find security from the enemies around them. Jünger said much the same thing, that in the 20th century men knew they were surrounded not by people but by potential enemies, who could break the secret contract into which humanity had entered with complete impunity. In the 1930s he added, 'the impression is roughly as if someone in the room would raise their voice and say "Since we are now as animals together among ourselves..."'.[57]

Who were the Jews in 1945, those who were led so uncomplainingly to their death, but 'Anyone', 'subjugated', the victim of what 'Others' did to them? Who were they but 'unhoused human beings' in Heidegger's vivid phrase, who died, martyrs to a cause they never understood, victims of someone else's cause not their own. As Peter Sloterdijk argues, such a philosophy is a reflection of an industrial, bureaucratic age, a response to the phenomenon of mass death in the 20th century, in the absence of which it would never have been formulated, let alone taken root. Heidegger's philosophy should be read not only as an existential ontology but as 'the encoded social psychosis' of an age.[58]

Many soldiers in the 20th century did indeed see their death as significant precisely because they elected to die, to fight their way into history. The senseless death, the death that cannot be explained away or made sense of, is that of the soldier who has no ideas, who has not joined up of his own free will. Watching some young conscripts embarking on a train for France in 1916 Siegfried Sassoon regretted the fact that they had no future, that they were already dead. If they were not yet literally dead that was only 'from an oversight of the enemy' – they were not going to do anything, but rather to have things done to them. The martyr who chooses to be shot rather than betray his friends may be a hero. The soldier who loses his life anonymously in a mass attack is rarely seen in an heroic light.[59]

A few years later watching thousands of City commuters going to work, T S Eliot observed 'I had not thought death had undone so many'. As they swarmed over London Bridge he was reminded of masses of reinforcements going up to the Front. It is a memorable phrase, an image in fact suggested by Bertrand Russell who, after seeing troop trains departing from Waterloo Station, had a strange intimation of London itself going up in flames, of a whole city vanishing like a morning mist.[60] The anticipation of such a catastrophe was already widespread before the onset of the nuclear age amplified it profoundly. History by 1945 had indeed become what Hegel feared it might – 'a slaughterhouse in which man would sacrifice his virtue, even his happiness'.[61]

For a nuclear war, of course, could not resolve an ideological debate. A nuclear war would be a very different kind of catastrophe from any that Dostoevsky had imagined. Such a war could destroy both protagonists to the debate. As Bakhtin argued 'in dialogue annihilation of the opponent also annihilates the very dialogic sphere in which discourse lives'. Ideas might survive defeat in battle, but they could not survive a nuclear catastrophe. No ideas would live on in the consciousness of others, in part because there would be no survivors to continue the debate.

Everything in the 20th century consciousness led eventually to the threat of nuclear war, the fear of total destruction, of a commitment that had first been glimpsed at Verdun. The 20th century was the only century that looked as though it might be discontinuous with the future. In Kundera's words it left man precariously 'crouched on the narrow ledge of the present'.

Since the European Enlightenment men had hoped that one day mankind would be united in everlasting peace. In the Cold War the planet did indeed become an indivisible unit, but it was 'ambulant and everlasting war that embodied the long desired unity of mankind'. As Kundera wrote in the closing days of the Cold War the unity of mankind meant 'no escape for anyone, anywhere'. Such was the meaning in the 1980s of that grand phrase 'the brotherhood of mankind'.

WAR AND EUPHEMISM: KARL KRAUS AND THE IMPORTANCE OF THE COMMA

'I called out in exasperation "Why do we bother with a Commissarist of Justice? Let's call it frankly the Commissariat for Social Extermination and be done with it!" Lenin's face suddenly brightened and he replied: "Well put ... That's exactly what it should be called – but we can't say that."'

(Isaac Steinberg, *1918*)

'"The term 'pogrom' is not a German word", said Frank.
"Naturally, it is a Jewish word" and I smiled.
"I don't know whether it is a Jewish word", said Frank, "but I know that it never has been and never will be a part of the German vocabulary".'

(Curzio Malaparte, *Kaputt (1945)*)

One of the most regrettable developments of the 20th century is that whenever soldiers and politicians have had to confront their own actions they have tended to resort to a particularly invidious misuse of langauge: that of euphemism. As Paul Fussel maintains, while it would certainly be incorrect to trace the impulse behind all euphemism to the First World War, it was perhaps the first time in history that the horror produced by a unique event made public euphemism the 'special rhetorical sound of life'.[62]

If that was indeed the case, euphemism came into its own in the nuclear era, in part because it enabled man, in Hermann Kahn's immortal phrase 'to think the unthinkable' in a language which sometimes made it impossible to think through its implications.

Nuclear missiles soon became 'weapons of mass destruction'. War became 'conflict'. Winning was too loaded a term. Nations preferred not to win, but to 'prevail'. 'First strikes' and 'second strikes' masked the full impact of a provoked or unprovoked attack.

No-one wrote more extensively about this danger of the pernicious divorce of language and meaning than the Viennese critic Karl Kraus. Suitably, as Kraus himself observed, the Vienna in which he lived in the countdown to the First World War was itself a 'proving ground for world destruction'.[63] In such an apocalyptic context it is not surprising that Kraus should have been so much attuned to the stirrings of war. As he once wrote, 'an ear which hears the trumpet of the Last Judgment is certainly not closed to the trumpets of the day'.[64]

Kraus was an obsessive observer of the lexical and grammatical decay of literary journalism and political discourse. He was forever alert to the jargon of the time, to the debasement of thought by politicians, the debilitation of the mind through an excess of information, most of it trite, to the flow of words and images from the press which anaesthetised the public to the real meaning of words and resulted in an inability to comprehend the meaning of their own lives.

The work by which he is best known, *The Last Days of Mankind*, a play in five acts and 209 scenes, was written during the First World War. It is a large, sprawling, complex work, in part an impressionistic portrait of an age, in part a meditation on war, and, in the final analysis, an unrelenting attack on the distortion of language.

The play is set in the streets of Vienna and Berlin, in army barracks, in military hospitals and railway stations, and military posts. Its scenes juxtapose cheerful chatter in coffee shops with scenes of death at the Front. A father consoles his starving child with the thought that the enemy is starving too. A clergyman blesses the cannon. The poems of Goethe are transformed into war songs. Unborn children beg not to be born. After a great silence God speaks the words attributed to the Kaiser 'none of this was my wish'.[65]

The Last Days of Mankind is not really a play, it is a linguistic discourse in which the characters reveal and judge themselves through their speech. 'What is at stake in the war', he insisted, 'is the life and death of language'. In the play 'a world literally talks its way to perdition'.[66] Kraus brilliantly reproduces the empty rhetoric of the political speeches of the hour, emptied of reality and all meaning, the bureaucratic jargon of civil servants, the speech of simple people as well as self-important ones, the language of a people undone by their own words, killed off through their own linguistic imprecision.

Why, asked Kraus, were atrocities committed by soldiers at the Front or behind the lines which no-one would have imagined possible in 1914? Precisely because of Europe's poverty of imagination.[67] If such crimes had been imagined they would never have been committed. Kafka agreed. After the war he told Gustav Janouch that the poet Georg Trakl had preferred to commit suicide rather than witness the horrors of the war with his own eyes. He could not endure the war because he had too much imagination, because he had experienced the horror of war long before the soldiers did.[68] A man of letters who used language precisely and honestly had a better idea of the shape of modern warfare than those who rushed with such eagerness to join up in August 1914.

Kraus held the press to be particularly responsible for what had happened. He saw the journalist not as a messenger of bad news so much as a producer of it. He hated journalistic clichés, the jingoism of newspaper editors which encouraged men to join up, the references in newspapers to 'groups forming' and armies 'massing' when they meant that armies were on the march.[69] A newspaper, he once insisted, was as much an instrument of war as a grenade. The war correspondent killed imagination with his version of the truth. He threatened the reader's life with his lies. 'They sing prayers in battle for a fee', he once complained: 'kiss confederates on the mouth, praise the wonderful "tumult" of our day, ... compare a fortress with a beautiful woman, or vice versa (it depends) and in general behave in a manner worthy of the great times.'[70]

Satire apart, Kraus was deadly serious about his conclusions. Journalism, he maintained, had so impoverished the imagination that humanity was now prepared to fight a war of annihilation against itself. Deprived of the capacity to experience life, man now relied on the newspapers to implant the courage to join up. 'The abuse of language embellishes the abuse of life', he complained.[71]

In a word, Kraus's complaint was that language – the way a statement is made – bears within itself all the sense a man needs to understand the moral and ethical quality of that statement, as well as the quality of the man who makes it. Anyone lacking integrity was like the man of whom

Lichtenberg (whom Kraus much admired) had said, 'he can't hold his ink, and when he feels the desire to befoul someone, he usually befouls himself most'.[72] Kraus's critique of the way journalists used language was an implicit criticism of the society that the newspapers of the day reflected. In the peculiar circumstances in which Austria-Hungary found itself in 1914 he was not surprised that the state preferred to evade confronting its political problems by debasing the language of political discourse instead.

Kraus remained obsessed with the importance of language and grammar long after the First World War had ended. He believed that all political issues were fundamentally linguistic. Challenged for his preoccupation with punctuation while the Japanese were bombing Shanghai, he replied that if the commas had been put in the right place Shanghai would not be burning.[73] Later he responded to the rise of Fascism in his own country by organising language seminars.

He was not surprised by the rise of Fascism, indeed he had known that the First World War would never end in men's hearts, that the real struggle would only begin when the soldiers returned home from the Front. He was appalled but not astonished when in their post-war alienation they voted Hitler and Mussolini into power. Yet in the face of Nazism words finally failed him. It no longer seemed enough to rail against the abuse of language and imagery for purposes other than the expression of the truth. Hitler's rise to power rendered Kraus's life work, in his own eyes at least, irrelevant. After 30 years he was desperately tired of exposing the fraudulence of contemporary politicians. Sadly, his collapse expressed itself in the verbiage of his very last work, which was left unpublished on his death. The third *Walpurgisnacht*, a rambling, uneven, despairing polemic, relied largely on linguistic virtuosity rather than sustained thought.[74] It was an example of what Kraus had fought against all his life. It marked the extent of his mental degeneration.

But it also marked the degeneration of the European culture of which he had been so unrelenting a critic. In 1912 Kraus had foreseen a catastrophe far worse than the First World War, a time when the pyrrhic victories of progress would end in man making 'purses out of human skin'.[75] Perhaps even Kraus would have been astounded that his prediction would literally come true at Auschwitz. But the consistency with which he remained true to his own first principles enabled him from the beginning to see in Hitler the apocalyptic horseman whose arrival he had long feared. In the presence of such evil even he failed to find the right words.

Had he survived, however, he would have expressed little surprise that the enormity of Hitler's crimes was masked by euphemism, that the SS had a specific set of *sprachregelungen*, or language rules, to describe the Holocaust, code-names for killing, such as the 'Final Solution', 'evacuation', 'special treatment', 'pacification' and 'removal'.[76] It is after all easier to deny entry to a memory, as one of the survivors of Auschwitz once suggested, than to free oneself from an idea once it has been recorded.[77] This is precisely what the use of euphemism was designed to achieve.

Just as the liar knowingly affirms what he knows to be false, so a linguistic expression affirms what it knows to be untrue. Moral violation takes on the guise of a literary form. The Final Solution was a case in point, a figurative lie linking two contradictory literal references, while attempting to deny the contradiction and conceal it at the same time.

Individual features of language such as syntax, grammar and figures of speech were used by the Nazis as mere instruments to a political end. When the language was applied to works of genocide, language as a whole was subordinated to ends which were determined independently of it. It became detached from history and also from moral judgment, as Kraus feared it would. By the 1930s the corruption of language and politics were synonymous.

Nationalism, Kraus once wrote, was 'a love which tied men to the desecration of the German language'.[78] That is why the Austrian philosopher, Jean Amery, found Auschwitz a linguistic hell as well as a human one. As a philologist, the corruption of language horrified him. In the camps, wrote Primo Levi, the German language 'scorched his mouth when he tried to speak it'.[79]

German, unfortunately, was not the only language to be debased by military euphemism in the 20th century. The English language suffered more than most. Even during the Second World War George Orwell was complaining of a language which obscured real feelings, which excused soldiers displacing peasants from their farms by describing the process as 'a transfer of population', which justified killing defenceless villagers by calling it 'rural pacification'.[80] By using such expressions politicians were able to hide behind long words and exhausted idioms 'like a cuttlefish squirting out ink'.[81] Why had eternity not had the 20th century aborted, Kraus asked, when it discovered that ink ran in its veins.[82]

Jump 20 years on to the Vietnam War and we find euphemisms obscuring the ugly face of limited warfare. Terms such as 'protective reaction', 'forced draft modernisation', and 'free fire zones' allowed the soldier to differentiate his actions from routine killing. Free fire zones were intended to provide a 'killing ground' in which everything that moved, anything which impeded 'free movement', could be shot. It was easier to treat peasants as potential 'hostiles' rather than as non-belligerents or refugees. Even bombing became 'air support'. Men were not killed, they were 'degraded' or 'attrited'. The accidental death of civilians was written off as 'collateral damage'. If they were killed by 'friendly fire' they were the victims of 'accidental delivery'.[83] It was an idiom that reduced psychological insight into a collection of standardised observations, or ways of evading the truth. In time, the US military came to believe that it could see a meaning where none existed. In time, euphemism distorted its ability to think clearly. In the end, soldiers fell victim to their own specialist jargon.

Military spokesmen, complained Michael Herr, briefed the press in words that had no currency as words, or no meaning in the real world. Suffering was simply filtered out of military despatches: 'You got to the point where you could sit and listen to a man on television saying US casualties for the week had reached a six week low, only 80 GIs had died in combat, and you'd feel like you'd just got a bargain'.[84]

Even in their description of war psychosis, the medical authorities in Vietnam did what they could to disguise cases of illness. Post Traumatic Stress Disorder (PTSD) was the favoured euphemism to describe panic attacks, a preoccupation with traumatic events, the nightmares and dry dysphoria that takes the joy out of life and makes it difficult to associate with other people. It was an extraordinarily transparent term to describe the disorders associated with Vietnam, or for that matter any other war. Other psychologists would have preferred the term Post Combat Stress Disorder on the grounds that the words Trauma and Stress were bloodless. The term 'psychic trauma', of course, was originally devised by Freud to describe normal psychic wounds such as the loss of a parent, or abandonment, or a failure of a relationship. He never intended the words to be used of a massive *communal* disaster.[85]

By then the abuse of language had assumed proportions that not even Kraus had foreseen. Or perhaps he had, for writing in May 1918 he predicted that one day it would be possible to destroy whole cities simply by pressing a button. One day men might be able to incinerate London or Paris in a single *auto-da-fé*.[86] In this respect Kraus can be seen not merely as a satirist of a disintegrating Austrian empire, but as the prophet of an entire civilisation that found itself in 1945 poised on the brink of destruction.

3

War and the Human Condition

It was on the moral side and in my own person that I learned to recognise the thorough and primitive duality of man: I saw that of the two natures that contended in the field of my consciousness, even if I could rightly be said to be either, it was only because I was radically both.

(R L Stevenson, *The Strange Case of Doctor Jekyll and Mr Hyde (1886)*)

In the preceding chapter I have discussed at length some of the elements which made up 20th century consciousness – the persistence of historical meaning in life, the conscious wish to die for a cause and thus escape the oblivion of history, the claims that modernity made on modern man, the use of war for conscious self-invention. In this chapter I wish to scan the literature of the period not just for evidence of the ideas and beliefs framed by conscious thought, but also the fears and anticipations of the unconscious mind.

I want to discuss in particular what Stuart Hughes describes as 'a profound psychological change' that took place at the end of the 19th century, a move away from rational explanations of human behaviour in favour of irrational, unconscious forces. 'Since they are modern characters', wrote Strindberg of his play *Miss Julie* (1888), 'living in an age of transition more urgently hysterical at any rate than the age that preceded it, I have drawn them as split and vacillating ... conglomerations of past and present ... scraps for books and newspapers'.[1]

The world was aware of the psychological importance of neurosis long before Freud produced evidence for it, long before Freudian concepts became fashionable or well known. The psychological theories of war that I shall discuss in this chapter were as much a reflection as an expression of the times. Indeed, one theme that I might have developed, but for want of time, was the extent to which the theories of R D Laing – that in a crazy world the mad are effectively saner than the sane – drew their plausibility from the fact that the sane world seemed willing to blow itself up. The two theories I shall discuss – the idea of the death-wish formulated by Freud, and a compulsion for self-destruction described by Fromm – were stated by both men unambiguously in the form of concepts describing human nature. The third statement by Laing was considered to be descriptive, until one literal German anarcho-Laingian actually armed his mental patients and sent them out to be the vanguard of the world revolution.[2]

Psychologists such as Freud are to be congratulated for looking beyond the social expression of aggression, especially in the aftermath of the First World War. For it became fashionable in the 1920s to suggest that the cause of the war was capitalism or German militarism, or social bourgeois conditioning, not the human condition. There was truth in these explanations, but they were not of themselves entirely true. Sociological circumstances undoubtedly condition the form that aggression takes, particularly in the case of war, but they cannot account for the aggression itself. Sociologists cannot explain why men apparently enjoy conflict, nor can they help us understand the ferocity with which they are willing to fight it – their predisposition to engage in murder, or atrocity, or unnecessary (not necessarily unthinking) destruction.

Socialisation does not account for the values implicit in war, only for their perpetuation. Socialisation is not an explanation, only a description of a process. It is not and cannot account for the values themselves.[3]

It did, indeed, seem to many observers in 1914 that there were soldiers who embraced death quite willingly, who were prepared to die uncomplainingly for a cause. One French writer was struck by the pliant, almost worshipful posture of soldiers at the Front who had the air of supplicants offering the napes of their neck to the executioner.[4] 'Have you noticed', asked Marguerite Yourcenar in the interwar years, 'how men who are shot down collapse, fall on to their knees, bodies back … as if falling in afterthought … as if adoring their deaths?'[5] Why, Nietzsche had asked much earlier, were men willing to throw themselves into battle 'to destroy in order to be destroyed, to [compel] the powerful to become the hangman?' Why were they so willing to 'evade their human purpose', why did they not refuse to march to the sound of the guns and so escape destruction.[6]

Freud, for one, was never really able to answer those questions. Nevertheless, he tried. The concepts I shall discuss, the death-wish in particular, of course shocked a society that believed aggression could be dealt with through social reform and education, and that man would eventually *breed* true. Freud's theories did not accord with the Enlightenment's optimistic view of human nature, its faith in the perfectibility of Man, its insistence that aggression was alien to Man's true nature. Unfortunately, the 20th century suggested that the opposite was the case. As one writer wrote at the height of the Second World War, the insistence that Man was somehow better than his performance was a myth without any real evidential foundation.[7]

But before discussing Freud and his own explanation of 20th century conflict I wish to explore one other response to the phenomenon of war – Rainer Maria Rilke's lament that there was no such thing as an ordinary death, that in the 20th century man had lost the will to survive and experience his end as an affirmation, not a negation of life. In his most important novel on the First World War, John Dos Passos wrote of his central character 'he had not been driven into the army by the force of public opinion, he had not been carried away by any wave of blind confidence in the phrases of bought propagandists. He had not had the strength to live'. (*Three Soldiers*, 1927.) Rilke railed against the inevitability of that verdict. It is to his work that I shall now turn.

RILKE AND THE DENIAL OF ORDINARY DEATH

'I find it normal passing these great frontiers
That you scan the crowds in rags eyeing each side
With awe; that the nations seem real, but their ambitions
Having such a chief variety within one type, seem sane;
I find it normal
So too to extract false comfort from that word'

(William Empson, *'Manchouli'*)

Death is not only a terminus but a reference point in our lives, a point by which we can evaluate what we have achieved and what we have become. Death is for all of us a point of intersection between the finite and infinite worlds, the real and the eternal. It was for this reason that Walter Benjamin talked of the look of indefinable authority on the faces of the dying, in the photographs of those who were fortunate enough to die at home among friends or relations.

In the course of the 20th century a 'personal death' was something that many millions were denied. Rilke more than any other author was both sensitive to and appalled by this predicament. His main consciousness of war was the denial of the final recollection with one's own life which a personal death brings about. It was not the fact of death so much as the manner of it which he found so distressing and which still speaks to us most immediately when reading his work.

Of all Rilke's poems, the *Duino Elegies* are among the most perfect. The town of Duino, in the Gulf of Trieste, was where he retired in the early 1920s, the last years of his life. Before the First World War, however, he had spent many months there in the home of Marie and Alexander von Thurn und Taxis. The greater part of their castle was destroyed in the course of a number of closely fought engagements on the Izonzo Front (1915-17). Perhaps its main claim to fame in Rilke's story is that in the early summer of 1914 one of its visitors was the Archduke Franz Ferdinand. The Archduke came to Duino not to contemplate but to hunt. As a hunter he hoped to bring the number of animals he had shot to a million. His death shortly afterwards at the hands of a Serbian assassin resulted in exactly the same number of human casualties in a matter of months.

Rilke's immediate reaction to the war was not entirely negative. Like so many of his compatriots he was caught up by the stirring romance of the conflict. As early as the spring of 1904 he had predicted the onset of just such a conflagration, but one which he welcomed because it promised to redeem the world, to transform it into 'an Appoline product, fermented into maturity and still radiant with its inner glow'.[8] When the War eventually erupted, the promise of such a nihilistic vision soon dissolved.

On the outbreak of war Rilke was living intermittently in Paris. Forced to leave all his belongings behind, he lived out of a suitcase for the duration of the conflict. This was not so much an unfortunate twist of fate as an accurate reflection of his situation, that of an uninvolved but also unprotected traveller caught up in the midst of a frenzied mob.

Unfortunately, Rilke was not able to sustain himself with the patriotism of Hoffmanstahl, or Robert Musil, or Georg Trakl. He did not join up. He felt attached to Germany but 'only by language'. He could identify with it linguistically, but no more. He was not even prepared to subvert the language he loved by writing war propaganda. Originally called up as an army reservist with the First Reserve Rifle Regiment in 1916 he was excused service at the Front and sent to the War Archives Bureau instead. There he spent the next few months drawing lines in ledgers. He would not write as an apologist of the war, still less offer himself as a spokesman for the generals. He even refused a commission from his publishers to write a series of war poems which were then much in demand at the Front.

Quite early into the conflict, Rilke recognised that the war which was unfolding promised little hope of a better world, still less a redeemed one. The only consolation he was able to draw was entirely negative. War, he wrote to his friends, Elizabeth and Karl van der Heydt in November 1914, at least enhanced an understanding of the wretchedness of human life. The prospect of catastrophe was no more pervasive than before, only more real, more active, more visible. The misery of human existence could not be enhanced by any single event, not even by the war, but man's understanding of the 'unspeakable wretchedness of human life' might well be increased 'as though new dawns were seeking distance and space for their unfolding'.[9]

In a letter to another friend Rilke struck an even bleaker note, complaining with indignation that the war has accomplished what poetry could not. The chaos that the world was witnessing, he averred, was probably necessary to extract proof of human fortitude. It was wonderful that men could put up with misery on so grand a scale. The arts, alas, stimulated nothing at all in some people. Only in war was their steadfastness revealed, their fortitude finally vindicated.[10]

Unfortunately, fortitude was likely to avail men very little the longer war continued. Looking back to those early days in 1915 Rilke recorded how his mood had changed profoundly. At first, he had seen the war, as had so many of his contemporaries, as a 'monstrous god'; then as a monster, with heads, claws and a body devouring everything in its path. Months later he saw it as a spectre, then as a 'foul vapour in the swamp of humanity'.[11] Following news from the battle front, he remarked, was tantamount at times to being 'a witness to the world's disgrace'.[12]

When eventually, at the instigation of his friends, he was released from military service in June 1916, he found himself even more confounded by the willingness of the soldiers to endure the war with such fortitude, or such blind resignation. Why were men who were brave enough to die in battle too cowardly to stand in the middle of a town and cry 'Enough!'? At least, if they were shot for their defiance they would give their lives for a worthier cause than that for which they were fighting. In the meantime, those in the field died simply so that the horror could go on.

Rilke's sense of futility was to be a central factor in shaping his very idiosyncratic response to the slaughter, as well as the moral he drew from it. He did not flee from the presence of death, but he could not comprehend the inventory of terror. The modern battlefield was divided not between two armies but between the living and the dead, each repudiating the other. How was he, as a poet, to bridge that gulf when the dead seemed, on balance, to outnumber the living? How was it possible to render into the poetic imagination the death of so many, the 6,000 soldiers who died every day for 1,500 days of the Great War?[13] Looking back in 1920 at the catastrophe, he admitted that history had revealed many periods of destruction, but had any been quite as formless as the period through which Europe had just passed?:

> With no figure to draw all this around himself and expand it away from itself
> this way tensions and counter - tensions are set up without a central point that

first makes them into constellations, into orders, at least orders of destruction. My part in all of this is only suffering ... suffering with, and suffering beforehand and suffering after.[14]

The futility of the war (or its 'formlessness') made the task of rendering it into poetry more difficult still. All Rilke could do was to suffer, and, by so doing, bear testament to the suffering of others. The German Expressionist poet Gottfried Benn called poets 'the tears of the nation'. As poets, however, their suffering was greater than that of the common soldier. As poets they had very different ghosts with which to contend. In the words of Georges Bataille poetry was a sacrifice 'where the words are victims'.[15]

Stephen Spender has drawn an interesting parallel between Rilke's position and Keats's theory of 'negative capability' – the contention that the poetic character has no self, but is at the same time everything and nothing. Keats's contention that a poet can enter into the nature of things outside himself is an idea not entirely inconsistent with Rilke's belief that a poet's own identity might be compromised by empathising too much with what is outside his own experience. In a word, the poet is always in danger of trying to transform the world of reality into a language invented by the imagination. If true to himself, contended Keats, he must be one of those 'to whom the miseries of the world are misery and will not let them rest'.[16] This is what Rilke suffered in the Great War. Yet through his suffering he was able to create the *Duino Elegies* and the *Sonnets to Orpheus* after many years in which he had been silent. The war for a time fired his creative imagination.

Rilke did indeed suffer, but his experience of war enabled him in the end to produce a synthesis from the two antitheses of life and death. As he wrote to a friend in 1925, in his *Elegies* he had tried to illustrate how an affirmation of life and an affirmation of death were actually one and the same. Death was no longer what it had been in his youth, an enemy against whom the knight rode forth into 'the stirring world'. Death is with the knight from the very beginning, it is part of his *persona*.[17] It is not an enemy against whom the knight has to contend but a friend to be embraced at the appropriate moment. With a post-Christian sensibility Rilke rejected the concept of life after death. Death was in life. Life only had meaning in the finite, not the infinite world.[18]

Rilke's view of a man's right to an 'ordinary death' was, of course, very much in the mainstream of 20th century thinking. Old age provided man with an opportunity to come to terms with the two poles of existence – life and death. Old age, wrote Gottfried Benn, offered man an 'integrated ambivalence' – an opportunity to transit from one state of being to the other, or from being to non-being.[19]

Ambivalence was the key word. For Heissenberg and the scientific community it was the interplay between man and nature. For Freud it was the psychological mediator between love and hate. The Special Theory of Relativity argued that time and space, instead of being two different dimensions, were in certain circumstances factors of each other. The exponents of quantum physics, faced with the problem of defining the nature of so-called elementary particles, abandoned the distinction between mass and energy and posited the existence of a wholly ambivalent entity that was both particle and wave.

In the ideological conflict of the century Marxism offered an ambivalent synthesis which reconciled thesis and antithesis, a Hegelian synthesis that August Strindberg also saw as essential to all art:

> thesis, affirmation, antithesis: negation synthesis, comprehension ... you begin
> life by accepting all things. Then you proceed on principle to deny all things.
> Now finish your life by comprehending all things.[20]

If life was indeed a Hegelian mosaic offering a Judeo-Christian pattern of fall, suffering and redemption, without the final crowning of life (or comprehension) in death, life was meaningless. Deny a whole generation in 1914 the consolation of the final understanding, and you make a mockery of life itself.

This, of course, was the problem. War robbed man of more than just life. It was an affront to what Rilke called 'the identity of terror and bliss', 'the oneness of life and death'. It robbed him of an 'individual death'. That was the tragedy of the Great War. It made death anonymous and therefore meaningless. Meaninglessness *was* its anonymity. With so many dying all around him, how could a soldier's individual death be taken seriously? How could anyone, Rilke wrote in 1914, apply 'the standards of the individual heart' to the loss of any man in battle?[21]

Think what the cry of the drowning man used to be before the war, he wrote, even if it was only that of the village idiot. 'Clutching out of the water with a show that had suddenly acquired meaning', people would run 'to take his side against Death; they would even try to save him. How incredibly outdated all this has become.'

War, for Rilke, enveloped men in the larger picture, the long view. How could a soldier experience his own death when death meant so little, when dying on the battlefield represented merely a squandering of life?

It was a view that Rilke had formulated, in fact, shortly before the outbreak of the First World War. In *The Notebooks of Malte Laurids Brigge,* he had written that 'a death of one's own' had been denied the sick in those other institutions of the Modern Age, hospitals and sanatoria. Outside them, men died the death that belonged to the disease from which they had suffered. In hospital they died from one of the deaths which belonged to the institution. Men died as best they could, but the death of the indigent was banal, entirely without formality. Their death was as anonymous as their life. 'They are glad when they find one that fits'.[22]

Of course, we may well ask how many of those who died at the Front would have had 'a death of their own' had they survived the battlefield. There was nothing particularly distinctive about the death of Patient 57, a man without a name, whose squalid end George Orwell witnessed in a hospital for the poor in Paris in 1937. Number 57 was nothing more than a 'disgusting piece of refuse waiting to be carted away and dumped on a slab in the dissecting room'.[23] Such was the end to which many of the poor came in the interwar period. Such was the reality of life among the dispossessed and disadvantaged.

There was nothing normal either about the deaths of the victims of the Holocaust. Micheline Maurel, a survivor of Ravensbrück, wrote that those who lived in peasant hovels, who sat alone in despair in the cities, or those of a more metaphysical nature who tortured themselves over the meaning of life, were to be considered the happiest people in the world:

> Be happy, oh how happy, you who die a death as normal as life in hospital beds, or in your homes. Be happy all of you: millions of people envy you.

Those were the millions who were despatched to the Nazi death camps who never came back.[24]

There was little that was normal about life, for that matter, for the millions who passed through Stalin's *gulags*, the whole point of which was to simulate the imagined condition of death. 'Do you love life?', asked Solzhenitsyn, 'We love camp life, too, loved the life of a man who would gladly choose to live in a village of ten houses beyond the camp wire just to escape confinement'. 'Are you willing [to live in such a village]? ... Oh, not only willing, but Good Lord, please send me a life like that!'[25]

Had Rilke lived long enough to witness with his own eyes the years through which Solzhenitsyn and others lived, he would have realised soon enough that life in the 20th century has rarely been normal. Where was the ordinary life of men who were handed over from one political system to another, from Hitler's death camps to the *gulag*? What normal life was enjoyed by Margarete Buber-Neumann, a German communist transferred from a Soviet camp near Karaganda to the German concentration camp at

Ravensbrück? In *One Day in the Life of Ivan Denisovich* (1962) Solzhenitsyn mentioned Senka Klevshin who was transferred by Soviet
troops straight from Buchenwald to the same Soviet labour camp to
which the author had been condemned. It was Senka's story that inspired
Jorge Semprun's political reverie, his book *Quel Beau Dimanche*. Semprun
writes that for the Russian soldiers who liberated the camp Buchenwald
was life. It was 'ordinary' (not extraordinary): 'it was just like home'.[26]

For millions of people in the 20th century a personal death was a
privilege, almost a benediction, which, if they were fortunate enough, they
were not denied before their life was up. A normal death was exactly that,
a blessing, often artfully disguised.

And what of the nuclear age? Jonathan Schell writes of the 'second
death' - the death of death, the threat to the external cycle, man–birth–
life–death–mourning, a cycle which committed the poet Walt Whitman to
present death as the key, not the negation, of life. Those who lived under
constant sentence of death in the Cold War, under a suspended stay of
execution, often died intestate, fearing they had nothing to bequeath the
future.[27]

In a memorable phrase Edmund Burke once described civilised society
as a partnership of the dead, the living and the unborn. Deny the unborn
a future or break the cycle, then death can no longer affirm life. If the
dead are denied the chance to bequeath a future to the living, as well as
to the unborn, death itself will become absolute, final, in the final result
unfulfilling. The denial of 'ordinary death' in a nuclear age was not only
prejudicial to the future, but the 'death of death' diminished life itself.

The persistent threat of nuclear war in its most stark, unqualified and
ineluctably tragic form rendered life itself unrewarding for many. Perhaps, the moral of the story was that of Lord Marchmain's protracted
demise in Evelyn Waugh's *Brideshead Revisited*:

> I said to the doctor who was with us daily "he's got a wonderful will to live,
> hasn't he?"
> "Would you put it like that? I should say a great fear of death."
> "Is there a difference?"
> "Oh, dear yes. He doesn't derive any strength from his fear, you know. Its
> wearing him out."[28]

Life similarly wore out the survivors of Stalin's socialist Utopia. Life
outside the *gulag* was no more normal for Nadezhda Mandelstam than life
had been in the labour camps for her husband. When in 1938 a friend
commended her courage, the fact that she was frightened of nothing, she
begged to differ. She had never ceased to be afraid. Another writer, Anna

Akhmatova, lived constantly in fear not of death but of betraying her friends before she was liquidated by the state, just as a soldier fears through cowardice in the field that he may betray his fellow men in arms. 'Fear of ceasing to be oneself, fear of being frightened is what holds it all together', Akhmatova maintained. When an arrest came it was almost a relief.[29]

Solzhenitsyn felt a similar sense of relief *en route* to the Kuibyshev transit camp in 1950. The 25-year term which most of the prisoners were expecting to serve created a mood of hope – not despair – among many of the prisoners. The regime had tried to crush their spirit. Now it was the prisoners' turn to say a few words, words that would no longer be uttered under duress, words they had never been able to utter before.[30]

Denial of both a normal life and a normal death was surely the real tragedy of war in the 20th century, as well as the labour camps of Stalin's Russia and the nuclear peace that encompassed the world after Hiroshima. The terror of life for some was often more graphic than the terror of departing from it. Nothing in the 20th century was normal, not even death. In terms of odds defeated and probabilities denied, our escape from the Cold War, in fact, verges on the miraculous.

FREUD INVENTS THE DEATH-WISH

'Nothing is so completely at variance with original human nature as ... the ideal command to love one's neighbour as oneself.'

(Freud, *Civilisation and Its Discontents (1927)*)

There were many other explanations for human conduct in the 20th century; indeed, in terms of psychology such explanations were largely unique to the century. When soldiers went to the Front did they dream of redemption or destruction? Did their souls long for death? All that was detestable about war – the anonymity of the battlefield, the descent into the abyss, the 'postures of shame' which Drieu La Rochelle insisted distinguished the Great War from every other conflict – was what was so remarkable about 20th century combat. More remarkable still, was the sullen resignation with which so many millions went to their deaths.

In military terms the 20th century has been one of striking and disorienting confusion, and although in economic and social terms it was a century of striking net improvement in the condition of life, both world wars kept the minds of most citizens largely off these secular changes. In 1914 and in the run-up to the Second World War people had more urgent preoccupations. If, for the most part, in countries like England and France the chance of death was not, in fact, much higher than it had been a hundred years before, even those who knew this felt themselves and their families to be living on the edge of disaster. Yet it seemed a disaster willingly embraced. In taking to the battlefield did men wish to take possession of the future or repudiate their past?

To historians, the yearning for combat looks neither heroic nor promising. More than anything else it looks frightening, the object of too much desire – the desire for death. Was it also, as Freud claimed, a death-wish?.

* * *

In the years immediately before the First World War Sigmund Freud often used to take his children to the Vienna woods on mushroom hunts. The distinctly unmilitary Freud pressed his sons, Martin and Ernst, into 'joining the colours' in these 'Conquistadorial' forays into the countryside. Looking back on his childhood many years later, Martin recalled how, whenever he spotted any mushrooms, his father would use the whistle he carried in his waist-pocket to summon the 'platoon' into action. It was not long before the sergeants in the trenches were blowing their whistles for the men to go over the top.[31]

When the Great War came Freud was among the majority who welcomed it. 'For the first time in 30 years', he wrote to a friend, 'I find myself to be an Austrian'. Hurrying back to Vienna from Carlsbad he accused England, hitherto his favourite country, of gross hypocrisy for supporting Serbia's 'impudence'. For the first time in years, he wrote, he felt proud to be on the opposite side.[32]

In the early days of the war Freud lived from one German victory to the next, eagerly awaiting news of the fall of Paris. He was so caught up in the unfolding drama that he refused to provide his own patients with a medical note excluding them from military service.

If Freud had the courage of his convictions, so, too, did his sons. Martin joined up, anxious to see Russia without having to change religion, for in peacetime the country had been off-limits to tourists of Jewish descent. Another son, Oliver, a qualified engineer, found himself employed in military construction work.

As the first year went by Freud welcomed the fact that Germans had behaved decently. He expected the war to be fought with chivalry, with due regard for the lives of civilians. He also expected that both sides would show sensitivity to the acute suffering of their fellow men-at-arms.[33] Having made high demands of himself all his life he expected nothing less from the belligerent powers.

By 1916 his view of the war had changed completely. The fact that he had reached the age of 50, which he regarded as the threshold of old age, may have had something to do with his darkening mood. But the slaughter at the Front depressed him greatly.[34] By 1918 he was writing to Pfister, the first educational specialist to take an interest in psycho-analysis, that there was little that was good about human nature. Most of the people he had come across in person had no concept of ethics; those who did had departed readily enough from their ethical positions when it suited them.[35]

Later still, he refused to admit that his experience of the war had changed his view of humanity. Instead of expressing the disillusionment that any civilised man might feel at the horrors of the conflict, Freud claimed that his general view of mankind had been vindicated. 'Our unconscious will murder even for trifles ... In reality our fellow citizens have not sunk so low as we feared because they had never risen so high as we believed.'[36]

So what had the war revealed about the human psyche? What had led him to revise his account of man's mental pathology, what versions of the war were accessible to his imagination?

In the first place, Freud was confident that men had thrown themselves so willingly into battle because war had raised the stakes of life. Like Max Weber he was haunted by the intellectual impoverishment of the Modern Age. Modern society he complained, was emotionally sterile. Spontaneity and life were slowly draining away. War, at least, had changed this radically:

> Life is impoverished, it loses its interest, when the highest stake in the game of living, life itself, may not be risked.... War is bound to sweep away ... the conventional treatment of death. Life has become interesting again; it has recovered its full content.[37]

The 'sanction of death' was as essential to Freud as it was to his fellow countryman, the novelist Joseph Roth. The hero of *The Emperor's Tomb*, Roth's most enduring novel, is all too aware of the brittle, twilight world of Vienna. He joins the 9th Dragoons, not because he wishes to be killed, but to reassure himself that he is capable of dying well. In the shadow of death he can, at least, put his character to the test. Even a pointless death is preferable to an aimless life. But life undoes him in the end. Roth's protagonist returns from the war minus position, rank and self-esteem, minus past, present and future. Worst of all he has survived. 'The verdict of the Commission of Inquiry was without appeal: it read "Found unfit for death".'[38]

Is this the only reason why men volunteer for military service, conscious that death will stalk them every moment? The war, for Freud, seemed to have provided European man with an opportunity to release a pent-up aggression, one that hitherto had been denied expression by the state. Indeed, he maintained that the modern state had forbidden murder not because it was opposed to the use of violence but because it desired to monopolise its use for itself. The destructiveness of the Great War had arisen from an in-built human capacity for psychic regression, a phenomenon which the state had both repressed and permitted.[39] Governments had even encouraged deeds of cruelty, fraud and barbarity on a scale that, before the war, even Freud confessed he would never have suspected possible. The abrogation of all moral constraints in warfare permitted men relief from the constricting demands of civilisation. It afforded them a passing satisfaction of instincts that had long been held in check.[40]

But Freud went much further. He believed that there had been some consonance of surroundings and situation in the war that had allowed man to be more intensely himself. Inspired by this thought, Freud invented the concept of the death-wish as an explanation of an otherwise inexplicable human zest for self-destruction.

It was a concept which he had struggled against for some time. In the *Little Hans Case History* in 1909 he had written 'I cannot bring myself to assume the existence of a special aggressive instinct alongside of the familiar instincts of self-preservation and of sex'. Three years later he was so unmoveable in his insistence that a death instinct did not exist that he refused to accept a psychological paper entitled *Destruction as the Cause of Becoming.*[41]

Early in the war, however, he found in many test cases of war psychosis evidence of an aggressive instinct. The victims of shell-shock or trauma whom he visited in Hungary's hospitals dreamed of experiences in their past which contained so little potentiality for pleasure that they could no longer be explained away as impulses since repressed. So strong was the impulse of destruction that he could no longer treat the soldiers whom he analysed as patients. He began to see many of them not as victims but as responsible instigators of their own fate.[42]

The death-wish, he surmised, was not entirely at odds with the life principle. In war a soldier might act out of whim, from a momentary disbelief in the possibility of his own destruction. From that general proposition, Freud went on to formalise a particular proposition. War, he wrote: 'constrains us once more to be heroes who cannot believe in their own death; stamps the alien as the enemy, whose death is to be brought about as desired; it counsels us to rise above the death of those we love'.[43]

The guilt that men suffered, he argued, as manifested in the Christian belief in original sin, was probably the outcome of a blood-guilt incurred by primitive man. If the injunction not to kill was so strong a prohibition it would surely have been directed against an equally powerful initial impulse. It must therefore spring from a blood-lust still in the blood:

> We ask what is the attitude of our unconscious towards the problem of death. The answer must be: almost exactly the same as primitive man's. In this respect, as in many others, the man of prehistoric ages survives unchanged in our unconscious.[44]

Somewhat later in his study *Beyond the Pleasure Principle* he postulated a new psychological polarity between life and death. The death instinct inspired man to strive for his own personal obliteration. The life instinct impelled him to survive. It fell to the libido to divert the death instinct outwards into an urge to destroy. Man found it necessary to destroy some other person or object in order to escape destruction himself, to redirect his energy through a process of sublimation into activities other than self-destruction. Man must either destroy himself or destroy others. Holding back aggression, he wrote in 1938, was in general unhealthy and could lead to neurosis.[45]

Freud spent the post-war years trying to encourage people to consider how best to ensure that the life instinct emerged victorious in the end. Even so, he remained pessimistic. Civilised society, he often contended, seemed to be perpetually threatened with disintegration through the primary hostility of men towards each other. Men, alas, were not creatures who were concerned only to defend themselves if attacked. They were 'savage beasts to whom the thought of sparing their own kind is alien'.[46]

By 1925 he moved a step further, incorporating the death instinct into a more general theory of aggression. Perhaps it was the fear of obscurity or anonymity or final annihilation that drives men to war. Men who cannot achieve immortality through their creative work may try to postpone their death by killing others. Freud was quick to perceive a connection between a man's death and the brutality of his actions. Through the killing of an enemy, one's own death could be postponed. Hence the preference shown in the 20th century for killing, rather than dying, for an idea. Reading a German soldier's diary at the end of the invasion of Russia, Hermann Hesse too was particularly struck by the fact that the soldier was troubled a great deal more by the thought of having to die; having to kill was purely 'a tactical consideration'.[47]

The First World War, then, forced Freud reluctantly to conclude that he had overlooked the existence of non-erotic aggression, that the latter was innate and instinctual and that if unchecked it would represent a fearsome threat to civilisation. He was not, of course, entirely fatalistic. He genuinely believed that the conflict between the will to live and the will to die could be resolved by admitting to the existence of the death-wish rather than by suppressing evidence of it. Provided that the pleasure principle was gratified, he believed, provided the path to gratification was unblocked and erotic infantile impulse abandoned, then man could overcome his urge for self-destruction. As with other forms of neurosis, Freud wanted to make his patients more responsible for their actions, to restore some conscious control over their own lives.

There are many problems, however, with the idea of the death instinct which cast doubt on whether it can play any useful role in understanding war itself.

(1) Can it in fact explain anything? If all military struggles are produced by human destructiveness, or psychological alienation, then all causes of war are surely rendered irrelevant. In history only causation can explain anything. In rejecting causation and relying on alienation instead, Freud effectively turned his back on historical understanding. Perhaps this would not have mattered much if he could have cited history to illustrate the death instinct at work. He could not. He was unable to identify the presence of a death-wish independently of its manifestation, which was necessary if he wished to treat one as a cause of the other.

(2) Mary Midgley also takes him to task for failing to ask the right questions. He was always asking why people were unhappy, not why they acted as badly as they did. Whenever he did ask the latter question his stock answer was that they acted badly because they were unhappy. He never seems to have suspected that they might have been unhappy because they acted badly or not as well as they would have liked.[48] In this respect, he evaded the real problem of evil in the 20th century – the *conscious* (not unconscious) will to destruction.

Freud was not interested in the fundamental split between the individual conscience and the constraints imposed by society. But what of a society which demands we act badly? What of a state which provides its citizens with the moral authority to act wickedly? Didn't Hitler promise precisely that – to become the conscience of the German people?

It is otherwise difficult to explain why those who persecuted German Jews were not always SS or *Gestapo* members crazed with hatred, storming into homes, dispatching innocents off to the camps. The real evil of the Holocaust was that the little man, the anonymous bureaucrats, the pen-pushers in local government offices, adjusting edicts or dictating letters, or checking lists of evacuees, these were the men who connived in the murder of the Jews by acting badly without a purpose. The real guilty men were to be found among the two million employees of the *Reichsbahn*, the overworked clerks who were put to the trouble of throwing an already loaded railway system into confusion by sending cattletrucks full of fellow citizens to Auschwitz, spending their energies at a critical stage of the war working out complicated timetables for the transport of Jews.

In the modest little museum of the former Jewish quarter of old Cracow one can find a photograph of young German soldiers on their way to war. They are leaning out of railway carriages on the side of which someone has written 'Wir fahren nach Polen, um Juden versallen' - 'We are off to Poland to sort out the Jews'. The young soldiers display all the energy of youth, the enthusiasm of men little travelled, off to see the sights of Europe in the course of a sharp, short, relatively safe campaign. But then the enemy was in no way dangerous. The Jews were already victims of their own disbelief in the final catastrophe that was about to engulf them. Of 64,000 in the Cracow area registered in September 1939, only a few hundred survived the war.

Of all the institutions involved, the *Reichsbahn* came out ahead. It even made a profit, charging the state discount rates for large numbers of Jewish passengers, with groups of 400 travelling for half the third-class rail fare, and children paying less than half the usual children's rate. Despite difficulties and delays, despite Allied bombing day and night, the task was completed almost on schedule: no Jew was left alive 'for lack of transport'.[49]

Freud, however, did not have much to say about the proposition that evil can only be measured by the degree to which it did not penetrate human *consciousness*. Simone Weil once wrote that in François Mauriac's novel *Thérèse Desqueyroux*, the picture he had drawn of evil was defective, because it was 'lacking in colour'. Mauriac had failed to understand the monotony of evil, the feeling of emptiness it can so often produce, the way in which a crime can begin and develop until it takes on the monotony of a *duty.*

The 20th century saw ordinary, not necessarily very wicked, people coming to a point where they knowingly and inevitably damaged each other and themselves, causing the innocent to suffer, a point where evil seems not only inevitable, but also necessary.

As Georg Lukacs wrote of the Russian Revolution, the death of freedom was one of the tragic historical situations of the age, the tragedy lying in the fact that it was 'impossible to act in such a way as not to commit sin', that the ultimate measure of a man was not his choice of causes but 'the greatness of his sacrifice'.

'The individual when forced to choose between two evils', wrote Lukacs, 'chooses correctly when he sacrifices his lower to his higher self'. Worse still, Lukacs left his readers in no doubt that this tragic choice between evils showed man at his best, not his worst, in his willingness to sacrifice himself for the permanent good of others. Such sacrifices could be made not only by ordinary soldiers, of course, but by revolutionaries or terrorists, men like the anarchist Boris Savinkov, who in the run-up to the Russian Revolution of 1905 saw the ethical validation of his terrorist deeds 'in the fact that he sacrificed for his fellow human beings, not only his life, but his purity, his morality, his soul'. In other words, observed Lukacs, the just cause did not validate the violent act, violent acts validated the cause. Murderous acts could be described as ethical when those who committed them were prepared to imperil their immortal soul, when the terrorist was prepared to suffer the damnation of hell for the brief moment of redeeming mankind.[50]

What was Eichmann's defence when on trial for his life in Jerusalem in 1961 but his claim that the Third Reich had paid the ultimate sacrifice by carrying out the Holocaust? The troop transports that could have been used to carry soldiers to the Front were used instead to send civilians to the death camps. The Third Reich, he claimed, had made no economic profit out of the Final Solution, preferring to gas Jews rather than use them as slave labour. Was not Auschwitz, he asked, the ultimate act of redemption, a defining example of self-sacrifice in the name of the brotherhood of man?[51]

(3) By insisting that evil was *un*consciously 'willed' Freud also failed to ask whether it was not also a realisation of the conscious 'will to power'. Humanity, writes Georges Bataille, pursues two goals – one negative – to survive, to escape death as long as possible; the other positive – to intensify experience, to live life to the full.[52]

The second unfortunately can often run counter to the first, particularly in religious asceticism, in the acceptance, indeed craving for martyrdom as the ultimate enhancement of the spiritual life, the life lived in truth, the life enhanced through death. Did not Jünger once compare the soldiers with whom he served in the Great War to the medieval saints of old? Did he not extol them for their inner fervour, for their courage to live life to the full (on the threshold of death – and invariably beyond)?[53]

The wish to intensify experience, argues Bataille, should be seen as a value; survival as a good. Sometimes an intense life leads inevitably to death; usually it does not. War is one of the most intense experiences of all. If men often stop short, war never does. War introduces into life many experiences which may threaten existence but which can also enhance it, including, as Jünger noted, a criminal but legally sanctioned opportunity for destruction – destruction, but not self-destruction, because acts which in peace would lead to the gallows are often sanctioned, or tacitly permitted; not punished, but overlooked.

It can also offer for those of a more aesthetic disposition a host of 'heightened sensations' which can be more life-enhancing still. Moments of intensity are often moments of excess. And it is their excessive character which is often life-denying for everyone else. Value, as Nietzsche maintains, is situated 'beyond good and evil'. The pursuit of what is socially 'good' is based on the repression of our instincts. A good life is often a dull one – hence our pursuit of value of what is good for *us*, not for society. What is not socially good, however, is not usually in our interests either. In gratifying our instincts we often alienate others, at great cost to ourselves, the cost to life being the ultimate punishment for transgression. If we are victims, we are victims not so much of a death-wish as an error in judgement – a failure to understand the terms on which life must be lived.

I remarked in the introduction to this Chapter that the psychologists of the 20th century, for the most part, thought it enough merely to explain, not to prescribe or to change. They can be faulted for doing so. Indeed, the present trend in psychology is no longer content to help people under-stand themselves; the therapist tries to change them, he attempts to help them become more integrated into life.

Whether or not this is desirable does not fall within the scope of this book, except in one respect – the claim that had Freud or Jung been more politically committed, they would have understood their age better than they did.

The main problem with Freud's concept of the death-wish was that it ignored one of the attempts which made the 20th century different from the past, which made it definingly modern. Human nature did not change, even if men were made more conscious of their irrational impulses and thus tried to guard against them. Instead, governments, in the light of their own recondite understanding of humanity, tried to perfect human nature, to make men more historically responsive through social engi-neering. It was not Freud, but Hitler who changed or tried to change the human condition. It was not Freud but Stalin who tried to remake man, at least Soviet man, in the image of the political ideas that gained wide currency after the Russian Revolution.

The tragedy of the human condition in the 20th century was not the tragedy of man, but of those who tried to essentialise man, to make Soviet man more 'authentically' Soviet, or Aryan man more 'authentically'

German. The quest for authenticity would have mattered less but for the fact that it excluded others from its ranks, dehumanising them, or making them subhuman, or in the case of Stalin and the kulaks, rendering them without history. It is to the eternal shame of the early psychoanalysts not so much that they did not anticipate the attempt, but that they remained silent even at the very time that the engineers of human souls were at work. Where Jung and others failed most decisively was in that they did not take seriously (until too late) the aims of contemporary rulers. They said little in protest at the predisposition of states to judge who should or should not be human, nor did they foresee that their own analysis of the human condition might be used by politicians for far more cynical ends.

In the end, the real dilemma of the human condition was that mankind should have shown so little regard for its common humanity. The real tragedy of the 20th century was not that man was wicked or evil but that he was insufficiently attentive to what made him human, and thus gave him a reason to live in peace with his neighbours. In self-exile in Switzerland Jung was amazed that 'a time would come when I should be reproached for having said absolutely nothing about these things before 1934'. In 'After the Catastrophe' an essay which he produced at the end of the war and almost the last thing he wrote about the Third Reich before his death in 1961, he had much to say about 'the most monstrous crime of all age' – the Final Solution. In the course of the essay, Hitler was described as 'a psychopath', 'a psychic scarecrow', a man 'full of empty, infantile fantasies but cursed with the intuition of a guttersnipe'. Mockery is the violence of the metaphysician as warrior, Nietzsche once observed. If one's writings are to be mocking and violent they must hurt. In Jung's case they did little to help the German people understand themselves, even though this was his stated intention:

> 'When I say the Germans are psychically ill it is surely kinder than saying they are criminals'.[54]

In the Nuremberg trials the victorious powers chose to avoid psychology and applied the law instead. The Allies have been blamed subsequently for applying the law of the victors, for ignoring their own (mostly, but not entirely Soviet) crimes. The trials had many critics, but none, to my knowledge, who have ever blamed the Allies for denying the Germans a 'psychological excuse'.

One of the most important criticisms of Freud and Jung is that they failed to tell the truth, or rather that they failed to recognise it at the time. Jung was mesmerised by the Nazis: Freud loathed them; neither, however, understood the deeper forces animating the German nation. Neither took the Nazi outpourings seriously except as fantasy-driven expressions of protest. Freud did not live long enough to see Hitler's fantasies translated into fact. Jung spent much of the late 1930s dismissing Hitler's speeches as the outpourings of a political maverick more interested in winning political support at home than realising grand obsessions. Thus he reassured the Dutch psychoanalyst, G H van der Hoop, that Hitler's speeches carried no real conviction, that the Jews invited anti-semitism by looking for it everywhere, even in the Nazis. The Germans were no real threat to Judaism, Jung insisted. As a much younger nation, the Aryan race was given to banal infantilism. Hitler's ideology, Jung reassured his readers, was merely the expression of 'unrealised infantile wishes and unresolved family resentments'.[55] These ideas were all the more surprising when we remember that Jung himself was denounced by Nazi psychologists, who refuted both his analysis and Freud's as 'decadent' and untrustworthy. They are the more surprising still given Jung's knowledge in 1939 that patients in German mental hospitals were being systematically killed off in the name of racial purity.

Most ironically of all, both men reflected the age all too well in their intolerance of their own critics. In the case of Freud this was particularly true of his treatment of Sandor Ferenczi, the Hungarian doctor whose shell-shocked patients had inspired Freud to conceive of the death-wish after touring the hospital wards in 1915.

Of all the analysts of the time, Ferenczi had a reputation for being a successful therapist, unlike Freud who had only one (dubious) success to his credit. Late in the 1920s, however, Ferenczi came to the conclusion that he had been less than honest with his patients, particularly in suggesting that his women patients had fantasised episodes of child abuse. In confronting his patients with the knowledge that they would never know for certain whether they had imagined such episodes he had betrayed their trust. More to the point, on the basis of his years as an analyst he came to the reluctant conclusion that many of the stories he was told were true, that, at best, those patients who had submitted to therapy had done so for fear of not being understood or believed – a double blow for them, of course, if their stories were true.

It was greatly to his credit that his patients' protests struck a sympathetic chord. Unlike Freud, Ferenczi took their stories seriously. In his book *First Contributions to Psychoanalysis* he quoted from a letter that Schopenhauer had written to Goethe, in which he claimed that all the errors and follies of which so many doctrines and philosophies were full sprang from a lack of probity:

The truth was not found, not because it was unsought, but because the intention always was to find again instead some preconceived opinion or other, or, at least, not to wound some favourite idea, and with this aim in view subterfuges had to be employed against both other people and the thinker himself ... The philosopher must be like Sophocles's Oedipus who, seeking enlightenment concerning his terrible fate, pursues his indefatigable enquiry, even when he divines that appalling horror awaits him in the answer. But most of us carry in our hearts the Jocasta who begs Oedipus for God's sake not to enquire further; and we give way to her, and that is the reason why philosophy stands where it does.[56]

After quoting this passage Ferenczi added 'the deep and compressed wisdom of these remarks deserves to be discussed and to be compared with the results of psychoanalysis'. It was his misfortune to discover that Freud was unwilling, indeed bitterly opposed, to accepting as true the stories of child abuse that he was told. Freud insisted that Ferenczi was treating the fantasies rather than the memories of his patients. In despair Ferenczi recorded how little *empathy* Freud admitted having with his patients. Most of them, he noted in his diary of 1 May 1932, Freud had dismissed as 'riff-raff', only good for providing the analyst with material for his theories.[57] By 1930 Freud had indeed lost much of the earlier sympathy that he had once expressed for them. He saw the traumas of which his patients spoke as universal fantasies that made them undeserving of any real compassion. Therapy, he concluded, did not require any deep emotional commitment on the part of the therapist, only an intellectual grasp of theory.

In a sense, Freud had little sympathy too for the soldiers he interviewed during the First World War. What was the death-wish, but a convenient way of distancing himself from the struggle, explaining it away in terms of an archetypal neurosis and thus devaluing the pain of soldiers so shell-shocked that many were never able to return to civilian life. In universalising the suffering he had robbed it of its power to move society individually. It is this above all that renders questionable all unidimensional explanations of human behaviour – including most catch-all psychological interpretations of the human condition.

ERICH FROMM AND THE NECROPHILIC PERSONALITY

I shall hazard this conjecture: Hitler wants to be defeated. Hitler is collaborating blindly with the inevitable forces that will annihilate him.
(*Luis Borges on hearing of the American Army's entry into Paris in August 1944*)

When studying the Second World War in Europe we confront one figure – Hitler. It was, as historians have written, Hitler's war. Without him Europe might have escaped destruction. Without him much that was to perish might have survived. Half a century on we still have problems believing that an event of such magnitude could have had such a specific cause – the ambitions of one man.

The 20th century offers many explanations of human behaviour, one being Nietzsche's will to destruction. What Nietzsche wrote of philosophically, Erich Fromm wrote of in terms of psychology. In concentrating on the figure of Hitler and the degree to which the German people were his conscious or unconscious accomplices, is Fromm's psychological perspective adequate? Did Hitler indeed live life to the limit of his capacity? When you have only one life you cannot altogether ignore the question – are you enjoying it? In the post-war world of consumerism and low inflation we talk of 'the quality of life'. Politicians are elected solely to maintain it. Can destruction, however, be part of life as well? Can nihilism also be enjoyable?

It was a question which for much of his life absorbed Fromm's energies. It was in an attempt to answer it that he abandoned his original intention to become a rabbi, one of a long line of scholars on his father's side of the family.

The Great War interrupted these plans. The conflict marked him for life. Indeed, writes one of his biographers, it is tempting to speculate that the work for which he is most well known, *The Anatomy of Human Destructiveness* (1973), was conceived in response to the questions first thrown up by his experience of the First World War, by the anguish and confusion which the struggle produced in a sensitive, gifted, insecure adolescent.[58]

Fromm was only 18 years old when the war ended. By then he was already, in his own words, 'A deeply troubled young man who was obsessed by the question of how war was possible, by the wish to understand the rationality of human mass behaviour, by a passionate desire for peace'.[59] What explained the blood-letting through which Europe had just passed; how was such a war possible in a supposedly enlightened era; what were the origins of the pernicious rationalism which had beset the European powers? It was difficult, he wrote later, for a generation born after 1914 to appreciate the extent to which the war had shattered the foundations of European society. Had it not witnessed at first hand the increasing brutalisation that distinguished the 20th century from the 19th?

In a Freudian age, perhaps, it was not all that surprising that he should have abandoned his religious studies for a study of psychology instead, that he should have tried to find the answers to his questions in a study not of God, but of man.

In time, Fromm became one of the foremost psychoanalysts of his day, certainly the most widely read. When he moved from Berlin to the United States in the 1930s he became a best selling author equally at home writing in English or German. When the Second World War broke out he was safely ensconced in the United States. His only personal connection with the war and, more specifically with the Holocaust, came in July 1944 when he married Hetty Garland who had accompanied the philosopher Walter Benjamin in his attempted flight from France four years earlier.

Fromm was not a classic Freudian, still less one of the group of loyalists like Ernest Jones who remained doggedly faithful to Freud. If he was born too late to be a member of Freud's inner circle of friends, he was nevertheless taught by some renowned Freudians, Hans Sachs among them. He was fully conversant with Freud's work. On the death instinct, as opposed to their different theories of human aggression, their views were quite close.

Fromm did not fault the theory of the death-wish for being highly speculative, all the more so because it was based on the concept of repetition compulsion for which Freud offered very little, if any critical evidence. Ultimately Fromm was prepared to ignore these lapses. He believed that Freud in 1915 had displayed a more profound insight than most into the inner conflict between man's will to live and his compulsion to destroy himself.

In time, however, Fromm developed his own theory of 'negative transcendence' which, in its raw form, posited the existence of a blind impulse, a 'catastrophe complex' as he later called it, that might lead man to inevitable destruction. Later still he shifted his ground. Instead of construing it as the pre-eminent source of destructiveness, he subsumed negative transcendence under the title 'Compensatory Violence' and contrasted the latter with a new category of psychosis – necrophilia, a deep-seated hostility to life.

Fromm borrowed the term from a lecture given by the Spanish philosopher Unamuno at the University of Salamanca in 1936. When interrupted by a Falangist general who claimed that his own manifesto in life was 'long live death', Unamuno had characterised his protagonist's attitude as inherently necrophilic.

Because – Fromm argued – the necrophilic attitude to life is not autonomous but mechanical it makes no difference whether destructiveness is directed more towards the self than to others; it matters little whether it is suicidal in nature or not. If a man cannot create life he can, at least, destroy it. Indeed, that a man can destroy life is just as miraculous a fact as his ability to create it. Life itself is the miracle. Creation and destruction, like love and hate, are not mutually-exclusive instincts; they are both responses to a similar need: transcendence.[60]

A man can transcend his condition either by progressing or regressing. By regression, Fromm meant that by becoming a non-reflective animal again man could do away with awareness and reason, not by passively reacting to the world but by asserting his own nihilism. A person who cannot create or live productively may not wish to shuffle off the stage unseen or unmissed in the last act. He may wish to leave his mark on the world, even to triumph over it. Destruction can be his revenge against a world which has not permitted him to be productive.[61]

Fromm differed from Freud in his belief that human destructiveness is not fixed in the species. The intensity of pathological hatred for life varies from individual to individual. Moreover, he maintained, self-hatred and the hatred of others, far from being mutually exclusive, usually go hand in hand. A destructive personality is a man who knows himself all too well, who knows that his life is uncreative and therefore ultimately unrewarding, whose intellectual life is distorted by sensory deprivation and emotional numbness – a man whose wish to destroy is largely the outcome of an 'unlived life'.[62]

Fromm believed that the necrophilic personality could take many forms. In Hitler he found a man filled with an insatiable hate, a man who feared death because it would confirm his personal failure as well as his total extinction.[63]

In Hitler, Fromm found the most vivid illustration of a man whose political genius was the gift of being able to transmit and guide through the experience of his life the darker forces of his own age, principally the First World War, the only time during which he had ever felt personally fulfilled. The war of annihilation which Germany fought between 1941–45 also tells us something about the nation that almost perished in it. Did the German surrender in 1945 mark the resignation of a people who knew, too late, that they had tried to fulfil someone else's purpose? Or did they realise that they had also tried to fulfil their own?

Hitler had no interest in mourning the loss of German soldiers or the destruction of German cities which, but for one exception in February 1945, he studiously avoided visiting. What he promised the German people was a historical role, 'death in the continuity of life', the only immortality in his Thousand Year Reich. It is not irrelevant that the description of the privileges of the Aryan race in *Mein Kampf* culminates in the absolute meaning of sacrifice. The Aryan was distinguished from the Jew, argued Hitler, in the measure of his readiness to subordinate his life for the good of the community, 'and when the hour demands it ... to go so far as to sacrifice it' altogether.[64] 'Posterity forgets men who have only served their own interests and celebrates heroes who have renounced their own happiness'. The one who sacrifices himself is *the* sacrifice. It was an appalling doctrine, one that challenged Heidegger's insistence that 'the essence of being lies in its existence', not in its death, not in the negation of life but in its ontological affirmation.

The Nazis brought to this struggle for existence a language unique to themselves, replete with medical metaphors, plundered from the racial theorists of the late 19th century such as Stewart Chamberlain and Gustave Le Bon. 'Nations and governments mean nothing', Hitler wrote in *Mein Kampf*, 'except insofar as they contribute to the health and well being of the race'.[65] The decision to kill off the unfit, the degenerate, the irredeemably sick or parasitic was taken before the war, not during it, as the euthanasia campaign against the civil population in 1939 testified. Likewise, the decision to *quarantine* social elements regarded as dangerous and corrupting, such as Jews, homosexuals or gypsies, was taken earlier still with the construction of the very first concentration camps in 1934.

In *Mein Kampf*, Hitler had left no one in doubt that in order to 'cure' an era that was 'inwardly sick and rotten', an unusual courage would be demanded. The German people would have to confront without flinching the causes of the disease. When a Nazi doctor at Auschwitz was asked by a prisoner how he could reconcile his role with the Hippocratic Oath, he replied that his very respect for human life had required him to act against the Jews, to remove 'the gangrenous appendix from the diseased body'.[66] Quarantine camps were necessary. 'We don't want in the process of eradicating a bacillus to be infected ourselves', Himmler told a group of SS generals in 1943. In this respect, Rudolf Hess was right to declare that national socialism was merely 'applied biology'. As such, it applied to the patient as much as the disease.

The patient indeed, writes Robert Lifton, 'was not the Jews or the other people. The patient *was* the Nordic race'. Hitler always accepted that the purification of the German race through struggle was a high-risk policy. The war might well be lost. If it were not fought, however, he had no doubt that the nation would perish. In a word, there was no reason why Hitler should have felt any remorse for the deaths of seven million Germans in the war. We may rest assured that they were never on his conscience.

It would be quite wrong to say that Hitler planned the destruction of the German people, but he accepted that their *complete* destruction would follow from defeat. The nation would die anyway, he told a group of army cadets in December 1940, if it failed to assert 'its claim to existence'.[67] If people were not prepared to battle for their survival they could expect to perish. By going to war against Russia he had 'willed' the German people's destruction if they failed.

In this respect, Hitler's war was very Wagnerian. It was more than just a conflict, it was a *Nieblungentod*, a fateful struggle for existence, a struggle similar to that of the Nieblungs against the Huns, an epic drama on a universal scale. That is why Hitler remained so unforgiving. By 1944 he knew the Russians would win. The German people had not redeemed themselves, they had failed. The cost of failing 'the test of history' would be their total destruction.

Not content merely with 'willing' Germany's annihilation he tried to complete it before the Russians arrived. This time there were to be no more scapegoats as in 1918, no more fifth columns. The Germans would have no one else to blame but themselves. In September 1944, a month after his last meeting with the Nazi gauleiters, he gave the order for a scorched earth policy to be applied. Everything was to be destroyed in the wake of the Russian advance, not merely anything that might be useful to an invading army, but the collective memory of the nation itself. Every ration card, historical record, certificate of marriage, residency record, even bank account number; every castle, church, theatre and opera house – everything that made up the *German identity* was to be liquidated as the army retreated to Berlin.

If Hitler 'willed' Germany's destruction because Germany's 'will to power' had failed him, to what extent were the German people party to their own destruction, spared only the ultimate catastrophe by Albert Speer's refusal to carry out Hitler's scorched earth decree? Can Fromm's theories be substantiated for an entire people? Did Nazi terror alone foster that incredible 'passivity' which Joost Meerloo saw as a 'mass suicidal drive', inducing millions of Germans into unprotesting doom?[68] Was Hitler the Messiah that Wagner's friend von Bulow had concluded that the Germans needed 'an upside-down Christ', who would crucify his own people instead of suffering for mankind? In Hitler did the Germans unconsciously recognise, in Auden's phrase, such a 'psychopathic god'? Did the Germans believe in Hitler to the end like the priests of Tyre who, during the siege of the city by Alexander the Great, chained their gods to the pillars of their temples so that they would not desert them?

The fervour with which the Germans fought between 1944-5 in the rubble of the Third Reich astonished even the Russians. It is easy to say with Genet that the entire nation was 'on the index' that its criminality did not stop at the Wehrmacht HQ, that Hitler was an alibi that exonerated the ordinary German soldier. It is tempting to agree with Canetti that Hitler was not outside the crowd but was the crowd, its conscience, its voice, giving expression to its preciously suppressed desires, that his genius – in a memorable phrase of Konrad Heiden – was 'knowing better than any one else how to lead the nation, to guide by compliance'.

It seems more likely that their vote of confidence in Hitler's leadership tells us less about their necrophilic desires than the point at which they became accomplices *by default*, the point at which they could not afford to even contemplate defeat. Surely they continued fighting not to prolong the struggle, still less to ensure a suitably apocalyptic end, but to survive?

Knowing that Soviet retribution would be terrible they readily saw their counterparts in the Red Army as half-Asiatic savages who, once they burst into Central Europe, would destroy everything in their path. 'We must win the war', wrote a sergeant in the Sixth Mountain Division, 'in order not to be delivered to Jewish vengeance'. In projecting their own guilt onto the Russian people, the Germans peered into the abyss. They had to fight their own demons. They would either fight or perish. That is why they fought so tenaciously for so long.

As an officer of the Twelfth Panzer Division wrote after the defeat of Stalingrad, the battle might represent a defeat but it was not the beginning of the end, it was the beginning of a new, more profound struggle:

> Now the test has come. If we hold on now then we shall have a future ... If we do not hold on – then we don't deserve to have one ...

The rank and file of the German army, as well as most of its senior officers, gave Hitler their unquestioning support to the end. Without it he could never have survived so long. Even in defeat many were despairingly defiant. Another war, predicted one combatant, would soon ensue in which the German people would once again be called upon to make a sacrifice. 'In any case', he wrote shortly after the Reich's collapse, 'we have *provisionally* still not lost'. Chilling words indeed, but hardly signs of a compelling need for self-destruction.

In retrospect, what the German people sought to the end was a sense of security, and found it in the person of one man. Was it so perverse of Robert Ley to ask a crowd in the Sportspalast even as late as 1942, 'why did the Germans love Hitler?', or to provide the answer – 'that with Adolf Hitler they feel safe'?

It was, of course, a security for which they paid a terrible price. Ernst

Jünger considered that the Germans had only themselves to blame for the destruction that finally befell them. Had they not even been willing to join the *Volkssturm* battalions upon which Hitler had relied for his scorched earth policy to be carried out? But then all Hitler's inspirations, Jünger argued, had been experiments which had eventually been used against them – the burning of the synagogues, the extermination of the Jews, the bombing of London in 1940, the flying bombs towards the end of the war. In showing first that every deed was possible, that every unthinkable crime was not unthinkable, Hitler removed the safeguards against the use of similar methods against the German state. Having colluded in the destruction of others the Germans colluded in their own destruction as well. 'The frenetic applause', wrote Jünger, 'that accompanied his appearance, was the agreement for self-destruction, a highly nihilistic act'. Inviting the world to destroy them, the Germans confirmed what many had warned them against: that the greatest harm to themselves would come from their own actions.

In that sense the Germans *were* complicit in their own destruction. They were not seized by a collective madness, by an unconscious will to destroy themselves, but by their perception that others would destroy them in retribution for their own crimes.

In the spring of 1944 Harrison Salisbury left the Moscow office of United Press to join the Red Army on its march to Berlin. In the Crimea he saw with his own eyes the terrible fate visited upon the defeated German army, now reduced to a dejected force, its soldiers crippled by dysentery, moving listlessly among the burned-out tanks and personnel carriers, among pig-bellied bodies decomposing in the mud. What he saw was:

> 'the garbage heap of humanity ... here Hitler's Aryan man died, a worse death than any he devised in the ovens of Auschwitz, anus open, spewing out his gut until a Red tommy-gunner ended it with a lazy sweep of his chattering weapon'.

In Germany itself a more terrible fate still had been visited upon the citizens of Hamburg the previous year. In retrospect, had they not invited their own destruction? Among the dead in that summer of 1943 were the petty city bureaucrats who had issued new edicts and orders for the compulsory sale of art belonging to Jews, restrictions forbidding them from sitting technical examinations, orders confiscating their radios, cutting off their telephone lines, even soap rations at the end. The destruction of the Jews represented a slow countdown that ended finally in November 1941. On 2 August they were no longer permitted to use libraries. On 1 September all Jews over the age of six had to wear a yellow star. On 18 September they were forbidden to leave their residences. Finally, 20,000 of them were evacuated to Lodz where they were never heard of again.

Among those killed in the British raids were citizens who had taken advantage of the repossession of Jewish homes. Many of the 7,812 flats that had come onto the market went up in smoke that summer. If ever a people paid dearly for their indifference to their own fate, the citizens of Hamburg did in 1943. No other people paid quite so much for their civil reticence, for not speaking out in time.

* * *

Let me turn, however, to another interpretation of Germany's *Götterdämmerung*, which is not so much psychological as philosophical, and of which Fromm gave the best definition when he talked of the 20th century's 'catastrophe complex'. For if Hitler willed the destruction of the German people he did so in particularly Western terms, seeing death (or catastrophe) as a form of renewal, leading inevitably to rebirth and reaffirmation. If any fictional figure catches Hitler's own demonical obsession with self-destruction it is surely Wagner's Wotan, a god who rises to the tragic height of willing his own destruction. 'This is the lesson that we learn from the history of mankind', wrote Wagner in 1854, 'to will what necessity imposes and ourselves bring it about'. The world Wagner writes about is the self-conscious construction of man.[69]

Wagner was writing in very Hegelian terms. Germany existed as an act of self-consciousness; As a self-conscious people the Germans were definingly Western. Hegel was interested in the character of a culture, its *idea* of itself. 'The spirit of the age', he wrote, 'is the spirit present and aware of itself in thought'. It is the conscious description of itself that gives every culture its unique historical character.

By the mid-19th century most Europeans saw themselves as free, self-determining individuals who were no longer governed, as they had once thought, by natural laws or divine providence. It followed that their most important task was to understand themselves. For Hegel the main difference between Western and non-Western societies was not their different levels of material progress. Nor was it to be found in theories of race or explained entirely in terms of geography. It was the extent to which consciousness of itself was or was not lacking that made Europe different from every other community or nation. Because the Europeans were consciously self-determining beings they were free. It was because they were free that they were in a constant state of flux. They wished to become something more than they were.

In the cycle of operas that constitute Wagner's *Ring*, Wotan is the ultimate Hegelian god – a god who wants to rule the world but is ultimately prepared to renounce that ambition and thus seek his own destruction, if that is the price of self-knowledge. Wotan wishes from the beginning to become a whole person, to represent in himself all the contradictions of the world of the Ring – love/evil; heroism/ignominy; hatred/redemption. Only by becoming a whole person can he find meaning in the order of things, through the dialectic of the Ring, the discourse between gods and men. Only through self-consciousness can Wotan aspire to become more than a god, to become an *individual*.

'Paradoxical as it may appear', writes one of the *Ring*'s modern interpreters, 'we do not become individuals by clinging wistfully to the purposes we shape for ourselves in the conscious ego, but by letting those conscious purposes adapt themselves to the underlying purposes shaped for us'.[70] Individualism is, in Jung's sense, a growth of character. But the growth of character is produced, according to Jung, 'through integration'. When we are at one with life we can master it; when we are unreconciled to it, we no longer consciously determine our own fate.

Wotan has many great scenes in the course of the *Ring*, three of which stand out as markers on his quest for self-knowledge. In the first part Wotan, heeding the warnings of the all-seeing Erda, surrenders to Alberich the Ring fashioned from the Rhine maidens' gold, the Ring that brings absolute power to whoever possesses it, though it is a power that could only be obtained by renouncing love. By surrendering the possibility of redemption, Alberich is prepared to accept this bargain. Wotan in the end is not. In offering the giants the Ring as payment for the construction of Valhalla, Wotan implicitly accepts his own end, even if he only dimly glimpses the inevitability of that resolution at the time.

In a celebrated letter to August Röckel, Wagner wrote 'Alberich and his Ring could do no harm to the Gods if *they* were not already ripe for evil', if they were not in need of redemption themselves. 'Where, then, is the root of this evil?' Wagner asks. It is to be found in Wotan's second great act of renunciation, in the second act of *Valkyrie* when he forsakes Siegmund, the one hero who could save the gods. He does so at the urging of his wife Fricka, who as goddess of love and the family demands Siegmund's death for offending the moral order, for committing incest with his sister.

Fricka's voice is clearly that of the old order. She will have nothing of Wotan's argument that taboos like social conventions, are meant to reflect changing conditions, that they should not be used to arrest change in the name of the *status quo*. Men and women should live for themselves, that is, whatever is or has become necessary to life. The natural order is fashioned by man, not man for the natural order.

As Wagner adds, it is an instinctive error to wish to prolong an order of things when change has become inevitable: '... the whole unfolding of the drama [*Valkyrie*] illustrates the need to recognise and accept diversity, the perpetual changing, the eternal renewals of reality and life'. Siegmund, of course, does indeed die, but Brunhilde saves Siegfried, Siegmund's unborn son, the hero who is destined not to save the gods but to bring about their final destruction.

The last of the three scenes in which Wotan comes to terms with his destiny is his final encounter with Siegfried, as the hero is about to brave the flames and restore Brunhilde to conscious life, initiating at the same time the events which will lead to the destruction of Valhalla. As Wagner wrote to Röckel, if there was any 'underlying poetic theme' in the works that he had composed prior to the *Ring*, it was 'the supreme tragedy of renunciation, the abnegation of the will, which ... is necessary and unavoidable and alone capable of achieving redemption'.[71]

Wotan meets Siegfried on equal terms and, in allowing himself to be vanquished, is transformed from an arbitrary god into a rational man. He dies redeemed because he sacrifices himself to transform the world, to create a new order which could only emerge, of course, from the old. The very last scene of the *Ring*, the last act of *Götterdämmerung* is the blaze that sweeps through Valhalla – in whose burning interior Wotan awaits, resigned to whatever future the transforming fire may bring.

Wagner's *Ring* had a powerful impact on the European consciousness in the early 20th century in the *image* it offered of the 'will to power'. Let us not forget, Shaw wrote in *The Perfect Wagnerite*, that Wotan's principal desire is towards 'a higher and fuller life' which can only be attained 'by his own undoing'. Shaw was a confirmed believer in catastrophe. In the last preface he wrote in 1922 to the fourth edition of his book, he concluded that the sociological thesis of the *Ring* remained as relevant as ever, even if the First World War had not really changed the world that much:

> Indeed, the war was more a great tearing off of masks than a change of face: the main difference is that Alberich is richer, and his slaves hungrier and harder worked when they are so lucky as to have any work to do. The *Ring* ends with everybody dead except three mermaids: and though the war went far enough in that conclusive direction to suggest that the next war may possibly kill even the mermaids with depth charges, the curtain is not yet down on our drama, and we have to carry on as best we can.[72]

If the West succeeded, he added, his book would not require another edition. If not, the world itself would have to be 're-edited'.

The 'transforming fire' in the 20th century, more often than not, was war. Wagner and Hitler have always been associated in the popular imagination. I have offered one interpretation of Wagner's 'will to destruction', as an act of transformation, not nihilism. It is quite possible, however, to interpret Wagner's myth in more critical terms, to see in the philosophy of self-abnegation one particularly compelling theme of the 20th century's 'catastrophe complex'.

What appalled people most about Hitler appalled people most about Wagner. Nietzsche took issue with Wagner's self-abnegation, his celebration not of the love that overcomes death but the idea that death can only be overcome through an act of self-destruction, in the case of Brunnhilde her own immolation. Does not Wotan will the end of the gods, as Brunnhilde wills her own death? Could not their destruction have been avoided? Does Wotan not allow Siegfried to survive and later to break his own spear, the symbol of his power, retreating to Valhalla there to await his own end?

There is one particular aspect in which the *Ring*, wrote Theodor Adorno in 1938, was in agreement with Hegel's philosophy of history. Wagner too believed in 'the cunning of reason', a force in the world that he considered to be not positive but negative, indeed largely self-destructive.[73] Wotan's act in allowing his spear to be broken is the apotheosis of his self-knowledge which, on becoming conscious of itself, withdraws from the world of action. Whatever is opposed to Wotan's universal will to power is also in accord with it. His spirit seeks out its own annihilation.

Towards the end of his life Wagner, too, wanted Europe's destruction, so that a new age could be forged. He looked forward to a new twilight of the gods brought about by the purging fire. Hitler too was obsessed by fire, by the image of Germany consumed in flames. Did he not set the torch to Berlin as decisively as Rostopchin did to Moscow, during Napoleon's invasion? Was not the twilight of the gods, wrote Adorno, 'a homecoming without a home, an eternal rest without eternity' for both Hitler and Wagner, a mirage of peace all the more alluring because no human beings were left to enjoy it? Did not both men ascribe to the dead a happiness denied the living?

Towards the end of his life Wagner too glorified war. In one of his last essays on 'Art and Revolution' he wrote:

It can but arouse our apprehension to see the progress of the art of war departing from the springs of the moral force and turning more and more to the mechanical: here the rawest forces of the lower powers of nature are brought into an artificial play, in which for all arithmetic and mathematics the blind will might one day break its leash and intervene with elemental force.[74]

Wagner looked forward to the mechanisation of warfare, precisely because the generals of the future would no longer have to depend on the courage of their men. They would no longer be inhibited by the fear that their armies might melt away, or that mankind might revolt against war itself:

> Just as in nature everything has its destroying foe, so Art invents torpedoes for the sea and dynamite cartouches, or the like for everything else. It is conceivable that all of this, with art and science, valour, points of honour, life and chattels, might one day fly into the air through some incalculable Accident.

By 1945 an accident was only waiting to happen. By then war had indeed been mechanised with the invention of the atomic bomb. All it lacked in the end was its ultimate *metteur en scene*. For whatever Stalin was, he was not self-destructive. The Soviet Union even survived him. Germany, denied nuclear weapons, survived Hitler – only just.

If our historical consciousness has changed, so too has our understanding of the century's 'catastrophe complex'. We have not renounced the concept of catastrophe, of course. We have merely given it a new meaning. We are no longer haunted by fears of war, but by other anxieties, which are no less compelling. We still fear the future, only now we fear other things: environmental ruin most of all. It was Chernobyl which, symbolically at least, alerted many more people to the fear of provoking a different kind of nuclear threat: not a conscious act of war but the accidental meltdown of a nuclear reactor.

Why do we love catastrophe so much, even when there is little enough evidence of it? Why do we still project our existential anxieties onto history? Catastrophe is a very Western idea. We may have renounced an absolute belief in progress, but we are still dreaming of eras of transition – and crises as the turning-point or catalyst of them. We still love transitions because we still wish to escape the present – fear of an ecological catastrophe is one way of rendering imminent what we also believe to be immanent. We still tend to turn catastrophe into a historical force.

The writer Pitirim Sorokin considered other people's crises to be also 'painful transitional situations'. But he regarded the 20th century for the West 'as the period of the greatest crisis of all – a catastrophic transition to a new culture'.[75] That culture may be for some the forerunner of a post-historical or post-political era. It may even be post-modern. Many of us have no doubt that the twenty-first century, like the one through which we have lived, in Adorno's words may 'radiate disaster triumphant'.[76] The fact that we are standing on the eve of a new century merely gives our thoughts even more millenarial appeal.

We are haunted still by apocalyptic fears and intimations of our own mortality. Only moments of crisis, wrote Auerbach, enabled Europeans to become fully cognisant of their true character. It was significant perhaps that Auerbach too was somewhat apocalyptic in his thinking, that he also believed that European civilisation was approaching 'the term of its existence', that if it were to survive at all it would survive in a truncated form.[77]

Ultimately, we still dream of apocalypse because we are still obsessed by acts of violence committed against ourselves. We see the degradation of the planet as an act of violence; we may have disinvented war but we have not disinvented martyrdom. In his book *Violence and the Sacred*, René Girard writes:

> The sacred consists of all those forces whose dominance over man increases or seems to increase in proportion to man's effort to master them. Tempests, forest fires and plagues, among other phenomena, may be classified as sacred. Far outranking these, however, though in a far less obvious manner, stands human violence – violence seen as something exterior to man and henceforth as a part of all the other outside forces that threaten mankind. Violence is the heart and soul of the sacred.[78]

Girard's point is that what man should hold sacred is not nature but himself. In committing violence against nature he commits violence against the human race. Isn't the environmental crisis a sacrificial one, asks Girard, in that it is man's existence that is at stake? Are not flooding, forest fires and diseases themselves 'acts of violence' whose *consequences* are ecological because what is endangered is the survival of a world which sustains mankind?

In that respect, our reinterpretation of the catastrophe complex of the age is not so different from the old. Man is still rebel and executioner, policeman and victim, a martyr to his own acts in a world in which suicide, not murder, is still the greatest threat of all to his well-being.

MAN IN THE CROWD: ELIAS CANETTI AND THE QUEST FOR ANONYMITY

A fine dust of extinction, a grain or two for each man is scattered in any crowd like those black London war-crowds ... Wars begin with this huge indefinite interment in the cities.

(Wyndam Lewis, *Blast, no. 2, July, 1915*)

I remember once in London the realisation coming over me, of the whole of its inhabitants lying horizontal a hundred years hence.

(Alfred Tennyson, Notebooks)

Even those who were sceptical of many of the philosophical and psychological profiles of the human condition, or those who found concepts such as Freud's death-wish morally limiting, were preoccupied with an even larger transcendental reality – the crowd. Crowds dominated the imagination of 20th century Europe in the popular cinematic idiom of *Modern Times* and *Metropolis*, or in such popular classics as Spengler's *Decline of the West* where the masses were described as parasitical city dwellers, traditionless, religionless, ready for a Messiah or master builder to shape them for his own purposes. For the novelist Henry Green, writing in 1939 of a crowd milling in the concourse of Victoria Station, the masses were less protagonists in their own story than potential victims of aerial bombing.[79]

The crowd, however innocent or complicit in the events in which it played so significant a role was, itself a threat, for the causes of war in the 20th century are also to be found in the group mentality of the cities, in the phenomenon of mass urbanisation. Reading Ortega y Gasset's classic study, *The Revolt of the Masses*, many of his readers may have felt that the world he described was not one in which they wished to live. After due reflection, however, many more must have come to realise that most of them had been living in it for some time.

Readers of Elias Canetti's monumental autobiography, one of the most important accounts of the 20th century, will know how much the author is obsessed with crowd psychology. The behaviour of crowds is one of Canetti's central preoccupations, the mysterious phenomenon of humanity *en masse*, the interplay between crowds and human behaviour, between crowds and history, between crowds and power.

It was Canetti's imaginative contribution to reject the approach taken by Le Bon in *The Crowd* (1895), a book Freud much admired, and *The Psychology of Revolution* (1912). Whereas Le Bon had been content to assert the crowd's pathology and moralise about it, Canetti set out to explain its extraordinary destructiveness (often mentioned as its most conspicuous quality). He also differed from other German writers, Broch among them, in taking his bearings not from crowd psychology but from anthropology and history. Both writers saw the crowd as part of the unique tragedy of their own era, but Canetti dwelt more on the element of human fear that made it both wilful and aggressive.

In Baden in 1914, shortly before his family left for Manchester, the young Canetti encountered his first hostile crowd. On 1 August the band in the park struck up the German anthem to celebrate the declaration of war against Russia. It was the same tune as 'God Save the King'. The mood was anti-British. Undeterred, even defiant, Canetti sung the English words at the top of his voice. His young brothers, in their thinner registers, did the same. Only his mother's intervention saved them from being attacked. Only nine years old at the time, Canetti did not understand what he had done. Possessed by nothing stronger than curiosity at first, a sort of disbelief, he could not understand what had happened. For the rest of his life he was to observe the crowd in its many forms, glimpsed again and again in the wake of different experiences.[80]

What Canetti unconsciously discovered is that a crowd is defined not so much by its members as by its enemies, it is those 'outside' that a crowd seeks out. A crowd shares a common fate as well as a common hatred. Often it is motivated by few ideas other than the principle of exclusion, whether the manner of that exclusion takes the form of a pogrom or war.

How different was Canetti's experience from that of Stefan Zweig, for whom the crowds milling through the streets of Vienna in August 1914 represented a positive force, a force of unity, no longer an anti-Semitic mob. Joining the crowd, Zweig later recalled, he had felt part of a moral presence, a living embodiment of the spirit of the nation. Everyone believed they belonged to each other. In the crowd each man transcended his selfishness, as well as the differences of class, rank and language which separated him from his fellow citizens. Each individual felt no longer isolated but a responsible citizen, no longer 'an unnoticed person'.[81]

Writing after the event too, Drieu La Rochelle, although not a Jew and neither isolated nor unnoticed, found the crowd exhilarating. War might be meaningless but man could escape from consciousness of this fact by plunging into a crowd, casting off an independent persona. As his narrator explains in *The Comedy of Charleroi*: '... I was there, lost in the middle of it all, exulting in my anonymity'.[82]

How, asked Erich Fromm, could man escape from the loneliness of his existence? How could he be at home in the world, how could he find a sense of purpose? Facing the terror of historical dislocation and social alienation man could find a remedy not in philosophical doubt but by casting off reason and finding unity instead, the unity of purpose that a crowd represents.[83]

The young Canetti was never able to see the crowd in these terms. One brutalised crowd was as featureless and indistinguishable as another. Where Stefan Zweig had seen a refuge, Canetti saw a violent birth, one which forced Zweig himself to flee Germany at the end of his life.

No one understood crowd psychology better than Canetti. With his critical detached eye he observed the behaviour of one of his closest acquaintances, a young disabled student, Tomas Marak, who tried to take part in a May Day demonstration in Vienna in 1929. By joining in the demonstration, Marak hoped to find an anonymity which his physical affliction denied him. As a student studying philosophy he wanted to join the Academic Legion. The organisers of the march insisted instead that he take part in a demonstration of war invalids. Long did he protest that he was not a war veteran, that he had been crippled long before the call-up.

Canetti paints a vivid account of a bewildered young man protesting to the end that he had nothing in common with the war veterans who out of sheer 'cowardice' had mindlessly joined up, and been punished for their cowardice with the loss of their limbs. Now they were wheeling their way under a banner which read 'Never Again War'. Of course not, cried Marak – they would never go to war again; they couldn't. But everyone else taking part in the procession, including the students in the Academic League, would hurl themselves into the next war when it came, oblivious to all their fine May Day slogans.[84]

It was the enthusiasm with which many young Germans did indeed throw themselves into Hitler's war that stimulated Canetti's long interest in crowd psychology, and led him to publish his findings nearly 40 years later in a book that is still unsurpassed in its field. The contribution of the crowd to war, and its behaviour in it was for Canetti the central theme of his work.

The man in the crowd, argues Canetti, belongs in wartime to two crowds. From the point of view of his own side he belongs to the crowd of living fighters; to the enemy he belongs to the potential crowd of the dead. Men join up to avoid death, surprising though this may sound. A man can dream of escaping death, of course, but the dream is never enough to diminish his terror of it. What a man needs is the experience of a 'postponement', a stay of execution, and what experience is more potent than the death of the enemy? What does war offer, after all, but the comforting thought that the time has arrived not for one's own death but someone else's: 'Death to the English', 'Death to the French' represent more than merely conventional catchphrases. They constitute a remission of *one's own* sentence.[85]

Did not the survivors of the first atomic explosion, many of whom died days after the attack, feel threatened by the death of their own people? At one point it was reported that the Japanese had hit back, that several large American cities had gone the way of Hiroshima. The mood in the hospital changed, Canetti recalled in 1979. The people became a crowd again and believed that they were saved from death by this 'diversion of death' to others. As long as they were able to deceive themselves many believed that they would not die at all, that they had purchased immunity from the radiation.[86]

The factor then which drives men to war also explains its brutality. It is important for a crowd to kill the maximum number of enemy soldiers or civilians; it is important for the enemy's ranks to be 'thinned'. In the 20th century the victor is the country that kills the *larger* number. 'Each side wants to constitute the larger crowd of living fighters', Canetti wrote, 'and it wants the opposing side to constitute the largest heap of the dead'.[87] Had not Nietzsche predicted that in the 20th century victory would go to the side that killed the greater number, that built 'hecatombs' of a size never seen before?

In part, this explains why nations are not deterred from going to war by the thought of the casualty levels on their own side. They go to war out of fear for themselves. To win such a conflict is vital, whatever the cost. Victory goes to the crowd that imposes the greatest number of casualties on the opposing side. It goes to the side that reduces the psychological impact of its own losses.[88]

Hitler took that obsession to its logical conclusion. He himself, of course, was part of the crowd, a man whose face was first glimpsed by history in a photograph of a mob demonstrating its enthusiasm for war in the Odeonsplatz in Munich in August 1914. Later in his life he described how he fell on his knees and thanked God for the struggle. It was his decisive experience – the moment when he was released from his *anomie*, when he became part of a crowd, the strongest crowd of all – the German nation. He never forgot the experience. Indeed, his subsequent career was entirely devoted to recreating this moment – from the outside. As Canetti writes:

> The feeling for the crowd of the dead is decisive in Hitler. It is a real crowd. Without this feeling he cannot be understood, nor can his beginning, nor can his power, nor what he meant to do with his power, nor what his undertakings led to.[89]

Hitler lost himself in the crowd in the First World War. In the Second the crowd discovered him. 'That is the miracle of our age' he reminded the German people, 'that you have found me, that you have found me among so many millions, and that I have found you'. It was a crowd he would not relinquish.[90] His refusal to allow the army to retreat, beginning with the Winter Campaign before Moscow in 1941, was the sublimation of his wish to fight to 'the last man', even if in April 1945 this meant destroying the largest crowd of all, the German nation.

For their part, the fortitude of the German people at the very end, in the bitter street fighting in Berlin all the way up to the *Tiergartenstrasse*, arose, Canetti argues, from their own wish to maintain the crowd in being. The feeling was so strong that soldiers preferred to perish altogether rather than acknowledge defeat. The people acted as though death was the only thing outside themselves, as if to abandon the crowd would be to forfeit life itself. Hence their insistent belief in victory to the very end. Heinrich Böll recalls how, even a few months before Hitler's death, his fellow Germans were still reassured by radio broadcasts which referred not to the army's defeats, but its 'lost victories'.[91]

It was ironic, thought Canetti, that in fighting so relentlessly the German people ensured that never again would they seek to find themselves in the crowd of the dead. 'They love war so much', he wrote in 1945 'that they have pulled it into Germany and there too they refuse to yield it'.[92] But war was yielded up in the 1950s as both superpowers and their respective European allies came to acknowledge that in a nuclear war no one would survive. 'According to our defence experts', Canetti mused in 1980, the Third World War would last for only half an hour:

> What sort of contentment is even permissible as long as *that* lies ahead? ... Do not say that it may pass. For it will always be there, the menace of the last four hundred years swollen into an avalanche, that hangs heavier and heavier above the heads of the living.[93]

The defeat of Germany required the Allies to embark on the task of splitting the atom. Their very success denied the crowd recourse to war for in the nuclear age the battlefield was the city, the combatants the civil population, the crowd in its most extensive form. Death, Canetti wrote in *The Human Province*, would not be so unjust if it were not decreed in advance. 'Each of us, even the worst, still has the excuse that nothing he does can touch the wickedness of this advance verdict'.[94] But if we cannot avoid death we do not at least have to embrace it, or more particularly embrace a death we know we cannot escape – a nuclear war. The threat of nuclear catastrophe had, at least, inspired man to think twice. The indiscriminate nature of warfare had finally made mankind a little more enthusiastic about life.

In the nuclear age war between industrial powers was no longer a possibility. The crowd, a different crowd, now insisted on a different future. Production and consumption were now everything. Both superpowers wanted to surpass, not destroy each other; both wished to gain legitimacy in their own eyes as well as the world's through their ability, not to plunge the world into war, but to meet consumer demands.

Both superpowers had been forced to come to terms with the fact that even if they succeeded in motivating a crowd, in sending it forth to battle, the next war would still be measured in hours, not months. In a nuclear war there would be no survivors. Everyone would be a casualty, everyone would be part of 'the heap of the dead'. The crowd itself would cease to exist.

Even a future Hitler could not hope to find safety in a crowd, or even possess it for long. In the end, he would be repudiated by it. If political power had increased since 1945, so too had the vulnerability of the modern state. Nowhere in the world could a ruler be safe even from himself. No longer could he escape his own fear of the masses by 'thinning' out their ranks.[95]

Looking back at the 20th century we can see that Canetti was right to treat war as intensely associative, the ultimate attraction for an individual who wishes to lose himself in the crowd. War as an idea had an appeal of its own because the crowd in the 20th century has been an idea. Even such monstrous perversions of truth as Nazism inspired loyalty because they gave purpose to the individual life. At times the cause and community have been one. In a sense community *is* the cause; concerted action the only way men can defend themselves not only from an outside enemy, but also from one another.

Dostoevsky's Grand Inquisitor appreciates this truth. Why do men wish to worship secular gods as well as spiritual ones? Because of the wish of men to worship together, to embrace a cause embraced by all, believed in by the greatest number. 'What is essential', the Inquisitor observes:

> is that all may be together in it. This craving for community is the chief misery of every man individually and of all humanity from the beginning of time.

It was this craving for community, this willingness to submit 'to the general will', that Nietzsche recognised as one of the most worrying phenomena of modern times.

Nietzsche spent his life promising man a new God, a new divinity,

Chance (*Ohngefahr*), a God who would restore man's dignity by redeeming him from 'the servitude to purpose'. Man, he insisted, should be true not to a cause, or a mission, or a saviour, but simply to himself. This did not mean that he should live as he wishes, in a world in which everything is permitted. Nietzsche was not a nihilist; He merely wanted man to rediscover his true worth. He was appalled at the thought that a man should join a crowd, a party or political movement, simultaneously surrendering his freedom in the name of some value greater than life itself.

What does Nietzsche say in *Thus Spake Zarathustra*? 'If only you understood my words: 'by all means love your neighbour as yourself – but first be for me such that you *love yourself*.' He writes that man must learn to love himself 'so that one can bear to be with oneself and need not roam'. Nietzsche understood all too well that through lack of self-esteem men tended to seek refuge in a community of other men, to find sanctuary from themselves in a cause, a passion that needed self-abasement as a condition of its being. He hoped that 'the crowd' of which Canetti so despaired would be rendered obsolete if men discovered their true value. When he wrote of the 'will to power' he did not mean that states should master others in war. He wanted individuals to master themselves.[96]

Of course, Nietzsche was to be disappointed. In the 20th century men felt more alienated than at any other time from their own society and from themselves. A man who cannot live with himself is a man likely to submit to the will of another. Why, asked the Italian novelist Cesare Pavese on the eve of the Second World War, were men so intent on humiliating themselves? Why were they so anxious to attach themselves to other men, why were they so prepared to be bewitched by ideas that spelt their own destruction? 'Was this a presentiment of the brotherhood of man?'[97] A man who lacks self-respect can all too often end up prostituting himself, seeking refuge where he can find it – in a crowd. Perhaps it was not a presentiment of the brotherhood of man, but as Baudelaire had recognised in the previous century, 'the brotherhood of prostitution'.[98]

Dostoevsky also deplored the alienation of man from himself, the spiritual *anomie* that Marx not only recognised, but was the first to give a name to. Was not man, he asked, so disgusted at his own origins that he sought new parents? Would not modern man, he suggested in *Notes from the Underground*, prefer to be stillborn, conceived not by a woman but to contrive somehow to be 'born of an idea'? Was he not willing to die for an idea that gave him life, as he was unwilling to live life for its own sake? Did he not prefer the self-effacement of the dead to the self-confidence of the living?[99]

Throughout history, argues René Girard, man has been a prisoner of the myth of the 'sacrificial victim'. He has been willing enough to sacrifice himself in return for being 'numbered among the fallen'. The victimisation process, Girard asserts, was strong enough when men were prepared to die for a redeemer. It was stronger still in the 20th century, however, when men were prepared to die for an idea.[100] In Stalinist Russia Valery Tarsis was appalled by the 'crowd of Isaacs climbing onto the altars of their own free will – not even at their fathers' instigation'. Why did they not rebel against a demand for blood sacrifice, why did they act like lambs under the sacrificial knife 'instead of snatching it up and stabbing the priests'?[101] In sacrificing themselves, of course, they bound themselves to the community in death as well as in life. In remaining alive in the memory of a nation, a party, or a movement, they purchased a spurious form of immortality.

20th century man was bedevilled by 'the need to roam'. Only in the course of war was it revealed that a genuine community was one in which men lived for each other, fought for each other, and in striving not to be dishonoured in front of their friends recognised their worth as individuals. In time many recognised too that they had been betrayed by the causes they had espoused. Many more discovered that the reality of life, as Nietzsche had insisted, was more real and ultimately more consoling than the promise that life could be improved by political salvation. In time, many more discovered that political action was not the sole measure of man.

4

War and the Meaning of History

One of the characteristics of 20th century warfare was its apparent lack of purpose. Men found themselves conscripted to fight in anonymous military encounters, in brutal battles of attrition in which the cause of war, if there was one, was soon lost sight of. The enormity of conflict was such that there were only two legitimate responses. One was to impose a meaning on the catastrophes of 1914 and 1939; the other was to reject a meaning in history altogether, to refuse to accept that conflict could ever be a means to an end.

Nietzsche was not the first writer to interpret history as 'valued added', a means by which man could impose his will on an otherwise anarchic world. Nevertheless, it is in Nietzsche that we find some of the themes of 20th century warfare. In speaking of 'creating values', Nietzsche talked of endowing various things with 'value esteeming'. He argued that we do not discover that things happen to be valuable and esteem them accordingly; rather, he contended, man has 'placed values in things' by coming to esteem them – and in this respect, he observed, 'to esteem is to create'. 'Whatever has underlying value in our world now, does not have value in itself, according to its nature, rather it has been *given* value at some time ... and it was *we* who bestowed it.' Fundamentally considered, Nietzsche's opinion is that this bestowal of value upon things was intimately connected with the 'will to power' – 'valuation itself is only this will to power' – in a twofold way: it is both an expression of it and a means whereby the power of those in question is actually enhanced. Nietzsche might have been speaking of war when he added 'we have invested things with ends and values; therefore we have in us an enormous fund of latent force'.

Nietzsche was not content simply to make the point that 'we have to realise to what degree we are the creators of our value feelings – and thus capable of projecting meaning into history'. Celebrating 'the continually creative' rather than dwelling upon the fact that such values are only our creations, the attitude he considered appropriate was 'no longer the humble expression - everything is merely subjective' - but 'it is also *our* work - let us be proud of it'. The sort of value creation and state of mind of which he was thinking were inseparable in his view from the ethical health of the community, about which Hegel had written at the beginning of the 19th century.[1]

Of all the writers I shall be looking at in this Chapter Heidegger is, in this respect, the most important as the voice of Germany's national will to power. He was also a philosopher whose life spanned four changes of regime from the imperial era in 1914 to the more pedestrian, less heroic, but more rationally rooted Federal Republic of the 1950s. Heidegger was convinced that a nation without a historic role was not really a nation at all, merely a collection of individuals marking time. It was to take two world wars for the 20th century to recognise that surrendering life not for a cause or even a country, but for history is a curious, indeed questionable, form of redemption. One 20th century theme that does, indeed, appear to have been permanently discredited is the idea that without a historical role a people will die historically intestate.

Nations, however, were not the only 'units of account' to invest history with meaning. For Marxists the will to power came not from political élites, but from social classes working through history. One of the great Marxist writers of the 20th century, Georg Lukacs, did not use Heidegger's terminology, but for Lukacs too authentic experience was realised destiny.

For Lukacs the authentic life was one of human possibility, a goal to be achieved with means sufficient for its achievement. He was under no illusion that any class, including the proletariat, would ever entirely grasp the meaning of history but he considered that the privileged position of the latter might enable it to achieve a transparent consciousness of its own fate.

All bourgeois societies, he wrote, wished to avoid their historic transformation despite the fact that they could not escape it. To accept that history was catastrophic would imply, of course, the discovery of the transitional nature of late 19th century capitalism, which, in turn, would reveal the bourgeoisie's own historical transience, the terrible truth that it had been condemned to death.

It was in his treatment of the proletariat, of course, that Lukacs was most compelling. The proletariat needed war because it was the only class in history to recognise that it was in its own interests to want its abolition. It could only prevail by transforming society and thus transforming itself. War, in a word, was contained in its special insight into history.

Of course, these ideas have not worn well; they have not survived the test of history. But Lukacs put forward a view of socialism that was intended to educate the masses, to make them *self-conscious determinants of their own fate*, in the hope that in doing so they would invest history with meaning. What is most important, perhaps, was that most Marxists finally came to terms with the staying power of capitalism and the gradual *embourgeoisement* of the Western workforce. They did not, in the end, try to save themselves by unleashing the final catastrophe – a nuclear war. They wanted to re-educate their enemies, not to destroy them, to transform the world, not lay it to waste. In the presence of the ultimate catastrophic weapon they stepped back from the brink. In the nuclear age history could no longer 'be willed' if only because – in Khruschev's classic phrase – 'the bomb did not recognise the class principle'.

I have chosen to conclude this Chapter by looking at two other writers who saw the 'will to power' in somewhat different terms. The first is one of the great prophets of the 20th century, H G Wells. Wells dominated the popular imagination in the interwar years by his fictional works and his extensive, if often tendentious, commentary on modern life. He was one of the first novelists whose apocalyptic vision was translated in a more immediate message through the cinema, most notably in the 1935 film *Shape of Things to Come*. One of the great critics of the First World War, Wells nevertheless saw in the titanic wars on the Western Front an opportunity to disinvent war itself. His belief in the 'war to end wars' was compelling precisely because it touched on the hopes of his readers. Whatever the literary value of his works they were dramatic, and their drama involved moral and political issues of the greatest importance.

Ernst Jünger, by comparison, never wanted the First World War to end. On the Western Front Jünger saw the shaping of a new kind of man, the worker-soldier who was prepared to sacrifice himself if necessary for his own *Gestalt*. In the soldier he saw the primordial form of the modern worker and in the battle of material (the *materialschlacht*) the authentic vision of modern times. Appalled at the thought of permanent class war, Jünger hoped to transcend the class principle of history through an act of will, to mobilise society permanently, and thus heal the class rifts which made all advanced industrial societies inherently 'unhealthy'. There were many other German writers in the 1920s who tried to impose a meaning on the First World War in anticipation of the second. If only Jünger's views have survived, as Heidegger acknowledges, his writings have lasted because they speak 'the language of the century'.[2]

H G WELLS AND THE WAR TO END WARS

> Like most People of my generation I was launched into life with millennial
> assumptions ... There would be trumpets and shoutings and celestial phenom-
> ena, a battle of Armageddon and the Last Judgment.
>
> (H G Wells, *The Future in America, (1906)*)

In the summer of 1918 H G Wells received a letter from Eric Williams, a
young soldier in France, who wrote to thank him for playing the role of
an 'unseen parent' who had inspired him to seek 'a new and splendid
conception of life'. Wells never met Williams but he heard from him once
again, 21 years later, on the eve of the Second World War. Williams had
heard Wells deliver a lecture in Sydney during his Australian tour in 1939.
Unable to meet him at the time, Williams wrote to the novelist again:

> For every one of your followers who could be classified as 'distinguished' there
> are many thousands of ordinary men who look to you ... When I was a youth the
> discovery of your writing marked a complete revolution in my thinking. The
> continued reading of your books made me, in actual fact, a new man ...[3]

Misinformed, and frequently misguided in his writings about politics,
Wells was never misunderstood. His essential hope – that the experience
of mass warfare might mark the end of war itself – sustained him almost
to the end of his life before he succumbed to abject despair in 1945. It did
much also to sustain his readers who, in a world as depressing and
appalling as the 20th century, were in no mood to cast the first stone
against hope.

Wells was already a popular writer by the time the First World War
broke out. Like many of his contemporaries his outrage at the unprovoked
invasion of Belgium stirred him to action. With Hardy, Chesterton and
Belloc he was one of a group of authors who attended the first meeting of
the War Propaganda Bureau that was set up by the Cabinet in September
1914. In the early months he was to be found denouncing German
atrocities and demanding the most Carthaginian of peace treaties. Not
only did he demand that Berlin should be looted of its art treasures, he
also thought that after the war it would be fitting for the German people
to be punitively taxed by stamping on their railway tickets such remin-
ders as 'extra for Belgian Outrages – Two Marks'.[4]

As one of the most outspoken apologists of the British case, it was
natural that Wells should have been invited to tour the Fronts – the Izonzo
Front in Italy in August 1916 and the Western Front near Soissons a
month later. By then, however, though still committed to Germany's

unconditional defeat, Wells had begun to see the latter in wider terms, as part of a solution to a deep-seated crisis through which Europe was passing, of which the war itself was merely the most compelling sign. He came to Izonzo not only to look and learn but to draw a moral. It was a moral that he had been among the first to develop in a series of newspaper articles published as early as the first month of the war in which he had coined the phrase: 'The war to end all wars'.

What did Wells discover at the Front? On one level, he found an exotic world which he painted without economy of feeling. He discovered thousands of puzzled soldiers sitting about in cafés by the roadside, in tents and trenches looking thoughtfully into the future; Italian *Alpini* staring with a speculative eye across the mountains towards an unseen and unaccountable enemy; wounded troops staring out of ambulance train windows towards an uncertain future.

In France he found the whole world represented in the oddest of juxtapositions – Malagasy soldiers in French uniforms resting among shells waiting to be transported to the Front; khaki-clad Maoris sitting upon the steps of a horse-van; British soldiers weary and sullen, their shoulders drooped, 'their very outline ... a note of interrogation'.[5]

Unlike most other writers who visited the Front Wells came well prepared. He had predicted the outline of war years before. In 1901 in his first major work of non-fiction he had already foreseen that the next European war would involve massive universal conscription, 'a monstrous thrust and pressure of people against people'.[6] He had warned that such a conflict would degenerate into one of attrition, of trench warfare, of battles between lines of riflemen, a titanic conflict in which iron-clad vehicles would rove along the roads and fields unchallenged. He had forecast that the issue would be decided by a final 'knock out punch' which the generals on both sides indeed tried to deliver from 1916 onwards. He had no doubt that the conflict would be extensive and horrendously wasteful of lives. In other words, he came to the Italian and French Fronts fully prepared for what he found there.

Both Wells and Bertrand Russell thought the Great War a disaster. Wells differed from Russell in finding it a necessary one. It was necessary to teach mankind a lesson that could be learned in no other way. It was necessary to fight a war to end all wars, one which would end in permanent peace rather than an ephemeral one.

Wells's view of war was a quintessentially liberal opinion that progress, although arrested in 1914, could not be reversed, that a world civilisation was already in the making, that evidence for it could be found in the willingness of soldiers to die in such vast numbers, not for King and

Country, but for an idea, one which in his *Outline of History* he was to call 'the universal kingdom of righteousness'.[7]

What persuaded Wells that the steadily unfolding disaster across the Channel and in the north Italian plains offered hope of a universal *pax mundi*? He was particularly heartened by two developments: the war of the Common Man, and the war of the machine. Ever sensitive to historical turning-points, he saw in the heroism of the rank and file a truth about conflict that promised the end of war itself, a promise that should not be left unfulfilled. He believed he was witnessing a war of men rather than heroes, a new order in the making, an unheroic age, an era in which, to quote Canetti, the finest statue of man would be 'a horse that had unseated its rider'.[8]

The endurance of the soldier at the Front dwarfed the pretensions of 'great men'. The generals were no longer heroes but managers dealing as best they could with violence on a scale that even they found difficult to comprehend. The war had not thrown up an 'effigy' for the crowd to follow. In France Wells found instead a quiet determination to avoid history altogether. He was particularly impressed that George V had cautioned the Prince of Wales not to visit the Front so as to avoid any personal risk to himself. 'We don't want any historical incidents here', he had remarked.[9] The King's comment, Wells believed, should enter the historical record, for the life of the 'effigy' had been a series of 'historical incidents' in which the loss of vast numbers of men had been merely 'incidental'. On the last day of his visit to the trenches he found the soldiers were not prepared to talk of glory, or of King or Country, or even of empire. Such 'panoplies of effigy' appeared tawdry. The soldiers were engaged instead in a nobler and more significant crusade, that of finishing a job which had to be done and finishing it quickly in the hope that it would never have to be undertaken by anyone else.

Wells's enthusiasm for the steadfastness of the common soldier was not appreciated by the soldiers themselves. They saw in this curious secular prophet a man singularly devoid of imagination, oblivious to the carnage of which he had been told, but had not witnessed, for like all the literary commentators hosted by the generals he was never present during an offensive or 'big push'. Some accused him of lacking compassion for the misery of the soldiers, compared with his undoubted horror at the misery of the world.

Whether unimaginative or dispassionate Wells inevitably had to minimise the horror of war when promoting war itself as the maker of worlds. What he never admitted, perhaps because he never acknowledged it, was that he had made the war itself into a great effigy and the crusade to end war the greatest of all 'historical incidents'. The common soldier was not interested in a new political order. He was concerned only with whether he had a future or not. The soldiers may indeed have spoken little about King or Country, empire or glory; except for their survival, they gave little thought to anything else.

Wells's view of the war failed to speak to the soldiers directly of their own experience at the Front. In Wells they saw their own generals exhorting them to go over the top in the name of principles which had lost their capacity to inspire by the time the men found themselves mired in the mud of the Somme. Wilfred Owen saw in Wells not a great human-itarian, but 'a pair of bayonet-coloured eyes threatening me from over, as it were, a brown sandbag'.[10] They were eyes that were cold, even calcu-lating, the eyes of a humanitarian devoid of humanity.

Wells was much more interested in humanity than he was in the life of the common soldier, as the soldiers who met him realised early on. He tended to dismiss men at the best of times as agents of history, controlled by the force of historical necessity. Isaac Azimov, one of the legatees of the science fiction tradition which Wells established, once defined science fiction as a literary genre whose hero was not an individual but the human race.[11] And it was in Wells's concern for the human race, his unconscious callousness towards the individual, that the explanation for the hostility he aroused is to be found.

Like the hero of his Great War novel, *Mr. Britling Sees It Through* (1917), Wells believed that the common man was a weak vessel indeed, one who was in a state of 'perpetual perplexity from the cradle to the grave'. Mr Britling's mission – for which he is prepared to devote his whole life – is to transform the horror of war into the foundation stone of a new era by forging a new and altogether more commendable breed of men. In *A Modern Utopia* Wells had argued for a new society without its 'men of vicious minds, its cruel and furtive souls, its stupid people, too stupid to be of use to the community, its lumpish, unteachable, unimaginative people'. The species – he had added – 'must be engaged in eliminating them, there is no escape from that'.[12]

If Wells was disappointed in the human response to war, he had another reason for hoping that the end of war might be at hand. 20th century man had begun to invent machines so devastating in their power, so destructive of human life, that he might, at last, frighten himself into peace. Unfortunately, Wells made the cardinal mistake of thinking that men could be deterred by weapons as well as words. '*We must impose* upon this war the idea that this war must end war', he once declared.[13] But how was that idea to be imposed, and by whom? Wells came away from the Front confirmed in his opinion that artillery was now the essential instrument of war, the infantryman 'hardly more than a residuary legatee after the guns had taken their toll'.[14] His vision of the future was spare and unrelenting. If war was not disinvented, and disinvented soon, the inventions of the modern era would follow in the track of the new iron-clads – the tanks. If a permanent peace was not secured, the tanks would trample over 'the bickering confusion of mankind'.

Perhaps, Wells could be excused for exaggerating the impact of the machine age on modern warfare. He had been one of the first to prophesy the invention of the tank in his short story 'The Land Iron-Clad' (1903). He had also anticipated aerial warfare in his novel *When The Sleeper Wakes* (1899). At the turn of the century he had predicted that the nation which developed the most sophisticated machines would prevail. Between 'the more inventive and the more traditional' the more inventive would win. Later, he thought it particularly apposite that the war artist Pennell had chosen to draw scenes not from the battlefield but from the Home Front, scenes of the splendours and miseries of the forge and the furnace, a world in which the future was quite literally forged.[15]

Wells put his ultimate hope in the tank, the great land iron-clads of his early short story, with their 25in guns driven by engines so powerful that they would plough up the countryside over which they made their passage. His story had ended with the words 'they are the *reductio ad absurdum* of war'. So they were, he argued, as the Great War had shown. It was up to Britain's engineers and ironmasters to ensure that the Germans too learned about the absurdity of war. The tank could only be repudiated by repudiating warfare itself.

It was Wells's misfortune to live through a Second World War 20 years later. In 1940 as the Germans seemed everywhere triumphant he was still thundering away on the need for peace. 'Amidst the thunder of the guns', he wrote in *Common Sense of War and Peace* (1940) 'the search for *pax mundi* must begin'.[16] By the end of the war, Britain's victory over Nazism notwithstanding, he had a dire presentiment of what was in store: 'Our universe is not merely bankrupt, there remains no dividend at all; it has not simply been liquidated, it is going out of existence, leaving not a wrack behind'.[17] Wells lived to see the first years of the Cold War as well, the onset of an atomic era that, with his usual prescience, he had foretold 50 years earlier.

What had gone wrong? Why had the First World War not brought about the end of war? Was the fault in the peace, in the 'design for living', or the design for war? Why, to quote Wells's first nonfictional essay on conflict, *Anticipations* (1901), had 'the new order of men' not 'come into visibly organised existence through the concussions of war'.[18]

The fault, in fact, lay almost entirely in Wells's understanding of conflict. He was wrong to imagine that war itself could end war, that machines could be used against machines, or that men could be frightened by their own inventions.

In the first instance, the machines of which he had written before the Great War were not quite as monstrous as he had imagined. He did not grasp how unreliable many of his worst nightmare inventions were to prove, so that the tank did not make a decisive contribution to the First World War at all. Aerial war for that matter did not prove as important as he had imagined until well into the 1930s. If, like the generals, he believed in the knock-out blow, the High Command was astute in not putting too much faith in technology to deliver it. The Allied breakthrough in August 1918, like that of the Germans the previous spring, was achieved by old-fashioned infantry sorties, not by the intervention of the tank.

Wells also failed to see that when the tank did prove decisive it would give rise to a war of manoeuvre, not a war of attrition. He imagined that on the future battlefield the iron-clads would essentially constitute mobile artillery, slugging it out shell for shell in an even more desperate struggle than the war he had witnessed in 1916.

Wells also discounted the dynamic of technology. Machines were always smarter than their inventors; they could always be employed for purposes quite different from those intended by the designers. Wells the prophet was already an antiquarian by the time of his death. He refused to bring his ideas about technology up to date. Everything that he predicted, including the onset of atomic warfare, he predicted before 1914.

The truth was that Wells thought too little of his own powers of prophecy. As a prophet he was not without honour, but he dishonoured himself. His writings, he once confessed, were merely 'the easy dreaming of a literary man'. He did not take his nightmare scenarios seriously enough until 1940, when it was already too late. As he admitted on the eve of the Blitz, the idea of a future air war which he had worked out so thoroughly in *War in the Air* (1900) had never been intended to be more than an entertainment, if a black one, 'a preposterous extravaganza', which hardly merited further discussion.[19]

Wells's short-sightedness was the price he paid for being not so much a visionary as a prophet. He preached rather than predicted, admonished rather than advised. So confident was he of his own powers of persuasion that he produced a version of the world in which men should have been frightened into submission, into an obstinate fear of war itself, into a mute accommodation with history. His system was pre-Copernican: it was fixed, static, undynamic. It made no allowance for human ingenuity or the perverse inclination of men to devise weapons of even greater destruction.

So who was the true visionary in the 1920s? Was it Wells, with his hope that war would end war, or the forgotten historian Philip Guedalla who was quick to appreciate that the slaughter on the Western Front had been 'a war made by war for war', that all conflicts have a tendency to become self-generating, that machines do not cause wars or even end them, that the responsibility for doing so lies with men and no one else?

By the time the planes passed over Hiroshima Wells's innate optimism had deserted him; he knew his modern Utopia was forever out of reach. In a gloomy assessment of humanity Wells concluded that the moral improvement of man – if it ever came at all – would not come in the 20th century. Mankind had reached the limits of its understanding. On the threshold of his own death Wells could express only anger, even dismay, at the abject state of human nature. Unlike Dr Johnson he did not 'rejoice to concur' with the judgement of the common man. He was afraid of it. But then he had devoted his life (apparently without purpose) to showing the common man the way.

A man who wants to save humanity can often be over-sanguine about the fate of ordinary men. Even as a new darkness fell over Europe in the late 1930s Wells was indifferent, not to the fate of Jewry but to the fate of individual Jews. In his book *Travels of a Republican Radical*, which was published on the eve of the Holocaust in 1939, he recorded a conversation with a Jewish friend who had asked him – 'What's going to happen to the Jews?':

> I told him I had rather he had asked me a different question. What's going to happen to mankind?
> 'But *my people ...*', he began.
> 'That', said I, 'is exactly what is the matter with them.'[20]

By then Wells cut a sorry figure indeed. In Orwell's words he had become a man whose single-mindedness had made him a shallow and inconsequential writer, one who was 'too sane to understand the modern world of militarism and organised evil'.[21] A man who loved humanity and wanted to save it, grew to hate it for not saving itself. In his last major work, *Mind at the End of its Tether* (1945), he wrote that the entire human species was an anachronism which was in danger of extinction. Man 'in his present form [was] played out'. Wells had in a sense come full circle. Fifty years earlier in *The Time Machine* his time traveller had also thought little of the advancement of mankind, seeing in civilisation nothing but 'a foolish heaping that must inevitably fall back upon itself and destroy its makers in the end'.

Wells despaired of the future so much, argued Orwell, because he had such an imperfect understanding of the present. What was the use of arguing for federal world control of the air in the 1930s, or in support of a world state, when what had kept England on its feet in 1940 was not the vague idea of a better future but an aggressive self-respect translated into its willingness to continue the war, whatever the consequences. It was England, after all, that declared war on Germany, as it had in 1914. Wells was the victim of his class, and his time. He was a profoundly anti-militaristic member of the middle class for whom the jingle of spurs and the thunder of guns meant little. He was extremely optimistic about science, despite the fact that the most scientific nations, Germany included, were the most destructive. He was profoundly distrustful of wartime propaganda, even though Churchill could communicate with the English people in a way that Wells could not. Because he believed so little in patriotism he was incapable of understanding the force of nationalism, or of religion, or of feudal loyalties. He was completely unmindful of the fact that – in Orwell's words, 'creatures out of the Dark Ages [had] come marching into the present', and that if they were ghosts they were ghosts which needed strong magic to lay them to rest.

Wells's direst warnings of the future failed to materialise, not because he had an inadequate understanding of the nature of modern warfare, but because he had an incomplete understanding of the nature of man. He spent most of his adult life trying to tell his readers how to save the world, assuming that they could save themselves. His internationalism was a natural corollary of his belief that the way to heal mankind was first to heal society; that the life worth living was the life of an idea.

The question, how can someone who cared about the human condition have been so uninterested in the private condition of his fellow men, is begged, but not answered, by Wells's life story. The answer, perhaps, is that Wells the socialist planner, Utopian, visionary, and evangelist, never tried or wanted to try to understand human nature – he wanted to *change* it.

His work, like that of most other science fiction writers in the course of the 20th century, was obedient to the genre's central assumption about the course of history to come. That unwritten diktat was simple enough: it was a deep assumption that humanity would *breed true*, that it would breed a viable future out of its own nature, and imprint its countenance on the future world.

In that respect, Wells's work was rooted in a vision of scientific progress without its devastating side effects. He dreamed of the penetration of frontiers without any subsequent creation of Third Worlds, of the remaking of human society without any sense of violating the natural order. Science fiction literature generally assured its readers of an essentially unbroken uplift into future history. As Wells appreciated, belatedly, Hiroshima and Hitler had killed the dream of progress. Most recent science fiction by contrast has become a series of fables of exogamy, a deployment of various strategies not for breeding true, but for *marrying out.* Humanity, writes the critic John Clute, is no longer thought capable of handling the future unaided.

In post-modernist fiction we are seen as seeking help either from another species capable of saving us from the consequences of our ungovernable history, or from our own creations grown powerful enough to control us. In the most recent literature of all human protagonists are married into the electronic nirvana of cyberspace where they gladly surrender the management of the world to Artificial Intelligences.

MARTIN HEIDEGGER AND GERMANY'S HISTORIC MISSION

As far as the eye could see above the edges of the trenches the land had become the terrain of German idealism itself – every shell crater a philosophical problem, every barbed wire fence a representation of autonomy, every barb a definition, every explosion an axiom.

(Walter Benjamin)

Why is the German people the least exhausted of the white world and therefore the one on which may be placed the most hope? Because its political past had given it no opportunity to waste its precious blood and its great ability. This is the one blessed aspect of our wretched history since 1500; it has used us sparingly.

(Oswald Spengler, *Hour of Decision (1933)*)

'The essence of the modern industrial state', wrote Erich Kaufmann shortly before the First World War, was 'the will to assert itself and establish itself in history'. Writing after its defeat, another observer argued that the Germans would not be lost if they learned the meaning of their defeat – if they succeeded in 'asserting themselves historically'.[22] One of the many reasons why the German people were susceptible to Hitler's message, and, therefore, more than most nations complicit in their eventual destruction, was the excessive yearning for a historical role. Many believed that in the 20th century their country's moment in history had arrived. If Germany did not respond to the challenge, it was widely believed such a moment would never present itself again.

Would countries that passed up a chance to become a historical agent long survive? In October 1914 the painter Max Beckman described the artillery fire at the battle of Tannenberg as 'the angels' trumpets', and the battle itself as 'the opening of the gates of eternity'.[23] For many Germans saw themselves fighting not to win but to exist. Without war they could not survive. In defeat they would be extinguished as a nation. 'Who now remembers the Armenians?', Hitler asked a few weeks before the outbreak of the Second World War.

No one asserted Germany's claim to speak on history's behalf more forcefully than Martin Heidegger, its most influential philosopher this century. No one regretted more the profound loss of faith in what for the rest of the world marked Germany's greatest victory, its victory over itself: its repudiation of history's mission, its voluntary embrace after 1945 of historical forgetfulness.

Heidegger was by far the most influential philosopher of his generation, an intellectual who cast a shadow well beyond his immediate circle. This was unusual, perhaps, for a man whose writing style was so elliptical, not to say obscure. As a philosopher he is notoriously difficult to understand. His prose, unlike that of Wittgenstein or Freud, is full of short cuts and exasperating deviations. Stylistically his German is quite appalling. Some of his more persistent critics, including the novelist Günther Grass, have even related the 'disaster of his style' to that of his politics.

It is important to come to terms with his philosophy, nevertheless, even if it takes time to grapple with his arguments. It is important because long before his death in 1976 he was recognised as one of the three great philosophers of the century. How many German soldiers, asked George Steiner, died somewhere in Russia or North Africa after 1941 with a copy of his most important work, *Sein und Zeit* (1927), in their knapsacks?[24]

For a man so enthusiastic about the prospect of the struggle of nations Heidegger had remarkably little personal experience of it. In the full flush of patriotism he had enlisted in August 1914, only to be released from active service two months later. He never saw military service on either front. Indeed, he spent the years before 1917 as a postal clerk in Freiberg. Only in the last year of the war was he recalled to the colours as a rifleman in a quartermaster battalion.

Heidegger's somewhat quiet war did not quell his enthusiasm for combat. In the penultimate year of the conflict he published a book which put forward a theme popular enough among the members of the right-wing German intelligentsia – that the potentiality for death made war 'a superior reality'. But for the First World War, in fact, his philosophical enquiry might even have taken an entirely different direction. Wittgenstein concluded that nearly all the problems of philosophy had been solved, that those that remained required merely one last 'push' or offensive. Heidegger reached a quite different conclusion: that the Western intellectual tradition needed to be deconstructed, the better to be reconstructed again. What response was more natural than in the devastated hinterland of post-war Germany? What cause more compelling than a call to arms, the demand that the German people should question the soundness of a Western intellectual tradition that had been revealed by the war to be demonstrably false?

In the aftermath of war Heidegger did not hesitate to ask what for him was the most important question. What exactly was the German nation? In 1929 he asked the following questions of his own students:

> Who then are we? How do we comprehend ourselves now, when we say 'us'? ... This history of the spirit – is it only a German or Western and furthermore a European occurrence? Or shall we widen the circle in which we are standing?[25]

Sein und Zeit is full of terms such as 'existence' and 'resolution', 'the acceptance of fate', a willingness to 'serve history'. These are not just categories which happened to fit the Nazi jargon of the 1930s. They *were* the jargon, cast in a very Hegelian form. And even though it is true that Heidegger did not base his study on the German race, and that he provided only the barest elaboration in terms of the *volk*, in explicitly rejecting the *universal* significance of cultural values he proved an outspoken apologist of German nationalism, or its specific *volkisch-staatliche Dasein*, or cultural tradition. It was an interpretation of politics in which any idea of historical truth beyond that of the nation state was rejected altogether. Inevitably, it was a conception which minimised the dangers inherent in the will to power.

For Heidegger national identity was an understanding of a nation's place in history. Historical consciousness was for him, as for Georg Lukacs, 'historical knowledge as an act of self-knowledge', or, more probably, an act of self-knowledge which simultaneously involved a sense of community, an awareness of solidarity, an experience of 'the joy of belonging'.[26] Neither philosopher was alone in believing that historical consciousness *was* a nation's destiny. The Irish poet Yeats, for one, declared his own wish to replace 'logic' in a nation's life with 'historical sense' instead.[27] Later Sartre described his own nation's destiny as 'a singularity of consciousness before being'. Heidegger, nonetheless, took the argument much further in affirming that consciousness could deny a nation's most recent past while confirming its future. If Germany could not be history it could be the future and thereby be itself. If in *Sein und Zeit* he emphasised that individual freedom was an essential ingredient of a nation's authentic existence, he also wrote that it could not obtain this unless an entire generation were willing to submit to a common destiny. A common destiny meant a common mission. The language was common enough in 20th century Germany. As one philosopher had announced before the First World War, to be anything in the world 'we must have an ambition to win something in the world ... great incursions into the history of the world will follow of their own accord'.[28]

What gave Heidegger's ideas a special resonance in the 1930s was a widespread feeling of despair and abjection resulting from Germany's defeat in the First World War. His philosophical conception of historical mandates for nations grew out of his ideas about 'historicity', specifically that the authentic way for a nation to realise its historical potential was to fashion its future from out of its past, as Heidegger himself put it, 'to recapture, recuperate, in a more original form, the essential power ... concealed within the old'. From out of defeat could emerge victory, from denial, affirmation of the future. This philosophical conception is what Heidegger had in mind when he affirmed that his 'partisanship for National Socialism' lay in the essence of his philosophy, that his concept of historicity was 'the basis of his political engagement'.[29]

Indeed, he saw in Nazism the only political movement in his lifetime that seemed able to offer the German people an opportunity to realise their metaphysical authenticity, the chance to be themselves – the chance to be a people on whose 'decision' the destiny of Europe would depend.

Did Heidegger therefore actually desire Germany to go to war in 1939? Like many of his compatriots he suffered from an incurable *Angst*, an all-pervasive and rather German belief that the death of European culture was imminent, or that all that was best in that culture was about to be swept away to make way for something else. From a metaphysical point of view, he wrote in 1935, Germany was the only country of significance. Russia and America, he added, 'offered the same dreary technological future, the same unrestricted organisation of the average man'.[30] Communism was merely 'a variant of Americanism'. Against the uniformity of an Americanised humanity 'each people [had] to find and preserve the greatness and truth of its own determination'.[31]

In a more profound sense, however, Heidegger's philosophy did indeed suggest war was the only way, not so much of saving Europe, but of asserting Germany's mission. In his lectures on Nietzsche in the mid-1930s he insisted that the metaphysical quest for truth could only be pursued through struggle, not through the traditional philosopher's pursuit of the life of quiet contemplation. Five months before the outbreak of the Second World War he complained that the German character would never be 'fit for history' until it changed decisively, probably through war. Without a major struggle, he concluded, the Germans might be reduced to the status of a 'negro tribe'.[32]

The central point of his lecture on the poet Hölderlin (1934–35) was straightforward enough, namely that the truth of a nation is the revelation of its being. Once its being was revealed, after centuries of 'preparation', the nation would know what history had in store for it simply by 'being itself'. Being itself in mid-20th century Europe almost certainly meant going to war.

Heidegger never departed from this text once the war began. After the German defeat at Stalingrad he wrote:

> The planet is in flames, the essence of man is out of joint. World's historical thinking can only come from the Germans if, that is, they find and preserve the German essence.[33]

Later in his career, in his famous interview with *Der Spiegel* in 1966, he insisted that National Socialism had been on the right track from the start. True, the Nazis had failed Germany – they had not understood the authentic German character. The Second World War had in the end been nihilistic. But he did not fault Hitler for going to war, or for attempting to realise the promise of German authenticity. What Hitler had offered the German people was a chance to give birth to a new German Reich 'on the basis of which the people commits itself in its state to act for its destiny'. The fact that he had failed did not necessarily mean the attempt had not been worthwhile.[34]

Given Heidegger's own perspective, there was no reason why Germany should feel apologetic about its victories, or its destruction of moribund political orders. In 1940 he laid the blame for the fall of France on the fact that the French people were not 'equal to the metaphysics born of their own history'.[35] It was not enough, he maintained, for a state to possess tanks in large numbers, or squadrons of aeroplanes. It was not sufficient for a nation to have at its command individuals who could master the new technologies and employ them successfully. A nation in the modern age needed to be open to 'the metaphysical truth' of the machine age. France's defeat demonstrated a concrete example of a spiritually bankrupt democracy, one unable to respond to history's call.

After Stalingrad Heidegger found it more difficult to base his challenge
to the German people on their success in war. Instead, he changed tack
and insisted that the struggle would be a long one. In 1943 he told the
students who came to his lectures on Heraclitus that the German people
were about to be put to the ultimate test. The disaster at Stalingrad was
a challenge to which they must rise. Historical existence was, after all,
more challenging than mere existence and war more demanding than
peace. Any other role but a struggle for national survival, any other path
to authenticity, would be historically demeaning.[36]

Heidegger may have been frequently obscure in much of his philosophical writing, but it is most unlikely that his audience was left in any doubt
as to where he stood. Nor did he leave them in any doubt that he was still
confident as late as 1944 that Germany could still win the war. His
confidence stemmed from an unwavering insistence that the United
States and the Soviet Union were both intellectually exhausted. Heidegger may have despised both countries, but his contempt for the United
States was, if anything, greater. Indeed, he was more enthusiastic about
Germany's declaration of war against America than he had been about
the announcement that it was at war with Russia. The entry of the United
States into the war, he maintained, far from marking its re-entry into
history after years of isolation, would constitute its last historical act of
significance as a nation.[37]

In denying that Germany's chief antagonist had a historical future at
all Heidegger, like Hitler, insisted to the very end that victory was
inevitable. It followed that Hitler's apparent folly in engaging the world's
potentially two most powerful nations in battle at the same time was not
foolish at all but the gamble of a man who could trust in the hand that
history had given him. Germany had not overreached itself in Stalingrad.
Instead, it had reached out to grasp its destiny. In the metaphysical battle
between nations and 'being', how could the Germans not succeed?

In the end, of course, whether Heidegger actually personally wished
Germany to go to war or not, the struggle that Hitler unleashed proved to
be more history than the Germans could cope with. The Third Reich did
not survive its defeat. Heidegger lived on to see a new Germany which
rapidly 'sold out' to American materialism and reconstituted its political
life on the basis of democratic principles that were derived in large part
from the United States. He was particularly appalled that, of all European
countries, the image of America should be the most popular in the
Federal Republic. The United States served as an '*ersatzvaterland*' for the
generation of the 1950s and was the model for the youth culture which
grew up in the ruins of a former age. Even if the German idea of freedom

still derived from a political culture distinct from that of America, one that gave priority to the community over the individual, which preferred the 'positive' freedom of social democracy to the 'negative' freedom of pluralistic democracy, the Germans no longer challenged America or insisted on the primacy of their own model.

Worse still in Heidegger's view, much of the new Germany's energy was devoted to becoming something other than German. The Federal Republic, he wrote, was an attempt to teach Germans how not to be German. 'Whoever wishes to be a German', claimed the great nationalist of the 1950s Franz Josef Strauss, 'must see to it that he becomes a European while there is still time'.[38]

Heidegger was also appalled in later life that the new German republic had chosen to define success in terms of its ability to meet consumer expectations, that the will to power had been transformed into the will to wealth. The Germany he despised was that of the small state tradition, the Germany of *Heimatstadte*, or home towns. It was a small town reality that had existed in the 19th century, in a Germany squeezed between the contending grandees of Austria and the austere bureaucrats of Prussia. The Federal Republic was its heir, an unworthy heir at that, one preoccupied with becoming 'the sum of its own superficial occurrences', one that defined success in terms of profit and loss. All that was important in Adenauer's Germany, he complained, was whether life 'covered its costs or not'.[39]

Inevitably, Heidegger was profoundly depressed by the path the Germans had chosen to take, though his protest was largely disregarded until the mid-1970s. What Heidegger disliked most about the new republic was its lack of 'consciousness'. Like most Germans, of course, he was appalled at what had happened in 1945, the destruction of Bismarck's greatest achievement: a united German state. Its division persisted for more than 40 years. In the late 1980s a French philosopher could still write that Germany was no more a nation than it had ever been – that it still did not exist 'except in the distress of not existing'.[40] What Heidegger protested against was that the Germans seemed reconciled to forgetting their past, not reliving it. He was appalled that on his first day as President of the Federal Republic, Theodor Heuss had chosen to tell the German Parliament that 'fate had been kind ... to nations ... in granting them the ability to forget'.[41]

For Heidegger never departed from his initial script, that the United States was doomed as a society. The Second World War, he wrote, had 'decided nothing' because it had brought about no spiritual transformation. All it had achieved was the victory of one technological nation over another. In his 1966 *Der Spiegel* interview he set out his views quite plainly. The Americans, he argued, were: 'still entangled in a thinking – pragmatism – that fosters technological operation but simultaneously blocks the path towards the contemplation of what is characteristic of modern technology'.[42]

Technological language was 'historylessness' – it was a dangerous, because meaningless, indeed measureless, form of social action. It worshipped only power without understanding why or how it should be used. Europe, he concluded, had had to begin all over again without the United States, and without Russia. And in this endeavour he had no doubt that the Germans would play a role. Even as late as July 1945, after Germany had been almost annihilated, he could still write that the Germans could not go under because they had 'not yet arisen'.[43]

In one of the last lectures he gave in Athens in 1967 he insisted that the Europeans, with Germany at their head, must rediscover a historical role, or perish.[44] In one of his last letters, written only a few days before his death in 1976, he communicated to a friend his hope that, at least, in Russia 'old traditions of thought' would one day reawaken and reassert themselves. Only then could Russia and Europe embark on the same mission:

> History, if we experience it as what is destined for us, remains still and will always remain a new present: something which expects of us that we approach it thoughtfully and that we thereby put our own thinking and our own artistic creation to the test. For the beginning of a destiny is the greatest of things. From the outset it holds everything that comes after it in its power.[45]

Unequivocal words, indeed. But they were not taken up by the young generation of the 1960s who rediscovered Heidegger towards the end of his life. Instead, his views on technology, and environmentalism, in particular his outspoken criticism of the United States, had a superficial plausibility which endeared him to a young generation in revolt. The Holocaust and the fear of nuclear war certainly appeared to confirm that the world was heading for catastrophe, that the nihilism which Heidegger had predicted in 1940 would return soon enough.

Put simplistically, Heidegger did not change his opinions after the destruction of the Third Reich and much of the Europe he had hoped Hitler would save. He still believed that 'Being', remaining true to oneself, had been forgotten in the face of 'that which is', that Germany's redemption still lay in its 'reawakening'. He still hoped that one day the German people would renounce the technological progress which for many constituted material success, at a terrible price, the 'forgetfulness of being'. To the end he warned the Germans not to look for an answer to the spiritual crisis of the modern world in science and philosophy. Only a God could save them. Preparing for his appearance was the only option left.[46]

Even this message was not as fatalistic as it may sound. He did not urge upon the Germans a policy of *attentisme*, perpetually waiting for a new Messiah. He believed they had to earn God's return:

> The beginning of a new era does not occur merely because a God bursts in from hiding, or the old God in a new way. Where should he turn on his arrival if a place has not been previously prepared for him by man? How could there ever be a suitable residence for God unless the splendour of divinity had previously begun to shine in everything that is?[47]

In other words, society must make way for God, by preparing for his incarnation. In that respect, Heidegger's message was as dangerous as it had been in the late 1930s. It was dangerous not because he urged that Germany's 'reawakening' would end in war, or that it would find its true being in another struggle. Indeed, he turned his earlier thesis on its head, neatly suggesting that if Germany did not remain true to itself a nuclear war between the superpowers might well ensue.

It was this message which the German Left took so much to heart in the 1960s. For behind his notion of the world's spiritual crisis lay another, a notion that he had formulated for the first time in the rubble of Hitler's Thousand Year Reich. In the *Anaximander Fragment* (1946) he had warned that the Western nations were 'latecomers in history now racing towards its end'.[48] In a technocratic culture, security had been purchased in the form of the ultimate technocratic solution: nuclear deterrence. Nuclear weapons were popular in the West, in part, because they appeared to confront it with no immediate moral dilemmas. Men would not have to live with the consequences of their actions if deterrence were to fail. They would not survive.

What Heidegger was arguing was that the Western nations, led by the United States, had yielded to an 'unrestrained and complete technical-ization of man and the world' which had made modern man 'the functioning of technology'. Bernanos and others had felt the same. Yet we would be wrong to conclude that Heidegger disliked the new age so much because he disliked the possibility of war. In reality, he disliked nuclear weapons because they denied man a chance to sacrifice life for 'being'. No longer could it be said, as he had in *Sein und Zeit*, that 'as soon as man comes to life he is old enough to die'. In dying, a nation might take the world with it to the brink of total destruction and beyond.[49]

Heidegger did not change in the post-war world. His message was still dangerous. Those who think that the forces of technology lie beyond human control are likely to find this is indeed the case. Those who believe only a God can save them will probably be in need of such salvation quite soon.[50] Whether they were waiting for a benign God or a 'psychopathic' one, mattered less than the contention that they were helpless to change the world for better or worse. Quietism is inherently dangerous, for a people who need to be redeemed, who are awaiting the moment of awakening, are likely to be a danger to themselves as well as everyone else.

ERNST JÜNGER AND THE *FRONTSOLDATENSTAAT*

Time only strengthens my conviction that [life in the trenches] was a good and strenuous life and that the war, for all its destructiveness, was an incomparable schooling of the heart.

(Jünger)

The most celebrated writer of the Second World War was possibly the German novelist and amateur botanist Ernst Jünger. *The Marble Cliffs*, the book for which he is still best known, was an indictment of totalitarianism published on the very eve of the war, a novel whose chief villain is clearly Hitler himself, a caricature of a caricature that was a little too close to real life.

Jünger's novel was one of many examples of the phenomenon of *Innere Emigration*, the term used for the state of withdrawal into their own world of thought, which those opposed to the Third Reich were obliged to undertake if they wished to escape punishment. Perhaps, it would have been better to have sought refuge in what a Soviet dissident playwright once ruefully called 'the genre of silence'. But then silence would not have suggested itself to a man of Jünger's temperament. His dissent against the Thousand Year Reich was not that of a man morally uncomfortable in the face of the abyss. The war into which Hitler plunged the world in 1939 was for Jünger both the best and worst of times, fulfilling for the few, destructive for many, if bewildering for everyone else.

Jünger was attracted to war from a very early age. He was only 19 at the outbreak of the First World War. Some years before he had escaped the straightjacket of bourgeois family life to join the French Foreign Legion, from which he was forcibly removed by a long-suffering father. During the Great War he was wounded on no less than seven occasions. Only two months before Germany's surrender he received its highest military order, Le Croix pour le Merité.

Like many of his compatriots the war made Jünger the man. 'What had we known of life?' he once asked, 'we approached it with utter naïveté, troubled by a sense of inner discontent. War was the new, born of the impulse to heroism; we were fascinated by it'.[51]

So fascinated, in fact, that he was one of the few career officers who was allowed to remain in the *Reichswehr* after the war, although he found in Weimar Germany a world he was no longer prepared to take on trust. Unlike his fellow comrades-in-arms Jünger did not feel betrayed by the Armistice. The crumbling lines of trenches, the rows of guns silent behind the German lines, may have stood guard over nothing at all in November 1918 but it was the guns that Jünger clearly saw as the harbingers of the future. After such a struggle he knew that the next war would come soon enough. After such a conflict there could be no peace, only an armistice.

It was in the course of the struggle that Jünger first came to recognise that few combatants really understood what the war was about. His fellow men-in-arms looked for some meaning outside the struggle – they did not understand that the war *was* the meaning of their lives. They would never find the answer, Jünger wrote, for they had asked the wrong questions: 'They take the war to be not an expression but a cause and in this way hope to find outside what is only to be found within'.[52] As Jünger went on to contend, the mainsprings of war lie not in history or the clash of states but in ourselves. Death in battle, in that sense, is never in vain. Men die the victim of their own impulses, not the ambitions of countries or statesmen. No man dies for an idea, he dies for himself. 'Illusion and the external world are one and the same and he who offers up his life in error is still a hero.'[53]

He was disappointed to find that so many of the soldiers with whom he served were gross materialists, interested only in surviving, in living comfortably once the war had come to an end. Did they not know, he wrote in *Fire and Blood* (1924), a narrative about the offensive on the Somme river in April 1917, that war was the only theatre in which a man could discover himself? 'Life is the task, adventure its poetry. A sense of duty renders the task bearable, but the joy of facing danger lightens it.'[54]

Both Hitler and Jünger survived the battle of Langemark, a disastrous enterprise at the beginning of the First World War which cost 145,000 lives. It played a large part in Jünger's political fantasy life, as it did in Hitler's. The two men, however, drew different conclusions from it. At Langemark – in Hitler's words – man fought against man and heroes died with the German anthem ringing in their ears, and its words on their lips. At Langemark – in Jünger's words – a cosmic battle took place in which men were able to discover their inner selves for the first time:

> In the depth of its craters, this war had a meaning which no amount of arithmetic could possibly quantify. One could already hear it in the cheering of the army volunteers who sounded the voice of the formidable German daemon, a voice which combined weariness of old values with longing for a new life. Who could have thought that the sons of the materialist generation could have greeted death so ardently? ... Just as the real fulfilment of an honestly lived life is the gain of one's own deep character, so the result of this war cannot be anything but the recovery of a deeper Germany ... Deep under the areas where the dialectics of war aims are meaningful, the German met with a superior force: he encountered himself.

During the conflict, he believed, the German nation had become a reality for the first time, no longer an empty concept with its off-the-shelf icons, flags, hymns and marching tunes. Accordingly, what did it matter if Germany lost the struggle? To fight for such a cause in the last months of 1918 had been far more inspiring than to fight mechanically for victory.

William James wanted the 20th century to invent a moral equivalent of war. Jünger's contemporary, the conservative philosopher Hans Freyer, concluded that there was no moral equivalent. His political philosophy in the 1920s testified to his belief that only war, or the preparation for it, could create a degree of consistent political commitment that the state must and should expect of its citizens.

Had the First World War, he insisted, not seen Germany at its best? Had it not exacted the 'unconditional sacrifice' of its workers? Had it not shown that the state was ultimately founded not on a social contract but on a struggle against an external threat, one in which the 'spirit of class' had given way to an 'ethical socialism', a socialism which had reified the concept of nationalism?[55]

Jünger too prized the spilling of blood for its intrinsic worth. He went further, however, in discussing war's social function. In *The Decline of the West* Spengler had wanted a virile, assertive state so that Germany might pursue a more aggressive foreign policy. Jünger wanted to forge an integrated state, in which social harmony would be an integral part. A true worker's state could only be formulated by war, not because the workers would run it, but because those who had passed through war and emerged unscathed could never again return to a world of bourgeois values.

Jünger went further than anyone else in arguing that modern warfare had produced a new class of workers who had no parallel in civilian life. If the whole of life had become an industrialised phenomenon, war was merely the central hub of the machine. If Marx was right to claim that 'man creates himself through work', war was merely a more dangerous, if exciting, form of labour: 'The clatter of the weaving looms of Manchester and the rattling of the machine guns at Langemark', Jünger wrote, 'were aspects of the same process'. The worker and soldier technician were the most significant agents of the modern age.[56]

For those who bemoaned the divisive workplace at home, the clash between classes, the industrial war of all against all, the Front offered an emotional refuge. Life in the trenches had not been bedevilled by class distinctions. The old social prejudices had been obliterated in a storm of steel. Like Spengler, Jünger did not want to destroy capitalism, he merely wished to subordinate it to the national will. In a sense, one could say he believed that war was the last stage of capitalism in its most unadulterated form.

Likewise the real 'worker' was the man who was prepared to accept struggle and pain as part of his manhood. He was not a labourer looking to Marxism to bring about the end of history, dreaming of a socialist Utopia in which men would not have to work at all. The body was not man's to conserve but to sacrifice. If a soldier were buried under an artillery barrage, at least he would have lived; at least in that fraction of a second he would have experienced a moment of truth; – at least, he would have discovered within himself that elemental power or 'ground of being' of which, in its preoccupation with peace, the bourgeois world had no inkling. The worker-soldier was more than the sum of his forces and capacities; 'he is deeper than he can achieve in his deepest thought and more powerful than he can bring to experience in his most powerful deed'.[57]

Man might be part of the machine in Jünger's totally mobilised state, a functional cog in a completely planned society. But he need not be alienated, not suffer from a Marxist *anomie*. He need not be spiritually estranged from the machine age. As part of the machine his relationship with his own age would be symbiotic.

Such ideas, it should be added, were not unique to Germany. Even in Spain, a society largely cocooned from the cultural trends of the early 20th century, the young Ortega y Gasset forecast that the First World War would destroy the very concept of proletarian internationalism. 'This year', he wrote on 1 May 1915:

The international workers' festival has been broken.... Rich and poor will live this day together in the trenches of France, Belgium, Poland and Galicia.... A good lesson for all those workers to learn is that these things are not so simple as Karl Marx thought.[58]

Ortega's vision of war was, of course, less radical than Jünger's. But he was not alone in grasping the fact that something more profound had happened in 1914. War, he postulated, had been a form of escape, an escape from the conflict between classes that permeated 20th century life. War may not have offered peace, but it offered many peace of mind.

The fear of class conflict was so ingrained that the First World War was indeed a catharsis of a kind. Wasn't this a possible reason, asks Robert Wolh, for the outburst of belligerent enthusiasm in countries that before 1914 had been deeply divided internally.[59] 'But let us go forward!' Renato Serra wrote in what was one of the most probing and honest of self-examinations carried out by any member of the generation of 1914:

Behind me those that follow are all brothers, even if I do not see them or know them well ... after the first miles of our marching, all difficulties will have fallen drop by drop like the sweat from our downward cast faces ... There is no time for remembering the past or for thinking a great deal when we are moving shoulder to shoulder...[60]

It was certainly no time for mobilising the workers in the eternal class war. It was a dream that inspired not only Jünger, but Owen and Sassoon in the trenches, the middle class poets who discovered the workers for the first time. It was a dream that inspired J B Priestley and George Orwell in 1940 as the workers rallied once again to defend England against Germany. Of course, Jünger, in a very German way, took the issue much further in wanting to create a totalitarian state permanently mobilised for war against an outside enemy, a society in which everyone from the homemaker at her sewing-machine to the soldier at the Front would be involved in a total effort, a conflict in which the real 'age of the worker' would only just begin.

Jünger was not at odds with those who saw war as a release from the social tension and endless debates that had poisoned city life, the strikes and marches and demonstrations that were a feature of politics in the great cities of Europe, those great metropolises which Josiah Strong called 'the storm centres of civilisation'.[61] What were Europe's great cities but melting-pots of classes and races living in uneasy peace together, products of a civilisation that was both creative and destructive at the same time. This is what Serra meant:

Down there in the city, they are all still talking about party politics, bickering factions, people who cannot agree, people who would be afraid ... but I live in another place. In that Italy which seemed empty when I simply looked upon it, but which now I feel to be full of men like myself gripped by my anxieties and setting out with me along this road.[62]

War was for many an escape from the endless struggle between socialists and capitalists, between workers and bosses, between different classes and class interests. What he liked most about soldiers, remarked George Winterbourne, the protagonist of Richard Aldington's book *Death of a Hero*, was that at the Front they were no longer members of a class, or a subordinate rank, but men. What distinguished them as men was not their civilian occupations, but their membership of the same community. In the trenches no one hated the workers, or capitalism – nor, for that matter, did they necessarily hate the enemy. They drew their identity not from what they were against, but from what they were for: themselves. They retained their humanity by refusing to be labelled. What they retained was 'their essential integrity as men'.[63]

Could two mutually antagonistic classes constitute a nation? Perhaps, suggested Marc Boasson in a letter from the Front, in time of war. For what the First World War offered its participants – surprising though it might seem for those who had not joined up – was a glimpse of the 'virtues necessary for national life'.[64] It is a revealing phrase. What Boasson did not see was that for many soldiers, particularly in Germany, the war would continue long after the Armistice. He did not imagine that the soldier-worker would return home, a nationalist not a soldier on a lifetime's contract, bound by the small print of history. He had little conception of how brutalised many soldiers would become, or how unfitted many of them would be for civilian life. By contrast, Hitler grasped the new realities quickly enough – after all, he had served at the Front.

For Hitler the First World War never ended. It continued in the street fighting in Germany's cities. For him it was a way of preparing for the next struggle, of tempering the nation, by cutting out the cancer of defeatism. 'We have more than deserved this defeat', he told the German people in *Mein Kampf*. The mutinies in the army and strikes in the munitions factories that had marked the end of Germany's participation in the war convinced Hitler that its defeat had been inevitable. It was to be expected of a society that had been politically bankrupt in 1914, that had lacked the inner strength to fight to the end. If Germany was to win the next conflict it would have to find an inner strength at home that it had signally lacked during the Wilhemine period.

In other words, the real front was now the Home Front. After 1918 the war was internalised. 'Peace as a continuation of war by other means', argued Franz Schauwecker: 'We had to lose the war to save the nation'.

> The proper war is only just beginning, the real war ... for this peace is the continuation of war through other means, each goes to his own front ...[65]

In what Oswald Spengler called 'a war without war', in the paramilitary and political confusion that marked the last days of the Weimar Republic, the Front became their conscience. 'What does conscience call out to the addressee?' asked Heidegger in 1927.

> Strictly speaking – nothing. The call says nothing, gives no information about events in the world.... Nothing is called over to the addressed self, but rather it is called upon itself to be itself, that is to assume its own innermost possibilities.[66]

The political battles of the 1920s allowed many Germans to fight another enemy on another front, the enemy within Germany itself. Only when that war had been resolved, Hitler maintained, could Germany venture out into the wider world to become what its destiny demanded of it.

Many other writers, including Wilhelm Kleinau and Franz Schauwecker, wanted the soldiers to prepare for the next great struggle. In the paramilitary units of the *Freikorps* they saw a semi-professional force which provided military discipline in life. Although the Great War had ended in Germany's defeat Kleinau insisted that defeat would provide the means for winning the next round, provided, of course, that the *Frontsoldaten* could be kept in being.[67]

Jünger himself, however, remained largely detached from the *Frontsoldatenstaat* of which he wrote so enthusiastically. He did not deign to dirty his hands in the political violence of the 1920s, in the street battles in Berlin, the factional skirmishing which so disfigured the political landscape of Weimar Germany. But his writings certainly helped legitimise the rise of Hitler by providing yet another argument for the thesis that Germany's soldiers had not been defeated in battle, but 'stabbed in the back'; that the army had not failed society, but that society had failed the army. Had he not seen for himself, he once asked 'in lethally sparkling mirrors the collapse of an age which was hopelessly lost', even before the Great War had broken out?[68]

Like the trench warfare, the violent clashes on the streets of Germany's cities were largely a war of attrition. No one delivered a knockout blow, not even Hitler who eventually came to power by a constitutional putsch. But the tactical confusion of that warfare, in which energies were uselessly dissipated and politics denied the status of an heroic struggle, prepared Germany for the appearance of a great political figure.[69]

When the Second World War eventually came Jünger was among the first to join up. He had already enrolled as a captain of the *Wehrmacht* in 1938. It is not surprising that he should have won his second Iron Cross in the very first weeks of the fighting. No one ever doubted his bravery.

The difficulty of being alive to the problems of class warfare in Germany itself and the danger of trying to eradicate it was that Jünger had little interest in humanity as such. His totalitarian vision allowed for no loyalty other than to country. In his perfect workers' state values stemming from class, or family or religion were not allowed. Like all totalitarian visions it required war as a condition of its being. As such, it was an apocalyptic vision, a repudiation of life.

Even as a writer he turned his back on what most post-First World War authors such as Hemingway, Faulkner and Eliot had chosen to assert, that the events of the Great War were so horrendous that factual representation was often the artist's only possible response. Finding a meaning for the struggle in words was often best left to government propagandists:

> Few doubted that data had a meaning which transcended the factual ways of representation; most had little faith in the ability of the mind and language to describe transcendence. Many writers did not deny the possibility of the existence of mind and spirit but they refused to contemplate the meaning in words.[70]

Many more, in fact, believed that words might destroy the meaning of events for those who lived through them, that, unless used sparingly, abstract words would, in the end, promote only a 'shallow pose'. The shallowness of Jünger's thought is perhaps its main feature.

We must leave Jünger then with his own thoughts, still dreaming of a soldiers' community made up of men he despised, knowing full well that most Germans had little interest in war for its own sake, and despising them all the more for it. The man who lived for the *Frontsoldatenstaat* remained to the end detached from the soldiers themselves. Perceptive to the last, Goebbels recorded in his diary that in Jünger's dreams of a new Germany the really important thing was missing: any recognition that the task of reconstructing a new world would be carried out not by ideas, but by men.[71]

5

War and the Futility of History

The Great War was the first historical event of significance to confront modern man with a question whose implications were particularly grave: was it any longer possible to see progress in terms of a long historical trajectory, and could progress itself any longer be considered necessarily redeeming? Europe, of course, had known many earlier wars and catastrophes but by comparison even with the Thirty Years' War, the 'killing ground' of the Western Front seemed irredeemable. The carnage was absolute, the madness total. For a few, the catastrophe of trench warfare destroyed all possibility of belief in the future. 'So much energy wasted', commented Virginia Woolf of history, so foolish 'to believe in something so spectral'.

On the Western Front many of the war poets dismissed history as futile. No one was more representative of this point of view than Wilfred Owen who, though not widely known during the war itself, succeeded within a few years of his death in giving the poetry of anti-heroic protest as absolute an expression as the traditional heroic attitude had received in the form of the epic. Owen's poetry with its emphasis on human suffering may be limited in range but it reflects a momentous change in human sensibility: the realisation that traditional concepts of honour and heroism had ceased to be very convincing. Death was portrayed instead on the plane of historic futility.

Like most of the war poets Owen was overwhelmed by the phenomenon of industrialised warfare. The commitment to war was the subject of his poetry. Even with men like Sassoon who lived into the 1960s the best of their work is about the Great War. Their post-war work never gained so much edge or urgency as from the national tragedy that had inspired them. The problem, as Yeats recognised, was that confronted daily by the monstrosity of battle what theme was there available to them other than life in the trenches? More damagingly still, what attitude could they possibly express or attempt to instil in their readers other than outrage? The cruel upshot of this is that there is really nothing surprising about their poetry. They made no attempt to put themselves and the war itself into historical perspective. Seventy years on we know in advance where they are going to take us. In a word, while they may enlarge our perspectives they can never really transform them. History for them really did end in 1914. Henceforth, as we saw in Chapter Two, the future would forever be out of reach, the past always more attractive.

In the course of the 1930s, however, men began to see history as more threatening. W H Auden, revising his poem 'Prologue' in 1936, changed the line 'And called out a tideless peace by loving sun', to 'And out of the future into actual history'. It was a small change but a significant one, capturing the menace of the return of history from which the post-First World War generation had hoped to escape. The presence of the word 'history' was a consequence of the increasing pressure of historical events, 'the increasing volume of off-stage noises' in the late 1930s as the contending armies once again drew up their battle lines.

Several years later another poet of distinction, Ezra Pound, also found there was no escape from history. The *Cantos* are themselves included in the history they describe for they recall the way that Pound read Europe and Europe, in revenge, read Pound. The poem and poet were each other's destiny. Locked in a cage in Pisa for three weeks in 1945 as a fascist sympathiser, Pound found himself gazing through the legs of a prison guard, knowing, at last, that history was framed by power just as the historian was imprisoned in the system that he scrutinised: 'A sinistra la Torre/seen thru a pair of breeches' (*Canto LXXIV*).

In short, finding themselves, in the words of Jean-Paul Sartre, 'abruptly situated' in time they chose to break with Owen's view, to look history squarely in the eye for fear they would be overwhelmed by it. No longer was it possible to find in the futility of history a refuge from an escapable involvement in their own time.

Indeed, the French writer Ferdinand Céline did not expect the future to be any better than the past. As a writer he embraced the poor, the rejected, the socially disenfranchised, out of loathing for the intellectuals among whom he refused to count himself. In his work we find the ultimate *degagé* writer who poured scorn on the idea of fighting for a cause when the cause was so soon lost sight of. He was contemptuous of men who marched off for an idea whose time had already passed, who allowed themselves to be traduced by history, defrauded by their political leaders, betrayed by their own foolish beliefs. He found ridiculous appeals to heroism and patriotism in so profoundly unheroic an age.

Céline believed humanity itself to be on trial in the 20th century. He was far from confident that the ultimate death sentence could be indefinitely postponed. As a writer Céline (like Pound) expressed a mood that was typical of the 1930s – an end of the comforting pre-1914 belief in progress, a fear of the future that was real and therefore all the more intensely envisaged. Both men were driven by a sense of despair derived from their position, not as participants, but observers watchfully witnessing an age gone mad. Both men suspected that the age through which they were living might be the last, that the 20th century might be discontinuous not with the past, but with itself.

UNHAPPY WARRIOR: WILFRED OWEN ON THE WESTERN FRONT

The bloodletting will take the
Best blood

(Alain, *31 July 1914*)

What we know of the Great War we know through memory. Our experience of it is still a collective one. What we remember of the past depends on how it is remembered and how events are remembered depends, in turn, on texts which at any one time give them form. We experience life as we do because the texts we have predispose certain choices of interpretation. In the case of England and the Great War the major texts are poems; what we remember we know, in part, from the testimony of the war poets.

War not only influenced their writing, their writing determined the way in which war was understood by ordinary men trying to make sense of their own lives. To a man, the poets were caught up initially in the fervour of the hour. Almost to a man, if they survived, they did so disillusioned and embittered. The message they communicated was that modern war was meaningless, and contemporary history futile. Perhaps, that was its only meaning; perhaps, its pointlessness was the point.

Of all the English war poets the most celebrated by far is Wilfred Owen. As an autobiographical record his poetry is striking – few war poets are able to engage our sensibilities so compellingly; few are able to reach that depth of compassionate feeling which makes us think of him, rightly or not, as a great poet.

His war was not untypical of that of many other soldiers. He arrived at the Front in January 1917 very much a patriot, unquestioningly loyal, unreflecting about the war's purpose. Within weeks his letters home reveal that he had come to the conclusion that the war was an impersonal molloch, a machine which consumed millions of lives, which robbed death of any glory or nobility, that rendered heroism anachronistic. It was an experience which he insisted that the old men behind the lines, the

general staff officers who never visited the Front, could no more comprehend than the civilian population at home.

His sensitivity to the plight of the common soldier was shown clearly
enough when he returned to the trenches after recuperating from shell-
shock. Before he was sent back he worked as an instructor in the Northern
Cavalry barracks at Scarborough where he felt 'the conflicting roles of
leader and betrayer'. After a day's training, he wrote ironically, 'for
fourteen hours yesterday I was at work – teaching Christ to lift his Cross
by numbers'.[1] His bitterness was caught in his poem *The Send Off*:

> Down the close, darkening lanes they sang their way
> To the siding shed
> And lined the trains with faces grimly gay...
> Shall they return to beatings of great bells
> In wild train loads?
> A few, a few, too few for drums and yells
> May creep back, silent, to village wells
> Up half known roads.

Owen saw himself as betrayer as well as betrayed, an ambiguity which
adds poignancy to his poetry. His poetic achievement was to record the
war in its last, most critical phase in the 15 months between August 1917
and September 1918. Siegfried Sassoon was to write 30 years later that
while other poets had written 'trench sketches' which had illuminated
the darkness like military flares, Owen had made poetry out of horror.[2]
And what his poetry had to tell the generations that came after him was
that war was futile, its suffering meaningless.

Of course, the person we are discussing is not necessarily the true
Wilfred Owen, but Edmund Blunden's version of him. Blunden edited his
poems in 1931, 13 years after Owen's death. His biographical sketch of the
poet, using Owen's own words from letters he had sent from the Front,
helped to create what Owen had never had – 'a poetical character' of his
own.[3] Blunden's Owen is a sensitive, compassionate officer who returns to
the war out of love for his men and is killed ironically a week before the
Armistice. He is neither a hero nor a coward but a sacrifice, a man whose
brief life, as Blunden tells it, is meant to illustrate the futility of modern
war. Whether this is the true man or not it is impossible now to tell. As
Blunden wrote of the fighting he experienced himself near Ypres in 1917
a poet cannot tell a story. There is no story to tell. All he can do is record
the sights, faces and incidents which characterised the time. His poetry
lies in collecting them in their *original* form of incoherence; the poet's
task is not to make sense of it all after the event.

Whether Blunden's Owen is the real man or not, there is no doubt that Owen's message – the futility of war – has lodged in the collective consciousness of the English. Even Paul Fussell's *The Great War and Modern Memory*, a book which gained critical and deserved acclaim at the time of its publication, refuses to understand the Great War as anything other than a meaningless struggle. Fussell even attacks David Jones, the author of the last Great War prose poem, *In Parenthesis* (1937), for failing to show war as a shambles and its participants as 'victims'.[4]

Was this the true meaning of the First World War for those who took part in it? Its meaning can be found on two levels, that of the soldiers fighting waist deep in mud, shell-shocked or maimed, or waiting apprehensively for the order to go over the top in another 'push'. The meaning for the historian is somewhat different, it is 'what the war was about', a war which for many achieved nothing and changed even less, that was fought for questionable aims and by questionable methods. Are either of these graphically painted accounts historically true: can one even hazard that they are *poetically* true either?

In the preface which Owen provided for his projected volume of war verse he wrote 'all a poet can do is warn; that is why the true poets must be truthful'. But did he not violate one of his own canons? For if his poetry is really a truthful account, how could the ordinary soldiers have continued to fight in such conditions? The historian John Terraine, with characteristic bluntness, has argued that if the attitudes of Owen and Sassoon had prevailed throughout the British Army, British morale would have broken.[5] Owen's version of trench warfare was not untrue (in this he kept faith with his own credo), but it was not the *whole* truth. It was a reflection of a particular mood, or frame of mind expressed at a particular time, a time that was not necessarily characteristic of the soldiers with whom Owen served.

We must also ask why morale held in the British Army to the very end when it collapsed so precipitously in the French Army in 1917. The workers were promised a better world after the war, including homes fit for heroes. They were not, as Marc Ferro points out, passive victims who went to the slaughter unsuspectingly. They went to war expecting to improve their lot. They fought as much for themselves as they did for their country, or, put another way, they expected their country to recompense them for their service in due course. Middle-class officers like Owen had no reason to expect that the 'Home Front' would be a better place after the war. By 1917 it was all too clear it would never be the same again. The ordinary soldier, however, had very different expectations, in that he took the rhetoric of the politicians on trust. Many soldiers were willing to die to improve their world, to reject the 'shared past' that the poets diffidently held out to them. For them the Home Front was the *real* front, and the battlefield the future.[6]

Even those who returned to find the land for which they had fought was not fit for heroes nevertheless felt they had achieved something by their endeavours. For every poem denouncing the war as futile we can find a personal account, a letter, a journal entry, a personal affidavit denying, even decrying what one contemporary author in 1929 dismissed as 'the legend of disenchantment' that had arisen about the trenches.[7] Not all men returned to England in profound despair. One soldier wrote that the poets in 'piling corpse upon corpse', in 'heaping horror on futility' had produced so distorted a view of life in the trenches that he had looked in vain for scenes that he could remember.[8]

For every poet who as an officer lamented the stubborn inertia of his men there were officers who thought their men 'marvellous in their cheerfulness and the fewness (*sic*) of their wants'. Edward Thompson, who served as a padre with the 2nd Leicester wrote of men who had not furnished novelists with their officer heroes or poets with their caricatures. Far from being unhappy, sullen, even 'mute beasts' he recalled an extraordinary camaraderie among the men the poets had 'dishonoured'.[9]

In recent years, indeed, a number of military historians have attacked the war poets for distorting our collective memory of the conflict. Tony Ashworth quotes an officer from the 63rd Division who was fiercely critical of the 'disenchanted' authors for describing trench warfare as 'unremitting violent struggle'.[10] In exaggerating the presence of death they had made far too little of the boredom and inertia which were the soldiers' greatest enemy. Most poets were removed from the existence of their fellow soldiers or had little understanding of the lives they had led before the war. Blunden had been redefining his pastoral diction at the outset of 1914. David Jones had studied illustration at Camberwell; Wilfred Owen had taught English to boys of a French family near Bordeaux. In that sense their use of pastoral poetry, which later generations found so moving, was, in the main, meaningless to the soldiers with whom they served.

Of all the major poets Sassoon, in particular, should have known better. His first posting, after all, had been to a training camp on the outskirts of Liverpool where he would have seen at first hand how squalid were the industrial slums of the north. Instead, he found the eternal good humour of the troops surprising given the 'drudgery and discomfort' of army life.[11] Why should they have protested? For many the camaraderie of their fellow soldiers, the excellent rations they were given, even the excitement of war were not to be despised however much they might complain about another aspect of war – dying.[12]

By implying that the life of the ordinary soldier in peacetime was idyllic, the poets naturally made war hell by comparison. In fact, they were desperately out of touch with the condition of modern Britain. They needed but never attained a broader view than that afforded by their own privileged and secluded vantage point.

One million British volunteers and conscripts had to be rejected by the War Board because they were found medically unfit to serve. A grim picture was painted by C E Montagu of those who did pass muster, battalions of colourless, stunted, half-toothless lads from hot, humid Lancashire mills; their staring faces 'gargoyles out of the tragical-comical-historical pastoral edifice of English rural life.'[13] In a letter home another officer wrote that the transformation of new recruits in six months from stooped, wan, weak men to strong, well fed, clear-eyed soldiers would have made him a socialist when he saw what industrialism had done to them had he not considered war too high a price for physical fitness.[14]

Was not Owen's main complaint less the reality of death in battle than the experience of industrialised warfare? What he experienced in 1917–18 was mechanical warfare at its most relentless. No wonder he was overwhelmed by a sense of futility. And futile it remained for the poets who survived, who remained as implacably opposed to industrial England as they had been in 1914. When Blunden came to write *Undertones of War* he described himself as 'a harmless young shepherd in soldier's coat'.[15] Robert Graves took his protest one stage further. He retired to a mountain village in Majorca where he hoped to escape what he aloofly called 'the more shocking sights and sounds of pluto-democratic civilisation'.[16] The soldiers who returned to Manchester or Leeds were not so lucky.

As one ex-veteran wrote in the 1930s, the poets were also to be faulted for being so dispassionate about the war.[17] Nowhere were they more dispassionate than glossing over their own experiences. Rarely did they tell of the heroic deeds for which they themselves were responsible. As a creative artist Owen spoke eloquently of war's 'super human inhuman-ities, long famous glories, immemorial shame'. But as a soldier he engaged in those inhumanities enthusiastically enough. Owen's war, writes Andrew Rutherford, was not 'poetic'. His fellow soldiers saw in him a soldier who would kill with the rest, who was willing to fight to the end, who did not even question the morality of the war, only the incompetence of its execution.[18]

Owen's fear of losing face indeed required him to take risks that were not taken by the men under him. He welcomed his return to the Front in 1918 because of the 'ignominy' he felt in being shell-shocked on his first tour. He did not have Sassoon's self-confidence to turn conscientious objector. And even Sassoon returned to the Front in the end. What, asks Rutherford, was this if not tacit acceptance of the value of war even while disapproving of the value of the particular war being fought?

One discovers little of this in Owen's poetry. But then like Blunden, Graves and Sassoon, Owen subscribed to two conflicting ethics: one based on courage, the other on compassion. The former predominated in his life, the latter in his poetry, so that the claims of duty coexisted with those of dissent.[19] What his poetry represents is not his total experience of the war but a highly selective one, an edited, expurgated version of his own response to the challenge of battle. The essential difference between the war experienced by the poets and that experienced by the rank and file was that its 'truth' for each differed significantly. Truth for the soldier meant reality, his own, one that was necessarily subjective, of course, but recognisable to his fellow men-at-arms. The truth for the poets, claims Maurice Genevoix (himself a war writer) was 'not *their* truth but *the* truth', a truth that was as real for the next generation as his own, a truth that would eventually become part of modern memory.[20]

Owen invoked Keats in a variety of ways to help him define his own response to the struggle, but Keats's 'poetical character' was part of his dilemma. Keats argued that the poetic character is made up of light and shade; that it lives in 'gusto', that it exaggerates, indeed that it must do so if it is to have any character at all. 'What shocks the virtuous philosopher delights the chameleon poet' Keats observed.[21] The poet is Pascal's 'poet but not an honest man', forever writing poems, an expression of a despair greater than his own.

For Owen this meant exaggerating the pain and suffering of war, in order to contrast it with the apparent non-suffering of peace. From reading his poetry we would never guess that men such as Graham Greenwell could see the war as a 'great adventure' which, if for no other reason, invested the experience with meaning.[22] Battalions such as the Second Battalion of the Royal Welsh Fusiliers earned a reputation for aggressive trench warfare, for conducting raids into No Man's Land in order to combat the tedium of trench life. If Owen was a much better soldier than his poetry reveals so too was one of the Royal Welsh's best, Siegfried Sassoon. Yet one would never know from his own account of his career at the Front that he: 'spent a large part of his nocturnal watches crawling through the deep corn in No Man's Land with a couple of bombs in his pocket and a knobkerrie in his hand.[23] The dilemma, however, of writing poetry in time of war was more complex than simply the distortion of poetic character on the small canvas of the battlefield as opposed to the larger canvas of life. Since the war poets refused to give meaning to the suffering they described, they were unable to relate it to history. 'Of pity, grief and sorrow there is much in their poetry', writes Johnston 'but these emotions do not attain to the tragic'. The war poet, he argues:

> functions as conscience, as sensibility and as the voice of anger or pain, but he seldom rises above these functions and the aspects of ugliness or suffering upon which they are based. Enveloped in the tragedy of war he sees only magnified particulars and details – no event becomes 'luminous' in his mind.[24]

Instead the war poets robbed the dead of their dignity and death of its significance. Their poems lack an objective sense of restraint, certainly of self-proportion. And as poets they compounded these faults because the range of their experience was so narrow, because what they saw, horrific as it was, inspired them to write in a mood of understandable anger, without restraint, without inhibition.

It has often been said that, with the exception of Isaac Rosenberg, the war poets were of the second rank, not because of a failure of technique or of imagination, but because their experience was too narrow. But they can also be blamed for failing to rise above the genre of war poetry, by universalising the suffering. To have done so, of course, would have meant locating that suffering in a moral universe, to have invested it with meaning. And this the poets were not prepared to do. What they were prepared to undertake was to tell a story of futility. One of the few exceptions, David Jones, criticised his fellow poets for refusing to make 'significant for the present what the past holds'. To use his own term, none tried to 'transubstantiate' their material – to give point to the myth of war by explaining it to a future generation.[25] Owen refused to explain it at all on the grounds that the whole experience was inexplicable. Many found the experience endurable at all only on the understanding it would never be repeated, in other words, that it was historically unique, or more correctly ahistorical.

One of the most striking aspects of Owen's poetry is, in fact, how 'empty of historical sense' most of his poems are, how totally lacking in causes and consequences as though – argues one critic – 'No Man's Land existed in time as well as space separating these dreadful events from all other human experience'. In Owen's poetry the futility of war predominates so much that history is not part of the reality. The war is not a political conflict but a blood sacrifice. The soldiers have no independent identity. It matters not a jot whether they are English or German.

Perhaps, one of the reasons for denying the war historical meaning was that their poetry suffered from the limitations of its own technique. Many had difficulty coming to terms with history because the traditional poetic ways of dealing with historical experience, the epic and the heroic drama – were quite inadequate to capture an event on the scale of the Great War. One solution was to make war unhistorical. Another was to employ a poetic conceit that was already out of date. As pastoralists they remained stubbornly attached to a tradition of English poetry that had died some time before the Great War began.

Owen's poetic style was desperately old-fashioned. As Leavis said of Blunden's *Undertones of War* (1932) he was able to remain conservative in technique because of his attachment to a rural order which, if unreal for his reader, was real enough for the poet. The war poets have always been more honoured in their own country than they have abroad, where what they said, about the experience of war, if it struck a note at all, struck a false one. Wyndham Lewis recognised this early on when he wrote that the English had been left adrift at the beginning of the century by the artistic movements that had seized the continental imagination. The avant-garde poets on the continent, wrote Lewis, were 'the first men of a future that [had] not yet materialised'.[26] By contrast, Owen's generation could be said to represent the last men of a past with which the present had not yet come to terms. In a comment unusual for an English artist, Lewis correctly grasped the point that 'all that matters is so far ahead that it is beyond the sphere of these disturbances'. Continental poetry was hardly touched by the Great War.[27]

As Jacques Darras, one of the few continental authorities on the English war poets has written, the French poets were not 'overwhelmed' by the Great War. In France the war never became a literary event. The French, too, lost their artists: Péguy, Rivière, Fournier, Gaudier-Brzeska, but when the war came, in aesthetic terms, at least, it was considered to be a super-numerary event after the real upheaval had taken place – the Cubism of Picasso and Braque, the freeing of colour from line by Matisse and Kandinsky, the anarchy of the Dadaists in Zürich who took poetry in directions that Owen and his fellow English poets could not possibly comprehend. Modernism, so dominant in France, left the English largely untouched.

Darras is quite uncompromising. Owen, he believes, was as much a martyr to anti-modernism as he was a martyr to the war. His message was buried when T S Eliot wrote *The Wasteland* (1920): '"The poetry is in the pity" exclaimed Owen but cannot one detect in Owen and others a plea to the reader, not only sympathy for the plight as warriors but also pity for the inevitable inadequacies of the poetry itself?'[28]

Darras may be right about Owen, but is he right about Eliot? Did *The Wasteland* 'bury' the war poets? Clearly, in its structural form there can be no argument, but what of its first principles? Eliot, after all, insisted that his poem was based on the 'mythic' method, a way of controlling and ordering, of giving shape and significance to the immense panorama of what, in a vivid phrase, he called 'the futility of contemporary history'.[29]

Eliot and the poets of the immediate post-war generation wrote in order to make sense of the futility they saw around them. They did so self-consciously. If, as they suspected, the emotional appeal of words such as 'honour', 'courage' and 'patriotism' had led to war surely they had a duty to use words that would prevent another such conflict from ever again breaking out. The words they employed were deliberately intended to create what one contemporary writer called 'a sense of desolation, of uncertainty, of futility, of the groundlessness of aspirations, of the vanity of endeavour'.[30]

In that sense Eliot agreed with Owen that poetry could not make sense of war, or certainly the industrialised form it had taken after 1916. Both rejected history because it could not make eternally present the period in which so many soldiers had lived and died. The futility of history for so many veterans who returned from the war was represented by their inability to communicate their experiences to those back at home – in that sense the war was seen as a historical *caesura*, almost a non-event, an abstraction – in that sense it was ahistorical.

It was a view expressed, perhaps, most forcefully by one of the German survivors of the battle of Verdun who wrote years later of a quite exceptional bond that had linked the combatants on both sides. It was not the normal sensation of affinity, binding together men who had endured a common hardship. It was the affinity of soldiers whose souls had been transformed by battle. Whoever had passed through the hell of Verdun had crossed the last frontier of life, whoever had fought in the battle carried deep within them for the rest of their lives 'the leaden memory of a place that lies between life and death, or perhaps beyond either'.[31]

The soldiers who returned home from the Great War to pick up the fragments of their own lives were haunted by a truth that they could not communicate. It was a terrible truth that might have been exorcised or transcended through the act of retelling, but how did they communicate their anguish to a society that had little conception of what they had gone through? Often the survivors of catastrophes find the lack of interest or indifference of their friends far more painful to bear than the actual experiences. Frequently such experiences differ so much from the norm that they cannot provide points of reference for those back home, those beyond the range of the contending armies.

As the poet Robert Graves wrote at the time, the British infantrymen came back from the Front with 'new meanings of courage, patience, loyalty and greatness of spirit' quite different from those on the lips of the politicians. The meaning, alas, was 'incommunicable we found to later times'.[32] Graves himself felt so estranged from his own country that he withdrew to Majorca. Most of his fellow soldiers, like the hero of Philip Roth's novel *Flight without End* (1927), returned to find a world in which a homecoming was no longer possible. They brought with them their own estrangement.

When they wrote of their experiences at all they wrote largely for themselves, creating in the process 'a literature of separation'.[33] In the act of remembering they lost contact with the next generation. Richard Aldington talked about the 'self prisons' into which the veterans increasingly withdrew.[34] Graves referred to his fellow soldiers as 'cage mates'.[35] Another writer talked about 'the mental internment camps' in which most of the survivors found refuge.[36]

Céline wanted the poets of both world wars to bring order into the chaos of war. What could be more natural than that they should wish to create an order out of their own lives through the very act of writing it down? Frequently, however, they were reduced to silence, denied the catharsis of communicating their grief. Avitik Isahakian, Armenia's greatest symbolist poet, wrote in February 1916, at the height of the Armenian massacres, that there were no words in the dictionaries to describe the hideousness of the times – 'not a single poet can find words'.[37] The soldiers returned too from the Western Front to a world that would not have understood their words even if they had been forthcoming. In that sense history was indeed futile; in that sense they felt like exiles in an unfamiliar country, forced to live two lives, unable to resolve the contradictions between them. Their silence arose, not from a detachment from the events which they had experienced at first hand, but the sense of total division between war and peace.

Perhaps the main reason that so many First World War veterans renounced history altogether was their belief that only they could remember the war as it had happened precisely, as it had been *subjectively* experienced at the time. R H Mottram was one ex-soldier who lamented that 'his war', the war of those now growing middle-aged, had been turned into something 'fabulous, misunderstood and made romantic by distance'.[38] The distance of which he spoke was temporal, not geographical. The veterans lived in an eternal present. As Joseph Wehner wrote in his

book *Seven Before Verdun,* 'we went over the top into timelessness',[39] into
a void, a world without a future.

The next generation in contrast tried to repossess the past by making
sense of the war from their own perspective. In *Tender is the Night* Dick
Diver visits the battlefield of the Somme, equipped with all the 'sentimental equipment' necessary to honour the dead, not dishonour their
memory. When a member of his party argues that General Grant had
invented attrition warfare, the deliberate piecemeal destruction of the
enemy, Dick with his knowledge of history is able to object:

> No he didn't – he just invented mass butchery. This kind of battle was invented
> by Lewis Carroll and Jules Verne and whoever wrote *Udine,* and country deacons
> … and girls seduced in the back lanes of Wurtenburg and Westphalia. Why, this
> was a love battle – there was a century of middle class love spirit here.[40]

Dick's argument is that an overwhelming sense of obligation, honour
and duty for love of country had poured out against the machine-guns,
sustaining the soldiers to the end, even when they were mired in the mud,
or impaled on the wire, or blown to pieces by the guns.

Dick is able to commune with the past, to see in a little stream that it
took the British a month to cross 'a whole empire walking very slowly,
dying in front and pushing forward behind'. As he is the first to
acknowledge, a knowledge of history is essential if one is to remember it
accurately. Without a knowledge of 'Christmas postcards of the Crown
Prince and little cafés in Valence and beer gardens in the Unten den
Linden', how can one make sense of 1914? We read history, after all, to
render the past present, our present of course, not that of the soldiers who
served in the trenches.

Wehner was wrong to argue that the only reality is the timelessness of
a present which has now passed. Doesn't the next generation know the
past better than those who live through it? Do we not – in Eliot's words –
sense 'the past in a way and to an extent which the past's awareness of
itself cannot show'?[41]

If our capacity to understand history is deficient in many respects,
surely it is not in this one – standing outside it we can view the
consequences of a battle, or put it into its historical context. We can even
appreciate a campaign as far less significant than men thought at the
time. We can see it as one more battle that prefigured the next.

Can the past, in fact, ever be as accessible as 'the present' to those who
live through it? What Wehner meant by 'timelessness' was the soldier's
ability to remember what the past meant to him, outside and beyond the
collective memory, of what it means today to the world at large. Instru-

mental memory lacks involvement; personal memory does not. Eugene Minkowsky, who treated many First World War combatants and wrote at length about their psychopathology in the 1930s, found that their wartime recollections exemplified this distinction: 'Completely different attitudes towards the past are involved when we recount what we did during the war, when we try to relive what we experienced during that torment and finally what we feel is still present in the very fibres of our being, when we feel it thus become a part of our present even more than the *actual* present'.[42] As he went on to argue, 'even when we are conscious of participating in a great historical event ... we feel clearly that this event, as it will be inscribed in history, will be only a part of what it has been for us in the present'.[43] The soldier's timelessness, by comparison, is a 'present' that is outside history, it is his version of the truth, his way of making sense of his own life.

Our perspective is bound to be dictated by what we need from the past, in terms, for example, of what we require for our continued identity, whatever helps us make sense of our own world. Continuity depends wholly on memory. Recalling past experiences through the written or visual texts of history is vital in linking us with our earlier selves. All memory transmutes experience and distils the past rather than simply reflects it. We recall what we need to do – in that sense history is deeply hurtful to the survivors, for what we wish to view today determines what we may need to verify tomorrow. Memory sifts again when perception has shifted leaving us only fragments of what was initially on view.

Even when we rebuild what has been destroyed, when we reconstruct the past, we do so for the future, not to honour what was once someone else's present. In 1944 the Germans sacked the old city of Warsaw to destroy the will of its citizens, to break down their resistance. After the war the Poles rebuilt it exactly as it had been – 'it was our duty to resuscitate it', explained one of the architects responsible for the operation. 'We did not want a new city – we wanted the Warsaw ... of our future to continue the ancient tradition'.[44] The Warsaw of the uprising we know today is completely man-made, built to remind us of the past, built in that sense for the visitor, not those who survived the uprising.

If all historical memory is necessarily fragmentary, it has a unity of a kind, the unity we *impose* on it. Do not the massed identical crosses of First World War graves at Thiepval recall, not the courage of the individual soldiers who died, but the lesson of the general carnage? Are not war graves no longer repositories of the dead, but fields of remembrance for the living? When we visit the death camps, do we not subconsciously celebrate our own delivery?

Are we not, writes Adorno, all survivors of Auschwitz? It is surely our survival that makes sense of the Final Solution. It is our survival that we celebrate when remembering their sacrifice. All that is really important is that we should continue to visit the battlefields of the 20th century, that the Somme and Dachau should both be on our itinerary. For, in the end, the meaning of the 20th century as a 'theatre of atrocity' is the one we care to give it, of what we choose to bear witness to. If the First World War poets did not understand this, those who fought in the next war certainly did. By 1940, history had been rediscovered with a vengeance. That a new war might soon break out, sooner perhaps than imagined, Owen's generation had no doubt, even before the guns were silenced. Osbert Sitwell, writing in the month of the Armistice, had a presentiment that they would soon be asked to fight again:

It seems to me
That the cause for which we fought
Is again endangered.
What more fitting memorial for the fallen
Than that their children
Should fall for the same cause?

('The Next War')

When the next war came the poets of the period rallied to the cause readily enough. The case of T S Eliot is particularly interesting. Despite renouncing history in the 1920s, he found Britain's struggle in 1940 to have a historical meaning quite unique to his own predicament, that of an exile separated by three centuries from his ancestors who had left England for the New World. Eliot himself had fled from the United States, a society that seemed meaningless, to a country which provided meaning of a kind. During the war he clung to the few consolations of the English tradition. In *The Four Quartets* he wrote 'history is now and England' without a trace of self-doubt. For a moment, he became one of the voices of England's historical destiny in this, the last great moment in the English story.

The discovery of meaning, in fact, is what distinguishes the poets of the Second World War from those of the First. It was said of Sidney Keyes, a promising young writer who died while on patrol in North Africa in 1943, that of all poets he went further than anyone else in realising that mankind was once again at war because it was not yet ready for peace.[45] 'Where are the war poets?', asked *The Times Literary Supplement* in 1940. C Day Lewis provided an answer in a poem by the same title when he wrote 'they were defending the bad against the worst'.[46]

The poets of 1940 did not see the war as another futile encounter. Instead, they deliberately set out to locate it in history. They did not see the soldiers on their own side as victims. Nor did they think of the enemy as particularly villainous. They portrayed the soldiers on both sides as just that, men with a task to complete. The South African poet F T Prince, watching a group of soldiers bathing in a stream, was reminded of Michelangelo's picture of mercenaries being called away from their innocent ablutions to kill or be killed, of Paullaiuolo's 'brothers – naked warriors, hacking each other to death'. He did not see them as innocents led uncomplainingly to the slaughter.

Of course, the two world wars were very different. Of course, the poets of 1940 were more chastened, much wiser men. Of course, the Spanish Civil War had intervened, a conflict in which many had found their voice against fascism. Of course, the shock of war itself was no longer so immediate, or overwhelming. They came prepared for the worst and considered themselves fortunate largely to be spared it. In the Western Desert they escaped the carnage of the Eastern Front. The worst they saw with their own eyes was Belsen and the ruins of cities devastated by Allied bombing.

The acceptance of the task in hand created an empty space in which there was nothing to say, a space which produced – whenever there was – understatement. One can almost gauge, argues Paul Fussell, the merit or staying power of a Second World War poem by its very brevity.[47] But then the poetry of the Second World War was not intended to speak to the future. Its intensity was in its immediacy.

Keith Douglas, perhaps the greatest of the British war poets, who died in Normandy within days of the D-Day landing, wrote in a style of rapportage and documentary. To be sentimental or emotional about the war, he wrote to a friend, would be dangerous to oneself and to everyone else. His own style was deliberately spare. His intention was to communicate *a* truth about war, not *the* truth:

> To trust anyone or to admit any hope of a better world is criminally foolish, as foolish as it is to stop working for it. It sounds silly to work without hope but it can be done; it is only a form of insurance. It doesn't mean to work hopelessly.[48]

The poets of the Second World War lived for the present, not the future, and wrote accordingly. In the end, however, they rediscovered history and their own role in it. Unlike their predecessors in 1914 they did not lose contact with the past. As a result, they were not overwhelmed by the war when it came. To be sure, the fight against fascism made them responsive to history in a way that might not have been the case in any other war. But what really marked the change was something more profound: their acceptance that war had a meaning, a meaning which hastened the transformation of the lyrical poet into a historically responsive man.

W H AUDEN AND THE EXPLODING POETS:
THE ENGLISH AND THE SPANISH CIVIL WAR

We walked along the trenches.... 'We make a point of not allowing our front line visitors to be killed' said Nathan.... He told me to stoop because I was tall.... The Indian writer who was very short, took the order to apply to himself and stooped also.... Suddenly the Indian looked round from his bent posture and turned his face up to mine: 'I can see death's great question mark hovering between the trenches!', he said in a hoarse whisper. That was the only occasion in my life in which a lapse from dialectical materialism has irritated me.

(Stephen Spender, *World Within World*)

'When the fighting broke out on 18 July', Orwell later wrote of the Spanish Civil War, 'it is probable that every anti-fascist in Europe felt the thrill of hope'.[49] For those who joined up to fight for the Republican cause the struggle was intensely personal; it aroused a genuine fear that all that was of most value in the world was in danger of being lost; that this was a cause for which it was really worth fighting. 'You know how I feel about the whole mad business of war' the communist poet Christopher Caudwell wrote to a friend, 'but you also know how I feel about the importance of democratic freedom'.[50]

Interesting causes as such had not been uppermost in people's minds at the end of the Great War. Indeed, no one had been much interested in history. After spending a few weeks in the trenches Ford Madox Ford had turned his back on history altogether. Before the war, he wrote, if he had any interest, it had been that of a historian, basing his morality on everything that had gone before. 'But now it seems to me we have no method of approach to any of these problems'.[51] It was not so much that men distrusted the future as they no longer felt able to stand by what they had said about the past. History had played false. It had proved treacherous, even deceiving. Henry James had written to a friend shortly before his death that reality had betrayed them. 'Reality is a world that was to be capable of *this* – and how represent that horrific capability, historically latent, historically ahead of it?'[52]

It was precisely because history was latent that the Civil War poets were so self-conscious of their own actions. As Sartre was to write, from

January 1930 and the first significant appearance of the Nazis on the streets of the Weimar Republic, 20th century man came to recognise that he was at risk from the forces of history; that history was not futile, but dangerous. 'All at once' added Sartre 'we felt ourselves abruptly situated'.[53] It is a telling phrase. Perhaps, no other generation this century was so conscious of the fact that history was being made; that if history was to be survived it would have to be consciously forged. It was essential that the Great War itself should not enter the historical memory as a high point in a long descent into night.

From the standpoint of the Left André Malraux also noted that his generation, unlike that of the 1920s, was defined by its 'relationship with History'. Each citizen had to confront historical reality, not flee from it.[54] Sartre went on to conclude that the Spanish Civil War was the moment that history finally forced itself into modern consciousness. As the writer Jean-Pierre Maxence wrote on the eve of Hitler's war, 'modern man was stalked by history'; events now sought him out. There was no escape, no bolt-hole, no comforting (or perhaps not so comforting) consolation of the futility of history – history was to be confronted on its own ground in order that the future could be made on mankind's terms.[55]

For the English poets, in this respect, the war was an unexpected piece of luck. In the first book of war poems he edited in 1939 Stephen Spender, quoting Auden, wrote that the poets had 'exploded like bombs'. This was certainly the case. They exploded in energy, precisely because they found the struggle so inspiring. In a world in which the fight against fascism was lacklustre at best, in which the Western democracies seemed willing to compromise their own first principles, the Spanish Civil War came at the right moment. In a world in which they were accustomed to moral ambiguity the issues appeared to be relatively clear-cut.

Action itself seemed to be a kind of poetry to those who joined up, who chose to take part rather than remain on the sidelines. The poetry which emerged from the war was a hastily produced set of transcriptions of an experience expressed not in words but deeds.

'All a poet can do is to warn', concluded Wilfred Owen rather despondently in 1918. That was nearly always true of poetry written in the midst of a great social upheaval. But the poets who joined the International Brigade believed they could do more than warn; they could defend what was right against a force more deadly than German militarism. What they were fighting against was not even fascism but what they took to be the onset of a new barbarism, the triumph of a set of values almost entirely antithetical to their own.

The cause for which they fought in Spain offered them hope of redemption. Cyril Connolly on his first visit to the Front in 1936 told the readers of the *New Statesman* that he had found 'an absolutely new and all pervading sense of moral elevation' amongst the Republican soldiers, a marvellous 'flowering of humanity, something which it would be an unimaginable piece of human malignancy to destroy'.[56]

In Connolly we find a soft-headed democrat desperately anxious to find a democracy worth defending, a country with a future, a society that after three hundred years of slumber looked ready to re-emerge on the European scene, not a country like Britain, ageing, apparently sclerotic, on the point of dying, but 'in such a damned dull way, going stiffly and comatose instead of collapsing beautifully like France'.[57] Perhaps, it counted for something that Spain was not England in 1936. It counted for more that no one could accuse the volunteers of the International Brigade of being 'patriotic'.

Those who joined up did so for a cause. Many communists did so with alacrity. John Cornford, the youngest of the poets, who was to die on the day after his twenty-first birthday, reached the Front within a month of the war breaking out. Christopher Caudwell left for Spain in December 1936; Ralph Fox, the critic, and John Sommerfield, the novelist, left almost simultaneously. Fox and Caudwell were killed within a month of each other; Sommerfield survived. The first English casualty of the war, killed in an attack on an ammunitions train in August, was another Marxist, the sculptress Felicia Browne, who refused to leave for Britain at the outset of hostilities. She joined a militia unit instead.

Marxists, at least, knew the cause for which they were fighting; they went to their deaths unbowed and unapologetic. In an excellent critique of Cornford's poem 'Full Moon at Tiers', Samuel Hynes notes that Cornford locates the war in the intersection of the past and future where men are free to act and for once able to create their own history. As a communist Cornford succeeded in finding relevance to his continuing commitment even at the cost of his own life by turning the war into a Marxist parable of history in which events drew their meaning from the frame of 'historical necessity'. The certainty that had been lost in the Great War was restored in Spain, however uncertain the final outcome, however unpredictable the result.[58]

But what of those writers who were not Marxists? What inspired them to join up? In deciding to go to Spain in December 1936, Auden wrote to a friend that he did not believe that poetry needed to be or even should be directly political, but in the critical period in which they both lived the poet must have direct knowledge of political events. Academic knowledge was not enough. What the poet knows, or writes about, must be experienced during his lifetime. 'I shall probably be a bloody bad soldier', Auden added, 'but how can I speak to/for them without becoming one?'[59]

Auden eventually went to Spain not as a soldier but as a putative ambulance driver. In the event, he was refused permission to drive an ambulance by the Republican Government which wanted him to write propaganda for the cause instead. All his best endeavours to become a soldier were thwarted. His brief stay in Spain was marked by a series of setbacks, almost comic in scope. When he hired a mule and announced his intention of riding through Spain from Valencia to the Front, he only progressed six miles before it kicked him so badly that he was forced to abandon his plan. One has to conclude that some poets play-acted, in attempting to find a relevance to their lives that they could not find at home.[60]

In some cases they quite literally acted a part. One contemporary reviewer said of Sommerfield's book, *Volunteer in Spain*, that it seemed to be quite common in the Spanish Civil War for writers to behave as if they were characters in a forthcoming Spanish novel by Ernest Hemingway.[61] Writing about the defence of Madrid Esmond Romilly (a nephew of Churchill) claimed he could never really believe he was 'engaged' at any time in the conflict. 'We were only play-acting as soldiers, we were only amateurs.'[62] Those who like Romilly were 'privileged by birth',[63] that is, fortunate enough not to be born Spanish, could afford to return home whenever they wished. Many were invalided out to England towards the end. Many more didn't even wait for the excuse. Some of the poets, though seemingly committed, were simply not committed enough.

The problem with fighting a war in which the larger issue of the battle against fascism in northern Europe was likely to remain unresolved was a nagging feeling of irrelevance. What did it really matter if Spanish democracy collapsed? What was the point of dying in a Mediterranean backwater? The more self-conscious they became about their own role the more they saw themselves as outsiders, foreign to the conflict, uncommitted 'by birth', perhaps ideologically not responsive enough, unable, in the final analysis, to write themselves into history as could Cornford and his Marxist friends.

'There was something frightening, something shocking' Romilly concluded, thinking of the friends he had lost in the defence of Madrid, 'about the way the world does not stop because these men are dead'.[64] Who were the fallen, after all, the defeated, wrote Auden, of whom history might say 'alas, but cannot help nor pardon'? By 1938 history was invoked mostly by Marxists, a version of history to be sure but one which enabled them to keep faith, to play their hand well even if their optimism was never entirely convincing.

By 1939 many of the poets had begun to appreciate that it was not their war, that war itself was too hideous for causes. They were not combatants in the way that Owen and Sassoon, Blunden and Graves had been on the Western Front. When they were disillusioned by what they found they were able to book the first passage home. They were essentially 'scribblers' whose writing was immediately published, journalists who offered the Republican cause the best weapon, the chance to put its case.

The Spanish poets, Lorca and Raphael Alberti among them, were fighting for something much more than just democracy; they were fighting for civilisation itself against a new barbarism, against a political creed which took the lives of poets *as poets*, not only for being 'committed' men. As Salvador Dali records, Lorca knew he would probably not survive the struggle. With a macabre fascination for death he used to practise his own funeral in dress rehearsal with his friends.[65]

The more the English also saw of the war the more they were appalled by its atrocities. The Spanish Civil War was one of the most savage in European history. When the Prado museum exhibited some of its paintings in Geneva in 1939 the absence of Goya's depiction of the executions of 3 May 1808 was interpreted by many as an unwillingness on the part of the authorities to show anything that might conjure up an even bloodier, more recent struggle. Even Franco's friends like Bernanos deserted him because they were shocked by the brutality of the side they had originally supported. In self-exile in Majorca in 1937 Bernanos was horrified that 15 members of the 'fifth column' were executed a day. The bombing of cities like Guernica was one outrage too many, the final atrocity, one that so shocked Auden that he left Spain convinced that the threat of aerial bombing made it necessary to repudiate war altogether. With Isherwood he left for the United States in 1939 to escape a world war which everyone knew was coming even sooner than most governments were willing to admit.

During the bombing of Madrid, Saint-Exupéry had a presentiment of what was to come. Madrid, with its chimney-pots and towers, like portholes, resembled a ship at sea loaded with refugees ferrying from one shore of life to the other. An entire generation appeared to be on board. Yet the vessel loaded down by humanity was being torpedoed, bombed day and night, as if the purpose of the enemy was to sink Madrid, to see it slip under the waves.[66]

Not all the poets took Auden's line, not everyone despaired of the war, or discovered late in the day that war itself is in no way redeeming. Those who fought on to the end saw Spain as a dress rehearsal for the real performance, reassuring themselves that in putting up a fight against fascism for the first time, they had steeled themselves for the next battle. In the end the poets knew that they could only materially affect the struggle not by fighting but by bearing witness to what had passed.

Indeed, the Civil War, as a war recorded for a readership at home, gained a reality in England that it did not have in Spain. The Civil War for the English became the poet's war, a symbol of free action and a stimulus to free thought. The battles were turned into a text by writers using themes and metaphors which meant something to a largely English audience, not to a readership in Spain. The Civil War was experienced on a very different level. As Louis MacNeice wrote at the time 'our spirit found its frontier on the Spanish Front'.[67]

But to what did the poets really bear testimony? To the struggle for democracy, bravely if forlornly fought; to an intimation of an even greater struggle to come in the 'redemptive power of a cause' as opposed to a country?

By the end of the struggle Cyril Connolly had come to the conclusion that most of the poets had little idea of the cause they supported. He found that their poetry showed a poverty of diction, an absence of distinction, a use of clichés that were journalistic commonplaces in the 1930s. He complained that the poets had traded in slogans rather than ideas.[68]

The worst example possibly was one of the better poems to emerge from the war. In Auden's *Spain* (1937) two ideas stand out, one of conscious acceptance of guilt in what Auden calls the 'necessary murder'. The other that history has nothing to offer 'the defeated'.

Orwell later attacked the phrase 'necessary murder' as the phrase not of a poet but a belligerent 'party man'. In the December 1938 issue of *The Adelphi* he wrote that it was easy for Auden to write about the concept of 'necessary murder' because he had never committed one, and possibly had never even seen a corpse. When Auden himself later revised the poem for publication in *Another Time* (1940) he omitted three stanzas, amending the offending line to 'the conscious acceptance of guilt in the fact of murder'. He did so not because of Orwell's criticism but because, in the words of Edward Mendelson, 'he could no longer see the movement of history as a simple struggle between rising and dying forces'.[69] Nor could he any longer equate goodness with success. It was a very 20th century ideological position, success in war being a way of judging the morality of an action, moral action itself being determined by historical necessity. Hynes calls *Spain* a pitiless poem, the poetry lying in the pitilessness not the pity. Auden's revisions, notwithstanding, his poem even today does not deny that.[70]

Is this what the modern age learned from the Spanish Civil War? Was that its meaning? It was certainly part of its meaning. As early as his third visit to Spain in January 1937 Connolly's perception had changed. Now he informed his *New Statesman* readers 'it would be hard to find an atmosphere more full of envy, intrigue, rumour and muddle than that which exists at the moment in the capitals of Republican Spain'.[71]

Auden and Isherwood turned their back on Spain, on Europe, on the fight against fascism. They arrived in New York the day that the Spanish Republic finally fell in 1939. Isherwood's own description of their feelings during the voyage reveals their disillusionment with causes and crusades. As the Thirties ended, so too did false belief in the Cause:

> One morning when they were walking on the deck Christopher heard himself say 'You know it just doesn't mean anything to me any more – the Popular Front, the party line, the anti-fascist struggle ... I simply cannot swallow another mouthful'. To which Wystan answered 'Neither can I.'[72]

They fled to the New World not only to repudiate the Old; they did not believe in the 'old country' either. Orwell did. Orwell left Catalonia in 1938 thoroughly disgusted with the Republicans, particularly their communist supporters. Dying for a cause, a people's democracy, seemed no better than dying for a country. He had tried throughout the 1930s to bridge the gap between himself and the people by fictional imagination. After the Second World War he gave up.

What he saw in Spain was a totalitarian inclination which seemed to be at one, not at odds with, the popular will. After 1945 he dropped all pretence in believing in the popular cause. Inevitably, for him, this also meant a loss of belief in humanity. *1984*, his despairing vision of the future was his personal testament to the past. It offered a future in which totalitarian states were perpetually at war, a world in which the human spirit was permanently broken. It was perhaps a personal despair, writes Burgess, rather than a vote of no confidence in the human race, but it was a despair which had been first kindled while fighting in Spain in the 1930s.[73]

What the war really revealed was how difficult it was to fight for causes in another person's country, in a war in which the volunteers were geographically, even culturally remote from the fighting. Connolly's disenchantment with the International Brigade, Auden's horror at the destruction of Guernica, Bernanos's outrage at the fate of supposed 'fifth columnists', Orwell's disillusionment that the good cause was almost as irredeemable as the bad, in this the first and last set piece proxy conflict of the First Cold War, all have a familiar echo. They were to be repeated again and heard more volubly in Korea and Vietnam when the next Cold War staged its own proxy encounters. In Vietnam too the West found a regime largely undeserving of its support, as well as a people that were culturally different from the West Europeans.

It was unfortunate that for the United States, at least, it took two proxy wars to remind the American people that fighting for a cause was almost more effective when that cause was a country. *Pro patria mori* may have seemed an invocation of another age to Wilfred Owen in 1918. Twenty years later after Spain had fallen to Franco, dying for one's country seemed a good deal more appropriate, a good deal less like play-acting, dying that is for the reality not the idea of democracy in a battlefield hundreds of miles from home.

The poets who fought for democracy in Spain, Auden once claimed, travelled to distant places in order to reflect the better on their own past and own culture from the outside. 'Truth is elsewhere', he wrote in *On The Frontier.* By 1940 this was no longer the case. As the belief in the universal applicability of great ideas diminished so the Left was thrown back onto the defensive, into a gesture of self-assertion, of asserting the truth of its ideas at home, at the national, not international level, a level on which socialism could most easily be grasped. During the Second World War, writes Miles Taylor, 'many on the British Left were unequivocal in their support for a patriotism which was rooted in popular small-scale, often localised struggles for democracy. In this qualified sense patriotism was made acceptable'.[74] So too, Owen notwithstanding, was dying for one's country rather than a cause.

COMMUNITY REPUDIATED: THE ANGER OF FERDINAND CÉLINE

God is being mended.
(*Epitaph to L'Ecole des Cadavres,* Céline, *1938*)

Compared with the English poets, Céline, their contemporary, found in the Great War merely confirmation of his long-held opinion that mankind was fundamentally rotten. Both men experienced the First World War; both drew different lessons from it. In both cases their alienation from modern society cannot be understood outside the context of the trenches.

The Great War was the seminal event in Céline's life, one which shaped his own response to the real world by radically altering reality itself. It taught him that mankind was imbued with a capacity for living through, even enjoying, such 'destructive repetitions' as war.[75] What does the hero of his most important novel, *Voyage to the End of Night*, conclude at the end of the story? People who have nothing wrong with them are frightening, healthy people, the fit, not the infirm: 'as long as they are up to it they'll think about killing you'.[76]

Who else but Trotsky could have got the novelist's measure when he reviewed *Voyage to the End of Night* in 1933. It was a novel, he wrote, dictated not by a fear of death but a fear of life. The weariness life provokes usually leads to revolt; indeed active revolt is inseparable from hope. In Céline's case, however, all hope of revolt had been expunged because the author knew only despair.[77]

Céline's despair drove him to the conclusion that no political creed was worth dying for, that no political movement that promised Utopia on earth, let alone human happiness, was to be taken seriously. There was no happiness in the world, Céline insisted, only misfortune, more or less great, early or late in one's life, startling or secret, immediate or postponed. In his novels men are reduced to the status of meat, or guts. At best, men melt into the landscape; their hold on life – like their identity – is tenuous. In *Voyage* the climate of Africa claims as many lives as the battle of Verdun.

> In the climate of Fort Gono the European cadres melted faster than butter. A battalion was like a lump of sugar in your coffee: the longer you looked the less you saw.[78]

Céline's world was one in which men lived under a suspended stay of execution, a world in which mankind played both roles – that of executioner and victim. As one of his characters says when entering a restaurant: 'I got the idea that these people sitting in rows around us were waiting for bullets to be fired at them from all sides while they were eating. And why not? None of them are innocent.'[79]

In the 20th century death may be tragic but it is not the classical tragedy of the Greeks. In the 20th century the Gods are not needed. Of our fellow men, and of them only, should we be afraid.

Indeed, in Céline's world, far from being the victim of fate, men are accomplices in their own destruction. 'There are two main ways of dying, either through the total indifference of one's fellow men in peacetime, or their homicidal passion when war breaks out.' The First World War taught Céline that. 'It is war that created the feeling of revolt in me', he remarked in an interview in 1961 shortly before his death, 'it is *there* that I first understood'.[80] Who could have foreseen, he once asked, before the war broke out 'all that the filthy, heroic, good-for-nothing heart of man contains?' Man is so habitually blind that faced even with his own extinction he cannot imagine it.

As a doctor, Céline preferred to look after the dying, the wounded, the crippled, the spent, those who took leave of life bit by bit, little by little. He devoted his life to the sick, not the healthy. His commitment was to the human beings the world had rejected, not the world of political creeds and cardboard political heroes. He preferred to remain true to what he called the dreadful secret: that what man finds hideous in war he finds hideous in himself.[81]

Given his essential misanthropy, perhaps it is not surprising that during the Second World War Céline should have become a collaborator. He kept his distance, nevertheless, from some of the more notorious intellectuals such as Montherlant, Beraud and Robert Brassilon. He had no confidence in the Germans, and no faith in fascism as a political creed.

Always a pessimist, Céline could summon up no enthusiasm for the new Europe. His profound disenchantment with Germany's historic moment distanced him from most Germans. He neither welcomed German company nor sought out German friends. He did little or nothing for the occupation authorities. During this war of deceivers and deceived Céline could never be accused of self-deception. His distrust of the Germans was intuitive even if it did not always extend beyond the point of intuition.

By 1943 he knew that the war was lost, that 'the farce is played out', as he wrote to a friend.[82] Nevertheless, he considered himself sufficiently tainted by his collaboration to flee from Paris in July 1944 as the Americans marched on the city. He fled to Germany, accompanied by his wife, the actor Vigan (well known for his role in the film *Pépé le Moko*) and Bébart, his cat. After a short stay in Baden Baden, he journeyed to Rostock and Warnemünde on the Baltic coast before returning to Berlin and Ulm en route to the besieged French community in Sigmaringen. There one of the exiles described Céline's arrival, wearing a cloth-cap of a kind engine-drivers used to wear in 1905, dressed in two or three fur-lined jackets, a pair of moth-eaten mitts hanging around his neck with Bébart in his ruck-sack.

Céline's picture of these times is one of the most vivid and splendidly apocalyptic of its kind. 'The worst is being prepared: the Apocalypse' he had written in February 1939. Who better to write it than himself? One of his critics called him 'an angel of destruction convulsed with laughter'.[83] His account of the collapsing Reich in its last year is one of Grand Guignol at its most vivid, the description of an angry man seeking to interpret the incipient madness of war through the refinement of an aesthetic sensibility. The three books that he wrote about this period, including his masterpiece *North*, offer a frenetic meditation upon the meaning of war and history. If their exterior landscape is a public one, in depicting Berlin during the bombing, patiently awaiting the Russians, they are austere books nevertheless, which encapsulate large questions in sharp images as if seen through a war photographer's lens.

Céline has been called the greatest chronicler of Germany's destruction, the 'wordsmith' of its *Götterdämmerung*. His description of the ruins of German cities under a relentless siege from the air still has the power to draw the reader into his account:

Of Ulm:

... A notice, Ulm ... and that is all! ... flattened sheds around everywhere! ... mass of twisted metal ... houses as if it were grimacing and gigantic bits of wall here and there in enormous disequilibrium waiting for you to pass beneath them ...

Of Hanover:

... The comic thought was that on each fallen house, each mount of wreckage, green, rose pink flames were dancing in the round ... towards the sky.... It must be said that these streets of wreckage, green ... red ... pink ... flaming away, had a much more cheerful aspect, really like a festival than in their ordinary state, sad, melancholy, broken ...

Of Berlin:

We must be going through a suburb ... then some ruins, piles of stones ... another pile of stones ... and another! Perhaps, it's Berlin? Yes! Couldn't have believed it ... Nonetheless, there it is, written up! ... And, an arrow! Berlin! ...

Berlin itself in Céline's vivid account is a city on the verge of extinction 'all stage sets', a city of façades, of houses whose insides have caved in, a vast refugee camp full of the flotsam and jetsam of humanity: 'semi-Latvians, Afrikaano-Czechs, sub-Hebraics', anxiously awaiting the arrival of Stalin's Asiatic hordes.[84]

The apocalyptic end of the Third Reich confirmed Céline in his opinion that detachment was the only legitimate response to war. He himself was possessed not so much of a *nostalgie de l'apocalypse* as a positive enjoyment of the Last Judgment in dress rehearsal, an almost adolescent revenge against a world he loathed. His days in Germany were among the most vivid of his life. Céline puts so little ironic distance between himself and his protagonist (the German people) that it is possible to read his novels of the period as straight autobiography. His idiosyncratic style, with its short sentences, quirks of syntax, and his sparse, laconic language makes his voice plausible enough.

Céline's conclusion in 1945 was that the only sensible course was suicide or survival. To survive a man must remain detached. When he volunteered for the call-up in 1914 he realised as soon as the gates of the barracks had closed behind him that he and his fellow recruits were 'done for like rats'.[85] Never again would he be a willing accomplice in his own destruction. Never again would he join up, for a country or a cause. In peace too, the price of survival was a refusal to take part in political life. Céline's refusal to engage was merely another way of arguing that life is not important enough to die for: 'When you don't have imagination, dying is small beer; when you do have imagination, dying is too much'.[86] If life is so hideous, why should it be prolonged? Not because life is worthwhile but surely only to discover how far 'people can go in the way of crumminess'.

In short, Céline's collaboration in 1940 was confirmation not so much that he was no more committed to the cause of the Free French than he was to that of the Germans but that he was detached from the war itself. It was a position which the French inevitably saw as unpatriotic, even unpardonable. To declare one's detachment in 1940 was to declare one's neutrality in a world in which neutrality was no longer permitted. In occupied France few men died martyrs for their beliefs. Céline chose to make a martyr of himself by refusing to defend anything. Céline was persecuted not for his beliefs but for his disbelief. Even now he has still not been forgiven for being so uncompromisingly despairing, for claiming that war had no redeeming features at all, for refusing to deal in certainties, not even the certainties of his own convictions.

Céline was condemned not for taking sides with the Germans but for refusing to take sides at all, for his refusal to draw any moral from war except one that no government would admit to: its futility.

As Céline wrote to a friend during the occupation of Paris, the Nazis would like to have shot him as much as the French resistance: both execrated him for his 'lack of faith in mankind'.[87]

If Céline still deserves to be read it is because he offers a salutary corrective to the counter-argument, the myth of community which emerged from the modern consciousness of war.

There are always two wars, wrote Alain, 'the one we make and the one we talk about'. There is nothing necessarily ennobling about the first. The second is frequently a myth, a necessary lie which permits men to endure the worst, remembering only what they can afford to. The problem, however, with the myth of community is that it can so often be used to glamorise war itself. The trench can become, in Alain's words, 'the place in the world where men loved each other best; war, a school for humanity'. If this is true it would be a damning indictment of our age.[88]

The Great War which Céline witnessed at first hand was a theatre in which, to quote the historian Marc Bloch, 'men bear false witness in spite of themselves', false witness to their humanity, their comradeship and good faith.[89] Céline would have none of this. What he had seen of war convinced him that every soldier's thoughts had to turn to personal survival, that in war even the currency of friendship is debased.

Céline was certainly right to question some of the myths of community and friendship that had been forged this century. He was certainly right to challenge the literature of comradeship that established itself as a genre in the aftermath of the First World War. A preoccupation with emotions and the quality of relationships is a central *leitmotif* of many of these works. Unfortunately, the great majority of middle-class writers located the working-class soldiers they had met at the Front in a never-never land of emotional warmth, honest intimacy and a kind of classlessness that the soldiers never claimed for themselves. Many working-class heroes described in the books exist in a social no-man's land imagined by outsiders, whose own brief contact with working men inclined them to romanticise the community of the Front. Whether we are writing of Robert Graves, whose own memoirs betray a total ignorance of working-class life in the slums of the industrial north of England, or Ernst Jünger, who deceived himself into believing that the workers of Essen shared his own devotion to war, the truth of their pictures is often betrayed by concerns which are definingly middle class.

In rejecting the fellowship of the Front, of course, Céline committed the ultimate blasphemy of the modern age. He refused to testify to the meaning of his own experience and thus made light of life itself. He questioned one of war's few redeeming features. Comte had the idea that the miraculous never dared touch the soul, only the body. Echoing this thought, Alain commented that it was a pity that Achilles's friendship for his friend Patroclus should have been the occasion for his own death. It was a pity that, in the case of Achilles, the gods did not think to console him by killing friendship instead.[90]

Céline would doubtless have agreed. *The Iliad* might provide fine verse as well as a persuasive text, but it is not a very accurate portrayal of modern warfare. And yet surely the friendship of men at the Front *was* a redeeming feature of war. Many soldiers did find a community, one which demanded a temporary suspension of personal identity while at the same time offering a remarkable profusion of those experiences from which the identity of every group is derived: bereavement, comradeship in arms, pain, as well as the close bonds which men form in time of war. One thing the poets could not take away, wrote a First World War veteran, was the 'warm comradeship' between the soldiers, 'those slim erect figures' who had redeemed themselves.

Unlike the First World War the public too shared the events of the Second. Many of the photographic images which are familiar from the Second World War were lodged in the imagination while the conflict was being fought. Both combatant and non-combatant experienced events together. In bearing witness to history they were able to make sense of a shared past, to find refuge where they could find it – in memories of shared loss.

Something like this happened in Britain during the Blitz. Elizabeth Bowen tells how in the early days the unknown dead reproached those left living, not so much by their deaths which might be shared at any time, but by their unknownness which could not be mended. Who had the right to mourn them not having cared whether they had lived or not? The war created a community briefly in the autumn of 1940, an instinctive movement among crowds to break down indifference while they still had time. 'The war between the living and the living became less solid as the war between the living and the dead thinned.' Within two years, however, that sense of community had been lost. The losses were too great, the victims too many. Everyday news made the Blitz routine; every raid became 'one more nail [hammered] into a consciousness which no longer resounded'.[91]

In no country however did the war create a greater sense of common purpose than Soviet Russia. In the 1920s Isaac Steinberg had been appalled by the lack of community he saw around him, the hungry look in the eyes of people in the streets, or of passengers shamelessly stealing the seats from one another in trams. What he saw was not a citizenry but 'a mass of humanity, accidentally chained together', lacking all sense of 'human sympathy and understanding'.[92]

Soviet society was changed, perhaps permanently, by the intensity of the Great Patriotic War. Many Russians, observed one contemporary, knew that the regime was wicked, but they also knew they must fight. Everyone who had lived through the Terror felt hopeful for the first time since the Revolution. A number felt they were within 'inches of the open sky', that after the struggle their children might rediscover a new form of communism, not a war against the people, but a war of the people against oppression.[93] Even Nadezhda Mandelstam hoped that it would redeem a post-Revolutionary generation that had been corrupted by 20 years of Stalinism, that it would help young and old alike to regain a human conscience.[94]

Conscience is the keyword. Ilya Ehrenburg described the war not as a plunge into the depths but an ascent. In the midst of their travails the Russian people soared to a great height, a fact recorded not in panegyrics to Stalin, the 'military leader of genius', nor in military decorations, nor in the stylised battle pictures from the Front, but 'in the memory of those who did not return, in the inexhaustible tears – that living water of a people's conscience'.[95]

Why the Great Patriotic War should have forged such a bond will always remain something of a mystery, but a clue is contained in an article that Mikhail Bulgakov wrote in November 1919 at the height of the Russian civil war. The struggle into which the October Revolution had plunged Russia saw violence and brutality on a scale unparalleled even in Russian history. In the course of the civil war, wrote Bulgakov, the Russians had treated each other so abominably that future generations would have to pay for the sins of the old. The cup of retribution would have to be drunk to the bottom. 'The past will have to be paid for ... paid for in the figurative and literal sense of that word.' His generation of Russians would die pitiful bankrupts, relying on their children and even grandchildren to pay off their debt to history honourably.[96] Perhaps, through the appalling sacrifices that had to be made by the Russian people to survive Hitler's attack, Bulgakov's generation was able to atone for the blood-letting 20 years earlier. Of all the forms of 'historical sickness' which plagued 20th century Europe, perhaps history as an act of purification was one of the least demeaning of all.

A sense of community indeed has survived the 20th century, it remains one of the few redeeming features of modern warfare. As an English soldier wrote after the First World War, 'the greater the horror the nobler the triumph of the man who is not morally ruined by it'.[97] The soldiers could best avoid moral corruption by keeping faith with each other. In 1929 Frederick Manning produced a much neglected but seminal work, *The Middle Parts of Fortune*, which looked at the First World War not through the eyes of its officers, but the rank and file. Manning concluded that such soldiers, whether volunteers or conscripts, had only one concern throughout the war, that their nerve should not break, that their courage should not fail them. Their real struggle was not with the enemy but with themselves'. It was a struggle which was often inconclusive. Indeed, long after the war many were forced to wrestle with their psychologically scarred inner selves. The majority survived, however, because they managed to retain their self-respect.

In the Great War, as in every other conflict this century, the soldiers on both sides fought to survive if they could, but to die if they must, keeping faith with their comrades. 'Few soldiers', wrote the young Marc Bloch, 'think of their country while conducting themselves bravely; they are much more often guided by the sense of personal honour which is very strong when it is reinforced by the group'.[98] In fighting side by side with their fellow soldiers they were not victims, nor were they complicit in their own destruction. In choosing to fight they chose to bear witness to their fortitude as men. It was, writes Andrew Rutherford, 'an existential choice: an assertion of will which defines the self and asserts its value'.[99]

The tragedy, of course, was that the best died first. War asked too much of its bravest men. In every conflict the world is diminished by its lost generations. Here is Camus, writing to his friends in the Resistance in 1943:

> The law of sacrifice brings it about that finally it is always the cowardly and prudent who have the chance to speak since the others have lost it by giving the best of themselves. Speaking always implies a treason.[100]

And here is Primo Levi writing of the Holocaust just before he took his own life in 1987, haunted as he was to the end by the guilt of survival: 'Each man is his brother's Cain: each of us ... has usurped his brother's place and lived in his stead'.[101] And here is a Stalinist apologist, making the same point about the victims of Stalinism: 'It is precisely the most admirable, manly, principled, and by their own lights moral opponents who have to be killed; the others can be frightened or bought'.[102]

Solzhenitsyn confirms that the arbitrary arrest of ordinary Russian citizens during the Stalinist terror was not a 'lottery' as Ehrenburg claims. It was not arbitrary at all. Every citizen was at risk, but any person who objected publicly to the regime or its actions was immediately arrested. Those who were bold enough to protest were sent off to the *gulag*. As their numbers thinned so the entire society became 'more trashy'.[103] As Isaac Steinberg witnessed in the 1920s the Terror had robbed life of 'all that makes men out of men'; it had destroyed the social fabric, the link between men, between communities, even between parents and children. Stalin's tyranny killed the attachment to the family just as much as it broke the spirit of the nation.[104]

But there was another world in Stalin's Russia, that of the *gulag*, a community which Stalin could not break try though he might. How could anyone affirm life or a sense of community in the *gulag*, we may ask, we who have read about the servitude with horror but have never experienced it ourselves?[105]

Men soon discovered that if they could not love their neighbour they learned to love those close to them, those in the same predicament, facing the same terrors, attempting to exorcise the same ghosts. The inmates of the camps, claimed Solzhenitsyn in *The Gulag Archipelago*, one of the most moving testaments to human suffering, were 'enfranchised' in a way that those outside the camps were not. They were able to think their own thoughts, keep their own friends, knowing they had nothing to lose in declaring their friendship, knowing that no one could betray them, that they could no longer even betray themselves.[106]

Was the same also true of the German camps which the Soviet writer Vasily Grossman visited at the end of the war? Grossman, who had begun life a good communist, unquestioningly loyal to Stalin, began to have doubts on his first visit to Auschwitz, which suggested a painful association with the world of the *gulag*. In *Life and Destiny*, a book which was not published in his lifetime, he provides a moving account of the Holocaust in the East. A mother writes to her son from a ghetto in Eastern Europe:

> Do you know Vitia what I felt behind the barbed wire? I thought it would be horror. But would you believe it, that in this park for animals I felt relieved ... all around me stood people *with the same destiny*.[107]

This was the key to the camaraderie of the Front and for a brief moment the Great Patriotic War. It also explains why the experience of war for many soldiers reawakened a sense of community with the enemy, for did they too not share the same destiny? Were they too, if not neighbours, at least in Solzhenitsyn's words 'close to each other'? It was a sense of community that Drieu La Rochelle discovered to his surprise in the men under his command – both he and the rank and file soldiers despised the politicians behind the lines preaching undying hatred of the enemy.

It is perhaps appropriate to end on this note, quoting some lines by T S Eliot. *Little Gidding* was published during the Second World War in 1942. It was composed much earlier, however, during the Blitz.[108] It is an eloquent and unashamed celebration of 'community' in wartime:

> I think again of this place
> And of people, not wholly commendable
> Of no immediate kin or kindness
> But some of peculiar genius
> All touched by a common genius
> United in the strife which divided them.

But Eliot talks of a larger community still, a community of the defeated as well as the victors, of the Germans as well as the English:

Whatever we inherit from the fortunate
we have taken from the defeated.

History for Eliot was no longer 'futile' as he had believed in 1918. History was about the renewal, sometimes rediscovery, of values and ideas in the course of strife. No struggle, however relentless, no war, however uncompromising, could deny mankind membership of 'a single party'. For Eliot, survival unlike Céline, was an affirmation not denial of humanity itself.

For Eliot the community of men also included the dead, for those who did not survive did not die unsung or unremembered. None died in vain:

We die with the dying
See, they depart, and we go with them
We are born with the dead
See, they return and bring us with them.

Eliot claims that the 'fire and the rose' are the same, that 'the German bombers/and Pentecostal dove are one'. We must ask, of course, whether he would have written these lines a few years later after the Allied armies rolled into the death camps, when the 'flame' was associated with the ovens of Auschwitz. We have no reason to doubt, however, that he would not. All of us, wrote Adorno, are survivors of Auschwitz, all of us are from the same 'party' that was herded into the crematoria and consigned to the camps. All of us are the survivors of Hiroshima, recognising that what we have done to other people we are all quite capable of doing to ourselves. In that sense, Céline's essential misanthropy has to be denied, if we are to survive the next century.

6
20th Century War and the Aesthetic Imagination

Roosevelt was much more decent than Hitler or Stalin for that matter ... Of course, Hitler is much more interesting aesthetically, but you can't judge aesthetically. That's sheer romanticism.

(W H Auden, *Table Talk (1947)*)

In a choice between terror and slavery one chooses terror, not for its own sake, but because in this era of flux it upholds the exigencies proper to the aesthetics of art.

(Jean-Paul Sartre, *Situations (1965)*)

THE SOLDIER AS VICTIM

In former days war was men on their feet. War today is all the postures of shame.

(Drieu La Rochelle, *The Comedy of Charleroi (1927)*)

Of all the military engagements of the 20th century, perhaps none encapsulates the reality of fighting, at least in the popular imagination, more than the battle of Verdun. In 1916 the Germans tried to engage the French army on the narrowest of fronts, with the cynical intention of bleeding it white. Anxious not to alienate their own men the generals invented the euphemism that the Fortress of Verdun would be taken by 'precipitate methods'. But the methods soon became clear enough. The artillery was the cutting edge of the German attack, the infantry merely its expendable agent.

In 10 months of fighting nearly one and a quarter million men were killed or wounded. After the war another 15,000 unidentified corpses were interned in a huge *ossuaire*. Verdun remains the ultimate anonymous battle in which, acting alone, small groups of men fought blindly, even ferociously, on ground that became in equal parts earth, blood and bone as bodies were shattered by one shell and scattered by the next.

In the course of the campaign a 26-year-old Second Lieutenant of the 151 Regiment, Raymond Jubert, recorded in his diary a despairing account of the fighting. His topography of the nightmare landscape in which he served is as precise as any historical account. Verdun was not the battle he had imagined he would be fighting when he joined up. It presented not a grand *tableau* of sweeping strokes and vivid colours but a series of 'small, painful scenes in obscure corners of small compass, where one could not possibly distinguish if the mud were flesh or the flesh were mud'. It was not a battle in which men died heroically but an engagement whose significance most soldiers found difficult to comprehend. In the compressed area of the battlefield the trenches became an open cemetery as battalion after battalion, 259 in all, were literally decimated slowly by the German bombardment. 'In the middle of a combat one is little more than a wave in the sea', wrote Jubert, 'a stroke of the brush lost in the painting.'[1]

Out of the seething hell of Mont Homme which in May 1916 possibly saw the worst of the fighting, Jubert gazed with envy as French pilots passed overhead. Even their perspective of the battle, however, remote though they were from the immediate fighting on the ground, was equally bleak. An American volunteer later killed while flying in the Lafayette Squadron saw below an appalling picture of 'murdered nature':

> Every sign of humanity had been swept away. The woods and roads had vanished like chalk white from a blackboard. Of the villages nothing remained but a grey smear ... countless towers of smoke remind one of Gustav Doré's hell...[2]

In the hell below day after day went by when the soldiers saw no dawn, no sunset, no sun at all, no colour, only an inky blackness created by the smoke of the fires from the firing of the guns. When marching through this desert landscape few soldiers sang. Only when they marched away from the battlefield did their spirits pick up, knowing as they did that they were returning to a world of colour.

It may seem remarkable that in such a world man should have talked of the aesthetics of war at all. Yet it was equally true that colour could be found on many other battlefields, that the canvas of war could be painted with vivid brush strokes, at least in the imagination. For war offered a range of experience normally denied in peacetime. The Front experience (*Fronterlebnis*) was more than just an experience, it was an interior journey into the realm of pain and suffering in forms that could not have been imagined before 1917. It was an experience that many soldiers craved, or to which they soon became addicted.

'A craving for the extraordinary', is what Jünger himself called the criminal dimension which manifested itself early on in the First World War, among the soldiers who destroyed the cathedrals at Albert and Rheims and thought nothing of attacking even Nôtre Dame from the air.[3]

In that respect, war had long had an aesthetic appeal. In the late 15th century the Margrave Albert Achilles of Brandenburg was renowned for setting cities alight without a moment's hesitation. Arson, he claimed, gave glory to war in the same way that the Magnificat illuminated Vespers.[4] A few centuries later the novelist Stendhal's only complaint after Napoleon had put Smolensk aflame during the invasion of 1812 was that so fine a spectacle could only be appreciated by men of sensibility, not by common soldiers.[5]

War in the 20th century was different because of its philosophical presuppositions, in particular the one described by Rilke that the presence of death could throw life into relief, that it could open up a different dimension of experience. Transcendence of a kind could be claimed. Such transcendent moments from birth to death are necessarily short-lived, and often violent.

When we speak of transcendence we are using the term not only in its philosophical, or metaphysical sense, we are also talking of an opening up of an imagination that would never have been touched but for the reality of war. This is what Jünger meant when he complained that those who had experienced war only in terms of its inherent suffering had the outlook of a slave, not a soldier. They brought to it no inner experience, only an external response. War, Jünger maintained, produced moments of truth, or what Heidegger called 'epiphanies', in which the banality of everyday life could be transformed. As a consequence, life could never be the same again. The images that soldiers saw on the battlefield quite literally shook them into writing poetry for the first time, or discovering a beauty which they had seen every day without being aware of it.

It was in this sense that the priest Pierre Teilhard de Chardin, who spent the First World War as a stretcher-bearer at the Front, wrote home in 1917 that war provided an extreme boundary 'between what you are already aware of and what is still in the process of formation'. He did not see his own experience as a moment of transcendence. He used a word instead that could be equally applied to a religious or artistic experience. The word he chose was 'exaltation', accompanied to be sure by pain. Such moments, nevertheless, were not to be passed up: 'Not only do you see things that you experience nowhere else but you also see emerge from *within yourself* an underlying stream of clarity, energy and freedom that is to be found hardly anywhere else in ordinary life'.[6]

Could it even be said that war was romantic? There was, opined

Wyndham Lewis, a romance about fighting even in the First World War, hateful though it might be for many to admit it. For there was nothing more absurd than to complain that modern warfare, compared with the Napoleonic set-piece engagements of the early 19th century, was either drab or unromantic. To argue such a case, Lewis insisted, was to misunderstand utterly the nature of romance. Romance is only in part what we see. It is mostly what we feel. The observer is the romance far more than the observed. By definition the experience is existential.[7]

If the battlefield of the Great War offered few consolations to most combatants, it offered for Hugh Walpole serving on the Eastern Front in June 1915 'a magnificent, unforgettable spectacle'.[8] Such scenes seemed to have been consolation, at least, for the murderous conditions in which the 20th century soldier often had to fight. In the early days of the Second World War even the historian Marc Bloch was entranced at Dunkirk by the patterns cast on the sea by the black, rank smoke pouring from a burning refinery. Looking back on the episode he felt he had been 'cheated' into forgetting its tragic origins. Many spectators, of course, did not feel cheated at all. Some felt they had witnessed something worth witnessing.[9]

The battlescape of war offered a different range of experience to different men. 'Not a noise', as Walpole claimed, but a symphony for a British NCO on the Somme to whom, during one engagement, the air seemed to be full of vast, agonised passion 'bursting with groans and sighs into shrill screaming and pitiful whimperings'. 'It did not begin, intensify, decline and end', he wrote, 'it was poised in the air, a stationary panorama of sound, a condition of the atmosphere, not the creation of man'.[10] Writing almost 20 years after the event David Jones also recalled 'the drumbeat of the artillery' as a whole army kept time.[11]

Even in the cities war had its own scores – Wagnerian to the ear of Proust's St Loup. The sirens during an air raid over Paris reminded him of the 'ride of the Valkyries', all the more so because it was the only German music to be heard during a war in which every other German composition was censored.

Other writers in the 20th century have seen war in poetic terms. The poet Apollinaire was enchanted by the sight of the moon floating over the trenches, as the shells burst into sprays overhead: 'The Front lit up, hexahedrons were rolling, the steel flames were blossoming, the barbed wire was growing thinner with bloody desires'.[12] For David Jones there was 'something horribly fascinating about the appalling devastation', with its sharp contours and unformed voids. So profoundly did the panorama affect his imagination that he considered even the battlefields of Flanders to be 'a place of enchantment'.[13]

Fifty years later, thousands of miles further east, some of the conscripts who fought in Vietnam found the battlefield enchanting too. The war had an undeniable and immediate impact on impressionable young minds, in this, a young man's war. One soldier was fully aware that the war's beauty might be divorced from all conventional values but he refused to deny that its beauty was real:

> There is something about a fire fight at night, something about the mechanical elegance of an M-60 machine gun. They are everything they should be, perfect examples of form. When you are firing at night the red tracers go out into the blackness as if you were drawing with a light pen. Then little dots of light start winking back and green tracers from AK-47s begin to weave in with the red to form brilliant patterns that seem, given their great speeds, oddly timeless as if they had been etched on the night.... And then the flares pop, casting eery shadows as they float down on their little parachutes, swinging in the breeze and anyone who moves in the light seems a ghost escaped from hell.[14]

Although the high-tech war was most vivid at night, daytime fighting also had its aesthetic appeal:

> Many men love napalm, loved its silent power, the way it could make tree lines or houses explode as if by spontaneous combustion ... I preferred white phosphorus which exploded with a fulsome elegance, wreathing its targets in intense and billowing white smoke, throwing out glowing red comets trailing brilliant white plumes.

It would be wrong also to think that the war on the Home Front had no appeal either. 'If I had an aesthetic type of mind', confided the poet David Gascoyne in his journal in 1939, 'I should perhaps better be able to recall the fantastic element in the period we are living through':

> The spectacle of dense ranks of bombers zooming across the sky, the famous buildings tottering in the flame and smoke, of massed stampeding crowds, the sinking of giant liners, all would perhaps not be so difficult to bear if one were, above all, appreciative of the tragic-catastrophic-epic quality of the panorama from the artist's point of view.[15]

No city in the course of the Second World War suffered more grievously from bombing than Tokyo, but here its citizens discovered a rare beauty in their own destruction. One resident remarked that the fire-bombings of March 1945 that killed 200,000 people in a single night reminded him of a painting of Purgatory, a real inferno to match anything from the Divine

Comedy. The Vichy French correspondent, Robert Guillian, was also struck by the splendour of the spectacle. Witnessing a raid from the safety of high ground he described the city as a giant Christmas tree blossoming with flames as the B-29s passed overhead, bathed in a green light. The bombers, at times, flew so low that the Japanese even cheered them as they went past. Some emerging from the neighbouring bomb shelters expressed 'cries of admiration, at such a grandiose theatrical spectacle – the burning down of an entire city'. It was typical, he thought; it was a peculiarly Japanese response.[16]

What made the 20th century aesthetically unique was the era of the machine. It provided the battlefield with a simplicity and appropriateness of form which was recaptured on the industrial assembly line. Susan Mansfield writes that the First World War conjured up the sublime rather than the beautiful – 'the appeal of transcendent power and awesomeness as opposed to that of design, regularity, or grace'.[17] On the simplest level, it reflected an idealisation of the mechanical, a glorification of means, an aesthetic of form which was even more pronounced on the battlefield than in the factory. On a deeper level still it reflected a particular vision of the nature of mankind, the mystery of a culture that had subordinated itself to its own creations.

In his Cubist-related compositions the painter Léger celebrated his army comrades as titanic human machines who consisted of the same material as their own guns. In Jünger's eyes man was part of the machine reduced through war to 'a single concentrated determined release of energy'. The man of steel was a soldier whose physique had been mechanised, or, in part, displaced into his body armour. Canetti's description of the First World War soldier as a 'stereometric figure', the man/machine symbiosis in one, seems an apt description. The paintings of Oscar Schlemmer showed geometric men at once fragmentary but also immutable, made whole by geometry, by 'design' – men with a square for a rib cage, a circle for a stomach, a cylinder for a neck, a triangle for a nose. It is as though without geometry they would be automatically maimed.[18]

The First World War inspired a series of paintings in which most of the identifiable figures, the soldiers, disappear in kaleidoscopic fragments, characterised by straight lines, acute angles and brush marks indicating space and volume. Solid matter and paradoxically solid flesh seem to have been fractured and then reassembled according to the laws of war, not art. Two early 20th century schools of art, Cubism and Vorticism, did not hold up a mirror to nature so much as challenge the mind as well as the eye. What both sets of painters had already undermined before the war was many of the conventional notions of what art should be. By so doing they prepared the ground (as did the war itself) for styles even more radical and challenging.

Wyndham Lewis, who was already a Vorticist by 1914, discovered that: 'War, and especially those miles of hideous desert known as 'the line' in Flanders and France, presented me with a subject matter so consonant with the austerity of that abstract vision I had developed that it was an easy transition'.[19] As Samuel Hynes writes, a Modernist method that before the war had seemed violent and disturbing was found to be far more realistic after the same men had experienced the Western Front. It was not so much that Modernism had changed. Reality had. Even Nash's landscapes are geometrical in form, brutal, coarse, raw in design, with no sign of sunset or sunrise.[20] In Lewis's paintings we see a land disfigured by great gashes, by lines of trenches largely devoid of men. In the painting of both artists we find a world in which nature as well as man has been murdered by a new reality – that of the machine age.

It was Expressionism, above all, that emerged from the First World War, a style based on large areas of unbroken colour and dramatic brushwork which greatly enhanced the expressiveness of the artist's work. The chief visual characteristics of the new form – its broken lines, the nervous grotesque deformity of its figures, the lurid and cruel vindictiveness of its colours, inspired Joseph Brodsky to claim that the Second World War was its greatest exhibition.[21] Looking at some of the photographs of the battlefields of the Eastern Front Brodsky wondered whether the Expressionists had not wandered out of their frames and projected themselves 'across the landmass of Eurasia'.

By 1940, however, art had given pride of place to the cinema as the medium of capturing the essence of modern war. If photography in the First World War had been cinematographically disjointed, portraying war as more of a collage than a unified composition, the moving film came to its own under Hitler. Hitler went further than anyone else in treating war as a film script. The director Hans-Jürgen Syberberg understands this more acutely than most, perhaps better than Hitler himself. To quote from Syberberg's commentary from his film *Hitler: A Film from Germany*:

> Hitler understood the significance of film. Now we are just as used to regarding his interest in film pejoratively, as if he had only wished to use it for propaganda purposes. We might even wonder whether he had not merely organised the Nuremberg Rally for Leni Riefenstahl and taking the argument a little further, whether the whole of the Second World War was not indeed conducted as a big budget war film, solely put on so that it could be projected as newsreel each evening in his bunker ...[22]

The artistic organisation of the mass ceremonies of the Third Reich, even the organisation of its final collapse, seemed to be part of the overall programme of a movement. Hitler, claimed Syberberg, saw the war and its newsreel footage as his heroic epic. The newsreels of the war were in a sense the continuation of Riefenstahl's *Triumph of the Will.*

Hitler's end, of course, was the apotheosis of his love affair with opera, with Wagner's *Ring.* But then Adorno suspected that the modern attraction of Wagner's national epic was, in fact, its cinematic appeal. Bayreuth, with its vast stage and Wagnerian sopranos declaiming loudly against a background of music both thunderous and uninterrupted, surely represents, Adorno suggests, the Hollywood aesthetic itself – the mass soap opera with only the technical medium missing.

Syberberg rejects Adorno's description of the war as the Hollywood stereotype of the 'catastrophe movie'.[23] Instead, he insists that the Second World War was its inverted form: catastrophe as film. Did not the war confirm the opinion of Hitler's projectionist that he was not only the greatest general but also 'the greatest film-maker of all time'? And is it not as cinema that the Second World War is now largely remembered in modern memory?[24]

In Vietnam 20 years later many Americans lived the war in their imagination too. For many soldiers the conflict was not so much experienced as viewed by men who thought they were actors in their own film. Many felt the imagery of war to be so oppressive, that they were reduced in status to the role of passive spectators, not soldiers at all.

As a film Vietnam was not real. Yet as a movie it was for many participants more real than real life. 'Strangest [sensation] of all', writes Philip Caputo, was 'the sensation of watching myself in a movie. One part of me was doing something while the other part watched from a distance shocked by the things it saw yet powerless to stop them from happening'.[25] As a film script many veterans found the war in Indo-China easier to come to terms with than as a military engagement. As an engagement it lacked purpose. Only as a film did it seem to make sense. As a movie it didn't need to have a message, let alone an affirmative ending. It didn't even need to have heroes. In so disorientating a struggle heroism seemed to be pointless. As a movie, the war's pointlessness *was* the main point.

THE IMMANENT AS ART

Ultimately, however, what made the 20th century aesthetic of war so different from everything that had preceded it was more than its 'mechanical' message. It was its expression of modernity – what made the modern world 'modern'. If modernity means anything it is characterised in terms of an acute consciousness of discontinuity with the past, of a break with tradition, a feeling of novelty – the birth of the new, or history as perpetual motion, ephemeral, fleeting, contingent. Being modern lies not in recognising and accepting this perpetual movement, however, but in recapturing something 'eternal', something that is immanent, transcendent – words that will be found time and again in this book.[26]

Modernity, in this sense, differs from what has gone before, from the pre-modern view of eternity – that which lies beyond the present moment. Modern man was interested in discovering what lay behind it. He sought instead to discover eternity *within* the present instant. He sought to grasp the 'heroic' aspect of the present and so heroise the present itself. To be heroic was to transfigure the world – not to annul reality but to reveal the truth of it, to transform reality by grasping what it really meant.

Baudelaire, who was the first person to use the word modernity, captured its meaning in his remarks about 19th century art. He made fun of those painters who, finding modern dress excessively ugly, wanted to depict men wearing nothing but ancient togas associated with the revolutionary paintings of David. The modern painter was the one who could show the dark frock-coat as 'the necessary costume of our time', the one who knew how to make manifest in the fashion of the day the essential, permanent, obsessive relation that his own age entertained with death:

> The dress-coat and frock-coat not only possessed their political beauty which is an expression of universal equality, but also their poetic beauty which is an expression of the public soul – an immense cortege of undertaker's mutes (mutes in love, political mutes, bourgeois mutes ...). We are each of us celebrating some funeral.[27]

It is important, of course, to remember that Baudelaire believed that the essentialising of reality – the uncovering of modern life's essence – was purely an artistic phenomenon, that the 'heroisation' of the present had no place in politics and certainly not in war. Unfortunately, in the course of the 20th century men wanted to find the essence of war in the sound of battle, or the sight of an army on the march, or the view of a battle landscape. Some hoped to discover the transcendent reality of modern life on the battlefields of mid-20th century Europe.

Thus German painters during the Third Reich affirmed the negation of experience in a vain attempt to discover the greater truth of war itself. Looking at the Nazi artists and their creations, such as Walter Schmoek's

Soldiers, or Elk Aber's *Dispatch Courier*, or Franz Eickhorst's *Street Fighting*, or Paul Mathias's *Padua 10 May 1940*, we find that none can be taken to be a commentary on war at all, only an affirmation of history's mandate, of what the art critic Robert Scholz called at the time Germany's 'belief in its future'. Reviewing the frescoes of Franz Eickhorst, Robert Volz wrote that their beauty lay in 'the almost total absence of blood'. 'The readiness to fight and be sacrificed', he added, overshadowed the horrors of reality. 'What remains is the destiny of a people.'[28]

The central reality of what one historian called 'reactionary modernism', or fascism, was an attempt to free the creative spirit of man by reaching beyond morality to aesthetic immanentism. If an aesthetic experience alone justifies life, morality is suspended; desire has no limits. What fascism promised was engagement, commitment, authenticity – all of which were aesthetic standards by which to judge the value of political action. In the end, aesthetic standards replaced moral norms.

When Benjamin talked of the aestheticisation of politics he was right to contrast it with the communist politicisation of art. Communism did, indeed, reduce art to politics, giving it a political rationale, discriminating between 'good' and 'bad' art in terms of its social realism, or its social utility. The Nazis went much further in seeing art as the expression of the *volkstum*, a folk culture, the essence of a whole people or race. This is what Syberberg meant when he said that Hitler reduced everything to 'film'. Germany quite literally became a film, the German people extras, and it was as a film that it still lives on in our imagination, as a *Gesamtkuntes-werk*, an aesthetic project, reduced, perhaps, in terms of mass culture to kitsch.

As Jean-Luc Nancy explains, the Nazi obsession with what he calls 'immanentism' was predicated on the belief that a community could produce its own 'essence' as a work of art.[29] Essence is what, beginning in language, is reflected of a community in art, philosophy, religion and political life. In immanentism the community itself, the nation or the people, is fashioned into a work of art by its artists (its political leaders). If every community is self-creating, and all art self-producing, then the essence of a people is realised most forcefully in festivals or war, two modes of social action which quite literally fuse a community and delimit its scope.

The terrible problem with immanentism was that it led to extermination, to a radical break in history between man and God. Auschwitz did indeed reveal the 'essence' of Germany to the world (in Heidegger's view) by allowing the essential character of Western culture – the bid for technological domination to achieve a perverted apotheosis – when human beings dealt with other human beings as industrial waste.[30]

It was, of course, an outcome that Oswald Spengler had warned the German people of as early as 1932. In one of his last published works, *Man and Technology*, he cautioned against subordinating man to technology, warning that the attempt to control nature by transforming man would end not in communication with God but with the devil. In a famous passage he wrote that man no sooner sees a waterfall than he wants to transform it into a hydroelectric power station. He no sooner sees a herd of cattle than he begins thinking of its value as meat stock: 'Whoever was not himself seized by this will to almighty power over nature must experience it as devilry and one constantly perceived and feared the machine as the discovery of the devil'.[31]

Auschwitz in that sense represented the distortion of Western metaphysics when taken to excess.

It is precisely this point that Benjamin seized on in the epilogue to his most influential essay, 'The Work of Art in the Age of Mechanical Reproduction'. Quoting from one of Marinetti's more bellicose manifestoes, Benjamin concludes:

> '*Fiat ars, pereat mundus*', says fascism, and as Marinetti admits expects war to supply artistic gratification with a sense of perception that has been changed by technology. This is evidently the consummation of *l'art pour l'art*. Mankind, which in Homer's time was an object of contemplation for the Olympian gods, now is one for itself. Its self-alienation has reached such a degree that it can experience its own destruction as an aesthetic pleasure of the first order.[32]

Marinetti, too, wanted Italy to essentialise itself, for the Italian people to realise themselves as a work of art. One device was to turn the physical body into an engine of war, while, in true totalitarian fashion, transforming man into the object not subject of warfare. Marinetti saw the collective suicide of a nation as the expression of its will to power. 'Italian democracy was for us a body which must be liberated', he declared.

His most evocative invocation of the destruction of the body, and by implication that of the body politic, is to be found in a passage from a manifesto entitled 'The Birth of the Futurist Aesthetic'. Here war as the 'ultimate hygiene' has a bizarre, literal, as well as metaphorical truth:

> The plainest, the most violent of Futurist symbols comes to us from the Far East. In Japan they carry on the strangest of trades. The sale of coal made from human bones. All their powder works are engaged in producing a new explosive substance more lethal than any yet known. A terrible new mixture has as its

principal element coal made from human bones with the property of violently absorbing gases and liquids. For this reason countless Japanese merchants are thoroughly exploiting the corpse-stuffed Manchurian battlefields (1904-5). In great excitement they make huge excavations and enormous piles of skeletons multiply in every direction ... A hundred tsin (seven kilograms) of bones brings in 92 kopeks.[33]

In Marinetti's eyes, the aesthetic of war reached its final expression as a means of exchange, in the burning and recycling of corpses. In Manchuria the skeletons of Russian and Japanese soldiers who had been killed in the 1904 war were turned into gunpowder to make more skeletons out of future enemies. The aesthetic of the exchange was the harmony of death, or rather its continuity in life, the refusal to accept death as the inevitable end. For Marinetti the integration of death in life was the ultimate artistic realisation of politics.

For the Nazis the Holocaust was meant to be something quite different – a final accounting, the Final Solution. For Marinetti, artist as he was to the end, no final artistic realisation of a nation was possible or legitimate. Unlike the Nazis, Marinetti was very modern. In the end, an exchange is an exchange, an efficient *recycling*, which National Socialism was not. In that sense immanentism was the ultimate revolt against modernity as well as an ultimate denial of what fascism promised: the artistic self-creation of man.

In that sense too the nuclear era could have no aesthetic appeal since its finality promised to be as absolute as that of the Holocaust. The Futurists, who had indeed created an aesthetic of war, would have found little of value in the 'stony rubbish' of Eliot's *Wasteland*, the premonition of an ultimate war where 'the dead tree gives no shelter, the cricket no relief and the dry stone no sound of water'. The annihilation of man could never be an artistic product because it would be by definition nihilistic. To borrow another phrase from Eliot, from an essay on Joyce's *Ulysses*, it could not 'make the modern world possible for art'.

THE 20th CENTURY IMAGE OF WAR

Nietzsche Glimpses the Middle Ages in Disguise

I am greatly worried about the future in which I fancy I see the Middle Ages in disguise.
(Nietzsche, *November 1870*)

From the times of the barbarian invasions to the Second World War [German]
eruptions into history have been no different from the eruption of the plague
and the great epidemics. I'm reminded of that cardinal who called Hitler 'a
modernised Attila'.
(*Fernando Camon in conversation with Primo Levi, 1987*)

'We cannot determine to what height the human species may aspire in
their advance towards perfection', wrote Edward Gibbon in *The Decline
and Fall of the Roman Empire*, 'but it may safely be presumed that no
people, unless the face of nature is changed, will relapse into their original
barbarism'.[34] Gibbon thought he had no illusions about mankind. He
would have been surprised to discover that 20th century man, for all his
faith in progress, feared his own past might return when least expected,
as if time would be reversed or the future denied. In the comparative calm
of the late 19th century Nietzsche glimpsed an apocalyptic future, the
coming of a new Middle Ages, a period of darkness reminiscent of
Europe's distant past.

The Middle Ages that lived in the 20th century imagination was
interpreted in strictly 20th century terms, in that unique way employed by
the modern era of looking at history as the creation and invention of
modern man. The past is what the present makes of it. The Middle Ages
which Nietzsche foresaw was a working hypothesis, an aesthetic device
for understanding the sense of unease about the vulnerability of Western
civilisation, an intuitive feeling that war was the calling-card of the 20th
century.

(1) In a way, the Second World War can be seen as an act of self-conscious
medievalism. And it is as a medieval event that the war was understood in
Vichy France. A sensitive observer of the new republic, du Moulin de
Labarthète, maintained in his memoirs that it constituted 'a return to the
Middle Ages, an instinctive medievalism', something that the great
historian of the Middle Ages, Berdyaev, had not foreseen. Berdyaev had
preferred the virtues of the Middle Ages to the gloomy decadence of the
bourgeois age. And it was in reaction to that age that the Vichy Republic
was founded on such medieval principles of organisation as a system of
cités, baillages, pays and *provences*.[35]

On the German side self-conscious medievalism was far more developed.
In the 1930s Walter Benjamin had warned the German people that with its
instinctive mistrust of politics and its pervasive Utopianism it would be
peculiarly susceptible to a man ready to abolish politics altogether and
replace it with a grand *aesthetic* vision.[36]

In the case of the Nazis much of their aesthetic imagery was medieval.

If those images, in retrospect, seem excessively unreal, we forget that at the time the realm of medieval fantasy included within it a whole range of contemporary references. In the late 1930s the German people proved to be particularly receptive to what Hoffmanstahl called 'the damned up force of [their] mysterious ancestors ... the piled up layers of accumulated collective memory'.[37] No memory was stronger than that of the *Niebelungennot*, the anonymous 13th century epic, which tells of the betrayal and slaughter of the Burgundian royal family and its overthrow by the Huns.

As an artist-warrior Hitler had the chance to compensate for his lack of artistic talent by orchestrating in true Wagnerian spirit the greatest drama of all. When his Waffen SS divisions, which were significantly named *Siegfried, Wotan* and *Walkerie*, failed to prevail on the Russian Front, when the prospect of total oblivion could no longer be ignored, the minds of the more romantic Nazis turned to the end of the *Niebelungen* saga. Martin Bormann pledged to 'perish in King Attila's hall like the Niebelungs of old'. In the presence of his table companions in the Wolf's Lair Hitler mused that a hero without an heir should surely perish on a funeral pyre as Brunnhilde does in the last act of Wagner's great drama.[38]

Wagner's skills as a dramatist and *metteur en scène* were particularly appreciated by Hitler. Stagecraft and design were always crucial to the success of Nazi political theatre. Hitler was at his most theatrical in the closing months of the Third Reich. By then all the obsessive fears and expectations which had inspired his political career were reflected in a bogus, even kitsch, medievalism that it is difficult to take seriously years on.

The Middle Ages provided the symbols, Wagner the themes. Hitler was inspired not so much by the *Lay of the Niebelungs* as by Wagner's interpretation of it – a world in which ruler and ruled, good and evil, pure and corrupt, face each other in a simple, dualistic, almost Manichaean confrontation: Siegfried and Hagen, Wotan and Alberich, a pagan world of ambition, blood-lust, revenge and ultimately redemption. It was a world that spoke to the Germans more than it did to most other European peoples. Perhaps, of all peoples, they were the most attracted to its ascetic (as well as aesthetic) appeal.

The intensity of religious experience for which the crusaders were noted was especially attractive to late modern societies that had grown over-materialistic. The 'medieval moment' appealed to many 20th century Europeans because it offered a chance to experience what one writer termed 'the unreconciled opposition' between the finite and infinite worlds. At the turn of the century the American psychologist William

James had argued that the Middle Ages spoke clearly to an age which also believed that the world was sinful, which was also haunted by demons, this time secular rather than supernatural. Sin had to be squarely met and overcome, not ignored or evaded. In this mortal combat men would have to rediscover their 'heroic resources'. For the sin of the world could only be neutralised through suffering.[39]

James talked of the struggle in terms of a crusade against modern heresies. He spoke eloquently of men having to fight the sin of heresy within themselves as well as the outside world. In the mid-20th century many Germans found themselves susceptible to a political message that depicted the world as being at the mercy of a Marxist heresy financed and orchestrated by international Jewry – the killers of Christ. Fighting that temptation within themselves, purging the world of the menace, seemed justification enough. War offered a means of redemption, an opportunity to heal a deep and persistent social wound.

War as a crusade also offered modern man what it offered many medieval crusaders – an opportunity to break out of social constraints, to rediscover possibilities which though latent had long been suppressed. It offered a chance to explore the darker elements of the human psyche that had been denied by the Enlightenment or condemned in the name of reason. As James argued, war could be used by a society that was anxious to unlock previously locked doors, to enter into a realm of experience that had not been acknowledged, even less permitted.[40]

In a word, the neo-medievalism of the Nazis stood for the *tradition* – the Knights Templar, Rosicrucians, Alchemists, Neo-Cabbalists, the Holy Grail and the quest for it – a spurious medievalism to be sure, one that afforded an intimation of the end of history. It was a shabby medievalism, writes Umberto Eco, but 'the shabbier its heroes the more profoundly ideological its superficial naiveté.'[41] With its inevitably redemptive end – self-immolation – it was a medievalism which primed the German people for the final act in Berlin in April 1945, long before Hitler descended to the underground world of his bunker.

(2) If insecurity was another keyword of the mid-20th century it took a very medieval fear that the world was about to end in a final catastrophe. In the early Middle Ages the end had been imminent, quite real – reflected not only in fear of invasion by the barbarians, but the anticipation of a new millennium, the coming of the anti-Christ. In the modern age the recurrent theme of catastrophe, like that of the Late Roman Empire, was the fear that the barbarians would return.

Europe, in fact, had been preparing for such a reappearance for some time. Like Spengler, Max Weber had predicted the onset of an iron

Caesarian age in which war would bring 'not a summer's bloom ... but rather a polar night of icy darkness and hardness'.[42] Was Weber not right, asked Neumann in 1895, 'of what use is the best social policy if the Cossacks are coming?'[43] In Neumann's fears there was an echo of Hertzen's warning, a prospect of massacre and warfare on a new but at the same time depressingly familiar scale.

The world had to wait only 40 years. During a meeting in July 1941 with Marshal Kvaternik, the Defence Minister of Croatia, Hitler compared the Russian forces with the hordes of the Great Khan. Asia, he warned, had a disquietingly large reservoir of men against whom the Europeans would have to defend themselves for centuries to come.[44]

The war correspondent, Alexander Werth, was afforded his first glimpse of the 'Mongol' hordes, in the form of Kazakh soldiers driving hay-carts to the Moscow Front in September 1941.[45] Four years later in Berlin he was told by a Soviet commander, who was greatly embarrassed by the wholesale rape of German women, that the Kazakh troops under his command had been by far the worst offenders.[46]

The Poles had discovered this for themselves in 1944 when they found themselves treated much more harshly at the hands of Tartars, Uzbekhs and Kalusks than they had been in 1939 by their traditional Russian and Ukrainian enemies. Were the former exacting a revenge on the white man, those 'remnants of Calmucks and Uzbekhs' whom Gibbon had so confidently declared could no longer 'seriously excite the apprehensions of the great republic of Europe'?[47] In the 1940s the East Europeans seemed to exist precariously in a world of shifting armies and values, in which fears from the distant past were more potent than fears of an unknown future.

The war in the east did indeed conjure up images of the end of the late Roman Empire. As the Red Army erupted into Germany in 1944 its retribution was indeed appalling. In many villages women were beaten to the ground with rifle butts. In hospitals doctors were butchered, nurses raped, patients either shot in the head or thrown out of windows. In some villages the savagery was truly frenetic. Women were hacked to pieces; men were blinded or dragged to their death behind horses.[48] Perhaps, history had even greater resonance because East Prussia really did seem to be on the frontier between Europe and Asia, with its exotic flora and fauna including the Auroch or European bison and the wolf, two animals which were to be found nowhere else on the European continent.

As the Wehrmacht was driven west four years later so the threat of a Russian victory came to have an immediacy for ordinary German soldiers that the threat of 'racial pollution' by Jews did not:

Any German subjugation [wrote one lieutenant] would spell a total, one hundred per cent annihilation of everything German.... We are the last bastion – with us everything stands and falls to what German blood has given birth.[49]

In the last months of the war, in March 1945, a corporal insisted that the Germans were fighting to save European culture from 'the Mongol stream'.

(3) There was a third type of medievalism conjured up by the 20th century, an anticipation of the millennium, an intimation of the Last Judgement. From a sense of personal insecurity, the world moved into a sense of collective unease, or what the critic Frank Kermode called 'the sense of an ending', the final, terminal conclusion from which there was no escape.

'The dark ages are coming again', Wittgenstein forecast, a period in which he fully expected to see such horrors as people being burnt alive for witchcraft. Wittgenstein did, indeed, see such an age. He lived through it. Heretics in the mid-20th century were burned in crematoria, not at the stake. The modern *auto-da-fé*, as Karl Kraus had foreseen, claimed whole cities, not merely the religious faithful. What did it matter if the angels' trumpet of death had changed into the sound of the air raid siren?[50]

'I am the thunder, the cataclysm', Céline raged in *D'un Château à l'Autre*, his account of his peregrinations in the closing days of Hitler's Reich.[51] No other century, certainly no other war, provided such a peculiar but seductive evocation of the Last Judgement. Well might the survivors of the Minowitz concentration camp think that they had been delivered into the hands of the Horsemen of the Apocalypse when four Russian soldiers rode into their camp in 1944 wearing white capes, sitting astride white horses, harnessed in white to match the snow.[52]

The war, wrote the poet Horst Lange, 'is like a pestilence which overwhelms us and makes us sick'.[53] Here too was an invocation of the Middle Ages, of the Black Death that carried off a third of the population of Europe in the mid-14th century. Whenever there was a war, disease seemed to stalk the 20th century. An outbreak of typhus in Serbia in the First World War proved so virulent that the fighting on both sides stopped for six months. In the course of the Russian civil war 3,000 men from General Ydenich's White Army died in circumstances of despair, filth and misery so frightful that *The New York Times* refused to publish an account of it by Walter Duranty.[54] The fact that plagues did not carry off as many people in the Second World War was only because of prompt medical attention. The wholesale delousing of the population of Naples in 1943 stopped an incipient typhus epidemic in its tracks.

As a metaphor, however, the plague still spoke forcefully to the peoples of Europe. In the course of a conversation between Céline and an SS Major, the Frenchman was asked by his German host what had happened to the 'genuine 18-carat plague – why had the microbes lost interest, why had they gone on strike', why had the Allied armies managed to fight from Cairo to Milan without an epidemic breaking out in their ranks:

A calamity, Céline ... you saw the cables. Epidemics are washed up ... Even in Mongolia or India ... Under Dürer this would have been over two years ago ... and it can never end ... you will say that in your preface!
Two Horsemen of the Apocalypse instead of Four, pathetic, it will be written! The apocalypse inoculated? Impossible![55]

Well might Céline's SS interlocutor protest. The Führer would never have permitted it. Since then the bacteriological war centres have continued to produce man-made germs, hybrid strains, even more lethal than those produced by nature. It would seem that nothing can disturb the microbes waiting to strike when least expected, not even penicillin which brought the Allied armies a brief respite. In Alsace on 6 July 1885 a rabid dog bit the nine-year-old Joseph Meister. Meister was the first patient to be saved by Louis Pasteur with quinine. He was also the first janitor of the Pasteur Institute, and committed suicide 50 years later when, following the French defeat, the Germans occupied the building. As the poet Miroslav Holub later concluded 'only the virus remained above it all'.[56]

As a metaphor the plague had lodged so securely in the Western imagination that it suggested itself whenever the 20th century broke new ground in barbarism. A British correspondent, reporting on the effects of radiation at Hiroshima – vomiting, diarrhoea, bleeding gums, loss of hair – spoke of 'people still dying mysteriously and horribly [after the first few weeks] from an unknown something which I can only describe as an atomic plague'.[57]

(4) The most graphic theme of the new medievalism perhaps was the idea of a great peace breaking down, a great international power that had unified the world in language, customs, religion and art, collapsing under the pressure of its own decadence, or barbarian invasions. The latter could be either sudden or expected, relentless or pervasive. The 'Peace' could collapse as a result of the overwhelming assault from outside, or be relentlessly undermined from within by a gradual but debilitating loss of confidence. The collapse of the great peace in 1914 initiated a period of crisis and purposelessness, of drift and decay, particularly in the 1930s when, in the words of Jung, men were able to smell 'a faint whiff of burning in the air'. It was a period of almost permanent civil war marked by

clashes of opposing societies, each desperately trying to replace the old empire – at once to snuff out and transcend the old cultures in favour of 'a new order'. In the eclipse of the old order, war became a condition of life.

In the mid-20th century the Middle Ages were conjured up, not in the struggle between popularist Franciscans and doctrinaire and intransigent Dominicans but by other monastic groups, other 'isms', Marxist or Fascist in inspiration, who despised the old order as decadent or diabolical, or both:

> These societies of reformers, divided between a furious practical activity in the service of the outcasts in a violent theological debate, were ridden by reciprocal accusations of heresy and a constant to-and-fro of excommunication. Each group manufactures its dissidents and its heresiarchs; the attacks the Franciscans and the Dominicans made on each other are not very different from those of Trotskyites and Stalinists...[58]

Often the evocation of the Dark Ages was too contrived a metaphor, a dramatic creation whose anti-rationalism was too ironic to be brutal and whose images were often too pointed to be taken seriously. During the Spanish Civil War, however, thousands of intellectuals were rounded up and shot, and hundreds of museums and churches deliberately bombed. Even books were burned, including Spanish Bibles which the Republic had printed by the thousand and sold openly in Barcelona. Appalled by such wanton barbarity the poet Hernandez was moved to write:

> Singing I defend myself.
> And I defend my people when the barbarians of crime
> Imprint on my people their hooves of power and
> Desolation.[59]

But the Spanish Civil War spoke of a barbarism more sinister still. As Antoine de Saint-Exupéry observed at the time, it introduced a new type of warfare to the 20th century, one in which firing squads counted for more than soldiers of the line. Death became a sort of quarantine, as fifth columnists (a term first coined in the Civil War), the exponents of heretical ideas, or 'germ carriers', were shot with equal enthusiasm by both sides.[60]

Even before Nietzsche's warning of the coming Middle Ages Jacob Burckhardt had foreseen a disturbing new trend in the making, a barbarism of 'radical contemporaneity', an ingenious wish to transform society without reference to the past, without regard for what was being destroyed or constructed, a systematic and sustained rejection of history.

In the rise of ideologies such as communism and National Socialism Burckhardt would have seen an attempt to escape from history by transforming man through ideas alone.[61]

In the early 1930s Guigleilmo Ferrero was moved to ask whether Western man was really civilised or not? Had the Europeans become merely clever barbarians without appreciating the transformation? A Europe, Ferrero believed, unconstrained by its past, by its traditions, memories and values, would regress very quickly into barbarism. 'It will bring in its wake a new Middle Ages, without Giotto, Dante or the inspiration of Christ.'[62] Malcolm Muggeridge would have agreed. On a visit to the Crimea in the 1930s he came upon a German speaking colony still very close to the *volk*, to its medieval roots. Europe, he was led to conclude, was threatened not by one ideology but by two, both of them barbaric: the barbarity of the Germans belonged to the earth, that of the Russians went by the name of the Dictatorship of the Proletariat. The Germans were barbarians who were willing to make war on civilisation; the Soviets preferred to make war on life.[63]

In a word, the true barbarians were not hammering outside the gates of Gibbons's European republic; they were already within it trying to break out. Saint-Exupéry summed up the dilemma admirably:

> I once asked Lazareff what impression Hitler had made on Chamberlain who had just been in contact with him.
> 'Tremendous', he answered.
> It was to be expected. If you confronted Bergson with Attila, Attila would undoubtedly astound Bergson. As for Bergson, he could not possibly make any impression on Attila. A drunken sailor makes more noise than a philosopher. And the SS man who, thumbs stuck in his belt, walks up and down behind a humiliated physicist as he bends over to clean the latrine likewise astounds the physicist.[64]

Nietzsche had been right. He had foreseen how the endless quest for self-esteem or meaning in history would drive man to murder or worse. Germany did not collapse in 1939. It was corrupted. 'The German people retrogressed into all but prehistoric barbarism', Freud wrote not knowing that he himself would have to flee from Vienna when the German army entered the city, to be welcomed as 'liberators'. It took another Viennese intellectual, Karl Kraus, to appreciate the irony of what had really happened. It was not the barbarians who threatened the end of civilisation but the highly civilised European nations who had overreached themselves. The end would not come when the barbarians tried to break in but when they tried to *break out*.

The idea of a barbarism within was not a product of a fevered imagination, an aesthetic device to explain away as well as depict the barbarity of warfare. It was a symbol of all the forces at work within interwar Europe. It became a metaphor at the time for the explosive, largely negative forces which lurked beneath a decaying political fabric. It was a metaphor for a ferocious energy that, in the end, was directed largely against itself.

The Europeans should not have been surprised. Freud had already revealed the psychology of modern man. A host of other writers had written about man's instinct for self-destruction. Many of Nietzsche's contemporaries shared his anxiety about the future. Some had no illusion about the horrors which war might unleash. Not all men lived in a liberal world in which all things were the measure of man and every problem could be resolved by argument. If many late 19th century liberals had looked to the future with a confidence born of incomprehension, many others rightly suspected what lay in store. Far from being a philosopher who was misunderstood by his contemporaries, Nietzsche alas, was a visionary who was understood all too well.

THE 20th CENTURY AS HELL: THE LANDSCAPE OF MODERN WARFARE

Whosoever has built a new heaven has found the strength for it only in his own hell.

(Nietzsche)

In the end, what the writers of the 20th century captured in their accounts of war, even from the studied, sometimes contrived perspectives of a writer like Céline, was a literary image, part of our modern sensibility, an intimation of war as hell. When we use this term to describe the Great War or the death camps of Hitler's Germany we are not imposing a term on the past, we are accepting one which the past has imposed upon us. War as hell was not contrived as history was being written: it was in men's minds as history was being made.

For the soldiers on the Western Front the landscape of battle was infernal indeed – in the words of Edmund Blunden 'sickly, yellow and sallow, upheaved and brutalised, scrawled with leprous white and smudged with cinder black'.[65] In such a world, asked the official war artist Paul Nash, were not sunrise and sunset both 'blasphemous': 'only the black rain out of bruised and swollen clouds ... [was] fit atmosphere in such a land'. When Wyndham Lewis wrote about Flanders in the 1930s he recalled its festoons of mud-caked wire, its miniature mountain ranges of saffron earth and trees like gibbets – 'these were the properties only of those titanic casts of dying ...'.[66]

Looking back some years later, Lewis believed that the ideal artist for the Great War would have been the 15th century painter Luca Signorelli, 'the man who painted hell with such ability at Orvieto'. His fresco of *The Damned* is a compendium of naked figures being violently manhandled by devils, in a series of postures of muscular extremity. Lewis, too, saw the hell of war in the extreme physical demands it made of men, the more specialised the demand the more mechanical, the less human they could afford to be. In many of his war paintings soldiers are frequently to be seen escaping from the battlefield, reduced to not much more than a series of tense, muscular arcs in their rush to remove themselves to safety.[67] Such landscapes may not have been typical of the conflict but they were typical of the war the soldiers remembered long after it was over. For them it constituted, as it does for us, part of our memory of 20th century warfare.

The world of the Holocaust was more infernal still, even in an age in which men were stalked constantly by death, betrayal and disappointment. The Jews, writes one commentator, found themselves occupying the very centre of Dante's Inferno.[68] For another, Dante's Nine Circles of Hell had been replaced by the names of the death camps, names that haunt us still, that still wait to be exorcised from our imagination.[69] It was a peculiarly modern hell, of course. Even the most enlightened nations seemed to relish a nostalgia for barbarism; even the most scientifically advanced seemed willing to put science at the disposal of unscientific ideologies.

Was this *universe concentrationnaire* grasped at the time? Was the image of hell subconsciously aimed at?[70] Steiner has no doubt that the death camps were hell made immanent, the transference of the inferno from beneath the earth to its surface, the physical realisation in the modern mind of the Christian doctrine of damnation. As a moral reference point the Christian iconography of hell is perhaps the most immediate way by which we can come to terms with the death camp experience.

An infernal landscape apart, another intimation of hell captured in the photographs of the period was the look of bemusement in the eyes of the victims of 20th century warfare. In the photographs of the men who joined up so enthusiastically to fight the Great War what do we see but a look of mute incomprehension? Most of the soldiers look quite out of their depth. Many have the look of those who, finding themselves caught in history's slipstream, are desperately trying to reach the updraught without success.

In one of his many letters to the poet Ezra Pound, Wyndham Lewis recounted meeting a group of infantrymen returning from a raid. Their faces, he remarked, were 'all dull, their eyes turned inwards in sallow thought, or savage resignation; you would say *repulsed* if that were not too definite a word'.[71] Officers frequently commented on the apathy of their men – they seemed to them frequently to be 'children mourning in a haze of their own dreamworld', bearing a look of utter dejection as though defeated as much by life as by death.[72]

In the Holocaust those who survived seemed undone by life too. When the Allied forces liberated the camps they found that the few who had survived 'marched and laboured in silence, the divine spark dead within them, already too empty really to suffer'. As a former inmate recalls 'one hesitates to call them living; one hesitates to call their death, death'.[73] Beached by history, the survivors wandered around aimlessly, seemingly unable to comprehend the horror which had engulfed them.

Bemusement is what the first eyewitness accounts also noted in the faces of the survivors of Hiroshima. One witness recalls large crowds of people who moved silently away from the city towards the suburbs and distant hills. Their spirit broken, their initiative spent, they appeared to be walking to no particular purpose. 'Outsiders could not grasp the fact that they were witnessing the exodus of a people who walked in the realm of dreams'.[74] Another eyewitness recalled that many of the survivors were so blackened and bent that 'they didn't look like people of this world'. The 'Mask of Hiroshima', it was called, a look of bewilderment and disbelief:

> Their expressionless faces, the mask of imbecility, the face of an idiot, a face which had become a state of mind. The shadow of death had passed before their eyes, returned and passed on. The expressionless face was the mark not of the atom bomb but of Cain.[75]

As survivors many of them spent the rest of their lives trying to come to terms with the experience through which they had passed; their hell was a mystery that could not be shared, an experience that could not be communicated. Many returned to a world that had been irredeemably poisoned by war, to a people who had lost the capacity to give or receive either love or redemption.

Ultimately, the real intimation of hell was neither the grim reality of the battlefield, nor the sullen resignation of the survivors, but a belief, real or not, that their experiences had no meaning. No meaning, that is, other than that offered by Theodor Adorno that history is merely 'a progress towards hell'.[76] Mocking Hegel, Adorno went on to conclude that permanent catastrophe had become the only world spirit.

The despairing message that the Great War poets were eager to pass on was the purposelessness of individual suffering. Orwell later observed that most of the writing that came out of the First World War was the record of something totally meaningless, 'a nightmare happening in a void'.[77] Perhaps, he noted, this was not the only truth about the war but it was, alas, the truth about the individual response. A soldier advancing into a machine-gun barrage or standing waist-deep in a flooded trench knew only that the experience was appalling. After the conflict it was the sense of helplessness in the face of blind historical forces which the soldiers could not comprehend that persuaded many to bear witness to the horrors they had seen.

As for those who passed through the Holocaust most could find no reason for their suffering. Deprived of meaning they were almost as good as dead. They were denied a plausible symbolic world in which to place themselves, a framework of meaning with which to make sense of their fate. That was as much the pain of survival as the pain of guilt. That is why so many survivors spent the next 40 years interpreting and reinterpreting an experience whose meaning was ever elusive. That is why so many after surviving so hideous a fate took their own lives in the end.

It remains to ask whether in calling Auschwitz 'hell', we do not devalue the experience? People called Auschwitz 'hell' and its perpetrators 'devils' concluded one survivor, Michael Walser, because they could not comprehend how an enlightened age could treat a people in this fashion. 'Auschwitz was not hell', writes Walser, 'but a German concentration camp'.[78] The ease with which the camps were later dismissed as 'hellish' afforded an excellent excuse for not thinking about them at all. The reality of the experience was not translated into words but metaphors, which either belittled or distorted the experience itself.

For even the medieval view of hell was not quite as spare or tragic as the death camps of Hitler's New Order. In Dante's Inferno, the damned stand alone, suffering the travails and torments of a world that they have forged themselves in their own lifetime. It is their hell, no one else's. The souls of the damned have the freedom at least to speak to their visitors. They still live as they lived on earth, suffering the passions and inclinations which animated them in life. Dante's creations retain a tragic dignity, even courage. In Hitler's camps there was no chance of self-fulfilment, only the remote possibility of survival. A survival which was not worth surviving for some, for the philosopher Jean Améry, for the chemist Primo Levi, for the psychologist Bruno Bettelheim, all three of whom took their own lives 40 years later, in the twilight of a left-over lifetime.

In the work of Dante the image of man even eclipses that of God, such is the *heroic* nature of the Fallen, their awesome defiance to the end. In Hitler's inferno men were simply 'undone'. They were condemned because they were Jews, not men at all. In the 13th century imagination the inmates of hell were there, at least, by choice. They were their own free agents.[79] Even on the basis of an imperfect understanding of life, damnation was freely chosen. The Jews, gypsies and eight million others who were placed in the camps had no such good fortune. They were damned even before they entered the world. They were anonymous victims who did, indeed, find themselves in hell, in an inferno not of their own making.

WAR AS *TABLEAU VIVANT*:

MUGGERIDGE AND THE LONDON BLITZ

If you can blow whole places out of existence, you can blow whole places into it. I don't see why not.

(Elizabeth Bowen, *Mysterious Kôr*)

The novelist V S Pritchett recalls one of Elizabeth Bowen's characters observing the London Blitz, 'it will have no literature'.[80] In that sense, remarked Pritchett, it was like a car smash or a pile-up, a subject singularly without colour or distinction, a 'human accident' that had been waiting to happen – in a word, a mistake.[81]

It was much more than a mistake. It was an experience and for those fortunate enough to survive it, it was one which excited the imagination as a *tableau vivant*, a spectacle worthy of another more colourful age, one however which could only be staged in the 20th century.

No one drew a picture more vividly than Elizabeth Bowen, for whom the Blitz was much more than 'a car smash'. In one of her short stories she evokes a London which has come to resemble a lunar landscape, 'shallow, cracked, extinct'. Its soaring new blocks of flats and old houses look equally brittle under the moon. Not a light, not a voice, not a note from the wireless escapes into the silence. As she broods over its fate one of her characters is reminded of mysterious Kôr, a ruined, deserted city whose walls and towers stand forsaken 'beneath a lonely moon'. By the time the war came to an end, Bowen reflected, 'the abiding city' of Kôr might be the only city left.[82]

Bowen saw London in 1940 as lonely but defiant. Like many writers at the time she shared a special grief but also an unconcealed wonder at the vulnerability of a city whose streets sometimes vanished overnight. Not only did its inhabitants sometimes lose everything in a single moment, even its conventions and institutions exploded like bombs.

What most struck Louis MacNeice when he returned from America in 1941 was how much the Blitz had improved the look of the city: 'A block of shops which had been gutted and its pediments broken and its plate glass gone and its arches left open to the wind takes on a new dignity or patina it lacked in its ancient days'.[83] As for the many homes which had been cut in half by the bombing he was reminded of dolls houses, with one important difference: 'A bath in the bathroom and a dresser in the kitchen and wallpapers with roses and forget-me-nots and mirrors for the dolls to look into, not even cracked, but the dolls themselves have gone'.

What struck Kathleen Raine most were the stairways which led into space, the windows which opened up a threatening sky. Such writers were unlikely to represent the Blitz as anything more than a piece of social history, a unique piece to be sure, but one that suggested the bombing had a moral.

Later, Cyril Connolly expressed some regret for the loss of the London he loved, for the tall 18th century houses of Chelsea, their interiors blown out, gaping like ruined triumphal arches. Chelsea had been an area where social life had had some consequence; it had been one of the last strongholds of the cultured man of leisure. But who could feel any sorrow, he asked, for the loss of Leicester Square whose architecture was 'a standing appeal' to God to rain down death and destruction? Who could regret the passing of Victorian Bayswater with its stucco porches and lacy curtains behind which 'the hypocrisy of the century had been accumulated'?[84]

Radicals in fact welcomed the Blitz as a political statement which could be immediately decoded. The poet Julian Symons thought it splendid because it offered an insight into what life must have been like in post-revolutionary St Petersburg. 'For a few months we lived in the possibility of a different kind of history', of two worlds, one old, regressive going up in flames; the other new and egalitarian, waiting to arise from the ashes.[85]

For Graham Greene the Blitz provided a poetic retribution for the hypocrisy of the interwar years, for a society which had been fundamentally rotten. Could the world of the 1930s have ended in any other way? The urban wasteland that Greene saw when he travelled through England, the acres of abandoned cars around Slough, the industrial squalor of the north, had all cried out for destruction, to make way for something better.[86] This is precisely what the Blitz promised for the thousands who emerged from their shelters after the all-clear, who emerged into the dawn knowing they could expect something new. Buoyed up by such hopes Greene was inspired by the sight of 'flames like a sticky-coloured plate from a *Boy's Own* paper lapping at the early sky'.

Greene would often climb to the top of Primrose Hill with his friend Malcolm Muggeridge to survey the destruction from the best vantage point, the best front-row seat. There was something wonderful, Muggeridge later recalled, about London at the height of the Blitz, a city with no street lighting, empty of traffic once an air raid was on. For Muggeridge, the Blitz was the ultimate 'apocalyptic *son et lumière*', a nightly spectacle, a theatrical show on a scale which appealed to those of an aesthetic sensibility.[87]

Apocalyptic was the point. It offered a glimpse of hell, a foretaste, if a brief one, of the Inferno. Even David Gascoyne, who was personally appalled at the prospect of another war, appreciated that it would provide for many others 'a superb decor'. The future promised the world of van den Leydon's *Lot and his Daughters*, or that of El Greco, a veritable apocalyptic dreamworld.[88]

Muggeridge was reminded not so much of El Greco but the paintings of Breughel and Bosch. He was captivated by the emergence from London's underground stations early in the morning of large numbers of grey, dishevelled figures draped in blankets looking in the pale light of day like creatures from 'a Breughel painting of Resurrection Day ... predestined souls arising from their graves'. Even after the bombers had passed overhead these night-time habitués of the Underground continued to sleep on the station platforms, preferring their public to their private beds. 'Finally, they had to be dislodged by force', Muggeridge informs us, 'otherwise they might be sleeping there still'.[89] Was he so entirely off the mark? The shelters in the Underground must have fulfilled a social need beyond that of mere safety. Even at the war's end there were still bunks to be found on platforms, lined with chinz curtains, occupied by what the railways' own officials spoke of with pride as 'the loyal few'.

How do we explain the ability of writers like Greene to stand above the Blitz, to transform into literature so appalling an event? For one thing is certain, the war they wrote about was not the war endured by the 67,000 people who were killed in the bombing or the two million who lost their homes. Harold Nicholson probably spoke for the ordinary man in failing to find the Blitz at all redeeming. On Christmas Day 1940 he recorded in his diary that 'poor old London [was] beginning to look very drab'. Paris might be young enough to be able to take a little battering; London, alas, was not. As 'a charwoman among capitals ... [when] her teeth begin to fall out she looks ill indeed'.[90] But then Nicholson had an unpleasant war. His flat in the Temple was badly damaged by the bombing. For months he had to sleep in one of the study blocks of London University which had been requisitioned by the Ministry of Information. When he was on fire guard at the Palace of Westminster he found the snoring of his companions more unconducive to sleep than the monotonous drone of the bombers. Nicholson hated the war. Indeed, he was the only MP in the House who did not cheer the news that the *Bismarck* had been sunk with enormous loss of life. He could not – indeed would not – remain above the struggle.

Interestingly, Muggeridge was to recall how Greene remained totally detached whenever a raid was on. Coming upon him unawares he was surprised to find a total lack of sympathy for those around him.[91] Possibly Greene felt detached all along. His misanthropy after all dated back to the early 1930s when he had refused to visit the Soviet Union, not out of ideological animus, but because he had no wish to surrender a 'distrust of any future based on what we are'. The Blitz must have reassured him.[92]

Writing ten years after the event Greene, recalled that in the summer of 1940 London had appeared to him to be 'a corpse ... sweet with the smell of doom'.[93] Other, less misanthropic writers, remembered not the stench of death but 'the sweet scent of crushed glass'. Connolly and Orwell smelt a more hopeful future.

Greene, nevertheless, may not have been alone in his reserve. Most of the writers who recorded the bombing, including Elizabeth Bowen, insisted that the writer should remain detached. T S Eliot enjoined Stephen Spender not to get involved with his subject, but to treat it instead with reserve.[94]

Whatever their faults, however, no English writer to his or her credit ever realised the real detachment of an aesthete like Jünger, who tended to treat everything as an entirely solipsistic experience, the suffering of others as incidental to the plot, the victims of war as little more than extras on a film set. Jünger's writing captures the spirit of the age; to some extent, it is an explanation of the alienation. Alienation, deception, boredom, nausea, the vocabulary of Sartrean existentialism, works its way through Jünger's account of the Second World War, the account of a man who found meaning only in sensation.

Watching a bombing raid on the Renault works outside Paris in March 1941, Jünger found the entire spectacle rather tawdry, a cheap melodrama, worthy not of the theatre but of the pantomime. 'Seen from my quarter', he recalls in his diary, after noting in passing that several hundred workers had been killed in the raid and a thousand more wounded, 'the affair looked rather like stage lighting in shadowed theatre'.

Two years later he was fortunate to witness a raid more worthy of its spectators. Standing on the roof of the Hotel Raphael, a glass of Burgundy in hand, he surveyed Paris with its towers and cupolas, reddened by the sunset, stretched out in all its impressive beauty like the chalice of a flower flown over to be morally fructified. Everything was spectacle, a pure display of power intensified and sublimated by suffering.[95]

Apart from a brief tour of duty on the Eastern Front Jünger spent most of the war as a Deputy Provost in Paris where his social circle included such luminaries of pre-war Parisian life as Jean Cocteau, Marie-Louise Bosquet, the Paris correspondent of *Harper's*, and Alain Bonard, the travel writer, later Vichy minister.

Until Jünger left Paris he did not see the worst of the war. He certainly knew of it, however. To his eternal discredit he preferred to look the other way. As the war progressed, or regressed into even greater barbarism, he preferred to look on, unshocked, possibly unshockable. He once said of himself that he had 'no capacity for hatred'. Certainly, he showed no outrage at the atrocities he recorded, and no sympathy for its victims. His detachment is, perhaps, the most remarkable aspect of his life.

His detachment represented 'a grave defect of consciousness' claims the critic George Steiner. Admitting to no faith (secular or spiritual) Jünger's view of life was coloured by what the Germans call *die Versuchung zur Menschenvernachtung* – a temptation to despise other human beings. Even the language Jünger used to record his experiences was emotionally restricting. He often used jargon to minimise the impact of death, or dead words to anaesthetise himself to the horrors of the battlefield. The use of such language, Jonathan Stern argues, was quite deliberate. It revealed a contempt for those who did not share his set of values, a contempt not of death but of life lived on any other plane but an existential one.

What one critic calls 'the tone of ironical pessimism' which pervades Jünger's First World War writings is that of a man above the struggle, a narrator, or essayist, largely untouched by what he saw around him.[96] Like Hitler, Jünger was ultimately a solipsist. The world lived only for him. What he suffered on mankind's behalf confirmed his own authenticity as an observer.

Even in his First World War writing it is always the *other* person who is dead, the *other* soldier who is caught on the 'wire', the *other* whom Jünger observes with such meticulous detail, as if in the act of observing he was affirming his own life. He records how he spent hours staring nervously at corpses knowing that he himself might have been lying there instead.

Jünger frequently referred to himself in the third person. He wrote from a third person's perspective, from that of an outsider looking on. Not only did he tend to treat events as an outsider, he saw himself as an observer observing them. The act of remembrance was as important as the act remembered. That he survived to recall the events he had seen was all that mattered. His survival was the whole point of the events he describes:

> When I close my eyes I sometimes see a dark landscape in the background ... I recognise myself as a tiny figure, as if drawn with a piece of chalk. This is my outpost, right next to nothingness – down there in the abyss, I am fighting for myself.[97]

Whatever he was fighting for, it was certainly not to redeem the men he had fought beside in the First World War, or whom he observed with such cool detachment in the Second. In a diary entry for April 1946 he congratulated himself on his restrained recording of violent acts, his finely honed talent for appreciating them in terms that were essentially aesthetic and intellectual – in other words, for his ability to transcend the suffering of *others*. Unfortunately he spent so much time transcending the events he described that he never came to terms with them in their raw and most horrific expression.

As an aesthete, Jünger tried to interpret the incipient madness of war through the refinement of an aesthetic sensibility. As the war progressed it became increasingly difficult for British writers to do the same. What was once theatrical now appeared appalling. In the first volume of Waugh's War Trilogy, Guy Crouchback is reminded by the Blitz of the great liturgical celebration of Holy Saturday beginning with the lighting of a new fire and ending with a Pentecostal wind. By 1944, however, an attack by V2s conjures up a different picture altogether, not of a Pentecostal fire, but the Plagues of Egypt:

> 'It was something quite other than the battle scene of the Blitz with its drama of attack and defence; its earthshaking concentration of destruction and roaring furnaces ... was like a plague, as though the city were infested with an enormous venomous insect'.[98]

Muggeridge, too, was astounded by what he saw in Berlin in May 1945 when he set eyes for the first time on what had been accomplished by the Allies' unrelenting campaign of day and night-time bombing. How could one forget such a spectacle once seen, Muggeridge asked? Not all of the damage was created by bombers. The Russians had fought their way into the city street by street, house by house. By the end of the war a once proud city had been reduced to 75m cubic metres of rubble. The friezes and columns had been torn away from the Brandenburg Gate through which the most warlike nation in Europe had once despatched its armies to foreign fields. The trees along the Unter den Linden had been cut down for firewood, or charcoal. The subway had been flooded on the order of Hitler himself, leaving the victims of this internal shipwreck floating in black icy waters impregnated with soot, dust and sulphur.

The city presented a scene of utter desolation, a barren landscape permeated by the sour smell of rotting corpses, and the occasional glimpse of human badgers burrowing in the ruins, the 50,000 or so orphans who had been made so deranged by the bombing and the ferocity of the final Russian ground attack that they became hysterical at the mere sight of a uniform. Did all this, Muggeridge asked, represent the triumph of good over evil?[99] By the end of the war, even as a morality play, the bombed-out city offered little by way of aesthetic consolation, perhaps because in the nuclear age it offered little hope that the future would be survived.

WAR AS GRAND GUIGNOL:
CURZIO MALAPARTE AND THE EASTERN FRONT

As Grand Guignol chronicles, I can very honestly show you the very fine spectacle which it was, the setting on fire of powerful bastions ... the contortions and mimings.

(Céline, *Rigodon*)

As a war correspondent on the Eastern Front, the Italian journalist Curzio Malaparte discovered an even more bizarrely beautiful scene than the inferno of the Blitz. While walking one day along the edge of Lake Ladoga in the spring of 1942 he stumbled upon a translucent patch of ice through which were reflected the faces of Russian partisans who had been shot a few days before:

Imprinted in the ice, stamped in the transparent crystal, there appeared under the soles of my shoes a row of human faces remarkably beautiful, a row of glass-like masks like a Byzantine icon ... the lips were fine and consumptive, the hair long, the noses refined, the eyes large and exceedingly clear. What appeared to me in the ribbon of ice was a marvellous image filled with sweet and moving pathos. It was like the delicate and living shadow of men who had disappeared into the mystery of the lake....[100]

It is an account of an experience made romantic by Malaparte's sense of detachment. The writer succeeds in translating a scene of grim horror into a painting, a still life. The reader can almost hear the cracking of the ice underfoot, acting as a substitute for the partisans' lament.

Do Malaparte's images, these stark unexpected vignettes of the 20th century's most terrible conflict, reveal an excess of imagination? Are his accounts intended to be themes symbolic or real? What are incidents such as these supposed to conjure up in our minds?

To answer that question we need to know something of Malaparte's life. He was born Kurt Erich Suckert of German–Italian parents. He adopted the pseudonym Malaparte only in 1925. In his early journalistic years he supported Mussolini but fell foul of the Fascist Party in the early 1930s when his criticism of corruption hit home. During the Second World War he wrote despatches for the *Corriere della Sera* as a correspondent on the Eastern Front attached to the German army, before being expelled because of the over-critical tone of his reports. He spent some time in Poland, before moving to Finland. It was at Petsame in Lapland that he heard the news of Mussolini's fall.

Within days of returning home he was arrested for predicting that the German occupation was imminent and blaming Marshal Badaglio for not taking active measures to prevent it. He was released from the prison of Regina Coeli on the intervention of General Castellano, a friend upon whom it fell to negotiate the armistice terms with the Allies. Once out of prison he made for Rome and then for Capri where he awaited the arrival of the US Fifth Army. It was here that he completed his most memorable novel *Kaputt* from which the episode above is taken.

It has been said of Malaparte that in his novels war is not the protagonist but the spectator, that the chief character is not the war itself but what its soldiers witnessed during it, the destruction of a continent that was unable at the end of the struggle to look itself in the face.[101] Like Greene he treated the conflict with equanimity, in part because he believed the interwar years had been nothing but a sham, a mockery of everything Europe claimed to stand for.

It followed for those who were out of love with the past that the Grand Guignolesque moments which Malaparte recalls offered not a glimpse of a better world, but merely confirmation of human perversity. Indeed, was there a future after Dresden and Dachau? The world to which Malaparte returned gave him little reason for optimism. What he had glimpsed in the war, he believed, was Nietzsche's 'afterglow of European civilisation', not his 'age of the last man'.

How were writers like Malaparte to make sense of the horrors they had seen? How were they to invest their experience of war with meaning?

Beginning with the First World War and culminating in Auschwitz had not reality itself become so extreme as to outpace the capacity of language to represent it?[102] Was not the experience of war best communicated through deliberate and pointed exaggeration, rather than through factual accounts? What their accounts lacked in realism they might gain in insight; might they not be more truthful indeed, than straightforward reporting of the fighting?

Robert Scholes believes that realism died with the Second World War. If we cannot imitate the world we can construct a version of it. 'There is no mimesis only poesis – no recording only construction'.[103] The more poetic the account, the more the horror of war is transcended, the more real reality becomes.

It is a very unEnglish approach. But then the reality of war for both the Americans and the English has been quite different from that of the continental Europeans. What the Anglo-Saxons may dismiss as infantile, the translation of a reality denied into a fantasy asserted, other Europeans may find cathartic. Fantasy, at least, permits not so much detachment as a stepping back from the event. Creating a fictional past is not a way of displacing reality, but of recapturing its essence.

There are several ways of experiencing war (or any event) at second hand. We can start with a description, a poem, or a vividly written account, in short, with a word and imagine a battle or melée in our minds, or we can look at a photograph, an image, and find words to describe what we see, together with the wider scene from which the photograph necessarily excludes us.

Grand Guignol is surely an attempt to create something halfway between the two, to create a mental picture through words, but also to make an impact through the vividness of a bizarre, other-worldly event in the way that a picture does when we see it for the first time. Like a photograph it is, of course, an image the author wants us to see – it is his reality, rather than our own, but one that becomes our reality in the act of remembering.

An English or American audience frequently finds Grand Guignol artificial, or superficial, surreal rather than real because it is part hyperbole, often part pornographic. But is it also perhaps because the Anglo-Saxon imagination is limited? Malaparte's images are not familiar to the Anglo-Saxon experience and because they are unfamiliar are frequently dismissed as unreal.

However true to real life Malaparte's own account of the war may be, his intention was clear enough. He wanted to create an aesthetic of horror in the hope of conveying it in visual rather than verbal terms. Like Jünger he believed that the 'aesthetics of terror' could impose some order on a world in which the meaningful, indeed beautiful were to a high degree unreal. Malaparte scorned textbook accounts. He believed those who chose to tell a moral tale instead of painting scenes whose moral was implicit in the telling frittered away an important opportunity to reveal the nature of war. He chose the low ground, not the high, all the better, perhaps, to hit below the belt.

Malaparte's vividly baroque style is anyway far less unreal than his English readers may imagine. Take Helmut Becker, the Divisional Commander of the Totenkopf (Death's Head) Division, who on Christmas Day 1942 rode his horse to death before his colleagues in the regimental officers' mess. Their own eccentricities notwithstanding, the English knew nothing like this.[104]

Nor could they conjure up the scene in 1944 as Central Europe swarmed with armed men contracted out to the Nazis, modern versions of medieval *landsknechten* looting and raping with an abandon which had not been seen since the Thirty Years' War. As the Russians advanced in the winter of 1944 the people of Frisches Haff, an enclosed body of water on East Prussia's Baltic coast, attempted to reach the sea across the frozen ice before the Red Army arrived. Many fell through the ice with their horses, drowning with salvation in sight, envoking the scene of the Teutonic knights in the Battle of the Ice in Eisenstein's film *Alexander Nevsky*.[105]

Frequently, episode for episode Malaparte's grim images can be duplicated in real life. Take, for example, his account of a crowd of peasants stripping clothes from the bodies of Jewish prisoners ambushed on a stranded cattle truck in Podulea (Poland). In Malaparte's account, the corpses, protesting even in death against the indignities heaped on them, try to defend themselves against the further outrage of having their clothes and possessions looted, of suffering one indignity too many:

> Men and women dripping with perspiration, screaming and cursing, were doggedly trying to raise stubborn arms, bend stiff elbows and knees in order to draw off the jackets, trousers and underclothing. The women were most stubborn in their relentless defence. I never would have thought it would be so difficult to take a slip off a dead girl. Perhaps it was modesty still alive in them that gave the women the strength to defend themselves. Sometimes they raised themselves on their elbows, brought their white faces near the grim, sweaty faces of those who profaned them and gazed at them with staring eyes.[106]

The product of an overheated imagination? Unfortunately not. Take an account of the exhumation of murdered Jews at the Janowska death pits in Lvov. As the Russian Army approached in June 1943, the Jewish prisoners were employed to remove the bodies:

> The fire crackles and sizzles. Some of the bodies in the fire have their hands
> extended. It looks as though they are pleading to be taken out. Many bodies
> abound with open mouths. Could they be trying to say 'We are your own
> mothers, fathers who raised you and took care of you. Now you are burning us.'
> If they could have spoken maybe they would have said this, but they are
> forbidden to talk – they are guarded.[107]

Or take a similar episode in 1944 when the SS began burning the bodies
of prisoners who had been interred in mass graves outside the Plaszaw
Detention Camp. The surviving Jewish prisoners again had to disinter the
bodies and burn them. Many were horrified to see the temporary life that
the flames gave the dead. Often the corpses sat forward, throwing the
burning logs aside, their limbs reaching, their mouths opening as 'if for a
last utterance'.[108]

Another way in which the English and American experience differed so
much from that of the Italians was that both people were fortunate
enough to escape occupation. The Italians were not. No one in this respect
has surpassed Malaparte's account of the conditions to which citizens of
Naples were reduced in 1944. As a liaison officer with the US Fifth Army
he was in an excellent position to observe the onset of what he called a
unique plague, a disease which arrived when the Allies liberated the city.

It was a plague which attacked the soul, not the body. It was a moral, not
a physical illness against which there was no defence. Its first victims
were women who during the war had put up with every deprivation,
displaying a strength of mind and a quiet dignity as great as that of their
husbands or sons fighting in the field.

With the American occupation all too many were ready to sell themselves not for bread but for cigarettes. The men, too, soon lost what little
respect they had retained after Italy's surrender. Now they spat on their
country's flag and publicly sold their wives and daughters to the first
American soldier in the name of liberation.

Not even the liberators were immune from the disease. They were its
carriers. 'It is human to feel compassion for the afflicted' wrote Boccaccio
in the Introduction to *The Decameron*, referring to the plague which swept
Florence in 1348. But for Malaparte the source of the plague *was*
compassion, captured in the smiles of American soldiers, whose eyes were
full of human sympathy, who stretched out their hands in brotherhood to
a conquered people, an enemy that had turned ally overnight. Unfortunately, the price of freedom was paid not in the currency of 'gold but in
blood. Not in the most noble sacrifice but in cowardice, in prostitution, in

treachery, in everything that is rotten in the human soul'.[109]

During the war the Italians had fought to survive. In the early months of the liberation they endured every moral privation merely to live. The difference was profound. In fighting to avoid death they had preserved their self-esteem. After the liberation they were prepared to humiliate themselves for every food parcel and cigarette stub.

Malaparte's distress may have been translated into hyperbole, but other witnesses confirm his account. While walking through the city in the spring of 1944, Norman Lewis was accosted by a priest (a change from the usual pimps and whores) who offered him a range of small items, including umbrella handles and candlesticks uniquely carved out from the bones of saints he had filched from the catacombs. Lewis was intrigued more than distressed – after all, priests too had to live.[110]

What the Allies found in Naples was a society which had survived the war only to break down immediately as the old certainties – nation and nationalism – were challenged and lost their appeal. Perhaps, it was simply the impact of the 20th century.

An English reader may feel removed from Malaparte's account, but the English have never experienced the ultimate horror of occupation. Even the American GIs who swarmed into English towns during the war did so as allies, not liberators, an important distinction which enabled the English to maintain their self-esteem, while forcing the Americans to observe some 'social distance'. The American presence in London was very different from what the French journalist, Jean Lartéguy, described as 'the green sickness', the plague of dollars which he saw in the streets of Seoul, and later Saigon.[111] Like Malaparte's Neapolitan plague it was profoundly debilitating. It undermined deep social rules and conventions. It accounted, in part, for the speed with which the South Vietnamese gave up the struggle when the Americans finally went home, leaving behind them a society in which everything and everyone had had a price denominated in green dollar bills.

The fate of Naples, of course, was doubly tragic, for the corruption that followed the benign occupation of the Americans was following immediately upon the far more corrupting experience of 21 years of Fascism. After the war Italy produced few intelligent accounts of the war years and even fewer important novels. The country was shell-shocked in more than the literal sense of the phrase. As Jean Améry put it, in a telling image, a terrible war coming so quickly after a terrible peace had 'sucked nearly all the intellectual marrow out of the country'.[112]

Malaparte took war as it came. By 1945 men had come a long way from the time of the First World War when so many artists had felt, initially at least, fortunate indeed to find in the shell-cratered battlefields and lunar landscapes of the Western Front a subject-matter so consonant with the austerity of that abstract vision that we identify with the *fin de siècle* Europe of 1914. Like Vorticism itself, their depiction of war, once so progressive, half a century later struck a discordant, even hollow note. It was out of key with the times; it belonged to a past beyond recovery.

The problem with Grand Guignol, is that it portrays a world populated by stock villains rather than ordinary men, monstrous atrocities not thoughtless brutalities, bizarre events not coincidental collisions. It belongs to that unique moment in the 20th century when men were inclined to consider life itself a lesser art.

7

Waiting for the End of the World

'Ah, Gentlemen, if I had been able to read and write I could have exterminated the whole human race.'
(Michael Caruso, *A Sicilian Bandit in his Address to his Judges in 1863*)

So far we have looked at several aspects of war in the 20th century which relate to modern consciousness and what is specifically modern about it. The questions raised by Nietzsche's war of the spirits were profound indeed for they involved nothing less than a post-Enlightenment inquiry into human nature.

Looking back at both World Wars, does one feel pity or not for the fallen? Was 20th century man complicit in his own destruction or was he the innocent dupe of Big Ideas and the political leaders who represented them? The plight of 20th century man has certainly been horrific, probably pathetic, but has it in any way been tragic? Was Cesare Pavese necessarily wrong when he was moved to observe during the Second World War that 'we feel pity only for those who have none for themselves'?[1]

Twentieth century man did not pity himself particularly because he felt that war was inherent in the modern condition. By 1945 there could be no illusions. The threat of nuclear catastrophe challenged Western man's idea of himself; it challenged his belief in progress, in his headlong rush into the future; it challenged the West's faith in science, in the pursuit of intellectual endeavour. Above all, as André Malraux suggested, it called into question the 'credentials' of Western civilisation.[2]

Perhaps, most damning of all, it challenged faith in reason, in the positive power of rational discourse. The ideological struggle between East and West, between communism and capitalism began to look increasingly absurd. Both value systems promised their followers off-the-shelf salvation, but both also threatened each other's survival.

Both sides were prepared to destroy each other in a nuclear war, both possessed weapons that could be launched as a result not necessarily of political design but miscalculation, by technical accident or human error. 'What to do if the machines turn traitor?' asked Walter Lipmann in 1914.[3]

Was this the apotheosis of modern man?

In the pages that follow I have chosen to look at the response of three men to the post-1945 world. Benjamin did not live to see the first atomic explosion; Bernanos died soon afterwards. Only Brecht lived on into the 1950s. The terrible knowledge that mankind had acquired the power to destroy the world inspired many tales of Armageddon, long before the Hiroshima raid. One of the explanations for Benjamin's remarkable insight into the logic of the new age is the fact that the age itself was merely a working out of earlier ideas and inventions. The ultimate totalitarian terror of strategic bombing, the idea of war as peace and peace as war, implicit in the concept of the Cold War from the beginning, the realisation of Benjamin's 'permanent state of emergency' of the 1930s, all looked back to the past, not forward to the future.

When the first nuclear strategists wrote about the new age they looked more than anything else at the way it distorted one of the great factors of continuity in human history, time. The destruction of Hiroshima took place in an instant. The bomb exploded at 8.15 am on 6 August 1945. The blast and resulting shock waves lasted only for a few minutes. Yet both they and the fires that raged in the hours afterwards accounted for 'a desert of clear swept charred remains', 'the vast expanse of desolation that the city became'. As the American strategist Tom Schelling remarked, Hiroshima had changed the concept of war forever, war that is, between advanced industrial societies

> To compress a catastrophic war within the span of time that a man can stay awake drastically changes the politics of war, the process of decision, the possibility of central control and restraint, the motivations of the people in charge and the capacity to think and reflect while war is in progress. It is imaginable that we might destroy 200 million Russians in a war of the present, though not 80 million Japanese in a war of the past. It is not only imaginable, it is imagined. It is imaginable because it could be done in a moment, in the twinkling of an eye, at the last trumpet.[4]

What is common to all three of the writers I shall discuss is the sense of how the invention of nuclear weapons altered the meaning of time itself. Benjamin had already glimpsed the coming of an era which would rob man of hope in the future. Brecht believed that the collaboration of scientists and the state required both to live in an eternal present, not at the threshold of time and eternity. Bernanos believed that the concepts of peace and war had themselves changed permanently, that after 6 August the world had to place its existence before its essence, that 'being' must take precedence over 'becoming', even if this meant questioning the ultimate meaning of history, a quest that had begun with Hegel on the battlefield of Jena.

WALTER BENJAMIN AND THE ANGEL OF HISTORY

'Deus ex machina –
God has waited patiently and steps forth from the atom.'
(Elias Cannetti, *The Human Province, 1948*)

Perhaps, suggests Jean-François Lyotard, the nuclear threat followed too soon after the Holocaust, an event which ensured that many of the great ideas which had animated Western civilisation, philosophy included, lay in ruins. 'The writing of survival is itself gripped by the shame of not having succumbed, by the shame of being able to still bear witness and by the sadness engendered by daring to speak.' European man, he added stood after 1945 'in the ruins of ethics'.[5] The West may have produced, wrote Susan Sontag, the most sublime, subtle and arresting works of creative speculation, yet as a result of its intellectual efforts Western man found himself:

> Standing in the ruins of thought, on the verge of the ruins of history, of man himself. More and more the shrewdest thinkers and artists are precocious archaeologists of these ruins in the making, indignant or stoical diagnosticians of defeat ... in an era of permanent apocalypse.[6]

Twenty-five years into the nuclear age Sontag saw the great thinkers as archaeologists of a past which they might have little time to study. The ruins of the post-Enlightenment world had become, in Sontag's words, 'the definitive image of a traumatised age in despair at itself'.

It was this sense of despair that Walter Benjamin captured in the last essay that he wrote, 'Theses on the Philosophy of History', perhaps, of all his works, the one by which he is most well known. It was a despairing time for Benjamin and his fellow intellectuals, who found themselves marooned in Paris waiting for the Germans to arrive. He himself was not to survive the occupation – he took his own life at the end of the year, despairing that he would be denied entry to Spain. At this critical moment of his life – a critical moment for Europe as well, Benjamin penned the following words on the concept of progress – the great consolation of the post-Enlightenment age:

A Klee painting named 'Angelus Novus' shows an angel looking as though he is about to move away from something he is fixedly contemplating. His eyes are staring, his mouth is open, his wings are spread. This is how one pictures the Angel of History. His face is turned towards the past. Where *we* perceive a chain of events, he sees one single catastrophe which keeps piling wreckage upon wreckage and hurls it in front of his feet.

The angel would like to stay, awaken the dead and make whole what has been smashed. But a storm is blowing from Paradise; it has got caught in his wings with such violence that the angel can no longer close them. This storm inevitably propels him into the future to which his back is turned while the pile of debris before him grows skyward. This storm is what we call progress.[7]

It is appropriate, perhaps, that in the 20th century Benjamin should have chosen as a metaphor for Progress a howling wind blowing all before it. In Eugenio Montale's *La Bufera*, perhaps, the best Italian work to come out of the Second World War, the Angel of Death is propelled into history 'shaking bitumen wings half stunted with fatigue', announcing to a disbelieving world that its hour has come.[8]

In some of his much earlier comments on historiography Benjamin had twice depicted the historian as a 'sailor setting his sails to suit the wind, the wind of history'. It was appropriate too that he should have written his Theses on History as he himself was forced to flee in the wake of the German advance. Like the Angel of History he was blown backwards into the future, a future he was trying to escape.

Benjamin, writes Hannah Arendt, invariably used metaphors in a way men had since the time of Homer, for poetic effect. In the *Iliad* the tearing onslaught of fear and grief in the hearts of the Achaeans is compared to the combined onslaught of the winds from the north-west skies across the dark waters (*Iliad* IX). In another context, Homer compared an approaching line of soldiers to the long billows of the sea which, driven by the wind, gather out at sea before bursting onto the shore in thunderous fury (*Iliad* IV).[9]

Throughout the history of philosophy authors have employed metaphors to illustrate their arguments. Often their use has told us little about human nature but much about the society engaged in its study. By 1940 however was not the wind an improbable, even debatable metaphor to use? After Hiroshima did not the word lose its 'value' as a positive force for good? Had it not become metaphorically devalued; was it not more resonant of a threat than a promise?

Paul Fussell has shown how for the English, at least, the word 'dawn' never again could conjure up an Arcadian innocence after the world had witnessed the first dawn attacks on the Western Front, 'the break of day in the trenches' (the title of a poem by one of the most accomplished of the war poets, Isaac Rosenberg).[10] The same is also true of the Second World War and the sunset, at least for Germans. As the protean narrator of Syberberg's film *Hitler* complains, addressing Hitler, 'You took away our sunsets, by Caspar David Friedrich.... The words 'magic' and 'myth'...., are gone, exiled to external time'.[11]

Did not the metaphor of the wind also carry a less innocent connotation after the fire-storms of Hiroshima had abated? The wind in the Gospels has always been used to describe the free play of the Spirit, to describe the infinite world of the soul. 'For the Spirit bloweth where it listeth.' Not only in English literature, but in European literature as a whole, the wind has been used to describe the noumenal, the breath of the unattainable but nevertheless defining freedom of what it means to be human.

In the nuclear era the defining wind constituted a very finite world in which human existence itself was now at risk. 'When the wind blows ...' the bombs might fall. For 40 years, writes Philip Windsor, that threat forced all of us 'to define ourselves in terms of what we can declare to be finite rather than in terms of what we can apprehend and join ourselves into, outside the condition of what we actually are'.[12] In that sense man was confronted with a terrible fate after 1945: the possibility that the 20th century might be discontinuous with itself – that the future might never happen.

Even before the experimental explosion of the first atomic bomb at Los Alamos, some of the scientists involved in the project had raised doubts about the wisdom of the experiment. Edward Teller, the man who was later to become the doyen of the US atomic establishment, raised the question whether the bomb might ignite the nitrogen in the atmosphere or the hydrogen in the oceans and burn up the world as a result. On the day it was tested the Italian physicist Enrico Fermi offered bets on whether the world or merely New Mexico, would be destroyed if the atmosphere were to ignite. Robert Oppenheimer took the threat seriously enough to advise the Governor of New Mexico that in the event of an accident he might have to declare martial law.

Fear of the Apocalypse was never far from the minds of the scientists on that fateful summer day. One spectator remarked that the sound of the bomb, a long hard thunder echoing around the mountains, warned of the Doomsday to come.[13] Another observed that being present at the first atomic explosion was like sitting in the front row of the Second Coming. For those who witnessed the Trinity test as well as those who heard about it at second-hand the explosion rekindled ancient thoughts of the end of the world.[14]

Many journalists at the time glimpsed the reality of Hiroshima from the very beginning. The life expectancy of the human species, observed an editorial in the *Washington Post*, had 'dwindled immeasurably in the course of two brief weeks'. 'In that terrible flash two thousand miles away' concluded *The New York Times*, 'men here have seen not only the fate of Japan but the future of America'. When *Time* magazine named Truman 'Man of the Year' it ruefully opined that perhaps the day of 'the great men' had already passed:

> What the world will best remember of 1945 is the deadly mushroom clouds over Hiroshima and Nagasaki. Here are the force, the threat, the promise of the future. In their giant shadows ... all men are pygmies ... even Presidents, even Men of the Year are mere foam flecks on the tide ... In such a world who dares be optimistic?

On the popular level, people had been preparing for the Apocalypse for some time. When the Second World War broke out in Britain it was confused in people's minds with the end of the world, with the dire promise of the *Shape of Things to Come*, H G Wells' stark vision of the future which had appeared as a popular film in 1935.[15] It seemed only appropriate that the catastrophe that the Allies escaped ten years later should live to haunt them long after their own bombs had fallen on Hiroshima and Nagasaki.

After 1945 it became impossible even in the United States, a society traditionally favoured by geography, to escape from the ever present threat of the bomber getting through. As he drove through Cleveland and St Louis one of the Manhattan Project scientists found himself measuring in his mind's eye the distance from ground zero, the likely range of lethal radiation from fallout, as well as the extent of the blast and fire damage that would result from an atomic attack.[16] For the Americans this was a novel, uncongenial experience. Never before in their history had they been vulnerable to an attack from the air.

The explosion at Los Alamos also ensured that Auden's 'age of anxiety', the age of the Common Man, was introduced by a funereal conch rather than a fanfare by Aaron Copeland. Up to then the anticipation of Armageddon had appealed only to fringe groups, mostly religious enthusiasts starved of a sense of purpose in their lives. Now it touched everyone. It was imagined even if the image was often suppressed. It was insidious; it would not be denied.

The prospect of a nuclear war threatened to rob man of his own 'immortality', to destroy his permanence in the lives of those to whom he bequeathed the only thing he could pass on: the memory of himself. To become extinct, of course, was a kind of 'forever', a kind of immortality through death.

The upshot was a profound malaise about the future. The playwright J B Priestley noted that characters in the novels of the 1950s seemed to be flat and withdrawn as if 'they were already on the side of the monstrous bomb threatening us'.[17] Siegfried Sassoon, who survived into the 1950s, was continually struck by the incongruity of 19th century paintings depicting prosperous citizens, 'complacently unknowing their great-grandchild's air-raid worried mind'.[18] The fear of nuclear war, unforeseen, sudden and inescapable seemed to be encoded in the consciousness of 20th century man. Perhaps, many surrendered too easily to humanity's worst fears. Too often, they seemed unable to look the future in the face. Many more lived entirely for the present, hemmed in by a past that was too massive for them and a future that was too slight.

There was a finality about the nuclear bomb which compromised man's consciousness of himself. Hiroshima cast a shadow, not of a new historical beginning, but of the end of history. In the 1920s Thomas Mann had spoken of the First World War as the determining factor in his life 'with whose beginning so much began that has scarcely left off beginning'. Hiroshima seemed to constitute a final chapter. For the first time in history man was haunted not by millenarian thoughts of the future but by the fear that he might be denied a future, a fear that was no less intense for often being acknowledged only subconsciously. The late 20th century world was haunted by the prospect of what one writer aptly termed 'a bomb induced futurelessness', in which the enforced peace of the Cold War was seen to be (in Christa Wolf's words) a *Vorkrieg* or prelude to war.[19]

What if there was no future? History, wrote Julian Gracq, had 'essentially become a warning addressed by the future to the present'.[20] The work undertaken at Los Alamos did not spell the end of history but it did mark a loss of confidence in history, a faltering of purpose that was widely felt.

In a time of anxiety it is often advisable to take refuge in a future more imagined than real, but did the dead ends of history reveal a new age or a new beginning? By the 1950s it was no longer possible to see history as Vico had 150 years before as a cycle governed by providence. Nor was it possible to see it as Hegel's progressive force that emerged through the dialectical development of the World Spirit. It was even more difficult to imagine it as a natural process governed by scientific laws which, reversing Hegel on his head, unfolded dialectically.

History offered no comfort to the spiritually bereaved, the anxious or fearful. For the Romanian philosopher Mircea Eliade the 'terror of history' was encoded in man's evolution. Eliade craved for an era in which history would be prohibited, in which men would seek to avoid any 'spontaneous gesture' with 'historical consequences'.[21] In the 1950s spontaneous gestures, or unconsidered political moves, could so easily despatch the B-52s to their targets.

Hegel had foreseen a time when happy people would be those without history. Somewhat ironically, Eliade's fellow countryman E M Cioran also hoped for an eternal *ennui* in which nothing would happen, a period of atrophy in which men would die, not in war, but from universal boredom. 'Revolted by the carnage of the 20th century', he wrote: 'The mind dreams of a provincial *ennui* on the scale of the universe, of a History whose stagnation would be so great that doubt would take on the lineaments of an event and hope a calamity'.[22]

Must we take history seriously, Cioran asked? And if we must, are we condemned to stand on the sidelines, looking on? The answer seemed to depend on man's ability to divine that 'mixture of waltz and slaughterhouse' which comprised his own 'becoming'.[23] This was not a *Weltschmerz* or *Mal du Siècle*, so common in 1914, a melancholic yearning for the end of the world. Men's thoughts might be apocalyptic after Hiroshima, but from necessity, not choice. Nevertheless, the end of the world remained demonstrably alive in the imagination. As late as the 1970s an American historian looked forward to a post-historical age in which the tempo of history might slow down altogether, a post-historic stage of human development in which progress would depend on marking time.[24]

Fear of the future was not confined to the world of intellectuals. In the popular imagination the science fiction writings of the era did not claim to show what inevitably 'would be', or even 'might be', but what 'ought to be' or 'ought not'. By the didactic criterion of 'ought', science fiction as a literary genre provided not so much an anticipation of future history as a reflection of present historiography, revealing the anxious apocalyptic presuppositions which were inherent in all late 20th century speculations about the world that lay ahead.[25]

What did this say of man? The prospect of nuclear war robbed man of what George Steiner calls 'the grammar of hope', an abiding optimism even in the face of catastrophe.[26] Man, of all animals, is the only one conscious of his fate. He is the only animal that can use the future tense to make something better of his situation, to project meaning beyond his own life. With the arrival of the nuclear age men were never quite sure if they would survive it. They may not have been reduced to quite so despairing a state as the Aztecs, a people so obsessively fearful of their own destiny that every 52 years they had asked the Gods for permission to go on living. Nuclear deterrence did, however, force a change in the way men thought of themselves and their future; it required the 'grammar of hope' to be recast in a different tense – that of the future conditional.

The threat of a nuclear war did more than prompt a change of tense. It represented a profound threat to a world that since 1929 had preferred to live *for* the future rather than the present. The whole basis of economic planning, and social engineering, whether Stalin's Five Year Plan or Roosevelt's New Deal had been predicated on projecting both economic growth and political development into the future. In the interwar years people had preferred to live in the future instead. The emphasis was placed not on the exact sciences with their inferential methods based on logical and mathematical premises, but the inexact sciences whose inductive and deductive methods of research were more informal. The latter were preferred in social planning because they dealt with the cultural, social and historical laws of evolution. And it was the inexact sciences which formed the basis for all economic planning, particularly in the United States where Herbert Hoover was the first president to bring social scientists into his immediate circle of advisers.

In the 1930s men had lived for the future in part because they despaired of the present, of ever understanding what Eliot called 'the futility of contemporary history'. The historians of the period fell back on relativism, a subjective approach to the study of the past which enabled them to explain what had happened in the past, at the same time as they acknowledged that history could provide no understanding of the present. In France a new historical school, the *Annales*, was founded on the principle that history was not about events, wars, or dynastic changes, or even diplomatic struggles. Its main characteristic was futility. The historical evidence was always slender, uncertain, disputable. Margins of error were so great that calculations were almost meaningless. As one of the most popular English historians of the 1930s wrote:

> Men wiser and more learned than I have discerned in history a plot, a rhythm, a predetermined pattern. These harmonies are concealed from me. I can see only one emergency following upon another as wave follows upon wave.[27]

Even in science, the phenomenology of Husserl and Heidegger gave every experiment the unpredictability of an adventure which had still to unfold. Reality was no longer neatly ordered according to the old categories of space and time, neither of which were any longer considered absolute values. Both were taken to pieces by the industrial system. In such circumstances it was easier to live *for* the future rather than *in* the present.[28]

By the 1930s men had concluded that the only creative space in a programmed society was the future; it was the only space in which society could be reformed, or men educated to be better citizens. On the eve of the Second World War the future was not a vision obtained from the present but an event for which Europe waited with hope. At the end of the war men suddenly realised that the event might come in the form of a catastrophe greater than anything they had imagined.

Benjamin's Angel of History is blown into the future by catastrophe – the ruination that history has become in the modern era. From a strictly literary point of view the angel recalls the allegorical progresses and triumphs associated with the Baroque theatre with which Benjamin was fascinated all his life.

With the decline of religious faith the world is full of objects no longer recognisable as the work of God but as allegories, ciphers of the consignment of humanity to fate and at the same time ambiguous pieces in a puzzle of redemption. Benjamin's angel, of course, reverses the allegorical tradition. Catastrophe lies not in the past but in the future. So does hope. Catastrophe becomes proleptic – it ruins time and blocks progress, even as it propels the angel along.

In modern allegories, Benjamin maintained, history appeared as 'a frozen primeval landscape' in which death was the only reality. Modern allegories rejected the assumption of an immanent meaning to human existence which was the basis of traditional art. Benjamin's allegories reject any meaning immanent in the world or the life of man. As the great theoretician of modernity it was a measure of his despair that he could write:

> History, all the suffering and failure it contains, finds expression in the human face – or, rather, in the human skull. No sense of freedom, no classical proportion, no human emotion lives in its features – not only human existence in general, but the fate of every individual human being is symbolised in this most palpable totem of mortality. This is the core of the allegorical vision of the Baroque idea of history as 'the passion of the world'. History is significant only in the stations of its corruption. Significance is a function of mortality, because it is death that marks the passage from corruptibility to meaningfulness.

Later, Benjamin returned again to the link between allegory and the annihilation of history: 'In the light of this vision history appears, not as the gradual realisation of the eternal, but as a process of inevitable decay ... what ruins are in the physical world, allegories are in the world of the mind'. Was there a future worth waiting for? In the ruins of Hiroshima through which the Angel of History had been swept, the 20th century contemplated its prospects for survival with caution. What does a political age do in the face of developments which reveal its ideals are running against the grain of events, not with them? In the face of such a predicament it can beat a retreat or dig in, or burrow through the ruins.

BERTOLT BRECHT REVISES GALILEO:
SCIENCE AND THE BETRAYAL OF MAN

Galileo spins a toy of the earth around
The spinning sun; he looks at the student boy.
Learning is teaching, teaching is learning.
Galileo
Demonstrates how horrible is betrayal
Particularly on the shore of a new era.

(Muriel Rukeyser, 'On Brecht's Galileo' (1973))

Towards the end of Bertolt Brecht's play *The Life of Galileo* the author puts a disturbing conclusion into the scientist's mouth. If scientists brought to heel by self-interested rulers limited themselves to piling up knowledge for knowledge's sake then science would be crippled. The invention of new machines would lead to nothing but new impositions. Progress would be nothing but 'a march away from mankind'.

In the original version of the play Galileo had been portrayed as a possible anti-hero, a man who, like Brecht himself, lived in a period of historical crisis, but nonetheless succeeded in surviving. Refusing to fall at the hands of the Inquisition he decides to live, to allow scientific research to take precedence over his responsibility to the Church. In the revised edition of the play Galileo is portrayed in a very different light, as a man who chooses to pass up a heroic role in order to survive. The two versions are not the same. If Galileo had only stood firm against the Inquisition, Brecht suggests, science might have developed a Hippocratic Oath, a vow to use knowledge exclusively for the benefit of mankind. 'As things are', he concluded, 'the best that can be hoped for is a race of inventive dwarfs who can be hired for any purpose'.[29] It was a despairing view inserted into the play after Brecht heard of the raid on Hiroshima.

In the most explicit reference to the dropping of the atomic bomb Brecht added a prologue to the play's American production. If the audience did not learn from Galileo's struggle 'the bomb might make a personal appearance'.[30]

Originally, Brecht had seen science as a great liberator. The war in which he claimed the scientists had sold out for new and upgraded research facilities robbed him of any illusion that science could create a better world. The atomic age which, in Brecht's own words, 'made its debut' in the middle of his revision persuaded him to recast Galileo as a man who temporises so much that he sides in the end with established authority. Galileo is no longer the hero who recants in order to live for another day, but a weak cowardly man who knows when he recants that he is aligning science and the Inquisition for ever. Truth becomes not what man demands for his own enlightenment, but whatever governments require.

Brecht was quite unfair to the historical Galileo but his distortion of the historical record does not weaken the force of his argument. With Dürrenmatt's *Physicists* his play remains one of the most searching examinations of the ethics of science written for the stage. Brecht's loss of faith in the power of science to redeem mankind still has the power to move an audience. His cynicism about scientific truth still strikes a contemporary chord.

In the 20th century the nuclear physicists chose to withdraw into a world of their own making, a private place of retreat, in the belief that all scientific endeavour was predicated on an absolute commitment to discover scientific truth, irrespective of the consequences of their research. If they gave little thought to the future that was largely due to the fact that governments now funded their research.

The scientific community is a 20th century invention. By comparing two very different communities which shared the same members, the group at the University of Göttingen in the early 1920s who came together of their own accord and the men who worked on the Manhattan Project who were brought together by the US Government, we can study two different communities at work.

The University of Göttingen succeeded in attracting nearly all the scientists whose names are familiar to us. There was the young Robert Oppenheimer who arrived deeply engrossed in Dante's *Inferno*, anxious to discover why the poet had located the 'eternal quest' in hell rather than in heaven. There was the young Heissenberg who arrived from Heligoland in 1925 with a revolutionary approach to quantum mechanics. There was the young Houtermans who was obsessed with harnessing the energy that fired the sun.[31]

All three men attended the Study Group on Matter which met weekly in Room 204. Here they debated such questions as had the discoveries in nuclear physics abolished the duality subsisting between the human observer and the world observed? Was there, accordingly, no longer any real distinction between subject and object? Could two mutually exclusive propositions on the same theme both be correct at the same time? More than just physics was discussed at Göttingen. Max Born, who was appointed to the Chair of Physics in 1921, later claimed in his autobiography that the theoretical physicist must be a philosopher as well.[32] Of all the philosophical discussions which dominated the thinking of the Göttingen Group, none was more important than Heissenberg's Principle of Uncertainty.

Briefly explained, Heissenberg was of the opinion that if an object has to be exactly the same before we recognise it we will never recognise it from one day to the next. We recognise it because it is much the same as when we saw it last. In the act of recognition a judgement is built in, an area of uncertainty charted. It follows that no event, not even nuclear fission, can be described with complete certainty. What makes Heissenberg's observation profound is that it allows for a certainty that *can* be reached: in the world of the atom, in the area of uncertainty mapped out by quantum physics.

Not every scientist was happy with Heissenberg's use of the word 'uncertainty'. Jacob Bronowski preferred the Principle of Tolerance in two senses of the word: the exchange of information between man and nature can only be effective within a 'ply of tolerance'; secondly, in the political world, as in the scientific, there can be no absolute certainty, no unquestionable dogma that demands blind obedience. Any form of thought that is inherently dogmatic must necessarily be wrong.[33]

It was the tragedy of the Göttingen circle that as they debated into the night the world around them gave way to the intolerance of Nazism. Those who chose to escape Germany in the 1930s, Born, Schrödinger, Einstein and Leo Szilard among them, fled to the United States. A few years later, in a race to beat the Third Reich from constructing the first atomic bomb, they found themselves working under government contract on the Manhattan Project.

Of the remaining members of the Göttingen circle, many were put to work on the German atomic programme in 1940. By a trick of history, the scientists working on the German nuclear programme were defeated by a chapter of unexplained accidents. Hitler himself was entirely indifferent to atomic physics. Albert Speer, who was responsible for continued investment in the programme, later noted that of the 2,200 recorded points of discussion in his conversations with Hitler the subject of nuclear fission came up only once.[34] The explanation for Germany's slow progress in building a bomb can be traced back, in part, to Hitler's lack of interest.

It can also be traced, however, to an amazing chapter of accidents, of chances missed, of experiments misrecorded and false trails followed up. A report on the feasibility of the use of plutonium as a fissionable material was locked away in a safe and forgotten. Tests on the suitability of using graphite as a moderator for irradiating neutrons were wrongly recorded with the result that German scientists abandoned the very line of research which provided the Americans with a breakthrough.

Was this the result of deliberate sabotage, or, perhaps, of an unconscious obstruction on the part of a community of scientists who were too loyal to resign but not loyal enough to the regime to unload their moral conscience altogether? Was it not so much an end-game as a refusal to play the game any longer? It would be reassuring to think so but the truth was rather different. We are afforded a chilling insight into the moral consciousness of the scientists who worked on the Third Reich's nuclear programme in a conversation that was recorded during extensive debriefing by British officials.

When they learned on the radio of the Hiroshima bomb their whole world collapsed. At one stroke their confidence in German technology gave way to a sense of profound despair. Six years of work had been wasted. Within hours the inquest began. The younger scientists began attacking their older colleagues for not having enough vision, for failing Germany in its hour of need. Walter Gerlach, the self-appointed *Reichsmarschal* of nuclear physics took the remarks as a personal affront and was profoundly depressed for several days. Why, asked some of the others, were the Germans not given credit for some of the achievements of Hiroshima – Otto Hahn, the discoverer of nuclear fission for one? And why did the British newspapers continue to give undue stress to the fact that Jewish scientists such as Lise Meitner had played an important role in splitting the atom?[35]

Later, they criticised the Nazis themselves for not funding the research adequately, forgetting that if they had exuded more confidence in their own research they would probably have had all the government funding they could have used. Their convictions clearly ran deeper than appeared. Regrettably, they showed more regard for each other than the morality of their endeavour. When the extent of their complicity became known the US National Academy of Sciences, instead of exposing them, set up a special committee which reached the extraordinary conclusion that their wartime service had been 'a form of political resistance' against the Nazi regime, that, by stubbornly staying in the ivory tower of pure rather than applied science, Germany's nuclear scientists had preserved 'an island of non-conformity' in the Nazi state.[36]

Perhaps those who worked at Los Alamos would have been treated similarly if the Allies, not the Germans, had lost the war. The episode is an eloquent commentary on the role that scientists have seen themselves playing in the 20th century. It is not, alas, an index of their moral standing.

What then of the Manhattan Project itself? Oppenheimer's contract with the military was essentially personal, a chance to recreate the Göttingen community which had existed when Max Born and James Franck had taught there. And Oppenheimer did just that, bringing together men with civilised, enlightened minds who had read Proust and Dante. None of them had much in common with General Groves, the American in charge of security, a man whose narrow Presbyterian upbringing was reflected in a countenance that suggested he was never plagued by doubt. A photograph of the two men, of Oppenheimer in his broad-brimmed hat, standing next to Groves at the Trinity testing ground, one so concave and elegant and curving, the other so convex, gross and steady, reminded Martin Green of a naive Pierrot and his brutal antagonist.[37]

The Manhattan community was, if anything, even more exulted than the circle at Göttingen. Robert Jungk wrote much later that it was probably the first time in history that so brilliant a group of minds had been assembled in one place. James Tuck, an English scientist who worked on the project from the beginning, claimed that he had found at Los Alamos the spirit of Plato's ideal republic, a gathering of 'the best minds of the western world'.[38]

Plato himself, might have quibbled at the comparison. For the scientists' commitment to building weapons of mass destruction did not stop at the nuclear bomb. When in April 1943 Enrico Fermi suggested that the products of radioactive fission might be used to poison the German food supply, Oppenheimer was sufficiently intrigued by the idea to recommend the use of Strontium 90. His enthusiasm was tempered only by his concern that no research project could be undertaken unless the government could be promised a 'kill rate' of at least half a million men.[39]

What disturbed the critics of science most in the 1950s was the extent to which progress was increasingly funded by government contracts. At Los Alamos the nuclear physicists had been forced to accept a new reality, that only laboratories run by governments and funded by research grants could furnish them with what they needed to continue their work. Who was really responsible for the nuclear age? The government of the scientists who allowed their enthusiasm for truth to blind them to their own moral responsibility, who, regardless of the consequences, contracted

with the government to press ahead with the pursuit of truth? Did not
governments in effect pay scientists *not* to think of the consequences of
their own work? Did not vast research programmes such as the Manhattan Project require them to live in the New Mexico desert hundreds of
miles from urban life, isolated from the real world, like medieval monks
who, in the course of time, grew 'unworldly'? Could man afford to
encourage the progressive divorce of science and society in the name of
progress? Should scientists like Enrico Fermi have been allowed to
dismiss the moral scruples of their colleagues as the ethical musings of
petty minds indifferent to the 'superb physics' of the atomic programme?
Could the quest for scientific truth for its own sake, asked H G Wells
shortly before his death, ever again be justified?

How could scientists lose touch with their own humanity in quite so
desperate a fashion? Let me suggest three explanations.

(1) One is the problem of specialisation. Ortega y Gasset once described
scientists as 'the specialised barbarians' of the 20th century who like the
'primitive savages' of old took everything around them for granted.[40]
They seemed to be without a sense of time, to have no respect for the past
and no understanding of the future. The modern barbarian, Ortega
argued, believed civilisation to be entirely self-sustaining. Specialisation
bred isolation from the wider community from which the scientists came
but to which they felt no obligation or sense of responsibility. Ignorant of
the outside world, the scientist was often a moral outcast hiding behind a
speciality.

Was Ortega right to be critical of scientists for not being Pascal, for not
knowing much of the human reality beyond science, for not understanding
anything of the world beyond their own mathematical reach? Like
Newton, Ortega believed that the modern scientist spent far too much
time on the seashore collecting colourful pebbles without raising his head
and recognising there was a whole ocean beyond.

Specialisation certainly encouraged the scientists to draw a false
distinction between thought and action. Jacques Ellul's ideal scientist was
the Christian hero standing at the point of intersection between the
material and the eternal worlds, the man who had responsibility 'as a man
as well as a scientist' to testify to the truth, not merely of one world but
both.[41]

Scientists often see things differently. For them science is not so much
an accumulation of particular pieces of knowledge, but an imposition on
experience of changing conceptions of reality, of how the world operates
and what counts for knowledge of it. Galileo's heliocentric universe was
not a development of the geocentric universe that preceded it, but of its

revolutionary overthrow. And its public acceptance was not a matter of adding one's own belief to an old stock of ideas, but of agreeing to see the world quite differently.

Surely this was the reason that the Inquisition harried Galileo? Surely his real sin, in the eyes of the more enlightened members of the Church, was not the questioning of its doctrines, including its assertion that the sun revolved around the earth, but the fact that, in the words of Lewis Mumford, he traded 'the totality of human existence' for a mere scientific proposition: 'for that minute portion which can be observed within a limited time span and interpreted in terms of mass and motion, while denying importance to the unmediated reality of human experience from which science itself is only a defined ideological derivative'.[42] In other words, to live life as if nothing exists except that which can be measured by science is the ultimate scientific detachment from the world of men, or the world of consequences. For Mumford this was as much an affront to civilisation as it was to Galileo's judges.

(2) The nuclear age also tended to cocoon scientists in a 'timeless' environment in which they were discouraged from thinking too much about the future.

There were probably many people, in the first night audience in New York, who believed that Brecht's revision of his play did not go far enough, that science itself should have been put on trial, not merely the scientists. In a bleak apocalyptic vision of the atomic age T E Huxley questioned whether Marx had been right to see force as the midwife of progress. Was not progress the midwife of force?[43] Did not the prospect of technological innovation provide men with instruments of ever more indiscriminate destruction while the unverifiable myth of moral enlightenment continued to provide an excuse for using those means to the very limit, and if necessary beyond?

Could the 20th century survive in spite of science, asked a despairing Bertrand Russell in 1952?[44] The explosion of the first atomic bomb conjured up many ghosts in the Western imagination, but one of the most compelling was the remorseless logic of scientific endeavour. Was not the loyalty of the scientist to truth, rather than humanity? The law of science is not the law of the good or what humanity thinks of as good, moral, decent or humane. It is strictly the law of the possible. The poet Archibald MacLeish, writing of Hiroshima, argued that humanity would never again be able to trust science. For what is scientifically possible, science must know; what is technologically possible, science must produce. It was a Faustian pact that produced infinite novelty, that offered unplumbed possibilities for their own sake.[45] Denied belief in God, scientists had become slaves to technique, as well as technology.

When he contemplated this scene, Russell's fellow philosopher, Lawrence Whitehead, was reminded of a Greek tragedy. In the 1920s Whitehead had argued that literature bore witness to a constant discord between the aesthetic institutions of mankind and the mechanical values of science. Science, too, lived with 'tragic incidents as its inevitable issue', the real tragedy being not the incident so much as the issue, its *inevitability*, or what Whitehead described as 'the remorseless working of things'.[46] The knowledge that a scientific discovery will be used as a state, not the scientist, deems necessary, often for purposes quite unscientific, constitutes the tragedy of inevitability in the 20th century. The scientist no longer has the right to choose whether to develop an invention or not, and to live with the choice once made. The state arrogates that right for itself. In the late 1950s Martin Ryle, discovered too late that his work on measuring the intensity of the Earth's gravitational field could also be used to improve the aim of intercontinental ballistic missiles.

(3) The Manhattan Project raised a third question in addition to the cost of government-funded research and the dangers of over-specialisation. In an age of scientific discovery made not by scientists working alone but as members of a team, was there a role for individual conscience? Could a conscience be collective? Was Robert Jungk right to insist that 'the individual is a brake on progress'?[47] Jungk had meant by this that in a team there could be no room for the gentleman rather than the player, for a scientist who is ambitious for personal recognition. The question he did not ask was whether there could be any room for moral responsibility when scientists are not held personally responsible for their actions. Are recognition and responsibility not the same? Could a scientist cast responsibility aside, by merging anonymously into a research team? Could a state that commissioned his research take all the guilt upon himself?

In the immediate aftermath of the Second World War both the United States and the Soviet Union, after all, had treated the Nazi scientists who fell into their hands as 'resources', not men. Some were put to work for communism, others for capitalism. It was assumed by both sides that they would not object to working for either provided they were allowed to continue their research.[48]

In Stalin's Russia nuclear physicists were as complicit with the state as their German colleagues. One of the most brilliant, Peter Kapitza, who had worked with Rutherford at Cambridge for 13 years, told Khrushchev that it was wrong to assume that 'the principal task of science' should be the solution of economic problems. Nuclear physics held out much more interest. In a letter he sent to the Soviet leader Yuri Andropov just before his death, he amplified his view about the relationship between scientific creativity 'which comes from dissatisfaction with what exists' and political dissidence 'which does not lead to such useful results'.[49] Kapitza's dissatisfaction with the natural world drove him to experiment for the sake of experimentation. His dissatisfaction with the political world was not as pronounced.

Jungk, too, had once confessed that what had kept him at Los Alamos was the possibility of using a special microscope that existed nowhere else in the world.[50] It was in that sense that Jan Myrdal condemned scientists as little more than the 'whores of reason' who were prepared to prostitute themselves in the name of knowledge, whatever the result.[51] Myrdal was somewhat disingenuous. Perhaps the sharper critic was the Austrian novelist Robert Musil who observed but did not pass judgement. The very virtues which made possible the great scientific discoveries, he wrote in the 1930s, were *au fond* the same type of virtues as were attributed to the success of warriors in battle. Long before intellectuals discovered the 'pleasure of facts', the world's warriors had known of them: 'In the struggle for life, there is no place for sentimentalism, there is only the desire to suppress the opponent in the quickest and most effective way: everyone else is a positivist'.[52]

The 'spirit of facts' as Musil called them, particularly in the realm of the intellect, favoured the triumph of the man of skill, cunning and tenacity, the man without scruples, with the courage to destroy as much as to create. If the scientist had, indeed, replaced the soldier by the 1930s perhaps Brecht's revision of Galileo should have been more extensive. Should he not have portrayed Galileo as the progenitor of the scientist triumphant, co-opted by a society in which scientific endeavour had become a secular faith, and the willingness to kill a sacred duty?

As time passed it became increasingly difficult not to think that the fault lay in the scientists as much as their inventions. 'If it had not been in you', Karel Čapek's fictional atomic explosives expert is told, 'it would not have been in your invention'. In time it became increasingly impossible not to regard the scientists who worked on the nuclear programme as culpable due to the peculiar bent of their vocation. In due course, scientists were seen to have a particular capacity for human suffering, to be susceptible to a 'dissociation of values' from which 20th century man had suffered once too often.

Early on in his study *On Thermo-nuclear War*, Hermann Kahn, a physicist by training, one of the founding fathers of nuclear deterrence, told a revealing story about himself. On one occasion, in the 1950s, during a public lecture he had explained that if every survivor of a nuclear war were to receive no more than 250 roentgens of radiation, only one per cent more children of the next generation would be born mentally defective. He added that he could well envisage a situation in which the United States and the Soviet Union might find such a figure an acceptable cost. At this point, a member of the audience interjected 'I don't want to live in *your* world, in which one per cent of children are born defective'. Kahn replied angrily that it was not *his* world, it was her's. If she did not want to live in a world in which one per cent more of children were mentally defective she would face a dilemma because four per cent already were.

For Kahn, peace was clearly almost as terrible as war. In the end, the two could only be distinguished by 'quantitative estimates': 'And it is proper with the kind of calculations we are making today to compare the horror of war and the horror of peace and see how much worse it is'.[53]

It is a revealing anecdote, one which confirmed the public in its suspicion that scientists were not entirely on their side. It is particularly telling that Kahn should have responded as he did, that the world he was describing was not his but the questioner's. His unconscious detachment made possible the equanimity with which he contemplated the prospect of nuclear war, a fact which was no less remarkable for being understated. At no time, of course, did he ever advocate that such a war *should* be fought, but he was clearly not as appalled by the thought that 'their world' rather than his own might be destroyed.

Occasionally, other writers let slip the mask. In the 1940s Wyndham Lewis had asked could an atomic war be survived? If 50 per cent of a wolf pack were destroyed would we notice any change? If 50 per cent of our friends were to be blown out of existence would we be inconsolable? If we lose a husband or wife we may marry another. If we were to lose our arms and legs we could set ourselves up as limbless men better off as 'curiosities'. 'We could lose eighty per cent of the population of the world tomorrow and not notice it much', Lewis concluded.[54]

Almost 30 years later, the North-East Thames Regional Health Authority arrived at the same conclusion in the driest and direst of terms. A nation, it concluded in its contingency war plan for 1980, was like a forest. The aim of war planning was to secure the survival of the great trees. If a sufficient number survived, if the felling of the rest was 'selective and controlled', recovery might be swift. 'There will remain brushwood enough if thirty million survivors might be so described'.[55] It was a metaphor which the public would not have found reassuring. Indifference to its survival, rather than complicity in its destruction, was the main public claim against scientists. In such a world mankind could easily become the victim of its own metaphors.

No wonder that men feared scientists as much as they did their own governments, or that William Lamb's old cry was occasionally voiced. Could scientific progress be reversed? he had asked. 'Can we ring the bells backwards? Can we unlearn the arts that pretend to civilise and then burn the world?'[56] If this was the march of progress, or victory of science, 'who shall beat the drums of its retreat?'. As Lamb concluded, no one would. The drums would be beaten in vain. Scientists would continue their advance.

And yet – in the end did Brecht really have cause for complaint? Would he have been happier if the world had condemned Galileo and embraced, instead, the astronomer's chief critic, Cremonini, a Professor of Philosophy at the University of Padua who had refused to look through Galileo's telescopes to observe the satellites of Jupiter because reason told him they could not be there. Was it foolish to blame the individual scientist as if the fault were really in the creator? Scientific discoveries are the result of an endeavour that can span cultures as well as time. Using different methods, with very different motivations, scientists stumble upon the truth. They do not create it.

Scientists did not create the bomb. They discovered the principle of nuclear fission. The discovery was not willed by any particular individual; it was determined by the way in which a society evolved, and by the circumstances which spurred on his research. An individual artist creates a work of art, a work that can be copied, or even anticipated but not created by anyone else. The scientist attacks a problem at the same time as other scientists; the first to discover a solution does so often only a few months or years ahead of someone else. In the 20th century governments tended to bring scientists together from all over the world to address the same challenge; the result was to produce a breakthrough years earlier than might have been the case had one or two scientists struggled alone.

The creations of artists come from within their individual imaginations. The atomic bomb, by contrast, was developed only after extensive discussion and collaboration. The principle of fission was discovered, not invented. Blame the age that required the weapon, or that funded the research, or the age that inspired the scientists to work on the challenge of splitting the atom. Blame the spirit of enquiry as the Church blamed Galileo, but do not hold the scientists responsible for their own enquiries – every age gets the scientists it deserves.[57]

Was this not appreciated even at the time by another German exile, the novelist Thomas Mann, one of Brecht's neighbours in Pacific Palisades, the suburb of Los Angeles that played host to a large expatriate German community including Arnold Schoenberg, Franz Werfel and Bruno

Walter. In 1945 Mann was engaged in writing one of his most important works, *Dr. Faustus*. It was an anxious time, especially for Mann who did not feel especially at home 'among the gentle barbarians' as he was given to calling his American friends and associates. Nevertheless, as he wrote to another German exile:

> Things look bad ... but I believe fundamentally that all in all, humanity has been nudged a good piece forward despite all appearances to the contrary ... Even the A-bomb does not make me seriously anxious about its fate ... What strange rashness or what gullibility that we continue to produce *works*! For whom? For what future? And yet a work, even one of despair, can never have anything but optimism, faith in life, or its substance, for despair is a strange thing: it already carries within it the transcendence to hope.[58]

BERNANOS AND THE TRIUMPH OF TECHNIQUE OVER REASON

> 'The prophets feel God's threat to humanity which appears just to them. Today, when human beings threaten themselves, the prophets are getting confused.'
> (Elias Cannetti, *The Secret Heart of the Clock (1974)*)

In 1946 Georges Bernanos proclaimed that the invention of the atomic bomb marked the final triumph of technique over reason. It was a sombre conclusion to reach based as it was on the fear that the doctrine and technology of deterrence would require their own set of rules and conventions, in an age in which unpredictable behaviour and unorthodox ideas could no longer be tolerated. The more that man found himself living in such a world the more he would lose any possibility of free choice in making the future radically different from or continuous with the past.

As a Catholic writer Bernanos saw the atomic bomb as a further sign of the world's madness, of the loss of moral authority. Whichever side won the Cold War, the world seemed to be moving inexorably towards an age that would be dominated by technology, not reason, an era in which it would appear that the Word had never been made flesh, a world in which mankind would take the opposite road to that of the Incarnation.[59]

Bernanos was surely right to fear not so much the misuse of nuclear weapons, as the false claims made on their behalf. Could the Manhattan Project be considered virtuous simply because the Allies had made a virtue of defeating Japan? Was nuclear terror not immoral? The potential for evil in the world was everywhere. Man could not be saved even by Christ's suffering on the Cross. 'Man has defiled the very substance of the

Divine Heart', Bernanos wrote, 'even the blood which flows from the Cross'.[60]

Bernanos died a year before the Soviet Union acquired its own nuclear weapons. He remained a pessimist to the end, holding fast to a view of politics in which governments were no longer accessible to rational argument. He died a self-professed Catholic but also a despairing one, convinced that the world would not be redeemed. He left unfinished a manuscript work on the life of Christ, as ultimate victim, crucified by a world that understood little of its own predicament, a world that was intent on crucifying itself.

For if religion offered only a remote hope of redemption, technology offered none. Machines had replaced Man. Deterrence required clearly prescribed rules of engagement that could not be broken. Technique cried out for stability not imagination. Ultimately technique required the systematic application of a sequential procedure, or a finite set of rules.

In a word, technology compounded a lack of meaning in people's lives because its own language was non-teleological. Nothing tells us why a given technique is desirable other than that it promotes a technique, the maximal application of a technological advance. The language of a technological society cannot 'refer' beyond utility because it can provide no encompassing structure of meaning.[61] This state of affairs really did reach an apotheosis, as Bernanos claimed, in the invention of the atom bomb. Up to that point the value of air power was derived from the need to kill the largest number of enemy soldiers in the shortest amount of time. With the invention of the atom bomb a technology was created that could annihilate mankind. By 1945 men were only able to refer back to themselves by reference to possible extinction of the species. The most they had to offer each other was not 'the brotherhood of man' – it was considered sufficient if the two superpowers offered each other not even a reprieve from extinction, but a sentence deferred.

Technique, in addition, represented power, in this particular case the power of one state to annihilate another. When power becomes absolute, Bernanos argued, values disappear. Power frequently eliminates the boundary between good and evil. In politics, as he had witnessed in the 1930s, the distinction between good and evil had been impossible to draw once the ground of action, the Nazi 'will to power' or the Marxist 'historical dialectic', claimed to incorporate all value in its person.[62] The upshot was totalitarianism. Deterrence, too, was seen by Bernanos as totalitarian in inspiration, not least because genocide had become the currency of military power.

Possibly, in his critique of nuclear weapons, Bernanos did not go far enough. If technique was suspect, so too was reason. It was common to talk of the 20th century's irrational behaviour, but was the century irrational at all? Did it not witness the triumph of a reason so absolute that morality was denied a voice?

Reason saw the possibilities inherent in modern science; it exploited those possibilities without moral qualms. Reason put a premium on the virtue of the assembly line, on productivity, on minimal input and maximum output, even on the industrialised battlefield on which soldiers were 'processed' at the Front. In the United States it did not take long for Bernard Brodie to introduce into strategic thinking such economic concepts as marginal utility and cost.

By 1945, the weapons of mass destruction had reached the point where it was possible for an air force to destroy a city such as Dresden every night. It had become 'rational' to sacrifice an entire generation for military ends as long as the means themselves were rational. The ability of a society to destroy itself represented the acme of scientific endeavour.

Nuclear deterrence itself was based on the most rational use of power. It took profound reason to construct the weapons systems, to think through the strategy which defined their use, to maintain and service the vast architecture of deterrence which was truly architectonic in conception.[63]

Thousands of scientists sponsored by governments worked at the outer frontier of scientific endeavour, crossing the threshold from the atomic bomb to the first thermonuclear weapon, from the V2 to the inter-continental ballistic missile which could retarget its warheads in flight.

Hundreds of thousands of technicians working in defence establishments ensured that the missiles were not despatched by accident, that the world would not be engulfed in a catastrophe by a renegade general, or a computer error mistaking a blip on the radar screen for a pre-emptive nuclear attack. Thousands more spent the best years of their life sharpening their wits on the quixotic quest for ways to *use* the weapons which they had designed, to fight a limited nuclear war. In the late 1950s interest focused briefly on the jungles of South-east Asia where a generation of American scholars thought that nuclear weapons could be used with minimum loss of life. In the early 1980s attention turned to Europe when new advances in technology appeared to make a limited nuclear exchange thinkable for the first time.

What troubled 20th century man was not the wish or willingness of states to go to war but their *capacity* to do so. Genocide had become not a reason for going to war but a means of conducting it. Genocide had become the currency of military power, not because the superpowers wished to eliminate each other, but because power happened to be located at the level of the species and exercised at the level of life itself.[64]

What modern man needed in Bernanos's view was a natural discourse that would allow him a future. It was a view that had been held in the 1930s by no less a figure than Ortega y Gasset. Writing in 1933 Ortega argued that 'modern man' had first appeared in 1600 when he began to question religious faith as the basis of intellectual security. The modern age began when pure reason took the place of revelation. The modern age was initiated when science began to serve as the foundation of man's entire system of conviction.

Ortega believed that man needed to make a new leap. If revelation had given way to pure reason in the 17th century then pure reason should surely give way to what he called *razon vital* – or 'reason from life's point of view'.[65] Over pure reason, Ortega argued, life itself should claim dominance. Instead of the perspective of science, 20th century man should view the world from the perspective of life. If this was true in 1933, surely it was true in the 1950s? If it was not a comment made lightly, surely it was a comment well made?

Did not the bomb, asked Octavio Paz, represent the universal Accident 'waiting to happen', an error of judgement that could unleash the bombers and missiles without design, by mistake – an accident that was all too 'imminently probable'? It was imminent because it might happen at any time; probable because God had been banished from the universe. An accident, Paz argued, is not an exception, it is a natural consequence of Western science, and the pursuit of rational enquiry. The universal Accident was part of an idea of progress, it was one of the attributes of Reason that the Western world so adored. And like totalitarianism it was essentially banal 'because in the final analysis the Accident is only an accident'.[66]

ALBERT CAMUS AND THE ABSURD

By definition the writer cannot serve those who make history; he serves those who have to live it.

(Albert Camus, *Acceptance Speech for the Nobel Prize for Literature, 1955*)

The events which gave rise to the explosion of the first atomic bomb marked a turning-point for many European intellectuals. Endurance was no longer enough even for those who had endured the world for 45 years.

The tears which they shed for mankind had crystallised into remorse and not a little anger.

Camus was the editor of the Resistance newspaper *Le Combat* when the atomic bomb was dropped on Hiroshima. In an editorial on 8 August he wrote that Western civilisation had achieved a new level of savagery. Appropriately, it now had the means to destroy itself in an act of collective suicide. Camus was highly perceptive even for the time. From the beginning, he saw the weapon as something quite new. It offered humanity one last chance; it confirmed that peace was the only goal worth struggling for. This was not a hope, it was a demand, 'a demand that governments choose between hell and reason'.[67]

In another editorial a few days later he was even more uncompromising:

> The 17th century was the century of mathematics ... our 20th century is the century of fear.... We live in terror because dialogue is no longer possible, because man has suffered entirely to history.... Science's latest advances have brought it to the point of negating itself while its perfected technology threatens the entire world with destruction.[68]

Were men not cut off from the future, living with their backs to the wall like dogs?

Camus' response to the explosion of the first atomic bomb was, to a large extent, influenced by a political philosophy that had been formulated during the Second World War after he left Paris for Oran in 1940. It found its full expression in his *Letters to a German Friend*, in his notes for *The Myth of Sisyphus* and, of course, in the work leading to the publication of his most significant novel, *The Rebel* (1951). He had seen, he once wrote, many people take their own lives because they believed life was not worth living, but he had also seen far too many getting killed for ideas that gave them a reason to live. He was determined to confront head on the monstrous paradox that 'what is called a reason for living is also an excellent reason for dying'.[69]

Like Cioran, Camus had an instinctive distrust of the incorruptible fanatic who is willing to destroy himself to redeem humanity. No human being was more dangerous than the martyr who suffers for a belief. 'The great persecutors', Cioran wrote in 1946, are recruited among the 'martyrs not yet beheaded':

> Once man loses his facility for indifference he becomes a potential murderer. Sceptics who propose nothing are humanity's beneficiary; believers its nemesis. We mistrust swindlers, tricksters, etc. but believing in nothing it is not they who betray man; they leave man to apathy, despair and uselessness; to them

humanity owes the few brief periods of prosperity it has known.[70]

Such were the somewhat despairing lessons Camus had begun to for-mulate before the war, but they were made more immediate during it by events he witnessed at first hand. The consolation of a secular faith did not console him for long. The Big Idea had become a monstrous perversion of human endeavour. In the nuclear age a man willing to die for his beliefs was likely to kill everyone else with him.

The Second World War influenced Camus' approach to historical meaning in several other respects. To begin with, he was compelled to 'enter history' for the first time. During the Occupation he had taken a direct part in the liberation, a step which was as much metaphysical as political, a declaration that he had joined up on the side of humanity because it had become too dangerous to remain detached.

Later, Sartre argued that Camus has mistakenly identified 'history' with 'war' and entered it for the sole purpose of fighting against it.[71] As a *soi-disant* Marxist, Sartre's own view of history was that it revealed certain universal values that man could only discover through participat-ing in it. It was a version of history which Camus rejected out of hand, a version, he claimed, with some truth, that had plunged man into an endless series of conflicts.

Man cannot uncover the meaning of history any more than he can be signed up to achieve a specific historical goal. Man must transcend history by rediscovering himself. It is in that spirit that true values are to be found, values which, being prior to history, are not anchored in time. Ultimately, man cannot invoke history to solve the most profound problems of the human condition. Such problems cannot be solved by political action alone. According to Camus, life, or Absurdity, has to be endured: 'We all carry within us our places of exile, our crimes.... But our task is not to unleash them on the world; it is to fight them in ourselves.'[72]

The onset of the nuclear age compelled Camus to go further than he had intended, to redefine his interpretation of the Absurd. Before 1939 he had been an anti-idealist, rejecting the existence of transcendent values which were not founded on daily experience. Yet he wanted more from life than mere meaninglessness. He had criticised Sartre's *Nausée* for declar-ing that the Absurdity of life was an end, not a beginning. The invention of the bomb changed that. He emerged from it convinced it must be an end.[73]

To deny all meaning, of course, would be nihilistic. Although he denied that states or secular religions could impose a meaning on life, he did not deny that life had meaning for an individual. To have argued otherwise would have meant following the Nazis in affirming that violence and deception were the only values that made sense of life. In his fourth *Letter to a German Friend* he wrote that he continued to believe the world had no supernatural meaning but he knew that something in the world had meaning – man. Indeed, man demanded it for himself. What does Zarathustra say? 'Only man ... creates a meaning for things, a human meaning, therefore he calls himself man which means "the esteemer"'.[74]

Camus' experience of war convinced him of the truth of an opinion he had long held: that only existential meaning exists in the world, that 'existence' must precede 'essence', that life must take precedence over ideas. In an essay penned in 1946 he argued that in a world in which murder by the state was considered legitimate and human life trifling, mankind should think twice before attempting to achieve some dubious political end. In an atomic age would it not be more sensible to sit out the century as a night watchman in order to hand on the torch to a generation better equipped to survive? After Hiroshima the existence of mankind could no longer be taken for granted. Surely survival had become the ultimate existential goal?[75]

Camus spent the years after the war vindicating life as God intended it to be lived. Mankind's task, he argued, was not to heal the wound of existence as Socrates maintained; it was to live life to the full and thereby realise mankind's potential. Like Nietzsche he rejected 'the unshakeable faith that thinking [can help us] not only to know Being, but also to correct it'.

Camus went one step further, in rejecting the proposition that to live life for ourselves we need to deny the existence of God. We need not admit that God ever lived, or that we killed him. It matters only that we should live life as if it is of no importance whether God ever existed or not.

In *The Myth of Sisyphus* Camus provides us with a uniquely valuable argument against suicide, the self-murder of the man who can no longer live because he feels life should be something else, because he feels cheated of a 'better life' he will never know. Camus believed that the only death that was warranted was that of the man who dies so that others may live, who fights an enemy that would deny him the right to his own life, who would force him instead into an ideological straightjacket. To die in order to live is a profound sacrifice – it is not the same, however, as dying in order to make life worth living; it is not the same as dying for a better world.[76]

We must work with what we have. We must live life as we find it. That too is Zarathustra's challenge – the ship *Perhaps* stands ready to voyage into the great unknown, but who will board it? No one. Men are not that tired of life. They would rather live than die for the promise of a better life, for the honour of sailing on *The Perhaps*.[77] Once we recognise that the Socratic delusion is precisely that, then any form of suicide, including nuclear annihilation, becomes banal – it vindicates not *the* truth but a truism that man has often adopted arguments inimical to his own best interests.

Camus could not believe it was sensible to blow up the world for an idea, or even to threaten to. Life might be Absurd but endurance was not to be despised. In *The Myth of Sisyphus* Sisyphus himself is portrayed as a tragic hero. He labours hard to roll the stone up the hill. He puts his whole weight against it. He pushes it up a hundred times, only to see it roll back to the bottom. His purpose achieved, he descends the hill to begin all over again. It is during his return that Sisyphus is vindicated. In the act of descending, he rises above his fate.

If the myth is tragic this is only because Sisyphus is all too aware that his punishment is eternal, that it will never end. What would that punishment be if he were to be sustained by hope of redemption? Sisyphus knows the wretchedness of his condition. But his endurance is his victory. He masters his fate by refusing to despair, thereby defying the punishment of the gods. 'The struggle itself towards the height', writes Camus, 'is enough to fill a man's heart. We must imagine Sisyphus happy'.[78] So we must, as we must also imagine man to be so.

In the first English edition of the book Cyril Connolly aptly quoted Camus' belief that if there is a cardinal sin 'it is not so much to despair of life as to hope for another life and to lose sight of the implacable grandeur of this one'. Ultimately, humanity should not lose sight of the fact that life, although Absurd, is still worth living. The heroes of Camus' novels are not nihilists. Their consolation is the discovery of companionship, friendship or love. They know very well that the world has no meaning and do not expect to discover it in the course of their lives. Usually they conclude their own existence with a gesture of affirmation, a vote of confidence in friendship. Instead of rejecting what Camus himself once called the 'ferocious hopefulness' of 20th century philosophy, they are willing, in the end, to live life to the full.

8

Savage Wars of Peace:
The West Encounters the
Non-Western World

By the end of the eighteenth century some of the audience could feel the pain
of delinquents on the scaffold. The implication, paradoxically, is that inter-
human identification had increased.

(Peter Spierenburg, *The Spectacle of Suffering*)

WAR AND THE 'MEANING' OF THE WEST

In Theodore Roosevelt's *Winning the West* (1896) the destruction of the
Indian tribes was justified in terms of their backwardness. 'The most
righteous of all wars', Roosevelt wrote, 'is war with savages, though it is
apt to be the most terrible and inhuman'. 'Savage wars of peace', Kipling
called them, not really wars at all but short campaigns which laid the
groundwork for future advancement. They were 'righteous' because they
had the sanction of history, 'savage' because like the countryside native
peoples were rolled back if they got in the way. Of course, the twentieth
century was to see far more savage and brutal wars between the
Europeans themselves. A people who could treat African tribes as part of
the scenery to be rolled back as the land was 'recovered' were bound to be
indifferent not only to the fate of other peoples, but their own fate as well.
Many of the phenomena that were to form part of the twentieth century
style of warfare – genocide as a tactic of war, the use of technology at the
expense of tactics, even the mass displacement of peoples – were practised
systematically, and consciously, in Africa after 1870.

Africa, in a word, became a testing ground not only for the introduction
of modern ideas, but also for the aggressive world-view associated with
modernity. In terms of laying the ground rules for the next century, the
imperial powers were predisposed to act in a way they themselves would
have considered unthinkable in Europe itself a few years earlier.

It would be wrong, of course, to see the scramble for Africa as the first such Western initiative. The settlement of the Americas after 1500 had an immense impact on the way the Europeans regarded themselves. So, to a lesser extent, did the slave trade, the 'middle passage' in which up to 15 million Africans were transported to work the plantations of the Americas and the Caribbean. What made the scramble for Africa different were the following factors.

To begin with it was a conscious initiative, even a historically determined one. That is why the British called it a 'scramble', the French a 'hurdle race', and the Germans a '*Torschluspanik*', 'a race to get through the door before it closed'. The door concerned was that of history. Some of the participants felt that if they lost the race, if they did not even take part in it, they would be dispossessed of the future.

The door that remained open for the Europeans, had, of course, closed on the Africans themselves. Hegel called them 'a people without history'.[1] Max Weber, who was critical of colonialism in Asia, called Africa '*kulturlos*', a continent without a culture. Africa, argued Hegel, was the victim of its own 'particularity', its failure to live in the universal imagination, its absence from the world of reason.[2]

As Eric Wolf writes, this was a highly Western understanding of history, one which condemned the rest of the world to obscurity. 'If history is the working out of a moral purpose [as the Enlightenment maintained] then those who lay claim to that purpose are by that fact predilects of history'.

Essentially, the historical relevance of other peoples was tied almost entirely, in a European imagination, to their so-called 'discovery' or 'rediscovery' as if they had had no independent existence of their own before the Europeans arrived. Unfortunately for Africa, the continent discovered in the 1870s was not a real world, but a creation of the Western consciousness. The Europeans uncovered a world which the indigenous people had never known themselves because it had never existed in their own imagination. If they had no consciousness of their collective identity, the Europeans gave it to them by writing up the history of their respective cultures. In the course of recording their past, Africa became everything that Europe was not – a continent singularly lacking in civic or moral virtue.

The second difference between the opening up of Africa and the Americas in the sixteenth century was the attempt to bring the former within a universal economic order that had only come into being in the industrial age. Hegel was the first European philosopher for 200 years to justify the institution of slavery, not for commercial gain or political profit, but as a phase of cultural assimilation. The Africans, he contended, could only be civilised by breaking them into the international economic order, if necessary on the basis of slavery. During the scramble for Africa 50 years later Samuel Baker, the Victorian explorer, advocated civilising the Africans through a compulsory system of trade, a corvée to extinguish African 'idleness'.[3]

The third difference is that there was a conscious or unconscious acceptance that if the natives got in the way of their own development they could be sacrificed with impunity. One of the most compelling features of European colonialism was that the Africans failed to register in the European consciousness, even in the travel writing of the period. Anders Sparrman, a pupil of Linnaeus, whose *Narrative of Four Voyages in the Land of the Hottentots and the Kaffirs* appeared in 1798, surveyed the landscape much like Adam alone in his garden. In his book we find him assiduously recording rock formations, plants and animals. But where is everybody, asks his most recent biographer?

> The human presence, European or African, is absolutely marginal, though it was, of course, a constant and essential aspect of the travelling itself ... Khoikhoi (Hottentot) servants move in and out at the edges of the story, fetching water, carrying baggage, driving oxen, stealing brandy, guiding, interpreting, looking for lost wagons. Referred to simply as 'a/the/my Hottentot(s)' (or not at all, as in the eternal 'our baggage arrived the next day'), all are interchangeable; none are distinguished from another by a name, or any other feature; and their presence, their *disponsibilité* and subaltern status are now taken for granted.[4]

The Africans were so taken for granted that the opening up of the continent had its genocidal features as well. In the Congo, Leopold II's appetite for profit led to a significant fall in the population by at least 10 million in only 20 years. 'Exterminate all the brutes', is Kurtz's famous exhortation in Conrad's *Heart of Darkness*. Exterminate them they did, in what the Belgian colonial administration euphemistically called 'administrative massacres'. In the use of euphemism, if nothing else, such measures can be seen as the precursors of the 'special treatment' that was soon to be meted out to European Jewry.[5]

So appalling was the colonial record in the Congo that the Europeans eventually bestirred themselves to appoint an international commission of enquiry which removed the colony from Leopold's personal control. Perhaps, Joseph Conrad best summed it up in a letter to Roger Casement, whose report on the Congolese atrocities had first alerted a disbelieving world to events in Central Africa: 'It is an extraordinary thing that the conscience of Europe, which seventy years ago put down the slave trade on humanitarian grounds, tolerates the Congo State today. It is as if the moral clock had been put back'.[6]

In other colonies, including the German Cameroons, plantation workers were treated just as brutally. Many were quite literally worked to death. Even in death they were still useful. In 1900 the *Deutsch Reich Post* reported that at their annual general meeting the plantation managers were able to reassure shareholders that 20 per cent of the workforce each year ended up as agricultural fertiliser.[7]

The main reason why the Western world tended to be insensitive to the suffering of non-Western societies was the lack of a single *moral* authority which they shared in common. In nineteenth century Europe, at least, it was presumed that all Europeans were Christians. In the Franco-Prussian War the life of a French or German soldier was not meant to be considered any more significant by either side. No country had a right to win a war by deliberately exterminating its enemy. In late nineteenth century Africa this was not the case. No African was considered worth the life of a single British or French soldier. The native population was treated as though its continued existence was a matter of little interest except to the subject peoples themselves.

Hegel had feared such a future for Europe. In Spain and Russia during the Napoleonic Wars he had argued that in a guerrilla campaign the enemy might be difficult to tell apart from the civil population. He was concerned that such wars might see an intense 'absence of mind', accompanied by an equally 'intense presence of mind'. By absence he meant a 'complete indifference' to the suffering of the civilian population; by presence the development of even greater weapons of destruction.

While serving with the Russian forces in 1812, the only aspect of war that Clausewitz found particularly distressing was the behaviour of the Cossacks. He was revolted by such habits of riding down stragglers at the point of a lance, selling prisoners to peasants for cash, or divesting the unsaleable ones of all their clothes. The Cossacks, of course, were outside the European order. Their cruelty, writes John Keegan, was a reminder of the 'visitations of steppe peoples, pitiless, pony riding nomads' that had lain buried in the darkest recesses of Europe's collective memory since the thirteenth century.[8]

Hegel hoped, at least, that the universal culture of which all Europeans were a part might persuade their governments to limit civilian casualties, to fight wars on the old terms. In some circumstances the civil population might even be spared.

As Hegel had also foreseen, the technology that the Europeans

deployed, from the breech-loading rifle to the Maxim gun, proved
devastating when used in a non-modern setting. Maxim, the inventor of
the first machine-gun, believed that 'only a barbarian general would send
his men to certain death against the concentrated power of his new gun'.[9]
Long before 1914 his optimism was found to be naïve.

The combination of technology and indifference to the loss of life made
some African wars terrible indeed. In 1905 the German commander in
South-West Africa thought that only the total annihilation of the Herero
people would ensure that they never rebelled again. In the course of one
campaign more than half the Herero were driven into the Omaheke
Desert. Their wells were sealed behind them. For months afterwards,
German patrols executed the remnants trying to break out to the west.
Those who escaped the desert were bayonetted or shot as a matter of
course. Those who surrendered were sent to the labour camps, where work
was heavy, food scarce and medical supplies almost non-existent. When a
census was finally taken in 1911, only one quarter of the Herero were found
to have survived. Worse still, a third of the Berg Damara people had
disappeared completely. They were massacred simply because German
soldiers could not tell them apart from the rebel forces.[10]

What was colonialism, asks Conrad's interpreter Marlow, but 'a wanton
smash up', the rape of a continent brought about by a superior force that
frequently never set eyes on the enemy? In the case of *Heart of Darkness*
it was a French man-of-war 'in the empty immensity of earth, sky and
space ... firing into a continent'. The English, Conrad reminds his readers,
had had a similar experience themselves. Throughout the novel there are
several references to England itself once being a dark place that attracted
its own alien conquerors:

> The Romans came here nineteen hundred years ago – the other day.... Darkness
> was here, yesterday. Imagine the feelings of a commander of a fine – what d'ye
> call 'em – trireme in the Mediterranean, ordered suddenly to the north....
> Imagine him here – the very end of the world, a sea the colour of lead, a sky the
> colour of smoke – precious little to eat for a civilised man.... Cold, fog, tempests,
> disease, exile – and death.

Just before reaching Kurtz's stockade Marlow experiences a similar
feeling of alienation: 'Never, never before did the land, the river, the jungle,
the very arch of this blazing sky appear to me so hopeless and so dark, so
impenetrable to human thought, so pitiless to human weakness'.

His displacement is ontological. The moral purpose of imperialism is
called into question.[11]

Just as the Romans also discovered that imperialism destroyed the old republic as their generals battled over the spoils, the theme of Conrad's book is not the rape of Africa but the corruption of the Europeans. Marlow finds a land that lacks for him, a European, the essentials of life: hope, pity and understanding. Instead, it brings out in him, *as a European*, the darker aspects of humanity: rapacious greed, and a merciless uncaring for his fellow men. Later his studied polemics about the superiority of the white race sound like the special pleading of a man seeking to control his own intuitive nature.

In policing an empire, the Europeans discovered themselves for the first time. In much of the literature of nineteenth century colonialism, the most significant moment is when white encounters white. 'The negro ... is the white man's fear of himself', wrote Mannoni in *Prospero and Caliban*. Kurtz wishes to exterminate 'the brutes' because they act in a way he is capable of acting himself. His own willingness to kill, however, merely confirms his terrible knowledge of himself. Kurtz's eventual response to this self-knowledge is madness, a madness that was to consume an entire nation in the twentieth century, when it, too, tried to remake man in the image of its own particular gods.

For the effort to reshape the habits of nineteenth century natives paralleled attempts back at home to improve the conditions of the working class. Colonialism was as much a social discovery of Britain as it was a rediscovery of Africa. The sickening English slum and the bestial African bush became representations of each other. The processes of social reform and imperialism went together, as Nietzsche had predicted would be the case with war and social welfare. If the Western programme to remake the whole world in its own image required environments such as Africa to be transformed through an act of will, so did social reform at home.

The poor were seen to be as uncivilised as blacks in the bush. The street urchins of London and Liverpool were actually called 'nomads'. In Mayhew's (1851) classic description of the London costermongers they are called 'skins' – after the beaver skin hats and moleskin collars which the poor often affected. Some reformers, James Greenwood and Mayhew amongst them, described themselves as 'social explorers' – 'travellers in the undiscovered country of the poor'.[12] Talk of urban jungles brought the dark continent disconcertingly close to home. The poor of London were as much strangers to Victorian England as the Africans were to England's empire builders. Indeed, as Mayhew noted in the preface to his book, less was known of the unfortunates in England's midst 'than that of the most distant tribes of the earth'[13]

In one sense the scramble for Africa helped promote the alleviation of some of the worst urban slums. Englishmen only a stone's throw away from the cathedrals and palaces of major cities rediscovered similar horrors to those which Stanley and the other Victorian explorers stumbled upon in the great equatorial forests. Moral improvement was necessary, indeed urgent. The poor had to be colonised and converted, redeemed from their misery, from a life that knew no rules of gender, and no experience of childhood. The metaphors of misery reverberated through the literature of outcast London, coupling the pauper and the primitive in a common destiny. After the mid-nineteenth century the transformation of the outside world became a model for the possibility of social transformation at home. The study of ethnography served at once to make the familiar strange and the strange familiar. In time, writes Levi-Strauss, the coloniser became self-evidently his own instrument of observation.[14]

If the poor of Western Europe, however, were rediscovered in the course of the nineteenth century, the other implications of imperialism were not quite so benign. Where they could not be redeemed they might have to be eliminated. In a series of books, starting with *Anticipations*, Wells outlined his own plans for a future in which there would be no physically or morally unfit citizens. 'The swarms of black and brown and dirty white and yellow people', he added, would have to go because they would not keep pace with Western technological advancements. Within Europe too 'the vicious, helpless and pauper masses' would have to be expunged. Their 'merciful obliteration' could be achieved by starvation, but killing might be necessary as well. The men of his Utopia, Wells predicted, would not shrink from exterminating 'weak and silly and pointless types', in part because they would be acting unselfishly, for the good of all, for 'an ideal that would make killing [worth the while]'.[15]

Wells was writing in an age when the study of humanity had become the object of precise observation in an attempt to determine a man's exact place in the social order. The founder of scientific taxonomy, Linnaeus, recorded the division between the inhabitants of Europe and Africa with the same scrupulous precision as that which he applied when describing the difference between crustacea and fish. The Europeans, in his eyes, were inventive, orderly, governed by law. The Africans were clearly unable to govern themselves. A mass of new information ordered and classified according to Linnaeus's own scheme of botany, was bolstered by the minor sciences of craniometry, phrenology, facial angles and other aspects of quantitative measurement. The result was a new 'chain of being' in which Africans were seen to constitute the last link before apes.[16]

Only 60 years later German anthropologists were to be found discussing the hooked noses of Semites; the flattened occiput of the Armenian race; the agglutinogen B frequently to be found in the blood of gypsies and Jews. During the Second World War Otto Blattschen, on detachment from the Ahnenerbe Institute for Research into Heredity spent months in occupied Russia trying to discover an as yet undefined Judeo-Bolshevik race, one which allegedly 'predisposed' the Russian people to becoming communists. The result of his research disappeared in the last days of the war – 150 numbered glass jars all carefully labelled, each containing a human head in formaldehyde, in a perfect state of preservation.[17]

'Let us look to ourselves if we can bear to and see what is becoming of us', wrote Sartre in the 1950s. Thirty years before, the Germans had set out with the same colonial zeal as the British and French who built the great railway and road systems of Africa. This time, however, they were more interested in 'engineering the human soul'. This is what Sartre meant when he argued that the dreadful history of 20th century Europe, the misery the Europeans had inflicted on themselves, was a product of their own *internal* colonisation. 'It is simply that in the past we made history and now it is being *made of us*'.[18] In the 1930s many Europeans became a people to whom things happened. By the mid-1930s the Germans had moved on from redeeming blacks to redeeming Europe by subjugating the Jews, the gypsies, the Slavs and any other subspecies of mankind considered to be 'primitive', 'ritualistic', 'superstitious' or 'alien'.

In pursuit of this ambition Hitler even invoked the language of late nineteenth century imperialism. Musing about the fate of the Soviet Union in October 1941, he looked forward to a different age of empire, one that would stretch across the Russian steppes:

> New territories in the East seem to us like a desert … We will take away its character of an Asiatic steppe, we will Europeanise it…. As for the natives we will have to screen them carefully.
>
> Above all, no remorse on this subject. We are not going to play at children's nurses. We are absolutely without obligation as far as these people are concerned. To struggle against the hovels, chase away the fleas, provide German teachers, bring out newspapers, very little of that for us! …. Let them know just enough to understand our highway signs …. There is only one duty – to Germanise the country by the immigration of Germans and to look upon the natives as redskins…'[19]

Hitler's order to the soldiers on the first day of the Russian campaign claimed that the war was a European crusade against 'the greater part of Asia'. The Russians, wrote one German soldier, needed war as a form of education, 'a good schooling' on how to become human.[20] Frequently, letters from the Front talked of the need to discipline the 'rabble', to introduce the Slavs to European culture as if the Slavs were a race apart. Writing from Lvov one officer reported that the Russians were 'a race that had been strenuously reared into subhumanity'.[21]

As the Prussian writer Heinrich Von Treitschke had written much earlier in 1862, in all colonial clashes, whether between Teutonic knights and the heathen Slavs, or the Africans and the British, 'the bloodstained savagery of a quick war of annihilation is more humane, and less revolting, than the specious clemency of sloth which keeps the vanquished in a state of brute beasts while either hardening the hearts of the victors or reducing them to the dull brutality of those they subjugate'.[22]

This classic work of historical scholarship waited 80 years for its first English translation, appropriately in 1942. Hitler's war in the East was indeed a war of annihilation but it was also one in which 'the dull brutality' of the conquerors was in evidence from the very beginning. As Kurt Vonnegut observed, looking back on his time as a prisoner of war in Dresden, he had been struck at the time by the contempt which his German guards felt for Britain's 'nigger wars'. 'What is really scary about Germans in Germany is that they enjoy fighting other white people'.[23]

The West did, of course, pay an enormous price for its own actions. Auschwitz destroyed any moral authority it had in its own eyes, let alone anyone else's. Even earlier, at the end of World War One, some of the more prescient European writers had begun to recognise that the reversion of European man to primitive savagery was hardly likely to inspire those 'lesser breeds beneath the law', whom it was Europe's obligation to redeem. In Barbusse's novel *Under Fire* one of the characters is described as 'an ape man, decked out with rags and lurking in the bowels of the earth [the trenches]'. The Europeans, wrote Frederick Manning, had become a people in 'the most primitive state of their development ... nocturnal beasts of prey hunting each other in packs'.[24] The soldiers at the Front were like 'beasts of burden marching under the lash of the ox driver', added Barbusse; like savages they were moved by brute instinct. Like the Africans they lived in 'a perpetual present'. It was no wonder that in the years that followed so many books appeared contemplating the decline, even the end of European history, books with titles like *The Decline of the West*, *The Passing of the European Age*, and Alfred Weber's *Farewell to European History* (the last two written during the Second World War).

Even before the war, in Mann's great fable of the alliance between creativity and disease, the plague that infects Europe is Asiatic in origin, a combination of dread and promise, degeneration and desire so effectively rendered by Aschenbach's psychology. In *Death in Venice* Europe, despite its art, its culture and its philosophy, is no longer invulnerable. Imperialism seeps through the cracks, and takes it back to its origins.

The rediscovery of Africa shocked the Europeans by revealing their own brutality. In 1884 Nietzsche had described the European powers meeting in Berlin to partition Africa as 'beasts of prey', who, having exploited one continent, would turn on themselves. He correctly saw that many of the imperialists who ventured out to Africa were 'a shrunken, almost ludicrous species, a herd animal ... mediocre'[25] men who could not reconcile themselves to what 'is outside, what is different, what is not itself'. If he spoke of a master race, he had no specific race in mind, certainly not the Germans (or the English). Both he concluded, were obsessional neurotics behaving exactly like the savages they suppressed. Both were savages leading modern lives.

Of all Western peoples it seemed only the Americans might be different. The refusal to take an interest in non-Western cultures was stronger in the Americans than it was in the Europeans. Was not the United States, after all, the ultimate discovered state, a continent whose discovery Adam Smith had declared to be the greatest event in human history?

The United States indeed did not become a major colonial power in the late nineteenth century, in large part because of its own self-confidence. It was not spurred on by fears of the future, by the need to reinforce its belief in itself. But its distance from societies such as Africa created, in its own way, a different form of alienation. Indeed, distance was to become the central feature of America's relationship with the developing world in the post-war years.

In 1943 during a Japanese air raid on Chunking, the wartime capital of nationalist China, the American scholar Owen Lattimer found himself in an underground shelter. As the bombers passed overhead he was surprised to overhear a discussion between two senior nationalist officials – not about the existing war with Japan but the coming war with the United States. The Chinese seemed to be more fearful of America than of the Japanese, more fearful, that is, of a country that although only 200 years old was so dismissive of a 2,000–year–old civilisation.[26]

Until the onset of the Vietnam War the United States never questioned its moral superiority over societies that were non-Western. In the course of the war, however, such feelings became inverted. 'We are the barbarians, not they', complained Susan Sontag.[27] In Vietnam a modern society which prided itself on a high level of technological proficiency finally came face to face with the destructive potential of that technology. Was technological capacity in itself a characteristic of a civilised nation or was a truly civilised nation one that employed technology for different ends?

Mary McCarthy, another critic of the war, writing of America through North Vietnamese eyes, depicted it as a primitive society. If it was sophisticated at all it was only in its militarism, and the very soullessness of its aims. For her, America, not North Vietnam, was unmodern, 'pitiably underdeveloped' because of its reliance on technology.[28]

These questions, raised and answered by the British and French 70 years earlier, were only publicly aired in the 1960s. The questions had already been asked, however, in 1900, when Mark Twain was at hand to record his own reflections on America's conduct of the Philippines War, one of its first military engagements in Asia. Indeed, he went on to identify a number of features that were to become all too common much later during the war in Indo-China. It is to Twain's account that we must now turn.

MARK TWAIN AND THE PHILIPPINES INSURRECTION

I bring you the stately matron named Christendom returning bedraggled, besmirched and dishonoured from pirate raids in Kiao-Chow, Manchuria, South Africa and the Philippines, with her soul full of meanness, her pocket full of boodle and her worth full of pious hypocrisy. Give her soap and a towel but hide the looking glass.

(Mark Twain, *A Salutation Speech from the Nineteenth Century to the 20th Century, 31 December, 1900*)

It was, perhaps, fitting that America's greatest ironist should have lived through the years which saw the rise of the United States from relative obscurity to the status of a great power, a player on the world stage, a country with colonies. 'God has predestined, mankind expects', wrote Melville in 1850, 'great things from our race, and great things we feel in our souls'.[29] The United States marked its entry into the 20th century, its aspiration to greatness, by going to war against Spain. It marked its coming of age by seizing the Philippines in the course of the struggle, provoking shortly afterwards a Filipino insurrection in which more Americans lost their lives than in the war against the Spanish.

When the West Coast was settled in the 1890s, it seemed for a moment that Manifest Destiny had come to an end, that the westward expansion across the American continent had reached its logical conclusion. By 1900 it had become apparent that the expansive urge had not dissolved, that the United States intended to push further West into the Pacific. Reminiscing while on a tour of the Philippines in 1902, Lieutenant

General Nelson A. Miles was moved to reflect: 'At that time the regiment was on the frontier, has been on the frontier ever since and I now find it still on the frontier, on the frontier of our island possessions; on the frontier of progress ... even on the frontier of civilisation'.[30]

How civilised, however, was the United States itself? For Mark Twain believed America's emergence as a colonial power marked not its coming of age but its loss of innocence. The United States had chosen to contract into a Faustian Pact with the future in which it had reaffirmed the superiority of its own culture at the expense of everyone else. It now seemed that America's mission to redeem mankind would be pursued at the expense of its own redemption. More than innocence was lost in the Philippines rebellion. So too, Twain claimed, was America's self–respect.

Twain's opposition to colonialism was not a product of old age, the dyspeptic anguish of an old man nearing the end of his life. He had opposed the proposed annexation of Hawaii in 1873 on the grounds that the United States had nothing to offer the natives, but 'the novelty of thieves all the way up from street-car pickpockets to municipal robbers and government defaulters'.[31] He saw all wars, but especially colonial strug-gles, as a monstrous procession of pasteboard heroes marked by the thunder of guns and the cries of the dying, a tawdry *tableau vivant* which amounted to little more than 'a wanton waste of projectiles'.[32] He insisted that wars were mostly conducted for the glory of the few who despised the many, their own people. He hated colonial wars more than any other because they revealed that the most efficient killers in the world were Christians, men of good conscience who slept soundly at night, convinced they were bringing the blessings of religion and civilisation to a world desperately in need of both. Consistent to the end, he held that all territorial possessions, including the United States itself, consisted of 'pilferings from other peoples' wash'.[33]

Twain was unrelenting in challenging America's belief in its own progress. In 1901 he published a scathing critique 'Two Persons Sitting in Darkness' in the pages of *The North American Review*. His title came from Matthew 4:16, 'the people who would sit in the darkness saw a great light'. Shall we, Twain asked, continue conferring our civilisation upon the peoples that sit in darkness:

> Or shall we give those poor things a rest? Shall we bring right ahead in our loud, pious way and commit the new country to the game or shall we sober up and sit down and think it over first?

Would it not be wiser, Twain asked, to see how much stock was left by way of glass beads, theology, the maxim gun and hymn books? Would it not be more sensible to balance the books and draw up a profit and loss account before pushing on?[34]

Extending the benefits of civilisation had indeed been good for business. Doubtless, there was still money in the enterprise yet, but there was less than in the past. The stakes were getting higher; the risks much greater. What of the British in South Africa who had manufactured a war out of material so inadequate that it had been difficult to disguise the Boer War as anything more than a private raid for cash? The burning of Boer farms, the herding of women and children into block houses had been difficult to explain away. Unfortunately, for the British, the Boers were Christian too.[35]

And what of German behaviour in Shantung? China had surely been monstrously overcharged in 1900 for the deaths of several German missionaries in the course of the Boxer riots? Surely, $200,000 a piece for them in money, together with 12 miles in territory was an extortionate sum? The people sitting in darkness knew that they had been defrauded. Could China afford to import civilisation if that was the cost? If the Germans had lost two missionaries in America, would the United States have been charged $200,000 for them, and cowed into submission? Years before in *Tom Sawyer Abroad* Twain had written 'I asked Tom if countries always apologised when they had done wrong, and he says "Yes, the little ones does".'

Twain was unusually sensitive to the 'pious hypocrisies' which he saw all around him. His success in exposing them to an incredulous America owed much to what Freud, in an analysis of his humour, once called an 'economy of spirit'. Twain's gift was to distract his readers from pity, to make them almost as hard-hearted as the countries he described, almost as indifferent to the damage created in the name of progress and civilisation – 'almost', but not quite.[36] In making his readers complicit with the targets of his irony he brought home to them their own innate callousness. It was the cruelty of colonialism that Twain exposed to the light. In so doing, he described some of the features of 20th century warfare that were to become commonplace 60 years later in South-east Asia.

His criticism of the conduct of the American army in the Philippines is almost a faithful echo of later criticism of the American army's conduct in Vietnam. The insurrection in the Philippines dragged on for three years and cost more American lives than the Spanish–American war. It also cost the lives of many more Filipinos. The numbers were high because American generals prosecuted the war ruthlessly, justifying their actions in the name of military necessity.

General Wheaton dismissed every allegation of brutality out of hand.
'The nearer we approach to the methods found necessary by other nations
by centuries of experience of dealing with Asiatics', he had insisted, 'the
less the national treasury will be expended'.[37] Twain quoted these
remarks in an essay he penned on the atrocities of the war. He also
excoriated another soldier, General Smith, for issuing an order of the day
exhorting American soldiers not to take prisoners but to kill everyone
without distinction of age, to reduce the country to a 'howling wilderness'.[38] Smith was eventually court-martialled and retired from active
service but many other officers whose opinions and actions had been little
different were not. For them the Philippines was 'a good little war' which
presented unique opportunities for promotion.

What were little wars in the 20th century? One aspect of colonialism
which Twain particularly disliked was the assumption that because a war
was limited for a country the size of the United States, it was necessarily
limited for a native population. What was small for the United States
might be devastatingly destructive for everyone else.

Twain's most forceful criticism of the conduct of the war was perhaps
his description of a much discussed episode in 1900, the massacre of 600
Moros rebels. Of the Americans who attacked their defensive position,
only 15 lost their lives. Of the rebels, not one survived. Little if any interest
was expressed in enemy losses. Twain evocatively captured the spirit of
this double standard. Against the Moros rebels, he wrote, one Private had
had the misfortune to have one of his elbows grazed by a bullet; another
the end of his nose scraped. Both 'casualties' made the news in the
American press. Both had their names wired home at the cost of $1.50 a
word.[39]

Why, Twain asked, did America grieve so much over the loss of its own
soldiers on the battlefield? Why in the war with Spain had the Spanish
losses been 'felt' as human beings killed by other human beings; why in
the Philippines was the enemy not considered human at all?

Indeed, before the Second World War nearly every American schoolboy
used to know what Captain J W Philip said to his crewmen on the
battleship *Texas*, in Santiago Bay in 1898. When shell fire from the *Texas*
sank the Spanish cruiser *Vizcayo* and set it ablaze from stem to stern,
Philip had remonstrated with his men for cheering: 'Don't cry, boys, those
poor devils are dying'. It was important, perhaps, that the poor devils were
Europeans. The Moros were not.

Even the way in which the Moros rebels were dislodged from their
stronghold was to become desperately familiar in the course of the 20th
century. The Americans lost so few soldiers because the rebels were

shelled from afar over four days. The shelling made it impossible for the American commander to discriminate between the guerrilla force and the women and children who were with them. At the range at which the American soldiers were deployed, Twain added, they could not even tell 'a toddling child from a black six-footer'.[40]

Above all, Twain deplored America's attitude to the Philippines and its people. He was horrified at its casual willingness to destroy other cultures. In one of his later works, *A Connecticut Yankee at the Court of King Arthur*, he painted a compelling picture of an industrial culture confronting a pre-industrial one, in the figure of Hank Morgan, a 19th century foreman from a Connecticut gun factory who wakes up one day to find himself transplanted to sixth century England. Everything begins well, as he well-meaningly attempts to graft his own Victorian ideas onto a pre-feudal Arthurian culture.

Appalled by the ignorant superstition and illiteracy of sixth century England, Twain's time traveller sets out to make life healthier and happier through 'improvement'. Within a few years England is a prosperous community:

> Schools everywhere, and several colleges; a number of pretty good newspapers.... Slavery was dead and gone, all men were equal before the law.... The telegraph, the telephone, the phonograph, the typewriter, the sewing machine, and all the thousand willing and handy servants of steam and electricity were working their way into favour'.

Inevitably, the forces of reaction in the Church and Court rebel against the prospect of modernisation. The book concludes with a great battle fought between Morgan's small group of supporters and 25,000 knights. Yet it is Morgan's weapons, so much more advanced and deadly, that tell in the end. In only ten minutes all 25,000 knights are killed.

At the end of the battle Morgan cannot even calculate the number of dead because not much remains of them. Killed by a massive discharge of electricity they have been reduced to a 'homogenous protoplasm with alloys of iron and steel buttons'. And what has this great battle been fought for? For civilisation? Not in the eyes of Hank Morgan. Recognising the danger of a revolt against his attempts to reform Arthur's kingdom, Morgan had connected everything he had built, every factory, mill and workshop, to a pushbutton which when pressed would blow everything up in a single moment: 'In that explosion, all our noble civilisation and factories went up in the air and disappeared from earth. It was a pity but it was necessary'.[41]

Seventy years later, during the Vietnam war, an American commander on 8 February 1968 shelled the town of Ben Tre without regard for civilian casualties. The town was almost totally destroyed. When asked why he had devastated everything in sight, the commander answered in a memorable phrase: 'It became necessary to destroy the town in order to save it'.

Did the Americans in Vietnam display a callous disregard for Asians? Or did the battle of Ben Tre reveal the shape of modern warfare? Did the episode betray the lack of respect that a new civilisation such as America paid an ancient civilisation, once eminent, now emeritus, its glory behind it, retired, superseded, but not yet dead? Or was the Vietnam War no different from that much talked about but never realised conflict between the superpowers in which both would have been prepared to destroy each other at the push of a button?

In that sense, the greatest distance of all between the United States and the world it sought to redeem was imposed by time. As the most modern state in the world, the United States represented the 20th century, the future; any pre-modern peoples, by definition, represented the past. In Indo-China the US soldiers camping amidst a four-thousand-year-old Confucian-Buddhist civilisation, among the pagodas, temples and shrines of an old culture, found that it was totally inaccessible to their imagination. The countryside might be heavily populated and rich in monuments and villages, but it was called 'the jungle', or 'Indian country'. Where the South Vietnamese were recognised at all it was only when they were driven into strategic hamlets or urban refugee camps, a policy the US military tellingly called 'forced draft urbanisation'. How could a modern society recognise an unmodern one, or pay it any respect?

As Octavio Paz wrote in the 1980s, the United States was a 'historical project'. It was not a land with a history, but a virgin continent which, in the words of Robert Frost, the Pilgrim Fathers had possessed – in their imagination – long before they arrived. The birth of America was a triumph of the voluntary contract over the fatality of history, of private ends over collective ends, of the future over the past. America was an act of will and as such an archetype of modernity. The end of American society did not lie beyond it, but within. History was what the United States willed.[42]

The United States rejoiced that it had no castles, no dungeons, no palaces disfiguring the landscape, no aristocracy or monarchy. By definition, all were to be swept away so that mankind could be redeemed from its past.

What Twain bemoaned was in part the nature of modern warfare. But he was also critical of the willingness of Western societies to destroy non-

Western ones in the name of reason, to kill in order to civilise, to destroy in order to redeem. The poet, Robert Lowell, once noted how for America 'saving the world' often meant nearly destroying it. If such destruction came, he added, it would come 'in the guise of an idealistic stroke ... the Ahab story of having to murder evil and you may murder all the good with it', a reference to the ultimate American novel of redemption, *Moby Dick*.[43]

Yet there was a further problem specific to the United States which Twain ignored. In its best manifestation, he believed, the redemption of the world from tyranny had achieved much. He was particularly proud that the United States had been inspired to declare war against Spain, in part by the revolt of José Marti. Like the American public, he too had been outraged when half the population of Havana province had perished in the notorious Spanish *reconcentrado* camps, the first concentration camps in history, built a few years before the British resettled the Boer population in blockhouses in South Africa.

Twain's dislike of colonialism stemmed from his unequivocal commitment to the old Jeffersonian republic. He wanted to see the American message exported; he did not wish to see the United States engage in real estate land grabs of its own: 'We shall be ... what we were before, a real world power ... by right of the only clean hands in Christendom, the only hands guiltless of the sordid plunder of any helpless peoples' stolen liberties'.[44] An avid Republican, Twain believed that the country was only as strong as its Republican virtue. It was a formidable responsibility, not to be flung aside by the bullying of the pulpit or the empty catch-phrases of politicians. Americans *were* the message; they *were* the American idea. They had a duty not to fight foreign wars but to maintain their virtue, to fight crusades perhaps, but not limited wars.

His faith in crusades, however, was itself a problem. In an interview with *The New York Herald* he confessed that he would have been happier had the United States gone to the Philippines not to conquer the island but to redeem its people. Ten days earlier in an interview with *The New York World* he complained that the United States had occupied the islands instead of acting as the people's protector, liberating them from Spanish rule so that they could set up their own government. 'That would have been a worthy mission'.[45]

The word 'mission' gave him away for he never doubted that the United States had one. Why else did he want it to keep its hands clean? He was not an isolationist, but a redemptionist longing for something to redeem. He was unusual for his age only in criticising colonialism as a medium of redemption.

Here too his criticism was one thrust upon him by observation of wrong, not one that emerged from a conviction of right. It was negative, rather than positive, reactive rather than innovatory and therefore lacking the impact of innovation.

The Philippines War, it should be said, was not quite as bad as Twain made out. It was an extensive campaign in which nearly every battalion of the US army saw service. But the number of civilian deaths has been exaggerated. The Philippine forces lost 25,000 compared with 4,000 US soldiers. Atrocities were the exception not the rule. It does little good to make out, as American historians did in the 1970s, that the war was genocidal, or to talk falsely of 200,000 civilian deaths in order to exaggerate or amplify the suffering.[46]

Twain himself exaggerated of course in order to draw lessons that would have even more relevance towards the end of the 20th century than at the very beginning. What we find in the Philippines War, is a debate about America itself.

Twain's contribution to an understanding of America's own 'savage wars of peace' is an impressive memorial to his writing. He set himself against the tide and paid for it by being ignored after his death until his works were belatedly recognised in the early 1960s.[47] His message, after all, was not one that Americans wished to hear at the height of the Cold War when they were at their most self-confident. Twain was too critical, too acerbic, too penetrating in his analysis of America for a country that was so determined to realise the promise of the 'American Century'. Only later did the Americans begin to recognise that he had something to say to the generation of the 1960s. Only later did they recognise that in his criticism of America's mission, he had been disarmingly American.

WAR AS 'DEAD TIME' - VIETNAM AND THE CONSCRIPT SOLDIER

> To survive in combat
> a man must turn
> from the teachings of other men
> and come face to face with himself
>
> For some it is a joy
> to come to know such a man as he is
> for others, it is a nightmare
> which recurs so long as he may live.
>
> Steve Mason, '*Casualty*'

The Civil War apart, no other war in American history was quite so searing an experience for the Americans as was the war in Vietnam. It was the experience of the common man, the rank and file soldier, not the writer or poet drawing a moral from his own response to the conflict. Vietnam was significant, in large part, because the only other major conflict this century, the Pacific War, had engaged the nation hardly at all. Apart from Norman Mailer's novel *The Naked and the Dead* and the Oscar and Hammerstein musical *South Pacific* (writes John Elis) its impact on American literature was limited.[48] In its immediate aftermath Jean Amery wrote that because the Americans never faced a crucial existential situation in the Second World War, the war had no literary value. The literature of the Second World War, he concluded, in a compelling phrase, did not 'illuminate American man'.[49]

The Vietnam War, by contrast, most certainly did. It struck a chord with those groups who already felt estranged from their own society. For them the experience of the conflict provided an opportunity to create a better America, a chance even to rediscover or redefine the old. In the course of the war most Americans learned little enough about Vietnam, and even less about the Vietnamese, but they learned a great deal more about themselves. Indeed, every time a soldier served in Indo-China he felt he was leaving his identity behind to be 'rediscovered' upon his return.

As for the veterans who survived, 700,000 suffered the effect of delayed stress, with a large number committing suicide. Of married veterans, 38 per cent were divorced within six months of their return. Of those who saw combat, a quarter found it impossible to readjust on their return; another quarter were arrested on criminal charges. By the 1980s, 40,000 were registered heroin addicts in New York City alone.[50]

No other war in American history produced such a delayed reaction, a sentence of death postponed. But then no other society had repudiated its returning soldiers, the men who fought ostensibly in its name. The Peace Movement, which had opposed the war from the beginning, compounded the veterans' sense of alienation by denying them what was left of their self-respect, by shunning those who returned disaffected, shell-shocked, even morally distressed. Ultimately, there were no heroes or villains in Vietnam, no right or wrong causes. In the crucial years of the late 20th century America was a society that lost its way, as Twain had always feared would be the case when it had first embarked on its Asian adventure.

(1) 'For Americans to begin to understand the Vietnamese and probably any other people in the world, they first have to understand themselves with some objectivity'.

Thomas Bailey, Interrogation Officer, 525th
Military Intelligence Group, *January 1970–August 1971*.

Perhaps the most important aspect of the war was the way in which the United States tried to keep its distance from the conflict – to avoid what Mark Twain had written about so eloquently, the catastrophe that nearly always arose when a modern society encountered a non-modern one. If in one crucial respect the coverage of the war by television newsmen actually narrowed the distance between the American people and the war at home, in all other respects the generals tried, with no success of course, to put as much distance between themselves, or the soldiers under their command, and the theatre of war in which they had to operate. Distance both temporal and cultural is, in fact, one of the best ways to understand the Vietnam War.

One of the ironies of the Vietnam War, for both sides, was that in no other conflict in American history was the private soldier more likely to survive. Nearly two and a half million Americans were called on to serve but mostly for only twelve months at a time. Only one in 20 saw combat, less than five per cent came face to face with the enemy. The United States was loath to commit its soldiers to a sustained ground war with the attendant risk of high casualties. Casualties *were* kept down. On a monthly basis, battle deaths in the Korean War were twice as high as those in Vietnam; in the Second World War they were 15 times higher. By comparison the *per diem* rate of fire-power exceeded that of any other war in history.[51]

For the American soldier Vietnam was not a death factory swallowing huge numbers of men in an attempt to eliminate or defeat the enemy. No encounter in the war was as closely fought as that of Hurtgen Forest in the winter of 1944, a battle on the Franco-Belgian border in which 30,000 US soldiers were killed or wounded, one for every square yard of land gained. Vietnam's equivalent was the siege of Khe Sanh (1967) in which the concentration of American fire-power was truly astonishing. In the course of the battle 75,000 tons of ordnance were dropped by B-52s over a period of nine weeks, the largest number of explosives dropped on a single target in history.[52]

Distance made it easier to deal ruthlessly with the enemy. By counting the amount of ammunition expended and the number of sorties carried out by its aircraft the United States judged the success or failure of each military action. In the Mekong Delta in 1968–69 the 9th Infantry Division developed the strategy further than any other military unit. 'Exchange ratios' (i.e. the number of enemies killed) were used to determine the professional skill of a unit. Each unit was graded on what was called a contact/success ratio – the number of times contact with the enemy produced casualties on the enemy's side. A battalion commander producing only 50 kills a month had to boost his total. It counted for little if sometimes those killed might be innocent peasants rather than members of the Vietcong.[53]

Distance, alas, did not reconcile the American soldier to his fate. If anything it increased his disorientation. For the Vietnam War was a war without front lines, without an enemy that massed its forces prior to an attack, without territory to be captured or recaptured. It was a war in which the old rules no longer applied, in which victory proved elusive because it could no longer be defined. It was a war in which soldiers who did see combat never knew the satisfaction of retaking a village or moving the front forward, of maintaining the momentum of an offensive, storming a beachhead, or holding it against heavy odds over time.

Americans as a whole, wrote the novelist Saul Bellow while the war was still being fought, were unpractised in introspection, badly equipped to deal with opponents whom they could not undo in daring, or despatch like big game. Some of the areas in Vietnam harbouring guerrillas were dubbed 'Indian country' by US soldiers. But it was Indian country without the Indians, with an enemy that was far more insidious and lethal, one with whom it was far more difficult to get to grips. When there were no fronts, retreats, forced marches or movements forward that could be traced on a map, no knockout blows or great offensives, how was success to be measured except introspectively?

The American army, in short, blundered into an Asian 'heart of darkness'. Like Kurtz, its good intentions were perverted and undone by a geographical and ethical wilderness. Philip Caputo's memoir *A Rumour of War* states this Conradian theme most unequivocally:

> Everything rotted and corroded quickly over there: bodies, boot leather, canvas, metal, morals ... Our humanity rubbed off us as the protective blueing rubbing off the barrels of our rifles ... It was no orderly campaign, as in Europe, but a war for survival waged in a wilderness without rules or laws.[54]

The heart of Conradian darkness is the discovery of the 'fascination of the abomination', the last stage of Kurtz's slide into murderous madness in the African jungle. Many American soldiers made the same discovery, killing both the enemy and the South Vietnamese with abandon. When questioned about their responsibility for this collapse into moral darkness, both at the time and after the event, blame was typically ascribed not to the individual but to the environment in which he had to fight.

In such a conflict what was the point of losing one's life for a cause? In the vernacular of the soldiers themselves men were not lost in the Vietnam War, they were 'wasted'. After all, what had they lost their lives for? Not for their country to judge from the anti-war protesters at home, the flag burning students, the *jeunesse enragé* who were vociferous in their protests about the immorality of the war from the beginning.

The Americans who were asked to risk their lives for South Vietnam also found themselves distant (culturally and psychologically) from the society they were supposed to defend. They also found a society they did not think worth defending.

Too often the civilians seemed to be the enemy. The Vietcong blended in with the local population. The enemy was often anonymous. It was a war that challenged the soldier to perpetual vigilance. A child of 10 could throw a grenade as successfully as a guerrilla soldier. Women could not be trusted. The old certainties of war were replaced by a moral environment in which disorientation was inevitable. The soldier in Vietnam found himself culturally and racially isolated from the population he was supposed to defend. Within weeks of his arrival, his isolation was usually complete. Denise Levertov's poem 'What Were They Like' succinctly catches the inadequacy of the rather vague ideas held about the Vietnamese people on whose behalf young Americans were conscripted to fight the longest war in American history. As Michael Herr wrote:

> Even the most detailed maps didn't reveal much any more; reading them was like trying to read the faces of the Vietnamese and that was like trying to read the wind. We knew that uses of most information were flexible - different pieces of ground told different stories to different people. We also knew that for years there had been no country here but the war.[55]

It helped, of course, that the casualties on the other side were not European, that American soldiers were often able to distance themselves from the enemy as a people. Less happy was their ability to distance themselves from their own allies. In 1967 a Japanese reporter expressed his profound misgivings about the war and the American role in it. Helicopter gunships, he recorded, certainly conserved American lives, but in a way that suggested that the Vietnamese themselves were not considered worth saving:

> They seem to fire whimsically and in passing even though they were not being shot at from the ground. Nor could they identify the people as Vietcong. They did it impulsively for fun, using the farmers as targets as if in a hunting mood. They are hunting Asians...[56]

This was one of the principles of survival made necessary by the US army's own logic of fire-power. In the Mekong Delta, heavy helicopter gunships wreaked havoc. Peasants often fled whenever they heard them coming. Unfortunately, their decision to flee was frequently interpreted by helicopter pilots as evidence that they were Vietcong irregulars. On the basis of this misunderstanding many lost their lives.

In a war milieu in which loss of life was rendered meaningless, survival became the only concern, the sole value in a war without values. War was not even the private act of men feverishly exorcising their personal obsessions. 'What had begun as an adventurous expedition', recorded one GI, 'had turned into an exhausting, indecisive war of attrition in which we fought for no cause other than our own survival'.[57]. The only way out of Vietnam, apart from death, was to fight one's way out. Each man fought for himself, often without regard for his fellow soldiers.

War is about many things, but one of the most important is what the Germans call *Vergangenheitzbewaltigung* – or coming to terms with experience. We can only master what we can understand. If we cannot master our experience we cannot master ourselves. We cannot, in Sartre's words, 'internalise the external', or inscribe in our personal history our own experiences.[58] Of course, a soldier who despairs of ascribing any meaning to his experience is dangerous. He is usually a man devoid of imagination, so overwhelmed by history that he is poorer in spirit, unlikely to consider important the petty decencies of war.

Moreover, a soldier who cannot commune with himself or his fellows is unlikely to be able to communicate with a society that cannot share those experiences except vicariously, through television. Such a man is neither a victim nor a survivor. He is more often than not complicit in his own destruction.

Survival in Vietnam was not an existential struggle as it was on the Western Front. Instead, it was entirely solipsistic. A psychological profile of Vietnam veterans that was conducted in 1971 found that many soldiers considered the war to be meaningless because they had 'delimited' the scope of their concern.[59] Such was the strength of their preoccupation with themselves that they were able to retreat into indifference, or indiscriminate violence, or unpredictable behaviour, frequently stimulated by drugs or drink. Those who conducted the profiles discovered that the soldiers had remained untouched by everything around them, including the fate of their friends. For them, the real tragedy of the war was that they did not feel it at the time. Indeed, they did not feel it at all. One veteran called his period of service in Indo-China 'dead time'. He functioned, no more.[60]

Even as a group they put as much distance as possible between themselves and each other. Each soldier had to work out his survival in his own way. One veteran acknowledged:

Most people dealt with Vietnam by getting juiced, or zonked, or by daydreaming about the world. 'The world' was any place except 'Nam'.[60]

Another soldier insisted, 'We went to Nam by ourselves; we survived by ourselves; we came back by ourselves'.[61] Unfortunately many of those who came back did not survive psychologically for long.

> (2) But we burnt the village down. Any kind of holes that were found in the ground were blown up. There were a couple of weapons found, nothing that significant. A fair amount of rice was destroyed...and the graveyards were bulldozed. The whole thing was turned into a big parking lot.
>   (David Ross, Medic, First Infantry Division, *December 1965–July 1967*)

In distancing itself from the enemy America also failed to understand the impact of modern warfare on a Third World society. It did not understand that the technology on which it prided itself was likely to make the war more lethal, more morally exacting, more unacceptable to the viewers at home watching the war unfold on their television sets every evening. The death of so many civilians, frequently dismissed as 'collateral damage', was an inevitable consequence of a high technology society fighting a low technology one.

B-52 raids offer one example. At the height of the conflict they averaged 42 sorties a day. On average, their *per diem* release of bombs was 3,891 500-pounders. The B-52, alas, was not an ideal plane for the job. It had been designed to carry nuclear bombs in the planned strategic bombing of the Soviet Union. Flying at 30,000 feet in a nuclear war the planes did not need pinpoint accuracy. Lack of accuracy was compensated for by carpet bombing.

But carpet bombing in Vietnam meant something very different from what it had in the Second World War. As early as 1942 the journalist Alexander de Seversky had warned that total war against an underdeveloped country might be futile. 'One of the most curious features of the most modern weapons', he wrote, 'is that they are especially effective against the most modern types of civilisation'.[62] Against a Third World society bombing was likely to prove useless. It might well devastate a country without undermining the enemy's will to fight on.

Moreover, although the strategy employed by the US army was not genocidal, it appeared to be so to those who were not out in the field. Since the First World War the purpose of warfare had not been to capture territory or defeat the enemy in the field, but to deprive it of an army. But what of a war in which the enemy was impossible to locate? What of a war in which it was impossible to tell the difference between the enemy and the civil population?

Hegel had predicted what might happen if such a war were to be fought in Europe. 'Complete absence of mind coupled with the most intense presence of mind...in the moment of acting', an absence of mind which might result in 'complete indifference' to the fate of an entire people. Hegel had hoped that such a threat could be offset by universal principles governing the conduct of war which would exclude hatred of the enemy population as a 'principle of action'.[63] Even if this was never the case, at the height of the Second World War only 30 per cent of the bombs dropped were aimed at civilians. The rest were directed at soldiers in the field, in an attempt to deprive the leadership of its army. In Korea 70 per cent of all bombs were dropped on civilians. In Vietnam it was as high as nine in 10.

At times it appeared that the old rule of thumb of eliminating the enemy's main force had been replaced by a quite different principle altogether – in Sartre's phrase 'destroying the enemy population now appeared to be the norm, or ridding Vietnam of all Vietnamese'.[64] The Vietnam conflict was the first 'techno war' in which one side tried to inflict so many casualties that the enemy would be unable to make good the gap between desired and available force levels. This was what General Westmoreland called 'the cross-over point', the point at which the Vietnamese would not be able to replace their casualties fast enough to maintain an adequate force in the field.[65]

It is also estimated that 12 million South Vietnamese fled from one side to the other, of whom 900,000 were wounded and a quarter of a million killed. In Vietnam the forced resettlement of the population was intended to deny the enemy access to safe havens. A government report on the refugee problem published in January 1968 found that of those who had not been relocated but chosen to move of their own volition, most had done so 'only when military operations, *usually friendly* bombing and shelling, made it impossible for them to continue living and working in their homes'.[66] In all, there was no deliberate policy to maximise the loss of life, but the war was prosecuted as though the civilian population did not matter.

Massacres on the ground like My Lai and Quang Ngai were not commonplace, but they were not entirely uncommon either. My Lai was fully consonant with the way in which the war was fought with the massive displacement of people. Villagers were often caught between the two sides when they were not herded into strategic hamlets. What was so different about the murder of civilians at My Lai and the daily tally of death counts in the Mekong Delta was that Lieutenant Calley made the cardinal mistake of executing people on the ground, reducing the distance between the soldier in the field and the enemy he had to kill. Worse still, he narrowed the distance between the population at home, watching the conflict on its television sets every evening, and the soldiers who had been sent out to fight in the viewers' name. As the war progressed so the distance narrowed even further.

It was not a comfortable war for the spectator. Too many harrowing scenes were broadcast, too many atrocities reported by the press, too much suffering displayed to be ignored altogether. The radio and television stations which had imposed their own ban on over-graphic battle reporting in the Korean War did not feel impelled to do so in Vietnam.

In order to cope with this distorted perception of events the army changed the ethical ground rules as well. It was considered 'perfectly ethical' to shoot peasants who were on the run (often fleeing the Vietcong), but not to shoot them standing in front of you. It was ethical for pilots to drop napalm on a village but wrong for soldiers to destroy a village with white phosphorous grenades. Ethics became a matter of distance as well as technology. Killing people at long range was sanctioned. Killing them at close range was not. The object of the exercise was to kill the maximum number of the enemy without committing soldiers to a long, psychologically debilitating conflict on the ground.

What saved the GI in the field should have gone some way to lancing the criticism that the United States was wasteful of the lives of its own citizens. But those like Robert Kennedy who resigned from the Johnson Administration did so, not in protest against the war, so much as against the methods by which it was fought, or what he called 'thoroughly un-American means'[67] - the use of napalm, defoliants and chemicals, as well as indiscriminate bombing. In fact, the means were very American, designed to save American lives at maximum cost to the enemy by exploiting the technological gap between a Western and non-Western society.

The logic of attrition which dominated the psychology of the war also explained, if it did not excuse, the manner in which it was fought. This in turn raised a crucial existential question, first asked by Susan Sontag in 1968, whether anyone's life other than an American serviceman's was really worth preserving.[68] The Americans, as Twain had recognised, were a dangerous people indeed, possessed of a profound cultural chauvinism that was as much existential as ideological. Many really did not think that other peoples and countries were really worth saving if a cost had to be paid in American lives.

(3) If it happened in World War Two they would still be telling stories about it.

> But it happened in Vietnam so nobody knows about it...they don't even tell recruits about it today. Marines don't talk about Vietnam. We lost. They never talk about losing.
>
> (John Muir, Rifleman, Second Battalion, First Marine, First Corps,
> *February-November 1966*)

One other definition of distance must be looked at, that which the American people put between themselves and the young men who returned from the war. What the anti-war movement at home found so traumatic about the Vietnam War was also peculiarly American: a violent self-questioning about the nature of the American Idea.

The silent majority on whom a series of presidents relied for support throughout the war was prepared to endure every vicissitude, trained as it was in the art of mute accommodation. It remained faithful to the national myth, although its faith was sorely tested. It turned its back on the veterans when they returned home because they had not vindicated the myth, because they had returned defeated. They remained a perpetual reproach to a nation that had begun to lose its belief in its Republican 'virtue'.

For the counter-culture, the Vietnam War was far more important than just a defeat, it represented, in the words of Charles Reich 'a major breach in consciousness'. It created a gap so large that Americans began to question all the other myths that had previously sustained them. For a small minority, the rent in the fabric of consciousness was so irreparable as to make repair almost impossible. Todd Gitling, one of the more sensible and sensitive members of the New Left, looking back at the 1960s, acknowledged that 'only true believers in the promise of America could have felt so anti-American. Ours was the fury of a lover spurned'.[69] Susan Sontag, Norman Mailer and Mary McCarthy did not feel themselves victims of unrequited love, but they too shared the disenchantment of youth, they too felt disappointment with what the American Idea had become.

Twain had written about a war in the Philippines which had reasserted America's sense of self; only by reaching out had the Americans seemed able to understand themselves. The war in Vietnam represented an inner search for meaning. A conflict thousands of miles from home fuelled an internal debate that had no parallel in American history. If Vietnam was essentially different from most other American wars, the reason lay not in the fact that the United States lost the war, for the first time in its history, but that American innocence was lost in the course of the fighting – the innocence of individual soldiers, but worse still perhaps, that of the nation itself.

Innocence was the subject of Grahame Greene's novel *The Quiet American*. Greene's book is often taken to be an indictment of the harm that American idealism and innocence wrought in the 1950s. Greene's criticism, however, went much further. 'What is the good of critising Americans', asks the British reporter Fowler, 'they will always be innocent, you can't blame the innocent, they will always be guiltless. All you can do is control or eliminate them. Innocence is a kind of insanity'. Greene's point is that setting out to restore a political order in South-east Asia for purely political motives, in a country about which the United States knew almost nothing at all, is not innocence. Belief in one's own innocence is not the thing itself. 'Only a virtuous republic is capable of freedom', Benjamin Franklin claimed at the moment of America's creation. By the time the United States left Vietnam many Americans had begun to suspect that a free people might be incapable of virtue. In future the Americans would not have to make the world safe for democracy, but make democracy safe for the world.

It was in an attempt to restore that sense of innocence that had been lost in the Mekong Delta that Norman Mailer set out in his own words 'to clarify the nation's vision of itself'.[70] America, he believed, was the most dialectical of nations, the best of its history being coupled with the worst. In protesting against the worst, an American could acknowledge the best, 'the energy, wildness and undeveloped possibility that is part of the American scene'.

In the great Pentagon demonstration of 1967 he found his patriotism renewed, not denied. Did not the anti-war chants represent 'the echo of far greater rites of passage in American history'?[71] America had been founded on a rite of passage. Few settlers had emigrated without each undergoing a test 'even if it were not more (and no less) than eight days in the stink, bustle, fear and propinquity of steerage on an ocean crossing'. Each generation of Americans had forged their own rite, at Valley Ford, at Gettysburg, at Argonne, at Pusan. Mailer looked forward to a day when Americans might once again embrace the radical ideas that had inspired the pioneers who had founded the country. The Vietnam War, he believed, offered a choice between the United States as an Eden in which its children were innocent, and a new Israel, a militaristic debasement of its faith in itself.

What the war protestors suffered from most was the most telling distance of all, an estrangement from their own idea of themselves. Estrangement, not alienation. In that sense critics were rather too prone during the war to dismiss as 'anti-American' some of the works of mainstream and fringe writers alike who were critical of the old America, if perhaps rather too naïve in embracing the new. What was frequently identified as a predisposition to hostility towards the United States was often far more important than that – a chance to rediscover a virtue that had been lost when the United States set out on its road to becoming a great power, a virtue that could be recovered by renouncing its role in Indo-China. Much of the protest against America's role was the expression not of revolt against the idea of America, still less a reflection of political alienation. It was a wish to reinvent America anew. What did Mailer write in his novel *The Armies of the Night?* 'Brood on that country who expresses our will. She is America....'

On that note his novel concludes. That is why Mailer may have come as close to defining the mood of the 1960s America as Scott Fitzgerald did in the 1920s. Both addressed 'a nation sprung from a Platonic conception of itself'. Both were inspired by a vision of what still could be. Both felt responsible for what America did in the world, as Americans, if discontented ones.

For most non-Americans, of course, the endeavour seemed a hopeless one. Could a virtuous Republic become a great power, could a great power ever attempt to be virtuous? Naïve or not, these questions were still of critical account in American history as late as the 1960s. Even earlier, during the Korean War, the American army discovered the depth of disenchantment that lack of virtue could produce among even battle-hardened troops. Early into the hostilities, on 9 July 1950, only four days after US ground forces first engaged the enemy in Korea, an officer of the 24th Infantry Division, taken prisoner some 48 hours earlier, made a 900-word broadcast apologising to the Korean people for American aggression. Nothing like this had been seen before in American history.[72]

In the prisoner of war camps disenchantment was equally evident. Fellow prisoners from different allied armies reported the general listlessness of American prisoners. Not one US soldier successfully escaped from a permanent prison camp during the war. Nothing like this had been seen too.

Conditions in the prisoner of war camps were bad, but not as bad as they had been under the Japanese. Brutality was commonplace, but most prisoners managed to deal with it. The main enemy that the American prisoner faced was despair, a feeling of betrayal by his own country. Forty per cent of American prisoners died during the war. One in seven collaborated with their captors. In its aftermath the US army concluded that the prisoners' response to their conditions was not so much one of war-weariness as a feeling of disenchantment.

Even behind the lines the US Army Medical Corps was surprised to find that most other Allied soldiers recovered faster from their wounds than did the Americans. The Europeans, in particular, were determined to get better as quickly as possible so that they could go home, so that they could restart their lives. The Americans, by comparison, were haunted by such a sense of self-pity that many had no wish to return to a country from which they felt estranged.[73]

Those who returned from Indo-China often found that their 'homes' no longer existed. Some remained marked for the remainder of their lives by what they had undergone. Others lost the capacity to feel or share their experience with others. Some were unable to communicate with the community at home; as they had failed to communicate with their comrades in battle. Withdrawal into depression was frequently followed by disengagement from all human contact, by psychosis, and even suicide. 'The Vietnam veteran', claimed Robert Lifton, testifying before a Senate Sub-Committee during the war, 'serve[d] as a psychological crucible of the entire country's doubts and misgivings about the war'. He was both 'the agent and victim of that confusion'.[74]

Looking back over the 20th century it would seem that one of the most important phenomena of 20th century warfare was the extent to which soldiers returning from a theatre of battle were dispossessed of their national identity, or estranged from the ideas which previously they had believed their country to represent. Of all the major testaments to war Erich Maria Remarque's novel *All Quiet on the Western Front* comes closest to making this point. The First World War for Remarque's generation had two quite different meanings 'we did not disintegrate, we adapted', claims the novel's hero Paul Bauner, the last of the friends to be killed. He acknowledges that war has its morally uplifting features, including the positive affirmation of comradeship. Its destructive element lies in its future implications. 'War has ruined everything for us', Bauner laments. Fear of the future and self-pity are the emotions experienced by Remarque's generation, a generation that was destroyed by the war 'even if it escaped the grenades'.

In a brief but forceful prefatory comment to his book, Remarque added that his account of the fighting was neither an accusation nor a confession, least of all an adventure. He had simply tried to tell of a generation of men who, even though they may have escaped its shells, were destroyed by the war, a generation that in every sense was 'lost'. Remarque did not write so much of the war as its consequences. Indeed all the scenes and incidents in his novel illustrate how the war had destroyed the ties between the soldiers and their society back home. 'If we go back', claims Paul 'we will be weary, broken, burned out, rootless and without hope.... We will not be able to find our way any more'. That was the tragedy of the lost generation, the soldiers who found themselves cut off from their roots, of men who returned home to a society which meant nothing to them.

When one is estranged from others, one is frequently a stranger to oneself. The Vietnamese veterans discovered that fate more convincingly than most. It was only when the nation finally decided to honour its dead, to erect a memorial to those who had fallen, that the United States at last accepted its own share of the blame. The veterans were not exonerated but they no longer had to carry the burden of guilt on their own. In the act of communing they became true survivors.

9

Not The End Of The World News

We have talked our extermination to death.

(Robert Lowell)

'History, ultimately is not the devastating bulldozer it is said to be. It leaves underpasses, crypts, holes and hiding places. There are those who survive.'

(*Eugenio Montale,* La Storia)

'A frightful queerness has come into life', wrote H G Wells in his last published work. Perhaps the most frightful thing about life in 1945 was that it did not seem queer enough. The world had grown used to crises. It was Wells's generation that seemed naïve in ever thinking that war could be fought to end war itself. In the ruins of Europe after the fall of the Third Reich, Wells seemed confirmed in his re-evaluation of the future of mankind, in his conviction that war would never end war but might well extinguish the human race. 'There is no way out, round or through ... It is the end', he concluded.

The world had every reason to expect, in 1945, that another war would break out once it had recovered from the last. No one had reason to suppose that the century would not demand the usual blood tribute every 20 years. What did the Swiss playwright Max Frisch see in the eyes of the children playing in the rubble of Europe's burnt-out cities in 1946, in its bombed-out terraced houses, in its long lines of streets with truncated ends and bricked off perspectives? Passing through Arles, he saw a world in general decay, one which bore 'the corroding grimace of dissolution'. Not even the children radiated hope. Most would probably grow into adults, Frisch concluded, singing the Marseillaise with the fervent hope of their ancestors – 'le jour de guerre est arrivé'.

What saved the generation of the 1940s for whom Frisch already mourned was the invention of the atomic bomb. The craving for certainty did not die but states could no longer afford to do anything more than look after themselves first. The state chose to survive, rather than terminate its existence in the name of ideological orthodoxy. An intimation of this

257

had already appeared to Curzio Malaparte whilst stationed in Finland during the Second World War:

> 'The greatest problem of modern days is still the religious problem', said Bengt von Toine. 'On ne peut pas tuer le dieu – God cannot be killed'.
>
> 'But this is horrible!', exclaimed Countess Mannerheim.
>
> 'How can anyone conceive the idea of killing God?'
>
> 'The entire modern world is trying to kill God', said Agah Aksel. 'God's very existence is in peril in the modern consciousness'.
>
> 'The modern state', said Constantinidou, 'deludes itself into thinking it can protect God's life simply with police measures'.
>
> 'It is not only God's life. The modern state deludes itself that it can protect its own existence', said de Foxa.

In another story, this time by Michel Tournier, writing 30 years later, the frustrated death-wish of a young heroine is captured tellingly. Melanie, the hero of the piece, is a melancholic child, given to dark dreams and forbidden thoughts:

> When [in 1962] it looked as if a nuclear war might break out between America and the USSR over Cuba, Melanie was of an age to read the papers and to follow the news on radio and TV. It seemed to her that a breath of fresh air was sweeping through the world and her lungs swirled with hope. For to deliver her from her prostration, it would take nothing less than the immediate destruction and appalling hecatomb of modern war.

In Tournier's story the threat is dispelled, the lid of existence, which had been half lifted for a moment, closes on her again. As the author adds, 'Melanie realised that there was nothing to be expected from history'.

It is a graphic phrase and it was true. Long before the end of the Cold War men had begun to lose their belief in History, with a capital H, their faith in Kundera's Grand March. The invention of nuclear weapons persuaded states to take to the defensive, not the battlefield. It persuaded them to lock themselves up in garrison states, occasionally probing each other's defences instead of sallying forth to do battle. In his *City of the Sun* Campanella had proposed building seven walls around his perfect city to protect the virtue of its citizens. In 1961 the government of East Germany chose to build only one. It counted for something that 28 years later the Berlin Wall was breached by the people it had imprisoned, not by an opposing army entering the city in triumph.

Despite 40 years of the Cold War we have emerged intact. We are – in the words of Wyndham Lewis, writing of a different age in the shadow of a different catastrophe – 'the first men of a future that has not materialised'.

If in the opening years of the new era we have been reprieved from drowning in the undertow of violence that marked the last hundred years, our survival can be attributed, in part, to the meaning that we have imposed on 20th century war. The world survived because of a change in *historical consciousness*, to which some of the writers of the 20th century I have discussed in the course of this book made their own unique contribution.

Long before the end of the Cold War we had begun to recognise that war was as questionable a collective affirmation of life as it was an individual one. We had begun to confront our capacity for wickedness head on, instead of continuing to hide behind grand theories of the human condition. Grand theories indeed, like Grand Marches, have lost their universal appeal. We also began to recognise that in a world in which peace could for some be just as 'awful' as war, almost 'as hideous a reality', we were better advised to improve the quality of the peace we enjoyed, not merely to rely on the spirit of internationalism to avoid a major confrontation.

We also recognised that we had much to learn from the past. We came to reject Wilfred Owen's despairing credo that history was futile, and to accept instead Auden's claim that if we did not make history ourselves someone would make it for us. By the 1960s few writers believed that war had any aesthetic appeal either. Most accepted that it denied, not affirmed, what Coleridge called 'the reliques of sensation', that it would bequeath little to the next generation but anxiety and despair.

Writing in the aftermath of the collapse of communism Jacques Darras saw the new age as 'a privileged time, a watershed in history', one that invited mankind to rethink its identity and redefine its notions about politics, sovereignty and the nation state, forces that it had been in great danger of taking for granted. 'In many respects our century, the 20th century, is but an annex, a footnote to the 19th century',[1] Darras maintained, a working out of essentially 19th century ideas, those of Karl Marx and Adam Smith prominent among them. 'It is probably fair to say', the historian Norman Stone had written a few years earlier, 'that Europe before 1914 produced virtually all of the ideas on which the 20th century had traded: the rest being mainly technical extensions of these ideas'.[2] In the words of Hitler's first German biographer, Joachim Fest, what the people wanted in Warsaw and Prague in the closing months of 1989 was 'to be spared the political systems of redemption produced by the 19th century – the 19th century in which our opposing fronts, our ideals and visions, our understanding of roles and even of ghosts have their roots, has finally come to a close'.[3]

Not only has the 19th century finally come to a close; history too has been unmasked. In one of the most important critiques of one of the 20th century's leading Nietzschean philosophers, E M Cioran, Susan Sontag begins with a discussion of what has become 'definingly Western' – the intense historicising of the present. The West, as Nietzsche wrote in *Human All Too Human* (1878), was a culture which believed only in 'becoming' and as such was 'historical through and through'. As Sontag contends, this perspective on man's achievements fatally undermines their values, even their claim to truth: 'Meaning drowns in a stream of becoming; the senseless and overdrawn rhythm of advent and super-cession, the becoming of man as the history of the exhaustion of his possibilities'. The West was haunted by its ancestors, by its ideas, by its growing disbelief in its own virtue. War, for much of the century, was an act of exorcism.

Today we are confronted with a different problem. If the great ideologies of the 20th century tended to treat the past as a *tabula rasa* on which men could inscribe what they wanted to hear from their ancestral voices, do we not suffer from a very different problem, our inability to engage the future at all?

If political scientists are only just beginning to come to terms with this phenomenon, many writers of fiction have been dealing with it for some time. The hero of Saul Bellow's Pulitzer Prize winning novel *Humboldt's Gift* (1973) is silenced by the fear that he has nothing to say to a public that is no longer listening. The sacred words for him are still 'Poetry, Beauty, Love, Waste Land, Alienation, Politics, History, the Unconscious'. They are still capitalised. But what does Humboldt leave in the end – not a corpus of his work, but a mere movie script. As he himself puts it, 'he is the first poet who had power brakes', the first poet with a post-modern sensibility that finds the world too baffling to understand and history too difficult to grasp.

The next century, in that respect, looks as if it will be neither discontinuous with the past, nor with itself, but continuous with an eternal present. For the West the historical axis of time may change. It may find itself living without a future and without a past. It may become history-less in the sense that it will have no inherited memories, and no wish to make the future different from what has gone before. The Europeans, in other words, may no longer spend their time meditating on such transhistorical questions as truth or peace or human justice. In that sense they will become intractable material indeed for the stuff of drama.

Should we find this disconcerting? We should, if only because the West has become what it is, for good or ill, by asking itself questions about its direction and purpose. It lives in time, not in a self-enclosed present. It is linked to a past which has helped define its identity and a future which constantly puts it in question. It is the most self-critical as well as the most self- conscious of all the world's major civilisations. While it is fitting that many of the crusades and revolutions that made up its history should be written out of the script, to step out of history altogether would be to leave the field to other countries. For beyond the Western world, history is already being made faster than before. New political narratives are being constructed and new possibilities of democracy, social justice and sovereignty are being discussed. If the West continues to dispute whether its own history has any meaning, it may find itself becoming, in Hegel's words 'a people without history', a people to whom things happen, a civilisation that does not make war on others but has war made on it.

Notes

1. WAR AND THE TWENTIETH CENTURY

1   Cited Francis Clavdon, *A Concise Encyclopaedia of Romanticism* (London: Omega, 1986) p. 29.
2   M Sherry, *The Rise of American Air Power* (New Haven: Yale University Press, 1987) p. 9.
3   For this framework I am indebted to Philip Windsor. See his 'The Twentieth Century as Self-Conscious History' In N Hagihara, (ed) *Experiencing the Twentieth Century)* (Tokyo: University of Tokyo Press 1985) pp. 333–56.
4   Eric Leed, *No Man's Land: Combat and Identity in World War One* (Cambridge: Cambridge University Press 1979) p. 91. For one of the best accounts of the Eastern Front, see Omer Bartov, *The Eastern Front 1941–5: German Troops and the Barbarisation of Warfare* (New York: Oxford University Press, 1985) p. 132. See also his *Hitler's Army: Soldiers, Nazis and War in the Third Reich* (Oxford: Oxford University Press, 1991). There is a substantial new literature on the complicity of the German army in the criminal way in which Hitler fought his war with Russia. See, in particular, Michel Geyer, 'Die geschichte der deutschen Militars von 1860 bin 1945', in Hans-Ulrich Wehler (ed.), *De moderne deutsche Geschichte in der internationalen forschung 1941–5* (Gottingen: 1978) pp. 256–88; Manfred Messerschmidt, Introduction to W. Deist (ed.), *The German Military in the Age of Total War* (Leamington Spa Berg 1985).
5   Bartov, ibid., pp. 12–280.
6   Cited David Lubin, *The Art of Portrayal: Eakins, Sargent, James* (Yale University Press 1985) p. 15.
7   Henry Adams, *The Education of Henry Adams* (New York: Modern Library, 1931) p. 240.
8   Cited Leed, *No Man's Land, op.cit.,* p. 49. Ernst Glaser, who was only 12 years old at the time that he left Switzerland for Germany, recorded that the moment the train crossed the border the passengers felt a sudden cohesion of solidarity which made 'everything seem new'. *Ibid.,* p. 50.
9   Janet Flanner (Genet), *Paris Journal,* April 1945. See Mordechai Richter, *Writers on World War Two: An Anthology* (London: Chatto & Windus, 1991) p. 607.
10   Cited L. Kennett, *The Theory of Strategic Bombing* (New York: 1982) p. 8.

11 One of the best accounts of Germany after the bombing was written by a young Swedish journalist, Stig Dagerman, who visited the country in 1946. Essen presented a terrible dream landscape of denuded, freezing iron constructions and ravaged factory walls. Cologne's three bridges were submerged in the Rhine. Berlin was city of amputated spires and endless rows of shattered government palaces. In Hanover King Ernst August sat before the station on the only fat horse in Germany, practically the only object to have emerged unscathed in a city which had once housed 450,000 people. In Germany, Dagerman wrote: 'It often happens that people ask the stranger to confirm that their city is the most burnt, devastated and crumbled in the whole of Germany. It is not a matter of finding consolation in the midst of distress – distress itself has become a consolation. The same people become downhearted if you tell them that you have seen worse things in other places. It may be that we have no right to say so, for each German city is "the worst" for those who have to live in it.'

The bombing of Dresden in March 1945 was by far the worst experience of any European city. Kurt Vonnegut, who as an American prisoner of war found himself working in the city at the time, described the effects of the raid as 'one big flame that ate everything organic that would burn'. Fifty years later, recalling his experience after keeping silent for so long, he noted that there had not been much in the Dresden area worth bombing out of business, 'burning the whole place down wasn't an exercise in military science ... it was Wagnerian. It was theatrical. It should be judged as such.' (Stig Dagerman, *German Autumn* (London: Quartet, 1988) pp. 19–21; Kurt Vonnegut, *Slaughterhouse Five* (New York: Laurel, 1988) p. 173.)

12 Laurence Durrell, *Clea* (London: Faber & Faber, 1963) p. 21.

13 C Wright Mills, *The Abolition of War* (London: Collins, 1963).

14 Martin Stephen, *Never Such Innocence* (London: Dent & Co., 1991) p. 5.

15 Messerschmidt, *The German Military*, *op.cit.*, p. 19.

16 Cited John Keegan, *The Face of Battle: A Study of Agincourt, Waterloo and the Somme* (Hardmondsworth: Penguin, 1978) p. 247.

17 Herman Hesse, 'The Brothers Karamozov or the Decline of Europe' (1918) in Hesse *My Belief: essays on life and art* (London: Paladin, 1989) p. 95.

18 Keegan, *The Face of Battle, op.cit.*, p. 303.

19 Elias Cannetti, *The Secret Heart of the Clock: Notes, Aphorisms and Fragments 1973–85* (New York: Farrer, Straus, Giroux, 1989) p. 29.

20 Ian King, 'Kurt Tucholsky's Analysis of the 1918 revolution' in R. Dove and S. Laubfeds, *German Writers and Politics 1918–29* (London: Macmillan, 1992).

21 H. Stuart Hughes, *Oswald Spengler: A Critical Estimate* (New York: Charles Scribner, 1952) p. 150.

22 Herman Hesse, *If The War Goes On ...* (London: Panther, 1985) p. 135.

23 Richard Pipes, *The Russian Revolution 1899–1919* (London; Fontana, 1990) p. 734.

24 Sheila Fitzpatrick, 'The Civil War as a Formative Experience', in Abbot

Gleason (ed.), *Bolshevik Culture: Experiment and Order in the Russian Revolution* (Bloomington: Indiana University Press, 1985) pp. 57–76. The question as to the number of Russians killed by Stalin in the 1930s continues to excite controversy. The final speech for the prosecution in the trial of the Communist Party in 1992 quoted the head of Khruschev's Rehabilitation Commission to the effect that on the basis of KGB documents nearly 20 million 'enemies of the people' were arrested between January 1935 and June 1941, of whom seven million were shot and the majority of the others died in the *gulag*. At least half a million of those nationalities deported between 1941–6 can be added to the list, as can the victims of the 1930–33 famine, the kulak deportations and other anti-peasant campaigns. See *New York Review of Books*, 23 September 1993, p. 27.

25   Ivan Maudsley, *The Russian Civil War* (Boston: Allen & Unwin, 1987) p. 242.

26   Fitzpatrick, 'The Civil War', *op.cit.*, p. 66.

27   Alexander Solzhenitsyn, (London: Collins & Harvill Press: *The First Circle* (trans. Max Hayward) (London: 1988). For the *zak* trains, see Solzhenitsyn, *The Gulag Archipelago 1918–56: An Experiment in Literary Investigation* (New York: Harper & Row, 1974) pp. 498–99. See also, Eugenia Ginzberg, *Journey into the Whirlwind* (New York: Harcourt Brace, 1967).

28   Joseph Brodsky, *Less Than One: Selected Essays* (London: Penguin, 1987) p. 29.

29   See Christopher Coker, *Reflections on American Foreign Policy Since 1945* (London: Pinter, 1989).

30   Andrew Berding (ed.), *Dulles on Diplomacy* (Princeton: Princeton University Press, 1965) p. 103.

31   Cited Kurt Tweraser, *Changing Patterns of Political Beliefs: The Foreign Policy Operational Codes of John William Fulbright 1943–67* (London: Sage, 1969) p. 41.

32   Octavio Paz, *One Earth, Four or Five Worlds: Reflections on Contemporary History* (Manchester: Carcanet, 1985) pp. 31–2.

33   Cited Z Brzezinski, *Power and Principle: The Memoirs of the National Security Advisor 1977–81* (London: Weidenfeld & Nicolson, 1983) p. 541.

34   Cited Kim Holmes, 'The Origins, Development and Composition of the Green Movement', in Robert Pfaltzgraff (ed.), *The Greens of West Germany* (Institute for Foreign Policy Analysis, 1983) p. 4, n. 90.

35   Robert Abzug, *Inside the Vicious Heart: America and the Liberation of the Nazi Concentration Camps* (New York: Oxford University Press, 1985) p. 170. American soldiers did not always see the reality for what it was. Reports from the US Sixth Army who liberated the Naztwiller camp mentioned the artefacts of human destruction: its disinfestation units, lethal gas chambers and incinerator rooms without describing what they had actually been used for.

36   Robert Van Hallberg, *Charles Olson: The Skull is Out* (Cambridge, MA: Harvard University Press, 1978) p. 180.

37   Salvador de Madariaga, *I Americans* (Oxford: Oxford University Press, 1930)

p. 3.

38 Robert Park, *Race and Culture* (Boston: Little Brown, 1950) p. 144.

39 Michel Tournier, *Gemini* (London: Methuen, 1986). In England the word 'disposable' was introduced into the language in 1643 as a result of the chaos of the English Civil War.

40 Michel Tournier, *The Wind Spirit: An Autobiography* (London: Collins, 1989) p. 218.

41 Hermann Kahn, *On Thermonuclear War* (New Jersey: Princeton University Press, 1961) pp. 641-2.

42 Elias Cannetti, *The Conscience of Words* (London: Andre Deusch, 1979) p. 83.

43 W Deist, *The German Military in the Age of Total War op.cit.*, p. 123.

44 Richard Holmes, *Nuclear Warriors: Soldiers, Combat and Glasnost* (London: Jonathan Cape, 1991) p. 23.

45 Eli Wiesel, 1946 ... 'Suddenly I said to myself, maybe the whole world, strangely has turned Jewish. Everybody lives now facing the unknown. We are all in a way helpless.' Cited Robert J. Lifton, *The Genocidal Mentality: Nazi Holocaust and Nuclear Threat* (London: Macmillan, 1991) p. 1.

46 George Schwab, 'Eli Wiesel. Between Jerusalem and New York',. In Karl Rittner (ed.), *Eli Wiesel: Between Memory and Hope* (New York: New York University Press, 1990) p. 24.

47 Elias Cannetti, *The Human Province* (London: Andre Deusch, 1985) p. 57.

48 I Pisar, *Of Blood and Hope* (Boston: Little Brown, 1980) pp. 262-3.

49 Cited Lifton, *Genocidal Mentality, op.cit.*

50 Albert Camus, 'Notebooks 5 September 1945 - April 1948', in *Notebooks 1942-52* (ed. Justin O'Brien) (New York: Paragon House, 1991) p. 134.

51 E Rabinowich, *Bulletin of Atomic Scientists* (January 1957) pp. 2-7.

52 Gwin Prins (ed.), *The Choice: Nuclear Weapons Versus Security* (London: Chatto & Windus, 1984) p. xvii.

53 Joseph Conrad, *The Secret Agent* (Oxford: Oxford University Press, 1983) p. 26.

54 Octavio Paz, *On Poets and Others* (London: Paladin, 1992) p. 107.

55 Jean Baudrillard, *Fatal Strategies* (London: Pluto, 1983) p. 39.

56 Leo Labedz, 'On Trial: The Case of Sinyavsky and Daniel', in Melvyn Laski (ed.), *The Use and Abuse of Sovietology* (London: Survey, 1988) p. 31.

57 Arnold Toynbee, *Civilisation on Trial* (Oxford: Oxford University Press, 1948) p. 3. For Toynbee's own recognition of the importance of the First World War as the central 'turning point' in his life, see *A Study of History*, Vol. 12 (Oxford: Oxford University Press, 1964) pp. 606-9.

58 Cited J Bouveresse, 'The Darkness of this Time: Wittgenstein and the Modern World', in A. Phillips Griffiths (ed.), *Wittgenstein Centenary Essays* (Cambridge: Cambridge University Press, 1991) p. 35.

59 During the First World War the Turkish Government transported one and a half million Armenians by train to Syria where they were left to starve or were butchered in detention camps. Like the destruction of the Jews, that of the Armenians was not originally planned. Only their forcible resettlement

had been initially considered. After it became clear, following the Allied defeat at Gallipoli, that the war would be prolonged, the Turks became more emboldened. Like the Nazis at the Wanensee Conference, the Central Committee of the Party took the decision to exterminate the Armenians at a secret, specially convened meeting. The orders were communicated secretly to provincial party headquarters by cipher telegram. The execution of the Armenians was carried out be special units including the notorious terrorist irregulars, the Chete. See Girard Libardian, 'The Ultimate Repression: The Genocide of the Armenians, 1915-17', in Isidor Wallimann (ed.), *Genocide in the Modern Age, Etiology and Case Studies of Mass Death* (London: Green Court Press, 1987).

60   Cited Adam Watson, 'European International Society and its Expansion', in Hedley Bull and Adam Watson (eds), *The Expansion of International Society,* Oxford: Clarendon, 1984) p. 13.

61   Oskar Kokoschka, *My Life* (London: Thames & Hudson, 1974).

62   John Reed, *The War in Eastern Europe* (New York: Charles Scribner & Sons, 1916).

63   *Jewish Holocaust Theology,* p. 34. Not all Jewish writers see it in this way. Lucy Dawidowitz in *The Holocaust and the Historians* (Cambridge, MA: Harvard University Press, 1981) argues that the 'special Jewish sorrow' was the end of a thousand-year-old Ashkenazi Jewish tradition. The Holocaust in that respect destroyed not only the Jews but also 'the continuity of Jewish history'. (p. 14).

64   Nicholas Humphrey, *Consciousness Regained: Chapters in the Development of the Mind* (New York: Oxford University Press, 1984) p. 205.

65   Cited Richard Sonn, *Anarchism and Cultural Politics in Fin de Siecle France* (Lincoln: University of Nebraska Press, 1989) p. 27.

66   Cross, *Lost Voices of World War I, op.cit.*

67   Henri Barbusse, *War Diary,* cited *Penguin Book of World War I Prose op.cit.,* (London: Viking, 1989) p. 196.

68   Wohlfarth, 'On Some Jewish Motifs', in A. Benjamin (ed.), *The Problem of Modernity: Adorno and Benjamin* (London: Routledge & Kegan Paul, 1989) p. 193.

69   Robert Musil, *The Man Without Qualities,* Vol. 1 (London: Picador, 1979) p. 8. See also David S. Luft, *Robert Musil and the Crisis of European Culture 1880–1942* (Berkeley: University of California Press, 1980). Hannah Hickman, *Robert Musil and the Culture of Vienna* (London: Croom Helm, 1984) p. 95. See also, Italo Calvino, *Six Memos for the Next Millennium* (London: Jonathan Cape, 1992) p. 108-10.

70   Günther Grass, *From the Diary of a Snail* (London: Picador, 1974) p. 265.

71   Hayo Krombach, *Hegelian Reflections on the Idea of Nuclear War* (London: Macmillan, 1985) p. 93.

72   Cited Alan White, *Within Nietzsche's Labyrinth* (London: Routledge & Kegan Paul, 1990) p. 35.

73   Cited George Steiner, *Dostoevsky or Tolstoy: An Essay in Contrast* (London:

Faber & Faber, 1960) p. 21.

74 Friedrich Nietzsche, *Thus Spake Zarathustra* (London: Penguin, 1961) p. 10.

75 *Ibid.*, p. 116. Throughout his life Nietzsche strongly condemned 'the foul theory that one could only attain to a culture when armed to the teeth and wearing boxing gloves'. See Tracy Strong, *Nietzsche and the Politics of Transfiguration, op.cit.*, p. 199.

2. ON CONSCIOUSNESS AND MODERNITY IN MODERN WAR

1 Hitler was convinced by 1945 that Germany too had willed its destruction. As he told Albert Speer 'if the war is lost then the people will be lost too ... for the people has proven to be the weaker and the future belongs to the stronger Eastern people. All that will be left after this fight will be the inferior sort, for the good have fallen.' (Cited Elias Canetti, *The Conscience of Words* (London: Andre Deutsch, 1979) pp. 75–6.

2 See Peter Paret (ed.), *Makers of Modern Strategy* (London: 1986).

3 Cited Tim Travers, *The Killing Ground: The British Army, the Western Front and the Emergence of Modern Warfare 1900–18* (London: 1987) pp. 44–5.

4 Karl Polyani, *The Great Transformation: The Political and Economic Origins of our Time* (Beacon Press: 1944) p. 29.

5 Thurnwald, *Black and White in East Africa: The Fabric of New Civilisation* (1935); F E Williams, *Depopulation of the Suar District* (1933), *ibid.* pp. 291–2. In one of his more famous works, *The Time Traveller*, H G Wells paints the sad picture of a humanity grown 'indescribably frail' and decadent through too many years of peace. The Elio – like cattle – 'knew no enemies and provided no needs'. Their end was the same. The Time Traveller comes to the conclusion that moral strength is the outcome of a need, that security sets a premium on feebleness.

6 *The Diaries of Evelyn Waugh* (ed. Michael Davie) (London: Weidenfeld & Nicolson, 1976) pp. 250–1.

7 Friedrich Nietzsche, *The Will to Power* (ed. William Kaufman) (New York: Random House, 1968).

8 Friedrich Nietzsche *The Genealogy of Morals* (ed. William Kaufman) (New York: Modern Library, 1966).

9 Cited Theodore Schieder, 'The Role of Historical Consciousness in Political Action', *History and Theory,* 27:4 (1978), p. 2.

10 Octavio Paz, *One Earth, Four or Five Worlds* (Manchester: Carcanet, 1987) p. 22.

11 *Ibid.*

12 Robert Bellsch, 'Religious Influences in US Foreign Policy', in Michael P. Hamilton, *The American Character and the Formation of US Foreign Policy* (Grand Rapids, Michigan: Eerdmans, 1986).

13 Normal Mailer, *Of A Fire On the Moon* (Boston: Little Brown, 1970) p. 10.

14 Hermann Hesse, *If The War Goes On ... Reflections on War and Politics* (London: Panther, 1985) p. 58.

15 *Ibid.*

16 Friedrich Nietzsche, 'Use and Disadvantage of History for Life' (1874), *Untimely Meditations* (trans. R J Hollingdale) (Cambridge: Cambridge University Press, 1983).

17 Cited Peter Gay, *Weimar Culture: The Outsider as Insider* (Oxford: Oxford University Press, 1969).

18 J H Plumb, *The Death of the Past* (Harmondsworth: Penguin, 1972) pp. 149–50.

19 A J P Taylor (ed.), *Churchill: Four Faces and the Man* (London: Allan Lane, 1969) p. 121.

20 See Andrew Sinclair (ed.), *The War Decade: An Anthology of the 1940s* (London: Hamish Hamilton, 1989) p. 237.

21 J H Plumb, 'Churchill as Historian', in Taylor (ed.), *Churchill, op.cit.*, p. 36.

22 Cited Fritz Stern, *Dreams and Delusions: The Drama of German History* (New York: Random House, 1987) p. 182.

23 Raymond Aron, *The Century of Total War* (Paris: 1954).

24 Walter Benjamin, *Illuminations* (1968) p. 262.

25 Canetti, *Conscience of Words, op.cit.*, p. 77.

26 Joseph Roth, *The Emperor's Tomb* (London: Chatto and Windus, 1979).

27 Cited Agnes Heller, *A Philosophy of History in Fragments* (Oxford: Blackwell, 1993) p. 77.

28 Cited Tim Cross (ed.), *The Lost Voices of World War I* (London: Bloomsbury, 1988) p. 384.

29 *Ibid.*

30 *Ibid.*

31 Theodore Zeldin, *France 1848–1945*, Vol. 2, *Intellect, Taste and Anxiety* (Oxford: Oxford University Press, 1977) p. 1084.

32 Cited Martin Green, *Children of the Sun: a Narrative of Decadence in England after 1918* (London: Chatto and Windus, 1979) pp. 468–9.

33 *Ibid.*

34 Taylor, *Churchill: Four Faces, op.cit.*

35 E M Cioran, *The Temptation to Exist* (Quartet, 1987) p. 22.

36 *Ibid.*

37 Tracy Strong, *Friedrich Nietzsche and the Politics of Transfiguration* (Berkeley: University of California Press, 1975) pp. 214–5.

38 David Beetham, *Max Weber and the Theory of Modern Politics* (Polity Press, 1985) p. 47.

39 Cited Jeffrey Perrett, *The American People: Days of Sadness, Years of Triumph 1939–45* (New York: Conrad McCann, 1973) p. 417.

40 Arthur C. Danto, 'Some Remarks on the Genealogy of Morals', in Robert Solomon (ed.), *Reading Nietzsche* (New York: Oxford University Press, 1988) p. 17.

41 *Ibid.*

42   Friedrich Nietzsche, *The Dawn of Day* (New York: Garden Press, 1974).

43   *Pages from the Goncourt Journal* (ed. Robert Beldick) (Oxford: Oxford University Press, 1988).

44   Elias Canetti, *The Human Province* (London: Andre Deutsch, 1985).

45   Milan Kundera, *The Book of Laughter and Forgetting* (Harmondsworth: Penguin, 1978) p. 179.

46   Milan Kundera, *The Unbearable Lightness of Being* (London: Faber & Faber, 1984) p. 261. See also Robert Musil, *Diaries* (Hamburg: Rowoht Theebruck Verlag, 1952). Musil saw something immensely satisfying about the appearance of 'willed action' in war as opposed to 'passive receptivity' in peacetime. 'In war the will is directed towards movement of the legs: decisions that are always ultimately connected with oneself.'

47   Rory Maclean, *Stalin's Nose-Across the Face of Eastern Europe* (Flamingo, 1993) p. 146; for Hobsbawn see 'The New Threat to History', *New York Review*, December 1993.

48   Italo Calvino, *The Literature Machine: Essays* (London: Picador, 1987) p. 209.

49   Mikhail Bakhtin, *The Problem of Dostoevsky's Poetics* (ed. Rory Emerson) (Manchester: University of Manchester Press, 1984) p. 287.

50   Georg Lukacs, *The Theory of the Novel* (London, 1971) p. 71.

51   Anthony Burgess, 'Solzhenitsyn as War Poet' in Burgess, *Homage to Qwert Yuiop. Selected Journalism 1978–85* (London: Abacus, 1986) p. 452.

52   For a good analysis of Mann's *White Mountain*, see Laurence L Langer, *The Age of Atrocity: Death in Modern Literature* (Boston: Beacon Press, 1978) pp. 69–112.

53   Bakhtin, *Dostoevsky's Poetics, op.cit.*, p. 284.

54   F Dostoevsky, *The Idiot* (London: Penguin, 1987) p. 201.

55   George Steiner, *Tolstoy or Dostoevsky? An Essay in contrast* (London: Faber and Faber, 1960) p. 210.

56   Peter Sloterdijk, *Critique of Cynical Reason* (London: Verso, 1988) p. 197.

57   *Ibid.*

58   *Ibid.*

59   Siegfried Sassoon, *Siegfried's Journey 1916–20*, cited Jon Glover/Jon Silkin (eds), *The Penguin Book of First World War Prose* (London: Viking, 1989) p. 338.

60   Cited Paul Fussell, *The Great War and Modern Memory* (Oxford: Oxford University Press, 1977) p. 326.

61   W F Hegel *The Essential Writings* (ed.) F Weiss (New York: Harper and Row, 1974) p. 71.

62   Paul Fussell, *The Great War and Modern Memory, op.cit.*

63   Larry Wolf, *Postcards from the End of the World: An Investigation into the Mind of Fin de Siecle Vienna* (London: Collins, 1988) pp. 90–5.

64   Edward Timms, *Karl Kraus: Apocalyptic Satirist, Culture and Catastrophe in Haspsburg Vienna* (New Haven: Yale University Press, 1986) p. 67.

65   J P Stern, 'Karl Kraus's Vision of Language', *Modern Language Review* 61 (1966) pp. 76–7.

66 Max Spalter, *Brecht's Tradition* (Baltimore: Johns Hopkins University Press, 1967) p. 149.

67 Timms, *Karl Kraus, op.cit.,* p. 145.

68 Jan Janouch, *Conversations with Kafka* (London: Quartet, 1985) p. 99.

69 'War and the Crisis of Language', in Robert Ginsberg (ed.), *The Critique of War: Contemporary Philosophical Explorations* (Chicago: Henry Regnery, 1969) p. 47.

70 H. Zohn (ed.), *In These Great Times: A Karl Kraus Reader* (Manchester: Carcanet, 1984) p. 80.

71 Timms, *Karl Kraus, op.cit.,* p. 146.

72 Allan Janik, Stephen Tumin, *Wittgenstein's Vienna* (London: Weidenfeld & Nicolson, 1973) p. 90.

73 *Ibid.,* p. 190.

74 J B Stern, Karl Kraus and the Idea of Literature', *Encounter* (August 1975) pp. 37–48.

75 P. Lilienfield, 'Reflections on Karl Kraus', *The Nation* (23 April 1973) p. 536.

76 Hannah Arendt, *Eichmann in Jerusalem: A Report on the Banality of Evil* (New York: Viking, 1963) p. 80. The Polish poet Zbigniew Herbert, one of a generation of Poles who lived through the Nazi occupation, then the Stalinist repression, recalls the infamous massacre of natives in Indonesia by the Dutch Governor of the East Indies Jan Coen. Some historians maintain that Coen only issued an order for the evacuation, not subsequent murder of 15,000 natives, but, writes Herbert, the local governor probably knew what the word 'evacuation' meant. It was understood to be a 'final' evacuation – the removal of the natives to the other world. (*Still Life with a Bridle: Essays and Apocryphies* (Jonathan Cape, 1993) p. 137.

77 Primo Levi, *The Drowned and the Saved* (London: Michael Joseph, 1988) p. 18.

78 Karl Kraus, *Half Truths and One and a Half Truths: Selected Aphorisms* (trans. Harry Zohn) (Manchester: Carcanet, 1986) p. 82.

79 Levi, *The Drowned and the Saved, op. cit.,* p. xii.

80 George Orwell, Politics and the English Language' (1946) in *Collected Essays* (London: Secker & Warburg, 1975) p. 364.

81 Kraus, *Half Truths, op.cit.,* p. 82.

82 *Ibid.,* p. 40.

83 Herbert Kelman, 'Violence Without Moral Restraint: Reflections on the Dehumanisation of Victims and Victimisers', *Journal of Social Issues* 29:4 (1973) p. 48.

84 Michael Herr, *Despatches* (New York: Avon Books, 1978) p. 229.

85 Chaim F. Chatan, 'Afterword: Who Can Take Away The Grief of a Wound', in Boulanger (ed.), *The Vietnam Veterans Redefined* (New York: Erlbaum, 1986) p. 176.

86 Nigel Calder, *The Comet is Coming* (London: A. Dent, 1980) p. 59.

3. WAR AND THE HUMAN CONDITION

1 Malcolm Bradbury, *Modernism: A Guide to European Literature 1890–1930* (Harmondsworth: Penguin, 1970) p. 47.
2 *The Sunday Times,* 22 August 1993.
3 *Ibid.*
4 Cited Eric Leed, *No Man's Land: Combat and Identity in World War I* (Cambridge: Cambridge University Press: 1979) p. 30.
5 Marguerite Yourcenar, *Fires* (Aiden Ellis, 1982) p. 11.
6 Cited Joseph Nef, *War and Progress: An Essay on the Rise of Industrial Civilisation* (Cambridge, MA: Harvard University Press, 1952) p. 409.
7 D R Davies, *Down Peacock's Feathers* (London: Centenary Press, 1944).
8 Eric Heller, *The Disinherited Mind: Essays in Modern German Literature and Thought* (Cambridge: Bowes & Bowes, 1952) p. 110.
9 Rainer Maria Rilke, *Selected Letters* (trans. J B Leischman) (London: Hogarth Press, 1941).
10 Rainer Maria Rilke, *Fifty Selected Letters* (trans. C F MacIntyre) (Berkeley: University of California Press, 1947) p. 21.
11 Wolgang Leppmann, *Rilke: A Life* (Cambridge: Lutterworth Press, 1984).
12 *Ibid,* p. 308.
13 Gill Elliot, *The Twentieth Century Book of the Dead* (New York: Charles Scribner, 1972) p. 28.
14 Rainer Maria Rilke, *Letters* (New York: Norton & Co., 1969) pp. 214–5.
15 Jean-Luc Nancy, 'The Unsacrificable', in Claire Nouvet (ed.), *Literature and the Ethical Question* (Yale University Press, 1991).
16 Rainer Maria Rilke, *The Notebooks of Malte Lauridis Brigge* (Oxford: Oxford University Press, 1984) pp. 8–9. See also Stephen Spender, *Life and the Poet* (London: Secker & Warburg, 1942) p. 122. Spender claimed that the suffering caused by war was of no greater significance to the poet than the suffering that existed already in the world. He quotes the poet Geoffrey Grigson, 'the greatest intensities of suffering or evil are always being endured somewhere by somebody in peace or war'. In this way war did not have to be understood as war, as a subject of particular interest. It was part of the pain of life which the poet suffered.
17 Peter Gay, *Weimar Culture: The Outsider as Insider* (London: Secker & Warburg, 1968).
18 Rilke, *Letters* (1969), *op.cit.,* p. 112.
19 Detlev Peukert, *The Weimar Republic: The Crisis of Classical Modernity* (London: Allan Lane, 1991) pp. 185–6.
20 Cited James McFarlane, 'The Mind of Modernity' in Malcolm Bradbury, *Modernism, op.cit.,* pp. 86–8.
21 Jeremy Reed, *Madness: The Price of Poetry* (London: Peter Irwin, 1989) p. 44.
22 Rilke, *Notebooks, op.cit.,* p. 9.
23 George Orwell, 'How the Poor Die' (1946), in George Orwell, *Collected Essays*

(London: Secker & Warburg, 1975) pp. 345–6.

24 Cited D Enright (ed.), *The Oxford Book of Death* (Oxford: Oxford University Press 1983) p. 242.

25 Alexander Solzhenitsyn, *The Gulag Archipelago*, Vol. 2 1918–56) (New York: Harper & Row, 1975) pp. 179–606.

26 Georges Nevat, 'Man and the Gulag', in Philip Windsor (ed.), *Experiencing the Twentieth Century* (Tokyo: University of Tokyo Press, 1985) p. 221.

27 Jonathan Schell, *The Fate of the Earth* (New York: Aron Books, 1982).

28 Evelyn Waugh, *Brideshead Revisited* (Harmondsworth: Penguin, 1984) p. 167.

29 Nevat, 'Man and the Gulag', *op.cit.*, p. 220.

30 Solzhenitsyn, *The Gulag Archipelago*, Vol. 3, *op.cit.* A similar feeling was to be found in Poland in 1983. A Polish political prisoner, Eva Kubsiewicz, refused to petition for release: 'It isn't worth it. Here no-one can detain you for explanations. Here you have nothing to fear. It is paradoxical, I know, but if in the morning you are awakened by something banging on the door you are not afraid of uniformed guests. You know it is only your kindly gaoler bringing you your morning coffee. The bialoleka [the present] is a moral luxury and an oasis of freedom'. (Cited Edith Wyschorgrod, *Spirit in Ashes: Hegel, Heidegger and Man-Made Mass Death* (Yale University Press, 1985) pp. 163–4).

31 Frederick Morton, *Thunder at Twilight: Vienna 1913–14* (London: Peter Irwin, 1991) p. 52.

32 Ronald Clarke, *Freud: The Man and his Cause* (London: Jonathan Cape, 1980) p. 376.

33 Gerda Siaran, *The Counting of Aggression: Perspectives on Aggression and Violence* (Boston: Allen & Unwin, 1985).

34 In 1915 he began a series of major essays on war. In the second, *Attitude Towards Death* he argued that civilised man could no longer hold the idea of death at arms' length. Instead, in keeping with the times, he would have to alter the old saying 'if you want to preserve peace, arm for war' and substitute instead 'if you want to endure life, prepare yourself for death'.

35 Clarke, *Freud: The Man and his Cause, op.cit.*, p. 365.

36 J. Strachey (ed.), *The Standard Edition of Complete Works of Sigmund Freud* (London: Hogarth Press, 1955), Vol. 13, p. 297. See also Herman Hesse, *Reflections* (New York: Farrar, Strauss & Giroux, 1974) p. 68.

37 Paul Rozen, *Freud: Political and Social Thought* (New York: Alfred Knopf, 1968) p. 194.

38 Joseph Roth, *The Emperor's Tomb* (London: Chatto & Windus, 1984) p. 46.

39 Strachey, *The Standard Edition* Vol. 14 ('Thoughts for the Time on War and Death') p. 279.

40 In Ernest Jones, *Life and Work of Sigmund Freud* (New York: Basic Books, 1955) p. 300. This uncompromising notion of engagement appears in literature in the early 1920s. In one of his autobiographical short stories about the First World War, Drieu La Rochelle writes 'I was 24; in a few days I was going to enter life through the gate of the armistice. I foresaw dimly what I have felt since: that

the same deliberate abandonment to death would be the basis of all my actions …In any love, any work, one must go to the limit, toward the sanction of death.' (*Etat-Civil*, pp. 21–22).

41 See editor's note in *Civilisation, Society and Religion*, Vol. 12, *Penguin Freud Library* (Harmondsworth: Penguin, 1991), p. 248; Richard Boothby, *Death and Desire: Psychoanalytic Theory* in *Lacan's Return to Freud* (London: Routledge, 1991) p. 5.

42 Strachey, *The Standard Edition*, Vol. 19 ('Beyond the Pleasure Principle') p. 24.

43 Jones, *Life and Work of Sigmund Freud, op.cit.*, pp. 312–16.

44 *Ibid.*, p. 317.

45 Erich Fromm, *The Anatomy of Human Destructiveness* (Harmondsworth: Penguin, 1977) p. 261.

46 J Strachey (ed.), *Freud: The Standard Edition*, Vol. 21 ('Civilisation and its Discontents') p. 86.

47 Hermann Hesse, *If the War goes on: Reflections on War and Politics* (London: Panther, 1985) p. 19.

48 Mary Midgley, *Wickedness: A Philosophical Essay* (London: Ark Paperbacks, 1984) pp. 164–8.

49 Raul Hilberg, *The Destruction of the European Jews* (Chicago: Quadrangle Press, 1961) p. 640.

50 Cited Mary Gluck, *Georg Lukacs and his Generation* (Cambridge; MA: Harvard University Press, 1985) p. 207.

51 Jean Amery, *At the Mind's Limit* (Bloomington: Indiana University Press, 1980) pp. 25–6, 35–6.

52 Jean Bataille, *Literature and Evil* (London: Calder Boyars, 1973) pp. 51–3.

53 *Ibid.*

54 William McGuire (ed.), *G C Jung Speaking: Interviews and Encounters* (Princeton University Press, 1977) p. 118.

55 *Ibid.*, pp. 59–60.

56 Cited Jeffrey Mason, *Against Therapy* (London: Fontana, 1988) p. 139.

57 *Ibid.*, p. 131.

58 Daniel Burston, *The Legacy of Erich Fromm* (Cambridge, MA: Harvard University Press, 1991) p. 12.

59 Cited Gehard Napp, *The Art of Living: Erich Fromm's Life and Works* (New York: Peter Lang, 1989) p. 12. See also Rainer Funk, *Erich Fromm: The Courage to be Human* (New York: Continuum, 1982) p. 51.

60 Richard Evans, *Dialogue with Erich Fromm* (New York: Harper & Row, 1966) p. 11.

61 Erich Fromm, *The Sane Society* (Greenwich, CT: Fawcett Premier Books, 1955) pp. 41–2.

62 Erich Fromm, *Man for Himself: An Enquiry into the Psychology of Ethics* (New York: Rheinhard & Co., 1947) p. 184.

63 Erich Fromm, *The Anatomy of Human Destructiveness* (London: Jonathan Cape, 1974) p. 41.

64 Saul Friedlander, *Reflections on Nazism: An Essay on Kitsch and Death* (New York: Harper & Row, 1984) p. 194.

65 Joachim Fest, *Hitler* (London: Weidenfeld & Nicolson, 1973) p. 608.

66 Robert J Lifton, 'Life Unworthy of Life: Nazi Racial Views', in Randolph Brahan (ed.), *Psychological Perspectives on the Holocaust and its Aftermath* (New York: Columbia University Press, 1988) p. 7. See also, Robert J Lifton, *The Nazi Doctors: Medical Killing and the Psychology of Genocide* (New York: Basic Books, 1986) p. 31.

67 Paul Jackel, *Hitler in History* (New York: Brandeis University Press, 1984) p. 33.

68 Joost Merloo, *Suicide and Mass Suicide* (New York: Grun & Stratton, 1962) pp. 67-75.

69 Cited Richard Osborne, *Complete Operas of Wagner: A Critical Guide* (Victor Gollancz: 1992) p. 28.

70 R. Donnington, *Wagner's Ring and its Symbols: The Music and the Myth* (London: Faber & Faber, 1973) p. 118.

71 *Ibid*, p. 260.

72 Bernard Shaw, *The Perfect Wagnerite: A Commentary on the Nieblung's Ring* (New York: Dover, 1967) p. 12.

73 Theodor Adorno, *In Search of Wagner* (NLB, 1981) pp. 130-2.

74 'Art and Revolution', in *Richard Wagner's Prose Works*, Vol. 6, *Religion and Art* (New York, 1966) p. 252.

75 Frank Kermode, *The Sense of an Ending: Studies in the Theory of Fiction* (Oxford University Press, 1967).

76 T Adorno, *In Search of Wagner* (trans. Rodney Livingstone) (London: 1981) p. 76.

77 Kermode, *The Sense of an Ending, op.cit.*

78 Rene Girard, *Violence and the Sacred* (Baltimore: Johns Hopkins University Press, 1984) p. 167.

79 Cited Paul Fussell, *Abroad: British Literary Travelling between the Wars* (Oxford: Oxford University Press, 1980) p. 217.

80 Elias Canetti, *The Tongue Set Free: Remembrance of a European Childhood* (London: Picador, 1977) p. 90.

81 Stefan Zweig, *The World of Yesterday: An Autobiography* (New York: Harper & Row, 1945) p. 224.

82 Drieu La Rochelle, *The Comedy of Charleroi* (Paris: Gallimard, 1982) p. 195.

83 Erich Fromm, *The Heart of Man* (New York: Harper & Row, 1964) p. 117.

84 Elias Canetti, *The Torch in My Ear* (London: Andre Deutsch, 1989) pp. 349-51.

85 Elias Canetti, *Crowds and Power* (Harmondsworth: Penguin, 1973) p. 82.

86 Elias Canetti, *The Conscience of Words* (London: Andre Deutsch, 1986) p. 27.

87 Canetti, *ibid*, p. 108.

88 *Ibid*, p. 162.

89 *Ibid*, p. 74.

90 Cited Joachim Fest, *Hitler* (London: Weidenfeld and Nicolson, 1973) p. 611.

91 Heinrich Böll, *Letter to My Son: War's End* in *Das End Autoren aus nein Landern erinaernsich an die letzten Tage des Zweitenweltkrieg* (Cologne: Verlag Kiepenheuer, 1985).
92 Canetti, *The Human Province* (London: Andre Deutsch, 1985) p. 166.
93 Elias Canetti, *The Secret Heart of the Clock: Notes, Aphorisms and Fragments 1973–85* (New York: Farrar, Strauss & Giroux, 1987) p. 67.
94 Canetti, *Crowds and Power, op.cit.*, p. 543.
95 *Ibid.*, p. 546.
96 Friedrich Nietzsche, *Also Sprach Zarathustra*, (Harmondsworth: Penguin, 1961) p. 70.
97 Cesare Pavese, *The Business of Living: Diaries 1935–50* (London: Quartet, 1980) p. 61.
98 Baudelaire, *Paris Spleen 1847* (London: New Directions, 1970) p. 23.
99 Dostoevsky, *Notes from the Underground* (New York: New American Library, 1961).
100 Rene Girard, *Violence and the Sacred* (trans. Patrick Gregory) (London: 1977) p. 167.
101 Valerie Tarsis, *Ward 7: An Autobiographical Novel* (New York: E R Dutton, 1965).

4. WAR AND THE MEANING OF HISTORY

1 Richard Schacht, *Nietzsche* (London: Routledge, 1992) pp. 416–8.
2 M Zimmerman, *Heidegger's Confrontation with Modernity, Technology, Politics and Art* (Bloomington: Indiana University Press, 1990) p. 210.
3 Patrick Parrinder/Christopher C Wolfe, *H.G. Wells Under Revision* (London: Associate University Press, 1986) p. 237.
4 Peter Kemp, *Wells and the Culminating Ape: Biological Themes and Imaginative Obsessions* (London: Macmillan, 1982) p. 151. A measure of the intensity of his anti-German feeling can be found in a pamphlet he wrote after a trip to the Front in 1916. In *War and the Future* (1917) p. 12, he argued that the war was 'a gigantic and heroic effort in sanitary engineering: an effort to remove German militarism from life'.
5 Wells, *op.cit.*, p. 9.
6 Lovat Dixon, *H.G. Wells: His Turbulent Life and Times* (London: Pelican, 1972) p. 183.
7 H G Wells, *The Outline of History: Being a Plain History of Life and Mankind* (London: 1920).
8 Elias Canetti, *The Human Province* (London: Andre Deutsch, 1985) p. 153.
9 H G Wells, *War and the Future* (London: 1917).
10 Philip Guedalla came to a similar conclusion. In *A Gallery* (London: Constable, 1925, p. 71) he wrote of Wells: 'One thinks of him as a pair of bright eyes watching the world, alert, not without malice'.

11   Frank McConnell, *The Science Fiction of H.G. Wells* (Oxford: Oxford University Press, 1981) p. 194.

12   H G Wells, *Mr. Britling Sees It Through* (London: 1985).

13   Norman/Jeanne Mackenzie, *The Life of H.G. Wells: The Time Traveller* (London: Hogarth Press, 1987) p. 300.

14   *Ibid*, p. 138–9.

15   *Ibid*, p. 156.

16   H G Wells, *The Common Sense of War and Peace* (London: Secker & Warburg, 1940).

17   Nigel Nicholson, *H.G. Wells* (London: 1950) p. 95.

18   H G Wells, *Anticipations of the Reaction of Mechanical and Scientific Progress Upon Human Thought* (London: 1902) pp. 204–5.

19   R T Stearn, 'Wells at War: H.G. Wells Writing on Military Subjects before the Great War', *Wellesian* No. 6 (1983) p. 9.

20   Kemp, *Wells and the Culminating Ape, op.cit.*, p. 183.

21   George Orwell, *Collected Essays* (London: Secker & Warburg, 1975). Wells despaired only after he heard of the bombing of Hiroshima. A year earlier, in his book *42–44: A Contemporary Memoir* (London: Secker & Warburg, 1944) he had written with confidence that a better world would come into existence after the war was over.

22   See V R Berghahn, *Modern Germany: Society, Economics and Politics in the Twentieth Century* (Cambridge: Cambridge University Press, 1982); Gordon Craig, *Germany* pp. 488–9.

23   Cited Peter Vansittart, *Voices from the Great War* (London: Jonathan Cape, 1981) p. 68.

24   George Steiner, *Heidegger* (London: Fontana, 1978) p. 76.

25   Geoffrey Barash, 'Martin Heidegger in the Perspective of the Twentieth Century', *Journal of Modern History* 64 March 1992) p. 66.

26   Georg Lukacs, *History and Class Consciousness* (London: 1971) p. 237.

27   Yeats, *Letters* (ed. Allan Wade) (London: Hart-Davies, 1954) p. 693.

28   Ludwig Delio, *Germany and World Politics in the Twentieth Century* (London: Chatto & Windus, 1959) p. 89.

29   Cited Ernst Nolte, *Martin Heidegger: Politics and History in his Life and Thought* (Propylaen, 1992) p. 41.

30   Luc Ferry/Alain Renaut, *Heidegger and Modernity* (Chicago: University of Chicago Press, 1990) p. 123, n. 33.

31   *Ibid*, p. 124. Cultural criticism of the Americans was strong in Germany in the 1930s. Gottfried Benn declared himself against 'Americanism', against 'the philosophy of pure utilitarianism, of optimism *a tout prix*, of the permanent grin – keep smiling – is not appropriate to Western man and his history'. (Cited Detlev Peukert, *The Weimar Republic: The Crisis of Classical Modernity* (London: Allen Lane, 1991) p. 185). Hitler had a less negative view of the United States. He suspected it might be 'a giant with feet of clay' but he claimed in April 1945 that he would have been happy enough to have lived with the

United States in 'peaceful coexistence'. (John Lukacs, *1945 – Year Zero* (New York: Doubleday, 1978) p. 41).

32 Victor Farias, *Heidegger and the Nazis* (Philadelphia: Temple University Press, 1989) p. 216.

33 *Ibid.*, pp. 276–8.

34 *Ibid.*, p. 68.

35 Other philosophers, even theologians, saw Germany as the most exciting, dynamic country of the twentieth century. The Jesuit scientist/philosopher Teilhard Chardin write 'The world is bound to belong to its most active elements.... Just now the Germans deserve to win because, however bad or mixed is their spirit, they have more spirit than the rest of the world.'

36 *Ibid.*, p. 216.

37 Zimmerman, *Heidegger's Confrontation with Modernity, op.cit.*, p. 90.

38 William Pfaff, *Barbarian Sentiments; How the American Century Ends* (New York: Hill & Wang, 1989), p. 58.

39 Martin Heidegger, *Existence and Being* (London: 1949) p. 289.

40 Philippe Lacoue-Labarthe, *Heidegger, Art and Politics* (Oxford: Basil Blackwell, 1990) p. 80.

41 Cited *History and Theory op.cit.*, p. 18.

42 For the *Der Spiegel* interview, see Gunther Neske (ed.), *Martin Heidegger and National Socialism: Questions and Answers* (New York: Paragon House, 1990) p. 61.

43 Zimmerman, *Heidegger's Confrontation with Modernity, op.cit.*, p. 181–2.

44 Lacoue-Labarthe, *Heidegger, op.cit.*, p. 113.

45 John Sallis, *Echoes: After Heidegger* (Bloomington: Indiana University Press, 1990) p. 43.

46 James Demske, *Being, Man and Death: The Key to Heidegger* (University of Kentucky Press, 1970) p. 137.

47 *Ibid.*

48 Allan Megill, *Prophets of Extremity: Nietzsche, Heidegger, Foucault and Derrida* (Berkeley: University of California Press, 1985) p. 141.

49 Heidegger, *Existence and Being* p. 289. See also Peter Sloterdijk, *Critique of Cynical Reason* (London: Verso, 1988) p. 203.

50 Megill, *Prophets of Extremity, op.cit.*, pp. 179–80.

51 Klaus Theweleit, *Male Fantasies*, Vol. 2, *Male Bodies: Psychoanalysing the White Terror* (Cambridge: Polity, 1988) p. 162.

52 Cited Jonathan Stern, *Hitler: the Fuhrer and the People* (London: Fontana, 1990) p. 163.

53 Ernst Jünger, *Fire and Blood* (1924) in Gerhard Loose, *Ernst Jünger* (New York: Twayne Publishers, 1974) p. 29.

54 Theweleit, *Male Fantasies, op.cit.*, p. 161.

55 Jerry Z Muller, *The Other God That Failed: Hans Freyer and the De-Radicalisation of German Conservatism* (Princeton, NJ: Princeton University Press, 1987) p. 74.

[56] Cited Volker Berghahn, *Militarism: The History of an International Debate 1861–1979* (Leamington Spa: Berg Publishers, 1981) p. 34.

[57] Ernst Jünger, *The Worker* (1933) p. 59. See also Nietzsche, *The Will to Power*. 'Concerning the future of the worker: workers must learn to feel like soldiers. An honorarium, a salary but not wages.... The workers must learn to live as the middle class does now – but on a higher plane, that is as the superior caste whose needs however are few. Hence they will be poor and live more simply. Power will be their sole possession.' (p. 37).

[58] Andrew Dobson, *An Introduction to the Politics of Ortega y Gasset* (Oxford: Oxford University Press, 1989) p. 51.

[59] Robert Wohl, Introduction to Jim Cross, *The Lost Voices of World War I* (London: Bloomsbury, 1988) p. 10.

[60] *Ibid.*, p. 328.

[61] Cited Malcolm Bradbury (ed.), *Modernism* (London: Penguin, 1976) p. 98.

[62] *Lost Voices, op.cit.*, p. 329.

[63] *Ibid.*, p. 12.

[64] *Ibid.*, p. 385.

[65] James Diehl, *Paramilitary Politics in Weimar Germany* (Bloomington: Indiana University Press, 1971) p. 214–6.

[66] Joachim Fest, *The Face of the Third Reich* (Harmondsworth: Penguin, 1973).

[67] Diehl, *Paramilitary Politics, op.cit.*, pp. 214–6.

[68] Berghahn, *Militarism, op.cit.*, p. 35.

[69] Erid Leed, *No Man's Land: Combat and Identity in World War One* (Cambridge: Cambridge University Press, 1979) p. 76–7.

[70] Laon was the only medieval city in the region left intact in the tramp and counter-tramp of the French and German armies. Even today it is still 'insulated from the depradations of history, cocooned through time, frozen like Pompeii in the past' (Jacques Darras, 'Beyond the Tunnel of History', *The Listener,* 4 January 1990, p. 11).

[71] Omer Bartov, *Hitler's Army op.cit.*, p. 216, n. 15.

5. WAR AND THE FUTILITY OF HISTORY

[1] Johnston, *English Poetry of the First World War: A Study of the Evolution of Lyric and Narrative Form* (New Jersey: Princeton University Press, 1964).

[2] Bernard Bergonzi, *Heroes' Twilight: A Study of the Literature of the Great War* (London: Macmillan, 1980) p. 127.

[3] Samuel Hynes, *A War Imagined: The First World War in English Culture* (London: Bodley Head, 1990) p. 437.

[4] Paul Fussell, *The Great War and Modern Memory* (Oxford: Oxford University Press, 1975) pp. 146–7.

[5] See John Terraine, *The Smoke and the Fire: Myths and Anti-Myths of War 1861–1945* (London: Sidgwick & Jackson, 1980). Terraine notes that on the first

day of the Somme the British may have lost 57,470 men, more than any European army lost in any war on any one day in history. An appalling figure it may be, but it was never repeated. Moreover, although the day has entered English folklore, why should it be any more significant than a week or a month? In one week (4–10 June) that year the Austrians lost 280,000 men; in one year (1915) the Russians lost two million. The British experience was not part of the European experience of war. 'The truth is the only really exceptional thing about Britain's experience in 1916 was that she had been spared so long.' (p. 37).

Nor is the myth of the lost generation easy to sustain. The UK did lose a disproportionately large number of young officers at the Front but their courage was not the main explanation for high casualty rates. The Germans made greater use of the NCOs – for every 25 officers in the line in every British battalion in the last six months of the war the Germans would deploy only eight. Thousands of promising young officers were killed at the British army undertaking work that the Germans entrusted to lance corporals. (See Keith Simpson, *A Nation in Arms*, p. 87).

6   Marc Ferro, *The Great War 1914–18* (London: 1973) p. 26.
7   Charles Edmunds, *A Soldier's War* (1929). Cited in John Terraine, *The Western Front 1914–18* (London: Hutchinson, 1964) p. 18.
8   A C Ward wrote in 1930 that one of the reasons the poets distorted the war was their insistence on being dispassionate. The rank and file by comparison believed the war to be necessary, not futile. (War, 'The Unhappy Warriors', in *Literature and Ideas in the Post-War Decade* (London: Methuen, 1930)).
9   Hugh Cecil, The Literary Legacy of the War', in Peter Liddle, *Home Fires and Foreign Fields*, pp. 205–30.
10 Tony Ashworth, *Trench Warfare 1914–18: The Live and Let Live System* (London: Macmillan, 1980) p. 17. See also, J. Baynes, *Morale* (London: Cassell, 1967) for a study of the infantry battalion as a social community.
11 Siegfried Sassoon, *Memoirs of an Infantry Officer* (London: Faber & Faber, 1930) p. 130.
12 Correlli Barnett, *The Collapse of British Power* (London: Methuen, 1972) p. 432.
13 See E Montagu, *Rough Justice* (London: 1926) p. 68.
14 Terraine, *The Smoke and the Fire, op.cit.*, p. 42.
15 Blunden, *Undertones of War, op.cit.*, p. 266.
16 Robert Graves, *Occupation: Writer* (Bath: Portway, 1951) p. ix. Karl Miller accuses Owen of being interested not in history but experience, and a pastoral one at that. He sees him as an over-sensitive individual who sat apart in order to feel what it was like to be a romantic person suffering fits of melancholia ('Hello to All That', *New York Review of Books*, 16 October 1975, p. 28).
17 F R Leavis, *New Bearings in English Poetry: A Study of the Contemporary Situation* (London: 1963) p. 61.
18 Andrew Rutherford, *The Literature of War: Five Studies in Heroic Virtue* (London: Macmillan, 1978) pp. 79–80.

19 *Ibid.*, p. 85.
20 Maurice Genevoix, 'Commentaries on the War: Some Meanings' in Panichas (ed.), *Promise of Greatness*, p. 485.
21 Karl Miller, *Doubles: Studies in Literary History* (Oxford: Oxford University Press, 1985) p. 79.
22 Graham Greenwell, *An Infant in Arms: War Letters of Company Officer 1914–18* (London: Lovat Dixon & Thompson, 1935).
23 Keith Simpson, 'The British Soldier on the Western front', in Peter Liddle (ed.), *Home Fires and Foreign Fields: British Social and Military Experiences in the First World War* (London: Brasseys, 1985) p. 149.
24 Johnston, *English Poetry, op.cit.*, pp. 19–20.
25 Jon Silkin, *Out of Battle: The Poetry of the Great War* (Oxford: Oxford University Press, 1972) p. 333. See also David Jones, *Epoch and Artist* (ed. Harman Grisewood (1959) p. 243).
26 Julian Symons (ed.), *The Essential Wyndham Lewis* (London: Vintage, 1991) p. 19.
27 Jacques Darras, *Beyond the Tunnel of History* (London: Macmillan, 1990) pp. 65–69.
28 *Ibid.*
29 Samuel Hynes, *The Auden Generation: Literature and Politics in England in the 1930s* (London: Bodley Head, 1976) p. 29.
30 *Ibid.*
31 Cited Alistair Horne, *The Price of Glory: Verdun 1916* (London: Macmillan, 1962) p. 362.
32 Frank Richards, *Old Soldiers Never Die* (New York: Berkeley Publishing Co., 1966), p. 3.
33 J M Winter, *The Experience of World War One* (London: Papermac, 1988), p. 229.
34 Cited A C Ward, *The 1920's* (London: 1930), p. xxi.
35 Robert Graves, 'The Marmositos Miscellany', *Poems 1914–1926* (London: 1927), p. 191.
36 C E Carrington, *Soldiers from the War Returning* (London: 1965), p. 252.
37 Avetick Isahakian, *Notebooks of a Lyric Poet* (University Press of America, 1991).
38 R H Mottram, *Journey to the Western Front Twenty Years After* (London: 1936), p. 1.
39 H Williamson, *The Wet Flanders Plain* (London: 1929), p. 59.
40 Scott Fitzgerald, *Tender is the Night* (Harmondsworth: Penguin, 1979), p. 24.
41 T S Eliot, 'Tradition and the Individual Talent', *Selected Essays* (London: Faber & Faber, 1934), p. 16.
42 Eugene Minkowsky, *Lived Time: Phenomenological and Psychopathological Studies* (1933) (Reprinted Northwestern University Press, 1970), p. 153 and p. 167.
43 David Lowenthal, *The Past is a Foreign Country* (Cambridge: Cambridge University Press, 1985), p. 204.

44 *Ibid.*, p. 46.
45 Ronald Blythe (ed.), *Writing and War: Stories, Poems and Essays, 1939–45* (Harmondsworth: Penguin, 1982).
46 *Ibid.*
47 Paul Fussell, *Killing in Verse and Prose, and Other Essays* (London: Bellew Publishing, 1988) p. 130.
48 Ted Hughes, Introduction to Keith Douglas, *The Complete Poems* (Harmondsworth: Penguin, 1989).
49 George Orwell, *Homage to Catalonia* (ed. Peter Davison) (Harmondsworth: Penguin, 1989) p. 189.
50 Hynes, *The Auden Generation, op.cit.*
51 James Longenbach, *Modernist Poetics of History: Pound, Eliot and the Sense of the Past* (Princeton, NJ: Princeton University Press, 1987) p. 9.
52 *Letters of Henry James* (ed. Percy Lovelock), Vol. 2 (London: 1920) p. 462.
53 Jean-Paul Sartre, *What is Literature?* (Paris: Gallimard, 1972) p. 228.
54 André Malraux, Preface to Monique St Claire, *Cahiers de la Petite Dame* (Paris: Gallimard, 1973) p. xxiv.
55 Jean-Piere Maxence, *Histoire de dix ans 1927–37* (Paris: Gallimard, 1939) p. 12.
56 Humphrey Carpenter, *The Brideshead Generation: Evelyn Waugh and his Friends* (London: Weidenfeld & Nicolson, 1989) p. 313.
57 Paul Fussell, *Abroad: British Literary Travelling between the Wars* (Oxford: Oxford University Press, 1980) p. 16.
58 Hynes, *The Auden Generation, op.cit.*, pp. 247–8.
59 Charles Osborne, *W.H. Auden: The Life of the Poet* (London: Eyre Methuen, 1980) p. 130.
60 *Ibid.*, p. 134.
61 Valentine Cunningham, *Spanish Front: Writers on the Civil War* (Oxford: Oxford University Press, 1986) p. 21.
62 *Ibid.*, p. 28.
63 *Ibid.*, p. 50.
64 Esmond Romilly, *Boadilla* (1937).
65 Salvador Dali, *Diary of a Genius: An Autobiography* (London: Picador, 1966).
66 Antoine de St-Exupery, *Wind, Sand and Stars* (London: Heinemann, 1970).
67 Louis McNiece, *Autumn Journal*, cited Robin Skelton (ed.), *Poetry of the 1940's* (Harmondsworth: Penguin, 1968) p. 24.
68 Cunningham, *Spanish Front, op.cit.*, p. xxvi.
69 Edward Callen, *Auden: A Carnival of Intellect* (Oxford: Oxford University Press, 1983) pp. 126–7.
70 Hynes, *Auden Generation, op.cit.*, pp. 312–2.
71 Carpenter, *The Brideshead Generation, op.cit.*, pp. 312–3.
72 Christopher Isherwood, *Christopher and his Kind 1929–39* (London: Eyre Methuen, 1977) pp. 247–8.
73 Anthony Burgess, *1985* (London: Arrow Books, 1985) p. 102.
74 Miles Taylor, 'Patriotism, History and the Left in Twentieth Century Britain',

Historical Journal, 33:4 (1990) pp. 982–5.

75 Mary Green, *Fiction and the Historical Present: French Writers in the 1930's* (University Press of New England, 1986) p. 37.

76 Fernand Celine, *Journey to the End of the Night* (New York: 1983) p. 99.

77 Merlyn Thomas, *Louis-Fernand Celine* (London: Faber & Faber, 1979) p. 126.

78 Celine, *Journey to the End of the Night*, *op.cit.*, pp. 8–9.

79 *Ibid.*

80 Erika Ostrovsky, *Celine and his Vision* (London: University of London Press, 1967) p. 170.

81 Green, *Fiction and the Historical Present*, *op.cit.*, p. 37.

82 Patrick McCarthy, *Celine* (London: Allen Lane, 1975). See also J H Matthews, *The Inner Dream: Celine as Novelist* (New York: Syracuse University Press, 1967) p. 170.

83 Ostrovsky, *Celine and his Vision*, *op.cit.*, p. 48.

84 Fernand Celine, *North* (London: Bodley Head, 1972).

85 Celine, *Journey to the End of the Night*, *op.cit.*

86 *Ibid.*

87 Thomas, *Louis-Fernand Celine*, *op.cit.*, p. 135.

88 Alain, p. 47, fn. 10, *Making of Myth*.

89 *Ibid.*

90 Alain, *Gods* (London: Quartet, 1988) p. 60.

91 Elizabeth Bowen, *In the Heat of the Day* (London: Jonathan Cape, 1948).

92 Richard Pipes, *The Russian Revolution, 1899–1919* (London: Fontana, 1990) p. 839.

93 Bradley Smith, *The War's Long Shadow* (London: Andre Deutsch, 1986) p. 86.

94 Nadia Mandelstam, *Hope Against Hope: A Memoir* (Harmondsworth: Penguin, 1983) pp. 630–1.

95 Illya Ehrenberg, *The War 1941–5* (London: MacGibbon & Lee, 1964) pp. 124–5.

96 Mikhail Bulgarkov *Diabolid* (Harvill: Collins, 1991) p. ix (Introduction by John Curtis).

97 Carrington, *Soldiers from the War Returning*, *op.cit.*

98 Carole Fink, *Marc Bloch: A Life in History* (Cambridge: Cambridge University Press, 1989). See for his Great War friendships, Bloch, *Memoirs of War 1914–5* (Trans. Carole Fink) (Ithaca: Cornell University Press, 1980).

99 Andrew Rutherford, *Literature of War: Five Studies in Heroic Virtue* (London: Macmillan, 1978) p. 105.

100 Albert Camus, 'A Writer's Notebook', *Encounter* (March 1965) pp. 25–9.

101 Primo Levi, *The Drowned and the Saved* (New York: Summit, 1988) p. 81.

102 Cited Stephan Whitfield 'Totalitarianism in Eclipse - the Recent Fate of an Idea', in Arthur Edelstein, *Images and Ideas in American Culture* (Hanover: Brandeis University Press, 1979) p. 73.

103 Alexander Solzhenitsyn, *The Gulag Archipelago 1918–56: An Experiment in Literary Imagination* (London: Collins Harville, 1988) pp. 324–5.

104 Richard Pipes, *The Russian Revolution*, *op.cit.*, p. 839.

105   Rousset, *The Days of Our Death*, *op.cit.*

106   Solzhenitsyn, *The Gulag Archipelago, op.cit.*

107   Cited George Nivat, 'Man and the Gulag', in Hagihara, *Experiencing the Twentieth Century* (Tokyo: University of Tokyo Press, 1985) p. 145.

108   See Angus Calder, *T.S. Eliot* (Brighton: Harvester Press, 1987) p. 147.

6. TWENTIETH CENTURY WAR AND THE AESTHETIC IMAGINATION

1   Alistair Horne, *The Price of Glory: Verdun 1916* (London: Macmillan, 1962) p. 181.

2   *Ibid.*, p. 187.

3   Ernst Jünger, *In shahlgewittern* (Berlin: 1931) pp. 114–5.

4   J R Hale, *Renaissance Warfare Studies* (London: Fontana, 1983).

5   Stendhal, *To the Happy Few: Selected Letters* (London: Soho Book Co., 1986).

6   Tim Cross, *The Lost Voices of World War I* (London: Bloomsbury, 1988) p. 382.

7   Wyndham Lewis, *Blasting and Bombadeering* (London: Eyre & Spottiswoode, 1937) p. 119.

8   Robert Hart Davies, *Hugh Walpole* (London: Macmillan, 1952).

9   Marc Bloch, *The Strange Defeat* (New York: 1948).

10   John Ellis, *Eye Deep in Hell: Trench Warfare in World War One* (New York: Pantheon, 1976).

11   David Jones, *In Parenthesis* (New York: 1961) p. 216.

12   Guillaume Appolinaire, *The Poet Assassinated and Other Stories* (London: Grafton Books, 1985) pp. 137–8.

13   Modris Eksteins, 'When Death Was Young ... Germany, Modernism and the Great War', in R J Bullen (ed.), *Ideas Into Politics: Aspects of European History 1880–1950* (London: Croom Helm, 1984) p. 32.

14   Michael Herr, *Despatches* (New York: Aron, 1978) p. 170; William Broyles, 'Why Men Love War', *Esquire* (November 1984) pp. 62–63.

15   David Gascoyne, *Collected Journals 1936–42* (ed. Kathleen Raine) (London: 1991).

16   Robert Guillain, *Le Peuple Japonais et le Guerre* (Paris: Juillard, 1947) pp. 198–211. Christopher Isherwood also found the bombing of Hankow 'impressive' as a spectacle, in particular the sound of bombs exploding. 'It was as tremendous as Beethoven', he wrote, 'but wrong – a cosmic offence, an insult to the whole of nature'. (Christopher Isherwood/W.H. Auden, *Journey to a War,* p. 61).

17   Susan Mansfield, *The Gestalts of War: An Enquiry into the Origins and Meaning of a Social Institution* (New York: Dial Press, 1982) pp. 158–60.

18   Klaus Theweleit, *Male Fantasies,* Vol. 2, *Male Bodies: Psychoanalysing the White Terror* (Cambridge: Polity, 1981) p. 51; Elias Cannetti, *Crowds and Power* (London: Penguin, 1981) p. 365.

19   Ezra Pound was particularly struck by an exhibition of Wyndham Lewis's war

pictures in 1919. He believed it to be the best art that had come out of the war, although he believed, like so many artists, Lewis had got a good deal more out of art's resistance to war than war's much vaunted effect upon it. 'Indeed, Mr Lewis would seem to suggest that art is a cut above war; that art might even outlast it.' Ezra Pound, *Selected Prose 1909–65* (ed. William Cookson, London: Faber & Faber, 1978) p. 398.

20 Samuel Hynes, *A War Imagined: The First World War and English Culture* (London: Pimlico, 1990) p. 195.

21 Joseph Brodsky, *Less Than One: Selected Essays* (London: Penguin, 1987) p. 314.

22 Hans Jürgen Syberberg, *Hitler: The Film from Germany* (Manchester, Carcanet) p. 242.

23 *Hitler: A Film from Germany* is a breathtakingly perverse piece of cinema – a spectacular anti-film. No wonder, then, that Syberberg has scarcely made a film since but devoted himself to stage work and filmed readings from the classics, such as Kleist and Joyce.

24 Syberberg, *Hitler, op.cit.,* p. 241.

25 Philip Caputo, *Rumour of War,* p. 289. The first reference to war as a 'movie' that I can find is from the artist Paul Klee, writing in his diary in February 1918. A plane crash, one of many of which helped while away the time, offered for him 'a first rate movie effect'. (See *the Diaries of Paul Klee 1898–1918* (Berkeley: University of California Press, 1968) p. 388.

26 Paul Rabinow (ed.), *The Foucault Reader: An Introduction to Foucault's Thought* (Harmondsworth: Penguin, 1984) pp. 39–41.

27 *Ibid.,* p. 40.

28 Peter Adam, *Arts of the Third Reich* (London: Thames & Hudson, 1992) p. 159.

29 Philippe Lacoue-Labarthe, *Heidegger, Art and Politics* (Oxford: Basil Blackwell, 1990) pp. 47–52.

30 *Ibid.,* p. 51.

31 Cited Michael Zimmerman, *Heidegger's Confrontation with Modernity: Technology, Politics, Art* (Bloomington: Indiana University Press, 1990) p. 27.

32 Walter Benjamin, *Illuminations* (London: Fontana, 1979) pp. 244–5.

33 Denis McSmith, 'The Theory and Practice of Fascism', in M. Greene (ed.), *Fascism: An Anthology* (New York: 1968) p. 82. See also, Christiana Taylor, *Futurism: Politics, Painting and Performance* (University Research Press, 1979) p. 10. History, wrote Marinetti in 1905, was merely an infinite series of dress rehearsals for the final tragedy. Marinetti's point was not that history does not take place but that even when it occurs, in catastrophe, it only turns a rehearsal into a performance. (Manfred Hinz, 'The Concept of History in Italian Futurism', in Athanasios Mouoakis (ed.), *The Promise of History: Essays in Political Philosophy* (Berlin: Walte de Gruyter, 1986) pp. 188–9.

34 Edward Gibbon, *The Decline and Fall of the Roman Empire,* Vol. 4, pp. 167–9.

35 Nicholas Berdayev, *The New Middle Ages* (1924). See Donald Attwater (ed.), *The Bourgeois Mind and Other Essays* (New York: Books for Libraries Press, 1966) pp. 52–64.

36 Benjamin, *Illuminations, op.cit.*, p. 243.
37 Cited J P Stern, *Hitler: The Fuhrer and the People* (London: Fontana, 1975) p. 23.
38 Other members of Hitler's court went back to medieval history, not myth. Himmler saw himself as a new Henry I and liked to be referred to as 'the Black Duke'. Alfred Rosenberg had himself celebrated as the spiritual successor of Henry the Lion (Joachim Fest, *The Face of the Third Reich*, p. 452). Goebbels dreamed of a new Holy Roman Empire in which Burgundy would once again be united with the Reich.
39 T J Jackson-Lears, *No Place of Grace: Anti-Modernism and the Transformation of American Culture* (New York: Pantheon Books, 1981) p. 178.
40 *Ibid.*
41 Umberto Eco, *Travels in Hyper-Reality* (London: 'Picador, 1987) p. 69.
42 H Stuart Hughes, *Consciousness and Society: The Reorientation of European Social Thought 1890–1930* (1959) pp. 428–9.
43 J P Mayer, *Max Weber and German Politics: A Study in Political Sociology* (London: Faber & Faber, 1944) p. 35. Interestingly, it was the Germans not the Russians who were considered to be the barbarians in 1914. Baron Kervyn de Lettenhove despaired that the Huns were once again on the march, burning the most beautiful monuments as they passed through, destroying everything of artistic value, the town hall of Louvain and the Flemish Cloth Hall at Ypres being among the most noticeable casualties. (For the effect of the destruction of Ypres on the English imagination, see Paul Fussel, *The Great War and Modern Memory* (1973) pp. 40–1. For de Lettenhove see Silver, *Esprit de Corps, op.cit.*, pp. 6–7. The Russian invasion of East Prussia in the same year had very little that was barbaric about it. Indeed, compared with the atrocities of the German march through Belgium, which were real though exaggerated, the incursion of the Russian Second Army was almost without incident. Only two cases of rape were recorded. Forty years later, while serving a sentence in a forced labour camp, Solzhenitsyn composed a narrative poem, *Prussian Nights*, about his own experiences when his battery joined in the invasion of East Prussia in January 1945. Looking back he meditated on the coincidence that their line of advance was the same as that of General Samsonov and the Second Army in 1914. In Solzhenitsyn's own account, however, nothing is left out: the rapes, rapine, remorseless violence, the burned down houses, devastated farms. Only a clock 'surviving through it all' measures time 'honourably, between the others and ourselves'.
44 Richard Breitman, 'Hitler and Genghis Khan', *Journal of Contemporary History* 25 (1990) p. 341. Hitler was not alone in sharing this view. During the war Churchill often ruminated about the threat of 'Russian barbarism ... swamping the cultural independence of the old European states'. (Ernst Tropitsch, *Stalin's War: A Radical New Theory of the Origin of the Second World War* (Fourth Estate, 1987) p. 125). In fact the last nomadic (barbarian) attack on a European stronghold before 1989 was on Marrakesh in 1912. (See

Fernand Brardel, *The Mediterranean World in the Age of Philip II*, Vol. I (London: Collins, 1972) p. 179).

45 Alexander Werth, *Moscow '41* (London: Hamish Hamilton, 1942) p. 182.

46 Alexander Werth, *Russia at War 1941-5* (New York: Dutton & Co., 1964) p. 964.

47 John Lukacs, *The Last European War* (London: Routledge & Kegan Paul, 1976) p. 519. In Italy (1944) soldiers of the Eighth Army encountered Turcoman warriors, who had been pressed into service by the Germans. See Douglas Orgill, *The Gothic Line* (London: Pan, 1967) p. 242. Another soldier, Eric Newby, found himself taken prisoner of war by just such a man, 'a hideously cruel descendant of the warriors of Genghiz Khan'. (Newby, *A Traveller's Life*, pp. 130-1).

48 Albert Seaton, *The Russo-German War 1941-5* (London: Arthur Barker, 1971) p. 545.

49 Omer Bartov, Eastern Front *op.cit.*, p. 211. Germany's own history, of course, helped shape and transform its attitude towards its Eastern neighbours in a way that most West Europeans did not comprehend. The Germans after all had been invaded by the Mongols in the thirteenth century, though only briefly. When the Mongols appeared to return in 1944 history seemed to have reasserted itself. It was ironic that the two musicians responsible for aryanizing Handel's oratorios in 1942 renamed 'Israel in Egypt' – 'Mongelensturm' (or 'The Mongol Fury').

50 R. Rhees (ed.), *Ludwig Wittgenstein: Personal Recollections* (Oxford: Blackwell, 1981) p. 152.

51 Erika Ostrovsky, *Celine and his Vision* (London: University of London Press, 1968) p. 161. 'The horsemen of the apocalypse simply ride through the sky' Celine insisted. 'What does it matter if the angels' trumpet has changed its sound to that of the siren?.' In later stages of his literary career he compared himself frequently to Hieronymus Bosch, insisting that he saw the world mainly unfolding in a 'universe à la Bosch ... torture and jocularity'.

52 Anna Bravo, 'Myth, Impotence and Survival in the Concentration Camps', in Raphael Samuel/Paul Thompson (eds.), *The Myths We Live By* (London: Routledge & Kegan Paul, 1990) p. 106.

53 Horst Lange, *Under the Bombs: The German Home Front 1952-5* (Louisville: University Press of Kentucky, 1986) p. 150.

54 Walter Duranty, *Write as I Please* (London: Hamish Hamilton, 1937) p. 22. Primo Levi mentions that typhus was used as a weapon by some inmates of Hitler's concentration camps. Prisoners who washed and ironed SS uniforms would search for comrades who had died of typhus, pick the lice off the corpses and slip them under the collars of the ironed and spruced up military jackets. The SS rarely survived. 'Lice are not very attractive animals', Levi added, 'but they do not have racial prejudices'. (Carlo Levi, *Moments of Reprieve* (New York: Summit Books, 1985)).

55 Celine, *North* (London: Bodley Head, 1986).

56 Miroslav Holub, 'Distant Howlings', in *On the Country and Other Poems*

(London: Blood Axe Books, 1984) p. 73.

57 Spencer Weart, *Nuclear Fear: A History of Images* (Cambridge, MA: Harvard University Press, 1988) p. 109.

58 Umberto Eco 'The Return of the Middle Ages' in Eco *Travels in Hyperreality* (London: Picador, 1986) p. 81.

59 Valentine Cunningham, *Spanish Front: Writers at War* (Oxford: Oxford University Press, 1986).

60 Antoine de Saint-Exupery, *Wind, Sand, Stars* (1939) (London: Picador, 1990) George Bernanos recalls that in Palma (Majorca) in March 1937 there were an average of 15 executions of fifth columnists a day (*A Diary of My Times* (1938)).

61 Philip Rieft, 'The Loss of the Past and the Mystique of Change', in T R Urban (ed.), *Can We Survive Our Future?* (1972) pp. 46-7.

62 Guglielmo Ferrero, *Peace and War* (London: Macmillan, 1933).

63 Malcolm Muggeridge, *Chronicles of Wasted Time*, Vol. 2, *The Infernal Grove* (London: Jonathan Cape, 1975) pp. 59-60.

64 Antoine de Saint-Exupery, *Wartime Writings 1939-44* (London: Picador, 1986) p. 2.

65 Edmund Blunden, *De Bello Germanico: A Fragment of Trench History* (London: Hawstead, 1930). One might have to go back to Taddeo di Bartolo's extraordinary frescoes for San Gimigiano in Tuscany to see what the fourteenth century understood by horror. The scenes that men saw on the Western Front were more horrific still. Edwin Vaughan, the last officer left in his company during the battle of Langemarck records this memory on 27 August 1917: 'From the darkness on all sides came the groans and wails of wounded men; faint, long, sobbing moans of agony and despairing shrieks. It was too horribly obvious that dozens of men with serious wounds must have crawled for safety into new shell holes and now the water was rising above them and, powerless to move, they were slowly drowning.' (Edwin Vaughan, *Some Desperate Glory: The Diary of a Young Officer 1917* (London: Macmillan, 1985) p. 228).

66 Paul Nash, *Outlines: An Autobiography and Other Writings* (London: Collins, 1949) pp. 210-11; Lewis, *Blasting and Bombadeering, op.cit.*

67 Wyndham Lewis, *Creatures of Habit and Creatures of Change: Essays on Art, Literature and Society 1914-1956* (ed. Paul Edwards) (Santa Rose: Black Sparrow Press, 1989) p. 42.

68 Bolidan Wytwycky, *The Other Holocaust: The Many Circles of Hell* (Washington DC: 1980).

69 Lucy Dawidovicz, *The Holocaust and the Historians* (Cambridge, MA: Harvard University Press, 1981) p. 15.

70 George Steiner, *In Bluebeard's Castle: Notes Towards the Redefinition of Culture* (New Haven: Yale University Press, 1971) pp. 53-4.

71 Julian Symons, *The Essential Wyndham Lewis* (London: Vintage, 1991) pp. 23-4.

72 Keith Simpson, 'A Nation in Arms', *op.cit.*, p. 85.

73 Emil Fackenheim, *To Men the World: Foundations of Future Jewish Thought* (New York: Schockin Books, 1982).

74 Warner Wells (ed.), *Hiroshima Diary* (Chapel Hill: University of North Carolina Press, 1955) p. 54.

75 Cited Robert J. Lifton, *Death in Life: Survivors of Hiroshima* (New York: Random House, 1967) p. 27.

76 Theodore Adorno, *Negative Dialectics* (London: Routledge & Kegan Paul, 1973) p. 320.

77 George Orwell, 'Inside the Whale', *Collected Essays* (London: Secker & Warburg, 1975) p. 120.

78 Walser, in 'Holocaust in History', *Echoes of Genocide*, p. 30.

79 Erich Auerbach, *Mimesis: Representation of Reality in Western Literature* (New York: Garden City, 1953) p. 171.

80 Paul Fussel, *Killing in Verse and Prose and Other Essays* (London: Bellew Publishing, 1988) p. 130.

81 Ronald Blythe (ed.), *Writing and War: Stories, Poems and Essays of the Second World War* (Harmondsworth: Penguin, 1982) p. 27.

82 Elizabeth Bowen, 'Mysterious Kôr', in *The Demon Lover and Other Stories* (London: Jonathan Cape).

83 Louis MacNiece, *Selected Prose* (ed. Alan Heuser) (Oxford: Clarendon Press, 1990) p. 102.

84 Cyril Connolly, *Essays 1927–44* (London: Routledge & Kegan Paul, 1945).

85 Julian Symons, *Notes From Another Country* (London: London Magazine Editions, 1972).

86 Cited John Spurling *Graham Greene* (London: Methuen, 1983) p. 76.

87 Malcolm Muggeridge, *Chronicles of Wasted Time*, op.cit., p. 183–4.

88 Gascoyne, *Collected Journals, op.cit.*

89 Malcolm Muggeridge, *Chronicles of Wasted Time, op.cit.*

90 Harold Nicholson, *Diaries and Letters 1939–45* (ed. Nigel Nicholson) (London: Collins, 1970) p. 130.

91 Anthony Masters, *Literary Agents: The Novelist as Spy* (Oxford: Blackwell, 1987) p. 88.

92 John Spurling, *Graham Greene* (London: Methuen, 1983) p. 23.

93 John Lukacs, *The Duel: Hitler Versus Churchill* (Oxford: Oxford University Press, 1992 p. 149.

94 Stephen Spender, *Citizens in War and After* (London: Hamish Hamilton).

95 George Steiner, Introduction to Ernst Jünger, *On the Marble Cliffs* (Harmondsworth: Penguin, 1983) p. ix.

96 *Ibid*

97 *Ibid*

98 Evelyn Waugh, *Unconditional Surrender* (Harmondsworth: Penguin, 1964) p. 190.

99 Muggeridge, *The Infernal Grove, op.cit.*, pp. 183–4. As the first American journalists arrived in Berlin many were embarrassed to see the damage their

own bombers had inflicted. 'The ruin of the city was so immense', wrote John Dos Passos, 'it took on the grandeur of a natural phenomenon like the Garden of the Gods or the painted Desert'. At Stettiner Station Dos Passos saw crowds of dazed looking people with bundles and knapsacks over their backs, their skin hanging on their bones like candle drippings. It is a vivid if unpleasant phrase, 'Berlin was not just one more beaten up city. There that point in a ruined people's misery had been reached where the victims were degraded beneath the reach of human sympathy'. (John Dos Passos, *Tour of Duty* (Boston: Houghton & Mifflin, 1946) p. 319.) Stig Dagerman recalls meeting in Hanover an artist who was quite entranced by the ruined city. One evening they both saw a procession of nuns set against a series of buildings with clinging pipes and gallows like rafters. The artist was quite enthused. 'I'll paint that some day, not because it is a ruin but because the contrast so *so verdannt erschutternd*'. (Stig Dagerman, *German Autumn* (London: Quartet, 1992) pp. 166-7).

100 Curzio Malaparte, *Kaputt* (London: Picador, 1982). During the Second World War a Canadian padre Canon F G Scott came across the corpse of a young boy covered with a coating of yellow mud. He immediately thought of a 'statue made of bronze. He had a beautiful face with finely shaped head covered with close, curling hair and looked more like some work of art than a human being.' (Modris Eksteins, *The Rites of Spring: The Great War and the Birth of the Modern Age* (London: Bantam, 1989) p. 215.

101 Curzio Malaparte, *The Skin* (London: Picador, 1988).

102 Saul Friedlander, *Reflections on Naziism: An Essay on Kitsch and Death* (New York: Harper & Row, 1984) pp. 94-5.

103 Robert Scholes, *Structural Fabulation* (Notre Dame: University of Notre Dame Press, 1975) p. 7.

104 Charles W. Sydnor, *Soldiers of Destruction: the SS Death's Head Division 1933-45* (Princeton NJ: Princeton University Press, 1977) p. 318.

105 Albert Seaton, *The Russo-German War 1941-5* (London: Arthur Barker, 1971) p. 545; *The Price of Hitler's War: German Military and Civilian Losses Resulting from World War Two* (New York: Greenwood Press, 1986) pp. 123-7.

106 Malaparte, *Kaputt, op.cit.,* pp. 173-4.

107 Dan Colin-Sherbok, *Holocaust Theology* (London: Lamp Press, 1989) p. 11.

108 Thomas Keneally, *Schindler's Ark* (London; Sceptre, 1982) p. 275.

109 Malaparte, *The Skin, op.cit.,* pp. 22-4.

110 Norman Lewis, *Naples '44* (New York: Pantheon Books, 1978). Two particularly virulent strains of venereal disease, streptococci and gonococci, were reintroduced into Italy with the arrival of American troops. Lewis recalls that incidents of VD reached a pitch greater than ever witnessed in Italy before. So much so that there was one suggestion to smuggle prostitutes across Allied Lines into the German occupied north in the hope they would infect German troops and thus diminish the fighting efficiency of the German army. Twenty of the more attractive young Neapolitan prostitutes were actually rounded up

in January 1944 and taken to Capri from where it was planned that they would be smuggled into German occupied Rome. The girls rebelled, insisting that they get 1,000 lire a night from the Americans, and would be lucky to get 100 lire from the Germans.

111 Jean Lartéguy, *The Face of War: Reflections on Man and Combat* (Paris: Helmut Meyer, 1974).

112 Jean Améry, *Preface to the Future: Culture in a Conservative Society* (London: Constable, 1964) p. 8.

7. WAITING FOR THE END OF THE WORLD

1 Cesare Pavese, *The Business of Living: Diaries 1935–50* (London: Quartet, 1980) p. 83.

2 André Malraux, *The Psychology of Art* (Paris; Gallimard, 1949) p. 27.

3 Walter Lippmann, 'Force and Ideas', *The New Republic*, 7 November 1914.

4 Cited Michael Mandelbaum, *The Nuclear Question: The United States and Nuclear Weapons 1946–76* (Cambridge: Cambridge University Press, 1979) pp. 2–3.

5 Jean-François Lyotard, *Heidegger and 'the jews'* (Minneapolis: University of Minnesota Press, 1990) p. 44.

6 See introduction to E M Cioran, *The Temptation to Exist* (London: Quartet, 1986) p. 24.

7 Walter Benjamin, 'Theses on the Philosophy of History' in *Illuminations* (ed. Hannah Arendt) (London: Fontana, 1970) pp. 259–60.

8 See Italo Calvino, *The Literature Machine* (London: Picador, 1987) p. 187.

9 *Ibid*, p. 202.

10 Paul Fussell, *The Great War and Modern Memory, op. cit.*.

11 Cited Philippe Lacoue-Labarthe, *Heidegger, Art and Politics* (Oxford: Basil Blackwell, 1990) p. 23.71.

12 Philip Windsor, 'The Twentieth Century as Self-Conscious History' in Hagihara/Nobutoshi (eds.), *Experiencing the Twentieth Century* (Tokyo: University of Tokyo Press, 1985) p. 352.

13 Ray Lifton/Eric Markusen, *The Genocidal Mentality: Nazi Holocaust and Nuclear Fear* (London: Macmillan, 1991) p. 23.

14 Spencer Weart, *Nuclear Fear: A History of Images* (Cambridge, MA: Harvard University Press, 1988) pp. 101–2. The Manhattan chemist George Kistiakowsky predicted 'in the last millisecond of the Earth's existence the last man will see something very similar to what we have'. William L. Lawrence, *Men and Atoms* (New York: Simon and Schuster, 1959) p. 118.

15 Philip Sabin, *The Third World War Scare in Britain: A Critical Analysis* (London: Macmillan, 1986) p. 98.

16 Freeman Dyson, *Disturbing the Universe* (New York: Harper & Row, 1979) pp. 60–1.

17 J B Priestley, *Thoughts in the Wilderness* (London: Heinemann, 1957) p. 63.

18 Siegfried Sassoon, 'A View of Old Exeter', in *Selected Poems* (London: Faber & Faber, 1972) p. 68.

19 Christa Wolf, *Cassandra: A Novel and Four Essays* (London: Virago, 1984) p. 248. In the mid-1980s as a leading member of the East German Peace Movement Wolf wanted mankind to live by a 'new myth' – a peace that has a future in it'. See also, Anna Kuhn, *Christa Wolf's Utopian Vision*, Cambridge University Press, 1988 and Marilyn Fries (ed.), *Responses to Christa Wolf* (Detroit: Wayne State University Press, 1989).

20 Cited Fernand Braudel, *The Identity of France* Vol. 1, *History and Environment* (London: Collins, 1988) p. 27.

21 Mircea Eliade, *The Myth of the Eternal Return, or Cosmos and History* (Princeton, NJ: Princeton University Press, 1974) p. 150.

22 E M Cioran, *A Short History of Decay* (London: Quartet, 1988) pp. 5–6.

23 *Ibid*, p. 116.

24 Ronald Siedenberg, *Post-Historic Man: An Enquiry* (Chapel Hill: 1974) p. 237. Back in the nineteenth century Soren Kierkegaard had divined the way things were going. Surveying the nineteenth century he remarked 'he who fights the future has a dangerous enemy. The future is not, it borrows its strength from man himself and when it has tricked him out of this, then it appears outside of him as the enemy he must meet' (cited in Clarke, *Voices Prophesying War* (Oxford: Oxford University Press: 1966) p. 189).

25 Alasdair Spark, The Art of Future War: Starship Troops, the Forever War and Vietnam' In Tom Shippey (ed.), *Fictional Space: Essays on Contemporary Science Fiction* (Oxford: Basil Blackwell, 1991) p.§136.

26 George Steiner, *Real Presences* (London: Faber & Faber, 1989) p. 56.

27 Cited James Longenbach, *Modernist Poetics of History: Pound, Eliot and the Sense of the Past* (Princeton NJ: Princeton University Press, 1987) p. 9. After spending a few weeks in the trenches Ford Madox Ford was transformed into a historical pessimist: 'If, before the war, one had any function it was that of historian. Basing, as it were, one's mortality on the Europe of Charlemagne, modified by the Europe of Napoleon. I once had something to go upon. One could approach with composure the *lex allemannica*, the feudal system, problems of aerial flight ... but now it seems to me we have no method of approach to any of these problems.'

28 *Ibid*

29 Bertolt Brecht, *The Life of Galileo* (Trans. John Willett) (London: Methuen, 1988) p. 12.

30 *Ibid*, p. xxxiii. See the discussion between the Philosopher and Galileo:

    'PHILOSOPHER: Your Highness, Ladies and Gentlemen. I just wonder where all this is leading.

    PHILOSOPHER GALILEO: I should say our duty as scientists is not to ask where truth is leading.

    THE GALILEO PHILOSOPHER: Mr. Galileo, truth might leads us anywhere'

Ibid., p. 42.

31 James Cleugh/Robert Jungk, *Brighter than a Thousand Stars: The Moral and Political History of the Atom Scientists* (London: Victor Gollancz, 1958) p. 38.

32 *Ibid,* p. 29.

33 Jacob Bronowski, *The Ascent of Man* (London: Book Club Associates, 1973) pp. 365-6.

34 Albert Speer, *Inside the Third Reich* (London: Collins, 1970) pp. 227-8.

35 Sam Goudsmit, *Alsos* (Tomash, 1983). Goudsmit was placed in charge of a mission 'Alsos' (the Greek for grove) to investigate how far German atomic physicists had got in the development of the atomic bomb. The work has been superseded by the complete published transcripts from the British Public Records Office (1993) (available from TOP Publishing). The transcripts make sober reading. I quote just three:

> *'Gerlach*: If Germany had had a weapon which would have won the war, then Germany would have been in the right the others in the wrong and whether conditions in Germany are better now than they would have been after a Hitler victory ... I went to my downfall with open eyes but I thought I would try to save German physics and German physicists, and in that I succeeded.'
>
> *'Weizsacker*: History will record that the Americans and the English made a bomb and that at the same time the Germans under the Hitler regime produced a workable engine. In other words the peaceful development of the uranium engine was made in Germany under the Hitler regime, whereas the Americans and English developed this ghastly weapon of war.'
>
> *'Heisenberg*: If the Americans had not got so far with the engine as we did – that is what it looks like ... then we are in luck. There is a possibility of making money.'

History will, of course, record that the Germans never succeeded in making a nuclear reactor during the war.

36 Christopher Simpson, *Blowback: America's Recruitment of Nazis and its Effect on the Cold War* (London: Weidenfeld & Nicolson, 1988) p. 34.

37 Martin Green, *Children of the Sun* (London: Constable, 1977) p. 392.

38 Richard Rhodes, *Making the Atomic Bomb* (New York: Simon and Schuster, 1986) p. 12.

39 *Ibid,* pp. 510-11.

40 Ortega y Gasset, *The Revolt of the Masses* (London: Allen & Unwin, 1932).

41 Jacques Ellul, *Technological Society* (New York: Knopf, 1964), p. 435.

42 Lewis Munford, *The Myth of the Machine, technics and human development* (London: Secker & Warburg, 1967) (New York: 1970) p. 57.

43 Aldous Huxley, *Apes and Essence* (Harmondsworth: Penguin, 1949).

44 Bertrand Russell, *The Impact of Science on Society* (London: George Allen & Unwin, 1952) p. 96.

45 Cited Barry Commoner, *The Closing Circle: Nature, Man and Technology* (New York: Alfred A. Knopf, 1971) pp. 180-1.

46   Alfred Whitehead, *Science in the Modern World* (1927) (New York: Free Press, 1967) p. 14.
47   Jungk, *Brighter Than a Thousand Suns, op.cit.*, p. 199.
48   Ellul, *Technological Society, op.cit.*, p. 137.
49   J W Boag/P E Rubinin/D Shoenberg (eds), *Kapitza in Cambridge and Moscow: Life and Letters of a Russian Physicist* (Amsterdam: Elseiver Science, 1991). American scientists, of course, had their own reasons for contracting into a Faustian bargain with the government. One of the most eloquent spokesmen of the new science was Vannemar Bush for whom manifest destiny was very much alive. In his report to the chairman of the US National Defense Research Committee during World War Two, *Science: The Endless Frontier,* he spoke of science as the new horizon. See also, Vannemar Bush, *Endless Horizons* (Washington, DC: 1946). Manifest or not, the United States since the war has been responsible for nearly two-thirds of all scientific research in the world.
50   Ellul, *Technological Society, op.cit.*, p. 10.
51   Jan Myrdal, *Confessions of a Disloyal European* (London: Jonathan Cape, 1968) p. 189.
52   Robert Musil, *The Man Without Qualities* (London: Picador, 1983) p. 303.
53   Hermann Kahn, *On Thermonuclear War* (New York: Free Press, 1960) pp. 416–7.
54   Wyndham Lewis, *Rude Assignment: An Intellectual Biography* (London: Black Sparrow Press, 1984) pp. 103–4.
55   Gwin Prins, *Defended to Death: A Study of the Nuclear Arms Race* (London: Penguin, 1983) p. 106.
56   Cited Paul Johnson, *The Birth of the Modern 1815–30* (London: Weidenfeld & Nicolson, 1991) p. 1000. See also Daniel Borstein's despairing remark that unfortunately in history there is 'no technological counterpart to a counter-revolution' (*The Republic of Technology: Reflections on Our Future Community* (New York: 1978) p. 30).
57   John Barrow, *Theories of Everything: The Quest for Ultimate Explanation* (London: Vintage, 1992) p. 210.
58   Richard Winston (ed.), *The Letters of Thomas Mann*, Vol. 2, *1942–7* (New York: Alfred Knopf, 1972) p. 217. Brecht too, of course, had once shared that optimism. In the 1938 edition of *The Life of Galileo* he had written: 'Certain experiences could have brought you to a totally false view about what we always call the future of reason. But one man cannot alone corroborate them, or condemn them: it is too large an issue. Reason is something in which *people share a stake*. It is, that is to say, the egoism of humanity as a whole. This egoism is too weak, but even someone like me can tell that reason is not at an end but at a beginning.' (Manfred Wekwert, 'Questions Concerning Brecht', in Pia Kleber (ed.), *Reinterpreting Brecht: His Influence on Contemporary Drama and Film* (Cambridge University Press: 1992) p. 31.) This passage appears only in the 1938 version. Brecht did not feel as optimistic as Mann by the late 1940s, but surely the original version still has truth. Brecht died in 1956

rehearsing Galileo. The production continued despite his death. So did the world.

59 Frank Field, *Three French Writers and the Great War: Studies in the Rise of Communism and Fascism* (Cambridge: Cambridge University Press, 1975) p. 161. Bernanos was particularly appalled because he suspected the next war was not far off. Was it not the 'partial commitment' to peace that had produced the catastrophe of 1939? 'Merely by inhaling the air of the boulevards' in 1920s, 'you could have smelt the odour of the charnel houses, even though they were not to open their doors for another nineteen years.' [*ibid*]

60 Ernest Beaumont, 'Georges Bernanos', in John Cruickshank (ed.), *Novelist as Philosopher: Studies in French Fiction 1935–60* (Oxford: Oxford University Press, 1962) p. 42.

61 Cited Paul K Feyerbend, *Against Method: Outline of an Anarchistic Theory of Knowledge* (Cambridge: Cambridge University Press: 1969) p. 514.

62 Max Horkheimer, *The Eclipse of Reason* (New York: Seabury, 1974) pp. 8–9.

63 Cited Norman Moss, *Men Who Play God: The Story of the Hydrogen Bomb* (London: Victor Gollancz, 1968) p. 320.

64 Michel Foucault, *The History of Sexuality* Vol. 3, *The Cure of the Self* (Harmondsworth: Penguin, 1986) p. 167.

65 See Dobson, *An Introduction to the Politics and Philosophy of Jose Ortega y Gasset* (Cambridge: Cambridge University Press, 1989) p. 180.

66 Octavio Paz, *Conjunctions and Disjunctions* (New York: R K Publishers, 1982) pp. 111–112.

67 *Between Hell and Reason: Essays from the Resistance Newspaper Combat 1944–47* (Trans. Alexandre Gramont (Wesleyan University Press, 1991) pp. 110–11.

68 *Ibid.*, p. 117.

69 Albert Camus, *The Myth of Sisyphus* (Harmondsworth: Penguin, 1979) p. 11.

70 E M Cioran, *A Short History of Decay* (London: Quartet, 1990) pp. 5–6.

71 John Cruickshank, *Albert Camus: The Literature of Revolt* (Oxford: Oxford University Press, 1959) p. 122.

72 Henry S Kariel, *In Search of Authority: Twentieth Century Political Thought* (New York: Free Press of Glencoe, 1964) p. 176.

73 James D Wilkinson, *The Intellectual Resistance in Europe* (Cambridge, MA: Harvard University Press, 1981) pp. 61–2.

74 Cited Alan White, *Within Nietzsche's Labyrinth* (London: Routledge, 1990) p. 84.

75 Albert Camus, *Neither Victims nor Executioners* (Berkeley: World Without War Council, 1968) pp. 17–19.

76 Camus, *Myth of Sisyphus, op.cit.*, p. 111.

77 White, *Within Nietzsche's Labyrinth, op.cit.*, p. 76.

78 Camus, *Myth of Sisyphus, op.cit.*, p. 118.

8. SAVAGE WARS OF PEACE: THE WEST ENCOUNTERS
THE NON-WESTERN WORLD

1   G F Hegel, *Philosophy of History* (New York: Dover, 1956) pp. 91–99. As Hegel wrote in his lecture series: 'At this point we leave Africa not to mention it again. For it is no historical part of the world: it has no movement or development to exhibit'. This view was carried over into the twentieth century. In the Middle East T E Lawrence claimed that the Arabs had exhausted their possibilities – they had been around for too long. They had 'centuries of experience, but no wisdom'. Even the great Islamic scholar, Hamilton Gibb, in the 1930s adopted a similar view. The Moslems, he claimed, were an unhistorical people interested only in the after-life, in the religious not political world. Islam had no politics,no literature, no energy, no activity, no history of growth – the Islamic world was not historical – it was a historical 'fossil'. Eric Wolf, *Europe and the People without History* (Berkeley: University Of California Press, 1982) p. iv.

2   Stephen Haulgat, *Freedom, Truth and History: An Introduction to Hegel's Philosophy* (London: Routledge, 1991).

3   Frank McLynn, *Hearts of Darkness: The European Exploration of Africa* (London: Hutchinson, 1992) p. 273.

4   For Anders Sparrman, see Mary Louise Pratt, *Imperial Eyes: Travel Writing and Transculturation* (London: Routledge, 1992).

5   Hannah Arendt, *The Origins of Totalitarianism* (London: Allen & Unwin, 1967) p. 186. Arendt reports that the colonisation of Africa attracted particularly vicious men like Karl Peters (possibly a model for Conrad's Kurtz) who openly admitted that 'he was fed up being counted among the pariahs and wanted to belong to a master race'. (*Origins,* p. 189).

6   Thomas Pakenham, *The Scramble for Africa 1876–1912* (London: Weidenfeld & Nicolson, 1991) p. 656.

7   Lydia Potts, *The World Labour Market: The History of Migration* (London: Zed, 1990) p. 108.

8   Cited John Keegan, *A History of Warfare* (London: Hutchinson, 1993) p. 9. Establishing a code of conduct does not necessarily make war any the less brutal, of course – indeed, it may even make war more 'thinkable' than might otherwise be the case. This is what Tolstoy means in *War and Peace* when, on the eve of Borodino, Prince Andrei recognises two German staff officers in the Russian service riding past, one of whom is Clausewitz.

> 'The war must be extended over a wider area. This is a conviction which I cannot advocate too highly' one of them was saying.
> 'Oh, undoubtedly', replied the other, 'since the aim is to wear out the enemy, one cannot, of course, take into account damage and injury suffered by private persons'.
> 'Oh yes, spread the war!' said Prince Andrei with an angry snort, when they had ridden by. In that 'wider area' I had a father and a son and a sister at Bald Hills [his

family home]. He doesn't care about that. That was what I was just saying to you – those German gentlemen won't win the battle tomorrow, they will only make a mess of it.... They have nothing in their German heads but theories not worth an empty eggshell, while their hearts are void of the one thing that is needed for tomorrow ... 'One thing I would do if I had the power. I would not take prisoners.... Not to take prisoners! That by itself would transform a whole aspect of war and make it less cruel ... They prate about the wars of warfare, of chivalry, of flags of truce and humanity to the wounded.... All fiddlesticks.... They plunder people's homes .... kill our children and our fathers and then talk of the rules of warfare and generosity to a fallen foe.'

'If there was none of this magnanimity business in warfare, we should never go to war except for something worth facing certain death for, as now.... War is not a polite recreation but the vilest thing in life, and we ought to understand that and not play at war. Our attitude towards the fearful necessity of war ought to be stern and serious. It boils down to this: we should have done with humbug and let war be war and not a game.'

What Tolstoy means is that the best way of avoiding war is to make it irrational. Any effective counter to war calls for rational behaviour, magnifying violence to a point where it is its own deterrent or supernational, as where Christian love meets and opposes it by altogether non-violent means. The former alternative, as expressed by Prince Andrei, marks the apogee of Tolstoy's struggle to reach the truth of war in *War and Peace*: the latter is expressed, if not with the same dramatic persuasiveness in his later books *Christianity and Pacifism* and *The Kingdom of God is Within You*. (See pp. 118–119 in W P Gallie, *Philosophers of Peace and War: Kant, Clausewitz, Marx, Engels and Tolstoy* (Cambridge: Cambridge University Press, 1978).

9   John Keegan, *The Face of Battle* (Harmondsworth: Penguin, 1976) p. 326.
10 Pakenham, *Scramble for Africa, op.cit.*, p. 412.
11 Brian Spittles, *Joseph Conrad: Text and Context* (London: Macmillan, 1992) p. 87.
12 John and Jean Comaroff, *Ethnography and the Historical Imagination* (Boulder: Westview Press, 1992) p. 267.
13 *Ibid*, p. 291.
14 *Ibid*
15 See John Carey, *The Intellectuals and the Masses: Pride and Prejudice Among the Literary Intelligentsia 1880–1939* (London: Faber & Faber, 1992) p. 124–6. 'What will you do with us, we hundreds of millions who cannot keep pace with you?' ask the populations of China and Africa in *Anticipations*. Wells does not present anything approaching a properly worked out extermination policy, but nonetheless he appears convinced that genocide is the only answer. The 'swarms of black and brown and dirty white and yellow people who do not meet the new needs of efficiency will, he insists, have to go'. It is 'their portion to die out and disappear'.

16   In the comparison of the peoples outside Europe and the European masses, of
      course, the former often came out ahead. In his account of his sojourn in
      London's East End in 1902, Jack London compared the poor to the Inuit of
      Alaska and found the comparison invidious. He quotes Huxley from his
      knowledge gained as a medical officer in the East End. 'Were the alternatives
      presented to me, I would deliberately prefer the life of a savage to that of those
      people of Christian London.' Jack London *The People of the Abyss* (London:
      Journeyman Press, 1992).

17   Cited Michel Tournier, *The Erl King* (London: Methuen, 1984) p. 216. See also
      Theodore Zeldin, *France 1848–1945: Intellect, Taste and Anxiety* (Oxford:
      Oxford University Press, 1977) In the First World War a pamphleteer claimed
      that a phrenological study showed that German brains lacked the organ of
      comparison which explained not only their inability to make reasonable
      judgements, but also the depression of their skulls which made room perfectly
      for the vizor of their helmets.

18   Cited Marianna Torgovnick, *Gone Primitive: Savage Intellects, Modern Lives*
      (Chicago: Chicago University Press, 1990), p. 11.

19   For Hitler's colonisation plans for Russia, see H Trevor-Roper (ed.), *Hitler's
      Table Talk 1941–44* (London: Weidenfeld & Nicolson, 1973) p. 617.

20   Omer Bartov, *Hitler's Army: Soldiers, Nazis and War in the Third Reich* (New
      York: Oxford University Press, 1991).

21   Omer Bartov, *The Eastern Front 1941–56: German troops and the barbarisation
      of warfare* (London: Macmillan, 1985) p. 102.

22   Such views were not unique to Prussia. Take the following passage from *The
      Making of Western Europe* (1912) by C R L Fletcher:

      > Some will say, and in view of later and even modern history, I should be loath to
      > contradict them, that as the Slav has never shown any capacity for civilisation the
      > proper method was to apply to him that of Henry the Fowler and Otto the Great, to
      > push him steadily back eastward and to colonise his territory with sturdy Teutons
      > to leave him, if at all, only in a completely inferior position with no separate political
      > existence.

23   Kurt Vonnegut, *Fates Worse than Death: An Autobiographical Collage of the
      1980s* (Jonathan Cape: 1991).

24   *Machines as the Measure of Man* pp. 376–9.

25   Peter Bergman, *Nietzsche. The Last Anti-political German* (Bloomington:
      Indiana University Press, 1987).

26   Cited Robert Newman, *Owen Lattimore and the Loss of China*.

27   Susan Sontag, *A Trip to Hanoi* (New York: Farrar, 1992 Strauss & Giroux, 968)
      pp. 65–66. Some of the American planes shot down were cannibalised to make
      truck motors, small machine parts, spokes for bicycles: 'To observe ... in day
      to day functioning a society based on the principle of total use is particularly
      impressive to somebody who comes from a society based on maximal waste'.

28   Cited Hellman, *American Myth and the Vietnam War* (NY: Columbia Uni-

versity Press, 1987) p. 83.

29   Herman Melville, *White Jacket* (Oxford University Press, 1989) p. 152.

30   Cited Roy F. Flint, 'The U.S. Army on the Pacific Frontier, 1898–1939', in Joe Dixon (ed.), *The American Military in the Far East* (Washington DC: US GPO, 1980) p. 139.

31   Janet Smith (ed.), *Mark Twain 'On the Damned Human Race'* (New York: Hill & Wang, 1962) p. 70.

32   Mark Twain, *Following the Equator* (New York: American Publishing Co., 1987) p. 241.

33   Alex Ayres, (ed.), *Greatly Exaggerated: The Wit and Wisdom of Mark Twain* (London: Barry & Jenkins, 1988) p. 241.

34   Smith, '*On the Damned Human Race*,' *op.cit.*, p. 9.

35   *Ibid.* Saki (H H Munro) from the British side was equally damning about the South African war if from a rather different perspective. See Saki, *Alice in Westminster* in *Collected Works of Saki* (NY: Simon and Schuster, 1977) p. 26.

36   Sigmund Freud, *Jokes and their Relation to the Unconscious* (New York: Norton & Co., 1960) p. 110.

37   Smith, '*On the Damned Human Race*.' *op.cit.*

38   *Ibid*, p. 102.

39   *Ibid*, p. 114.

40   Ayers, *Greatly Exaggerated, op.cit.*

41   Mark Twain, *A Connecticut Yankee in the Court of King Arthur* (ed. Allison R. Ensor) (New York: Newton & Co., 1982).

42   Octavio Paz, *On Poets and Poetry* p. 49. The idea that the United States has a blameless past is an old one. In a best seller in 1846 an American visiting the dungeons of an English castle observes: 'Better the past should be blank than written over with such bloody hieroglyphics as these. When I consider these records and reflect upon the deeds of this crime-stained land I look upon our young nation as an innocent child.' (Cited David Lowenthal, *The Past as a Foreign Country* (Oxford: Oxford University Press, 1985) p. 110.

43   A A Ivory, 'A Talk of Robert Lowell', *Encounter*, 24 (February 1965) pp. 39–46.

44   Bernard Devoto, *A Pen Warmed up in Hell: Mark Twain in Protest* (New York: Harper & Row, 1972) pp. 9–10.

45   *Ibid*, p. 73.

46   Frank Freidel, 'Dissent in the Spanish-American War and the Philippines Insurrection', in Samuel E. Morison (ed.), *Dissent in Three American Wars* (Cambridge, MA: Harvard University Press, 1970) p. 95.

47   Even Twain's apparent anarchism made him popular with the counter-culture in the 1960s. 'Let us abolish policemen who carry clubs and revolvers and put in a squad of poets armed to the teeth with poems on spring and love.' (*A Pen Warmed up in Hell, op.cit.*, p. 12). Twain was being ironic. Irony, of course, is not something for which the counter-culture is much remembered.

48   For those who disagree, who see the Pacific War as 'the supreme collective social experience in modern American history', see Jeffrey Perrett, *Days of*

Sadness, Years of Triumph: The American People 1939–40 (New York: Free Press, 1973) p. 433.

49   Jean Amery, *Preface to the Future (op.cit.)* p. 73.

50   James Gibson, *The Perfect War: Technowar in Vietnam* (New York: Atlantic Monthly Press, 1986); William Appleman Williams/Walter La Febre (eds.), *America in Vietnam: A Documentary History* (New York: Norton & Co., 1975) p. 296.

51   Stanley Karnow, *Vietnam: A History* (New York: Penguin, 1984) p. 540.

52   *Ibid.*

53   Gloria Emerson, *Winners and Losers: Battles, Retreats, Gains, Losses and Ruins in the Vietnam War* (Bloomington: Westview Press) (1976).

54   Philip Caputo, *The Rumour of War* (London: Macmillan, 1978) p. xiv.

55   Michael Herr, *Despatches* (New York: Random House, 1977) p. 167.

56   Noam Chomsky, 'After Pinkville', in *Prevent the Crime of Silence: Reports from the Sessions of the International War Crimes Tribunal* (ed. Peter Weiss) (London: Allen Lane, 1971) p. 42.

57   Caputo, *Rumour of War, op.cit.*, p. 61.

58   Jean-Paul Sartre, *The Search for Method* (New York: Knopf, 1968) p. xxi, 79.

59   Murray Polner, *No Victory Parades: The Return of the Vietnam Veterans* (London: Orbach & Chambers, 1971) p. 144.

60   *Winter Investigations, op.cit.*, p. 163.

61   Peter Karsten, *Soldiers and Society The Effects of Military Service and war on American Life* (West Point: Greenwood Press, 1978) p. 224.

62   Alexandre de Seversky, *Victory Thru Air Power* (New York: Simon & Schuster, 1942) p. 102.

63   Cited Edith Wyschogrod, *Spirit in Ashes: Hegel, Heidegger and Man-Made Death* (New Haven: Yale University Press, 1985) p. 131.

64   Jean-Paul Sartre, 'On Genocide', in *Winter Investigations, op.cit.*, pp. 364–5.

65   Gibson, *Perfect War, op.cit.*, p. 2.

66   Andrew Krepinsevich, *The Army in Vietnam* (Baltimore: Johns Hopkins University Press, 1986), p. 227.

67   S L Vogelgesang, *The Long Dark Night of the Soul* (New York: Little Brown, 1974) p. 102.

68   Susan Sontag, *Style of Radical Will* (New York: Farrar, Strauss, 1969) p. 267.

69   Todd Gitling, *The Sixties: Years of Hope, Years of Rage* (New York: Bantam Press, 1987).

70   Joseph Wenke, *Mailer's America* (Connecticut: University Press of New England, 1987) p. 131.

71   *Ibid.*

72   Jean Larteguy, *The Face of War,* reproduced Paul Fussell, *The Bloody Game: An Anthology of Modern War* (New York: Scribeners, 1991) p. 672. The doctors found they could not break their research down on racial lines or even lines of origin, but they could along national fault lines.

73   Cited Paul Fussell, *Wartime: Understanding Behaviour in the Second World*

War (Oxford: Oxford University Press, 1989) pp. 140–1.

74   R J Lifton, 'Oversight of Medical Care of Veterans Wounded in Vietnam', *Hearings before the Sub-Committee on Labour and Public Welfare, U.S. Senate, 91st Congress, First and Second Sessions* (Washington DC: US GPO, 1970) pp. 495–6. See also, Louis A. Wiesner, *Victims and Survivors: Displaced Persons and other Victims in Vietnam* (Westpoint, Connecticut: Green Press, 1988); Myra MacPherson, *Long Time Passing: Vietnam and the Haunted Generation* (New York: Doubleday, 1984).

75   George Woodcock, 'The 1930's and 1960's', in Peter Aichingu, *The American Soldier in Fiction: A History of Attitudes Towards Warfare and the Military Establishment* (Iowa State University Press, 1975) p. 113. For Vietcong atrocities see Stephen Hosmer, *Vietcong: Repression and its Implications for the Future* (Lexington: Heath, 1970).

9. NOT THE END OF THE WORLD NEWS

1   Jacques Darras, *Beyond the Tunnel of History* (London: Macmillan, 1990) p. 61.
2   Norman Stone, *Europe Transformed 1878–1919* (London: Fontana, 1983) p. 390.
3   Cited *German Comments*, 19 (June 1990) pp. 80–93.

Index

301